*Old Stuff*
*in Up-Country*
*Pennsylvania*

"At the end of a day's threshing, there is nothing like a glass of cider
to cut the dust in a man's throat."

# Old Stuff in Up-Country Pennsylvania

*Earl F. Robacker*

*Photography by*
Stephen A. Karas and Bryden Taylor

*South Brunswick and New York: A. S. Barnes and Company*
*London: Thomas Yoseloff Ltd*

A. S. Barnes and Co., Inc.
Cranbury, New Jersey 08512


Thomas Yoseloff Ltd
108 New Bond Street
London W1Y OQX, England



Library of Congress Cataloging in Publication Data

Robacker, Earl Francis.
    Old stuff in up-country Pennsylvania.

    Bibliography: p.
    1. Pennsylvania Germans. 2. Art industries and trade
—Pennsylvania. I. Title.
F160.G3R56              917.48′06′31              72-5174
ISBN 0-498-01211-5

OTHER BOOKS BY EARL F. ROBACKER

*Pennsylvania German Literature*
*Pennsylvania Dutch Stuff*
*Touch of the Dutchland*


*Except as noted, illustrations are of pieces in private collections. Only the kinds of objects well known somewhere in the diversified territories of the country north of the Blue Mountain have been included, and, when positive ascription to a particular locality could be made, the fact has been noted. In a minimal number of cases when, for whatever reason, examples of known local provenance were not available for photographing, pieces thoroughly representative of up-country types but coming from farther afield were utilized. Commercially made articles are indicated as manufactured unless their nature seems immediately self-evident.*

Printed in the United States of America

*For Ada*

# Contents

|  | Acknowledgments | 9 |
|---|---|---|
| 1 | Places and People: Ups and Downs in the Up-Country | 13 |
| 2 | From Forest to Plank House | 22 |
| 3 | Poling down the River | 27 |
| 4 | Woodworking: Shoepegs to Ladderbacks | 34 |
| 5 | Over the Hill: The Wagon Wheel | 44 |
| 6 | Mills and Millers | 51 |
| 7 | Forge and Foundry | 59 |
| 8 | Glassworks and Glass | 68 |
| 9 | Droving and "Droviers" | 77 |
| 10 | Tanning Their Hides | 84 |
| 11 | Butter for Barter | 90 |
| 12 | The Egg Economy | 97 |
| 13 | The Peripatetic Trader | 106 |
| 14 | The Death and Reincarnation of Slate | 113 |
| 15 | Brick? Brick! | 120 |
| 16 | Potter and Pot | 126 |
| 17 | Schnitzelbank—and Other—Basketry | 134 |
| 18 | Fraktur | 140 |
| 19 | A World of Apples | 148 |
| 20 | Sap Bucket to Maple Sugar | 154 |
| 21 | The Honey and the Comb | 161 |
| 22 | Berrying: Pail to Preserve | 166 |
| 23 | Kitchens—Down and Out | 172 |
| 24 | All but the Squeal | 180 |
| 25 | Kootsches, Smokehouses, and Almanacs | 186 |
| 26 | The Lone Woman in the Up-Country | 194 |
| 27 | Warp and Weft | 202 |
| 28 | Quilts by the Dozen | 212 |
| 29 | Frolics, Bees—and Carpet Rags | 221 |
| 30 | Just Fooling Around: The Whittlers | 227 |
| 31 | A-Putzing They Went | 235 |
| 32 | Hickory Nut Dolls to Slingshots | 243 |
| 33 | The Receding Ice Age | 249 |
| 34 | The Ubiquitous Parlor Organ | 254 |
| 35 | Scrapbooks and Fancy Paper | 261 |
|  | Bibliography | 271 |
|  | Index | 275 |

# *Acknowledgments*

I am indebted to many persons who have given me assistance of one kind or another in the compilation of this book. At the head of the list would certainly stand Horace and Elizabeth Walters who, between them, are probably better informed on Monroe County history than any other two persons living today. In particular, I am humble before Mrs. Walters' remarkable memory and her inductive skill in genealogical matters.

To Albert Dillahunty, talented and versatile National Park Service historian, and to Peter DeGelleke, superintendent, both at the Delaware Water Gap National Recreation Area, I owe special thanks for the privilege of examining and recording documents in the possession of the Park Service. To John P. Cassidy, artist, of Easton, and to Kermit and Lovada Kutz of Gilbert, I am indebted for help, in one connection or another, in one of the most elusive of all fields—identification of eighteenth-century fraktur writers who, for the most part, took pains to work anonymously.

I am indebted to Thelma Weidman of Columbia, New Jersey, for information bearing on the early glass industry of that place, and to Elmer Gouger of Stroudsburg for his cheerful willingness to put aside personal affairs on my behalf.

I am permanently in the debt of my brother, Robert L. Robacker of Newfoundland, for his assistance in sudden minor crises—such as my immediate need for an obscure work of biography or an equally obscure bit of local history—and of his wife, Edith, for her tolerance while the pursuit took place. To Ralph Buzzard of Kellersville, I am grateful for such generosity in making his valuable personal library available to me when nothing but an actual early document would serve the purpose, and for other favors. I am equally grateful to the Monroe County Historical Society for the privilege of studying early ledgers in their possession.

I wish to express thanks to Joseph Smits, Frank and Carolyn Kerr, Vernon and Elsie Mack, and Edgar and Charlotte Sittig for their helpfulness in keeping me informed on relevant matters while the work was in progress; to John and Sally Ferrebee for lending a fine coverlet for photographing; to Dorothy Heberling and Helen Feigel for their prompt responses to my pleas for information having to do with early settlers in the Poconos; and to William J. Taylor for the photograph he supplied for the frontispiece.

Finally, my appreciation, my gratitude, and my love to the person who not only edited the manuscript from first draft through final typescript, but also uncomplainingly waited out the interminable process of checking and re-checking, revising, and updating; the person who knew more about the whole business, intuitively, at the beginning, than I knew, with benefit of documentation, at the end—my wife.

Earl F. Robacker

*Old Stuff
in Up-Country
Pennsylvania*

# 1
# Places and People:
# Ups and Downs in the Up-Country

There is an entity in what is commonly referred to as the Pennsylvania Dutch "country" of Penn's Commonwealth which has for years—centuries, for that matter—largely been passed over by those who write about or discuss the German-speaking element and their descendants. Not that the Dutch Country has ever been explicitly defined; from the time of Francis Daniel Pastorius in 1683, when the *Concord* put into harbor at Philadelphia with its load of emigrants from the Rhine country, there have been elements of vagueness attaching to the territory they set out to colonize.

At first it was just Germantown, outside the City of Brotherly Love, which felt the impact of the new non-English-speaking colonists whom William Penn, real estate promoter extraordinaire, had encouraged to cross the Atlantic. Then as the numbers continued to grow, as year followed year, the newcomers fanned out to the north, northwest, and west, settling in the fertile limestone valleys and rolling red hills up as far as what are now Easton, Bethlehem, and Allentown, and out to Harrisburg, down to York, and beyond. In all, perhaps a fourth of the total area of the Commonwealth came in time to be thought of as "Dutch Country," so thoroughly was it given character by the seemingly endless waves of emigrants from the German-speaking sections of Europe—not the Palatine counties alone but Switzerland and Alsace and spots still farther afield. It has been suggested that if one laid a map of Pennsylvania before him, put the point of a compass on Philadelphia, in the southeastern corner, and swung a 90-degree arc

half way to the top, he would have enclosed most of the Dutch Country.

The assumption is only very roughly accurate. Venturesome colonists do not stop short at a given point as birds are believed to do when establishing their feeding grounds; they keep on going as long as the spirit moves them, or as necessity compels them, once the close-in lands have been claimed. Thus it is that a broad, irregular periphery of Pennsylvania Dutch colonization goes beyond any arbitrarily suggested northern or western cut-off point, and penetrates further into English, Irish, Scotch, Welsh, or other territory than is commonly supposed.

The non-Germanic groups taking up their abode in colonial Pennsylvania staked their claims with what we should now consider a minimum of interference with one another. The Germans got the best farming land; they were there early, by invitation, and secured the kind of soil they particularly wanted. The few Swedish and Dutch holdings close to the Delaware, from Philadelphia northward, soon lost any individual character they possessed; a century after Penn's time they might as well have been English. Actually, there were fewer English immigrants than Penn might have wished. Many of them were Quakers who did not venture very far from Philadelphia—and many of those who did leave the city did not travel far.

The Scotch-Irish, less concerned with farming than with business or indeed with any nonagricultural enterprise, settled beyond the territory in which the Germans were most interested. The Welsh, who came to be thought of as slate-quarry workers, and the Slavs and the Irish, who were more or less stereotyped as coal miners, were of later vintage.

In fact, the principal difference of opinion as to who had the right to settle where he wished existed before the Revolution in northeastern Pennsylvania, where English-Irish "squatters" sent from Connecticut to occupy lands to which that state believed it had a legitimate claim tangled with the Germanic and other elements. Even this entanglement, which was more in the nature of a border brawl than anything else, while there were some hot and bitter clashes, was less than widespread. In the face of a common danger, those who participated most vigorously in the feuding largely forgot their differences during the Revolution, and by 1800 the boundaries of Pennsylvania, the point at issue, had largely been established.

More far-reaching than the disputes over boundaries in the period of the so-called Pennamite Wars was the mutual dislike or mistrust engendered between the *English*—which included all those ethnic strains emanating from Connecticut—and the *Germans*—all the non-English-speaking pioneers. In time, the coolness lessened, but to this day it has not completely disappeared.

Some of the lines of German penetration, as one might expect, kept on going so far that eventually the wanderers lost the sense of belonging to the southeastern sector. Among these are the hardy souls who went up to Kitchener and Waterloo in Canada; those who went west into Ohio—and ultimately to Indiana, Illinois, Iowa, and on to the state of Washington; and those who turned south to the pleasant climates of Maryland and Virginia. For the most part, the stories of these venturers have yet to be told; only in the case of the emigrants from Pennsylvania to Canada has anything like a comprehensive treatment by historians been given. By now it may be almost too late for most of the others—too late for the Ohioans, though there are enough church records to provide a good starting point; too late for the Iowans, whose identities are only too often confused with those of the members of the Amana community; too late for the growers of peas and oats in the state of Washington. Perhaps it does not really matter, since the whole story of the development of the colonies into the Union is one of diversity slowly growing toward an ultimate complete acculturation. Minor degrees of differentness have almost always been noted, tolerated, and then forgotten.

And yet, and yet . . .

In the peripheral territory beyond the one which

researchers and writers have in the past established by definition, however flexible, there are sizable communities and far-flung farmsteads with such obvious kinship to their better-publicized home country that to ignore them is like compiling a family history but omitting all members living more than 50 miles, let us say, from where Grandpa and Grandma started the clan. It is one of these territories, too extensive to be called merely a pocket, and yet with too great an impact by the English-speaking element to be regarded as a true enclave, with which we are here concerning ourselves.

Perhaps this concern can best be reduced to a query put to the author only a few years back in the village of Newfoundland: "What are we, really? You say that we're Pennsylvania Dutch—but since when are Gilpins, Carltons, and Lancasters Pennsylvania Dutch?" (They are not, of course.) The questioner might well have added, "And why, in a family of German background, is one likely to hear an expression which strikes back to Elizabethan England about as frequently as he does one which is obviously of German origin?" The answer is that here, in the up-country, one can actually sense the melding (or nonmelding!) of two different cultures—at least if he is watchful—and idioms, especially if they are picturesque, may have originated in England, by way of Connecticut, or Germany, by way of the Palatine immigrations.

Now let us examine our geographical territory. It is not exactly "handy" in shape; in its totality it extends from hither to yon; from fertile deep-loam farms in Berks and Lehigh counties northward to the thin-soiled subsistence acres at the top of the Poconos; out northwesterly to the places where one thinks of gaining a livelihood in terms of mining coal rather than farming. It represents the limits of the country which could be forced into a degree of productiveness by a Pennsylvania Dutchman with so many generations of the soil in his blood that it was hard for him to think of making a living in any other way.

With a map of Pennsylvania before him, let the reader omit the compass and trace a new line, starting at the city of Easton, and bring back into the fold villages and countrysides long unknown to or ignored by the writers of Dutchdom—the up-country Dutch Country. Be it noted that the term "up-country" probably originated because of the elevation of the land above sea level, but to any long-time resident it means north of the part of the Blue Mountain range which begins east of the Delaware Water Gap and runs westward across the Commonwealth toward

Harrisburg. "Up-country" in itself has little or nothing to do with "Dutchness" or "non-Dutchness." A resident of the village of LaAnna lives up-country from Portland, but in traveling the comparatively few miles from LaAnna to Hawley, for example, he goes from down-country to up-country. A well known writer uses the term "piedmont" for what many a bona fide Dutchman would simply call "up-country," scorning anything fancier. In other words, while in broad terms "up-country" means north of the Blue Mountain, once one is there he finds that any given spot is still relative to something else.

To sketch in the territory, start at Easton and go north along the Delaware on the Pennsylvania side. At Riverton, cross the river to Belvidere, New Jersey, and go up to the lovely old Moravian village of Hope. From Hope, return to Pennsylvania at the Delaware Water Gap, but include Columbia, on the Jersey side. With the twin towns of Stroudsburg and East Stroudsburg on the left, continue northward into Pike and then over into Wayne: Shoemaker's, Bushkill, Peck's Pond, Roemerville, Promised Land, Shohola, Honesdale. This is as far "up" on the map as it is reasonable to go, although there are Pennsylvania Dutch families, widely scattered, at least as far north as Hancock, New York. Swing left and down from Honesdale, keeping Greentown and Newfoundland inside the line. Now make a wide sweep west and south: Gouldsboro, Thornhurst, Stoddartsville, Hickory Run, Tamaqua. None of these last five is historically "solid" Pennsylvania Dutch—but true Dutch country is at their door. At Tamaqua, turn east to our starting point. Lands to the south are almost solidly our old, familiar "real" Dutch Country.

Not losing sight of the fact that this is peripheral Dutch ground, one should note, as he follows the line sketched above, that he has enclosed Stockertown (pronounce it "Stuckertown"), Ackermanville, Mt. Bethel, Newfoundland, Mountainhome, Albrightsville (considerably to the west), and then Lehighton, Weissport, and Bowmanstown.

What lies within this wobbly perimeter is up-country Dutch Country. Along all the boundary lines except the southern one it is far from being pure. The farther north one goes, the more English and Irish names one finds. However, within this larger territory there is another, more compact one so homogeneous that even today there are youngsters who speak Pennsylvania Dutch before they learn English—or so it is maintained—starting English just before they are old enough for kindergarten.

Let us take the pencil again and within the larger figure create a smaller one: again, start at Easton; then go to Richmond, Stone Church, the Stroudsburgs (which only partly belong, however), Reeders, McMichaels, Lehighton, and Weissport. This time we have enclosed a number of places which, in addition to those just named, are as Dutch as the proverbial sauerkraut—or as Dutch as Kutztown or Appelbachsville: Sciota, Bossardsville (pronounce it "Buzzardsville"), Appenzell, Neola, Effort, Gilbert, Brodheadsville, Kunkletown (and *Little* Kunkletown), Kresgeville, Trachsville, and the larger early Moravian town of Nazareth. Much of this territory, though not all of it, is in the western portion of Monroe County—and "West End" (locally, "Vest Ent") is completely synonymous with "Pennsylvania Dutch" in the thinking of people who live near enough to have any concern with the matter. In terms of persons, places, and, to a slightly lesser degree, of enterprises, we need to be more concerned with Monroe County than with any other.

Let us repeat one important point: *no* town, village, or crossroads settlement is any longer purely one thing or another in ethnic makeup. The melting pot has been simmering long enough that when one thinks of a Pennsylvania Dutch—or Welsh, or Irish—village, he is thinking of what *was*, historically, rather than of what *is*, here and now.

Place names once offered about a 50–50 clue as to the composition of a community. In some cases they still do; Bechtelsville, Krumsville, Zieglerville, and Kempton, along with a hundred others, took their names from local families of some importance. The clue is lost, however, in other cases, with the changing of the names of the village, sometimes to achieve something more euphonious, sometimes perhaps to lend hoped-for importance. The village of LaAnna in the Poconos will serve as an example: the postmaster did not like the sound of Houcktown, admirable as the Houck family might be. He was successful in gaining official sanction for a change to the name of his mother, LaAnna, and the word Houcktown gradually faded into a memory. It is of no significance to us here that a proud young father in a nearby community, learning of the change from Houcktown to LaAnna, exerted pressure to effect a similar change to honor his young daughter—from Panther to Gladys. The change was denied, as was another request to change the name of Panther to German Valley. German Valley, since it did not have its own post office, never made the map. The word "Panther" has all but vanished from officialdom since the community became an R.F.D. adjunct of Newfoundland.

It was not uncommon for even a tiny hamlet to be

known by several names in addition to the one used by the postal authorities. Paupac, near what is now Lake Wallenpaupac, was infrequently called by its "rightful" name—Ledgedale. There were those who called it Singertown, after one of the leading families, and in the 1870s it was Philipsburg. Sterling was Nobletown before people began to call it Sterling. Newfoundland started by being identified as the Dutch Flats, taking account of the German element, but both the church and the school bore the more dignified name of Hopedale. Fennersville became Sciota as long ago as 1867. One village was sarcastically dubbed Frogtown because of a little-liked prolific French family living there; the original name came into use again when the family moved away. Part of Canadensis was known as Hoke ("Hoch") Town, after another prolific family.

Paradoxically, up-country Dutchdom is, and yet is not, like the Pennsylvania Dutch Country about which so much has been said and written in the last several decades. At the outset, one who notes both similarities and differences must do so with recognition of the fact that some families in the Poconos go back in point of time only to 1848, when there was an extraordinary exodus of young men from Germany seeking escape from military service. While there was a more or less general distribution of these émigrés throughout the East, there were enough added to the comparatively sparse population of upper Monroe and the even more thinly settled sections of Pike and lower Wayne counties materially to affect the over-all character of the communities in which they settled. To many people today, these "1848-ers" are old families; in their own time, they were more often thought of as "Johnny-come-latelys."

Perhaps one should consider the differences first, since they appear to be more pronounced. At the head of these there is the land itself. Settlers in Berks and Lancaster counties, in particular, found rich limestone soil, well watered, of a quality surpassing even that of the Fatherland. With tireless industry and obvious know-how they turned it into some of the world's best—and most expensive—farm land, and have kept it that way for two hundred years and more. These were the earliest settlers; those who came later, as we have observed before, had to content themselves with "next-bests" on a declining scale —outlying farms with thinner soil, often acid, usually stony, often on hillsides and hilltops subject to erosion, sometimes in almost inaccessible spots, and subject to late spring and early autumn frosts. The hill farms of Pike County, most of which have long since reverted to the beech and hickory woods from which they first were carved, such as those in Panther, Simonstown, Carlton Hill, and Greentown, could be matched in lack of native productiveness only by the farms of what we now call Appalachia.

Yet these farms, most of them comprising a hundred acres or more of woodlot, wild pasture, and a minimal amount of arable land, were cleared, improved, and managed by men who expended on the total effort a greater amount of sheer physical exertion than the wheat grower of Lancaster County could have imagined. Generation succeeded generation, with one man in each remaining on the ancestral soil, while the rest of the children usually sought their fortunes—or at least their livelihoods—elsewhere. It was a back-breaking, everlasting struggle against odds which were surmountable only by the strong. Success was not financial; economic security was almost always out of the question. Instead, success was something equated, year by year, with comparative freedom from want and deprivation. In the long run, it was a losing battle.

Such farms are an extreme, of course, and do not fairly represent all of up-country Dutchdom. One wonders at the temerity which brought them into being; only a dedicated man or a desperate one fleeing from a hopeless situation elsewhere would have faced up to the job of turning this kind of wilderness into a homeplace.

Farther down-country, the situation was less stark; while a mountain top is usually a dubious place on which to create a farm, the flatlands at its base are at least less unsatisfactory—and the farther away one goes, the better the terrain becomes. Thus, the lands in Smithfield and Middle Smithfield townships, the fields in the neighborhood of Analomink and Henryville, and the acreages of Tannersville and Bartonsville, while they may still be too close to the hills for convenient or comfortable tilling, are much better than those a dozen miles to the north. And only a short distance to the south and west, with the Poconos still visible but far enough away that they pose no threat, the fertile acres of the West End, from Reeders to Nazareth, from Bossardsville to Kresgeville, can be matched in productiveness only by the "real" Dutch Country still farther south.

All of which is to suggest that the up-country Dutchman, after a number of generations, has become a little different from his down-country brother. He may have sprung from the same ethnic roots; he may, in fact, have the same surname, but he may be just a little more individual, a little more self-reliant, a bit more versatile than his favored relative—and a bit more of a fatalist, or at least a pessimist, and considerably more spare of frame the farther north you find him. In Monroe today he will have adjusted to modern farming methods in fields broad enough to accommodate the gargantuan machinery required. Up in Pike he will probably have given up farming and will be involved in some phase of the resort business, summer and winter. There is a limit to the lengths to which even the pioneer spirit can go. In one generation it can hold steadfast to the end, but eventually the realistic is likely to replace the idealistic.

Another facet of diversity is that of an accent in speech. For all the German background, the second- or third-generation Beehn, Ziegler, Schelbert, Moersch, Friebole, Heffele, or Heberling of the Poconos had so little of Germanic intonation in his speech that one had to look for it to detect it at all. Only in an occasional up-cadence toward the end of a sentence, when one would expect the sound to descend, did an elderly speaker now and then betray a German beginning. Moreover, it was a matter of pride in most families that German—or Pennsylvania Dutch—while known and used among adults in private, was almost never spoken in the hearing of children, lest they might pick up a foreign-sounding taint in their speech. (This condition did not prevail with the newer, 1848 Germanic element, however; Manharts and Siegs, living as close neighbors to Abels and Oppelts, could be identified as German—German, not Pennsylvania Dutch—the moment they opened their lips.)

South of the Poconos, intonation is a different story. One often hears a Pennsylvania Dutch inflection on the streets of Stroudsburg, and the farther he penetrates into the West End enclave, the more frequent the sound becomes. One hears it with no great surprise in Sciota, Appenzell, or Neola; he *expects* to hear it in Brodheadsville, Effort, Gilbert, Palmerton, and Nazareth, just as he expects to hear it in the heartlands of Womelsdorf or Reading.

*Pennsylvania Dutch*, as an identifying term for the early Germanic immigrants to Pennsylvania, was, of course, a name applied not by the people directly concerned, but by outsiders. Just how it came into being is a little obscure. It has been suggested that the word "Dutch" came about because so many of the immigrants journeyed to Pennsylvania by way of the Dutch port of Rotterdam, and an easy assumption was made that the people therefore were Dutch. Another theory is that the word is either a corruption or a mispronunciation *of Deutsch,* a broad term covering practically everything Germanic. Whatever the truth of the matter, the down-country Dutchman is not averse, at least at the present time, with the

spotlight of favorable publicity turned upon him, to being known as a Pennsylvania Dutchman. Not so his counterpart in German Valley or Roemerville or Angels, however—not that he would be either flattered or insulted; in his thinking he is no more Pennsylvania Dutch, whatever the term may connote, than he is American Indian or Greek.

He is at least partly correct. Germanic emigrants of 1848 have never been considered Pennsylvania Dutch, historically, although in drawing the line at this point there has had to be some hair-splitting. Pocono Germans who came earlier did not quite fit into the contemporarily accepted pattern of South German "belongingness," either. Taking Newfoundland as an example—admittedly because its early history is well documented—we find that a typical core of emigrants came from Gondelsheim, in the German duchy of Baden, in 1828. They had not been Moravians in Baden, as is commonly supposed; most of them, especially those whose surnames were Abel, Beehn, Beehler, Friebole, Raetz, Schneider, and Wolff, had been dissident members of the Lutheran faith in Germany. Nor had they necessarily been long-time residents of Gondelsheim; true, they emigrated from Gondelsheim, leaving Europe not by way of Rotterdam but from an unnamed port in France in 1828, and arrived in New York, not in Philadelphia, as was usual. But they had originally arrived in Gondelsheim as refugees from still other places, Switzerland, for one.

In the New World they were about as close to abject poverty and destitution as one could be and still survive. They appealed to the by then well-established *Unitas Fratrum* (Moravian Church) in Bethlehem for aid, and received it. A tract of land in the Poconos was available for purchase, and the Bethlehem Moravians arranged for loans so that the newcomers might carve out their destinies here. It was Daniel Stroud, son of Jacob Stroud, the founder of Stroudsburg, who had actually discovered that there was overlooked "unseated" land in the Poconos, and it was he who gave the territory the appropriate name of Newfoundland. It is by no means unnatural, then, that when the first church in Newfoundland was established, in 1837, the grateful settlers asked for, and received, permission to join the larger body of Moravians in Pennsylvania. Whether or not Moravians are Pennsylvania Dutch has always been open to question, particularly among members of the faith. If they are—and in some ways it makes good sense to consider them so—then Moravians by adoption should probably also be considered Pennsylvania Dutch, whether they came to the country before or after 1848 . . . but one may expect to have an argument on his hands, whether he is affirming or denying the point.

Why a Kutztown Pennsylvania Dutchman, after no matter how many generations in an English-speaking milieu, sounds "Dutchy," and why the remote up-country denizen does not is neither a paradox nor an enigma. There was no reason for the down-country Dutchman, at least for many, many years, to pay particular attention to his speech. Those who spoke *English* were the outsiders; English was the alien tongue. One never needed to feel self-conscious in speaking the language his relatives and friends spoke habitually.

At the northernmost point the situation was different. Again, taking the Newfoundland area as an example, one finds a peculiar situation persisting almost to the 1900s—and to a faintly recognizable degree even now: the community contained, almost from the first, an approximately equal number of English-speaking and German-speaking settlers. The English-Irish, who had originally come from Connecticut, may or may not have felt themselves superior, but the Germans believed that such was the case, and in worldly goods the English were indubitably better off. Carltons, Gilpins, Lancasters, Hazletons, Nevinses, Dunnings; Dietzes, Ehrhardts, Schaeffers, Heberlings, Uhls, Grims: they lived in almost two different cultural worlds at the outset, and only the passing of time convinced them that it was possible, if not really necessary or desirable, for the two worlds to become one. So marked was the feeling of separation at first that in the cemetery attached to the Albright's Church in Newfoundland a dirt road ran through the middle. German burials took place on one side, English on the other. At the time of the great flood in 1955, when Wallenpaupac Creek rampaged through the cemetery, bringing to light German and English bones alike, there were still those who deplored the fact that in the work of restoration it would be impossible to maintain the ethnic sanctity of the cemetery. And there were still those who took private satisfaction from the circumstance that the damage on one side of the road was less than that on the other!

In this scheme of things perhaps the real outsiders were the occasional French (Huguenin, Papillon) and later Irish (Field, Madden) families. The few Dutchmen from Holland (van Buskirk, Puffee) seemed to blend into the scene as German. The French pronounced their names as they would have done in the French-Swiss cantons from which they had come—but both Germans and English turned a deaf ear on such presumed affectation and pronounced them as though they were English.

The point of it all is that the focus in speech was consciously on English, even on the improvement of the quality of spoken English. As a kind of sop to an elder generation, some members of which may privately have remained unconvinced of the virtues of anything not German, an occasional "Dutch" sermon was preached to Moravian congregations at Newfoundland, German Valley, and Roemerville as late as the early 1900s. Whether the tongue was Pennsylvania Dutch or High German will probably never be known since there is no longer, so far as can be ascertained, any living person who can both remember and make a valid linguistic judgment. The chances are that it was German; the preachers were Moravian, and Moravian scholars tended to be well versed in foreign languages, including German.

The English did not attend Moravian churches, but established Methodist congregations at South Sterling, Hemlock Grove (Greentown), and Canadensis. Apparently the only other denomination to be represented by a church building was the Albright's (Congregational) previously mentioned, and that congregation had dwindled to the vanishing point by the early 1900s.

The entire matter of churches and church-going, especially as it is associated with ethnic similarities and differences, constitutes a significant point of separation between the country above the Blue Mountain and the country below it. It is probably safe to hazard a guess that nowhere in the upper Poconos in the nineteenth century were the words "Amish," "Mennonite," or "Schwenkfelder," so familiar farther south, used, or even recognized as belonging to the general body of words, let alone as names of religious denominations. Even in the "deep" West End, the churches were those of the "Gay" Dutch—largely Lutheran and Reformed—not of the sectarians.

So much for the differences. Broad-scale similarities may be less striking but should be noted. One of them was in food. There may have been no place between Pike County and the Maryland-Pennsylvania line which did not know about *Fasnachts*, call them by their non-English name, and eat them on Shrove Tuesday. Similar recognition is true of Dutchcake (Moravian sugar cake) and of such pork products as souse (pig's-foot jelly), *pannhaus* (scrapple), and "pudden" (liver pudding). Sauerkraut was a common denominator; so were sticky cinnamon buns; dried apples, corn, and string beans; molasses crumb pie; *rivel* soup; peas cooked with new potatoes; brown-flour potato soup; *latwerg* (apple butter) with or without accompanying *schmierkase* (cottage cheese); potato filling; sage dressing for fowl; potato salad with hot bacon-vinegar dressing; pepper cabbage; dried beef; spiced pears, and a dozen kinds of conserves and relishes.

At the same time, other Pennsylvania Dutch foods seem not to have made their way into the upper Dutchland: *schnitz* and *knep* (dried apples and dumplings in ham broth), although *schnitz* pies were usual; *drecher kuche* (funnel cakes), though doughnuts, crullers, and other deep-fat fried pastries were common; *boova schenkel* (potato dumplings), although other dumplings were popular; chicken-corn soup; saffron-colored and -flavored cakes, although saffron was used to deepen the yellow tone of butter; molasses-coconut pie; *hex* waffles (timbales); and *streivlin* or plowlines, a deep-fat fried pastry usually cut in strips with a pastry wheel.

One hesitates to suggest a similarity in clothing, in view of the more distinctive dress worn by various down-country religious groups. Excluding the Quakers or such sectarians as the Amish and the Mennonites, however, one would have to observe that there was a degree of homogeneity in clothing worn by those of Germanic background which did not exist among other people. A collarless short work jacket known far and wide among farmers as a *wammus* was available at country stores for years, and constituted a kind of badge among men who found that kind of garment more convenient and comfortable than any other. These men often wore homemade shirts long after the English were buying ready-made ones, and usually scorned mittens or gloves other those knitted by their own womenfolk. Long-sleeved homemade gingham shirts, blue bandannas, snap-brim straw hats, and sturdy leather shoes with hooks and rawhide lacers were *de rigueur* for summer use. "Sunday best" often meant a suit of black serge.

Women wore voluminous aprons to protect their dresses, and frequently an apron of lesser quality was put on to protect a better one. Since dresses were long, and were buoyed up and out by a number of underskirts, the total came to represent a formidable amount of yardage. Colors were somber; in fact, once a woman married, she tended to choose grays and blacks, oftener with an eye to their durability than to their attractiveness. Shoes were "sensible"; sunbonnets, almost always homemade, were standard, year after year. While there is no reason to suppose that women were totally oblivious to changing fashions, it would seem that change meant less to the Germanic than to the non-Germanic element. Most women made their own clothes and those of the chil-

dren of the family as a matter of course, and few persons had more than one special or dress-up outfit. The tendency to cling to conservative garb, with little or no change from year to year, was not necessarily a matter of aesthetic preference; in a good many cases it was a matter of economic necessity.

It is not inconceivable that the most pronounced characteristic held in common by members of Pennsylvania Dutchdom, up-country or down-country, was a quality of deliberateness in deportment and speech, coupled with contemplation often approaching caution, usually conveying an air of reserve and, especially in the initial stages of acquaintanceship, side-tracking or by-passing points of conversation that might become controversial. A long time was—and still is—required before an outsider in Dutchdom could feel that he had been accepted as an insider. Even marrying into a Pennsylvania Dutch family did not ordinarily speed up the process; the newcomer might remain on trial all the days of his life, and the condition extend to his children. A very recent example comes to mind: the author, engaged in ferreting out services needed in connection with the restoration of a stone house in upper Dutchdom, came to know rather well a personable, intelligent, well-informed young man of the community. This man, married to a local girl of Pennsylvania Dutch extraction, irreproachable in his conduct, and active in community affairs, stems from Greco-Slavic forebears. Not infrequently, in conversation, he would rather deprecatingly mention his origin, and one day the author asked him, "How long did it take you, with your name, to make the grade in this village?"

"I've never made it," he said, with unexpected bitterness. "I'm still an outsider, and I know now that I always will be. The Pennsylvania Dutch accept only their own."

The experience of one young man, extending over a period of perhaps 15 years, does not constitute a general truth and is not necessarily representative—but in an age in which people nationwide have agonized over the facets and ramifications of integration it does give us food for thought. In Dutchdom, one does not, on the strength of a mere prior introduction or yet of long acquaintance which has not progressed from acquaintance to acceptance, rush to his neighbor to ask whether he may, for instance, borrow a cotter pin until such time as he can get to town to replace a lost or broken one. He may call on his neighbor to ask his advice on an entirely different matter, and if circumstances permit, engineer the conversation toward his need for a cotter pin. The chances are overwhelmingly in favor of his getting it—but if he gets both the cotter pin and the neighbor's good will it will be because he has violated no iota of the neighbor's sense of the calm, unhurried fitness of things. One might actually spend less time by going to town to make the purchase.

Associated with the idea of all-deliberate speed is a practice likely to confuse the outlander who comes upon it for the first time—that of appearing to agree in words with the speaker but in the same breath veering to the opposite. Perhaps it is an attempt to forestall argument, though it is used as frequently in connection with such nondebatable subjects as the weather or the cost of living. Or it may be a throwback to the use of the German *Ja,* which might mean "Yes" or might approach the meaninglessness of such expletives as "Er" or "Uh," at the beginning of a sentence.

For example: "Mom, may I have a dollar?" asks Henry.

"Yes, I don't have a dollar to give you," avers Mom, who is likely to continue by asking "What for do you want a dollar?" and wind up by granting the request.

Or: "I'm going over to the post office for stamps," remarks Anna.

"Yes, why don't you wait until the rain stops?" demands Mom.

Or: "I told Junior he could go fishing with some other boys this after," says Mom at the dinner table.

"Yes, I need him myself with the hoeing," objects Pop. "He can go tomorrow."

Perhaps all this is lacking importance. Perhaps. There is evidence, however, to indicate that it is not. Learned societies have come into existence to study a cultural heritage which has no equal on the American continent—to study it, to understand it, and to preserve it. They have done and are doing a good job, and there have been some outstanding leaders. Since 1891, when the first of the societies of consequence began to function, an enormous amount of research, exploration, and explanation has been done. It made good sense to start those studies where most of them began—in the middle of a recognized, on-going situation. In later years, it made, and still makes just as good sense to undertake separate studies, limited in scope but in such depth as is possible, in order that we may broaden our horizons, round out our information, and perhaps make a few corrections. That there are still untouched areas—by now untouched only because they have not been recognized—should be a surprise to no one. However, the full story of what our German forebears did to shape us, our attitudes, and our thinking will not be told until such peripheral pockets as the West End and *its* periphery have been

analyzed and valid conclusions have been drawn.

There are still West Ends to explore. There are unpublished manuscripts in the dialect, crying out to be read, unknown music that calls for editing and publishing, and hidden fraktur records that could clear up many mysteries of time, place, and identity if they were brought to light. Within the past year the author has seen a number of pieces of superb fraktur never exposed to public view and never publicized. There are artisans of skill, artists of talent, workmen of ability, entrepreneurs of imagination. There are men who, vaguely remembered now, will be less than memories by the time another generation passes unless something is done to keep the names green.

No one, in the nature of things, can pry the invisible, submerged portion of an iceberg out of the water and thereby expose something new to the sight of man. But, with exploration and understanding, balances change and, given the right addition and subtraction, the total mass can fall into a position which will give a fairer picture of the whole. If enough researchers with enough avenues of exploration work quickly enough, we may get a markedly changed or completely revised view before time melts all.

Why the hurry?

Frankly, there is good reason not to dawdle. The peace and quiet of the deep Dutch Country as well as the leisurely pace of the villages farther to the north are, whether we choose to acknowledge it or not, already on the way to oblivion. The once lovely vistas of broad farmland from the highways leading west out of Dutch Country cities have all but disappeared. In their place are rows, endless rows, of boxy little houses, consciously cute now but with the seeds of future slums already sprouting within them.

Up-country, once modestly priced summer boarding places have vanished, front porches, wicker rockers, and all, along with the comfortable old farmhouses which, for a couple of months in the summer, catered to visitors from the city. In their place are pretentious hostelries with swimming pools, directors of recreation, bars, golf courses, and ski slopes—in many cases starting on a shoestring, rising to seemingly meteoric success, and disappearing or changing hands just as rapidly. One notes it without making a judgment. That is the way things are—and in such a picture the historical document from the past is often of less significance than the present dollar.

Eastern Pennsylvania can hardly escape the taint of the "metropolitan-suburban sprawl." Situated as it is within the wide strip of what has been dubbed *Boswash* ("Boston to Washington"), it is on the way to filling up with people, with houses, and with the complications the two create. Land can still be had, of course, for a summer place, for a second home, or for investment, but undeveloped land sold for a few dollars an acre little more than a decade ago now commands a thousand as a bare starting point.

The population is not exploding; it *has* exploded, and human beings must have and will find a place to live. That place will include—has included, does include—lower Dutchdom, the up-country, the remotest gully and crag of the Poconos. With good highways, a sufficiency of airports, and ample nonworking time, people—more kinds of people than the easy-going Dutch Country ever knew or imagined—are beginning to take over eastern Pennsylvania and are rebuilding it in their own image. Every problem known to the big city, every aberration in behavior, every vagary in dress or conduct can even now be matched in most remote country hamlets. What is worn in Greenwich Village in lower New York, what is thought in West-chester, and what is being protested by the would-be *avant garde* at college are being worn, thought, and protested in Appenzell, Gilbert, Snydersville.

If the past means something to us, we should have the good sense to do something to preserve it. We can not hold back the tide of population. We can not prevent the wholesale appropriation of property—whether humane or high-handed—for highways and their concomitant interchanges. We can not use David's slingshot when the government officially announces, "Your property is required . . . . ," no matter how long we have had it, how much we love it, or how pitiful the government's appraisal of its

worth seems to us as we scan the real estate listings for something comparable.

But we can consciously interpret and report such parts of the past as are known to us for the use of others who will come after us. By no means are all invaders barbarians; many are as eager as we are to fit themselves into the eternal, on-going scheme of human progress, with its past, present, and future. For the decaying buildings razed in urban renewal programs there is, eventually, the new high-rise apartment house. So, too, for the unique rural architectural gem with 28-inch thick stone walls there is at least a set of measured drawings on record somewhere in government archives; for seemingly wanton destruction of homeplaces and farmsteads there are, here and there, the charisma and benediction of the National Park Service.

In earlier times a farm grandmother who had reached the utter limit of her power to cope had a term for the next step: she simply "gave up," and from that point on, someone else carried the ball. Her situation and ours are not really comparable, though. According to the sun dial, time may take all —but not just yet, and not unless we choose, like Grandma, to give up and allow—not time, but other people—to do all the shaping of the future. We have two priceless attributes which not a soul among those who will eventually take our places has: the remembrance of and, in some cases, a partial first-hand acquaintance with things past. Putting them on record has, at the very least, all the absorption of a game. Any number can play. Let's start now: turn the page.

# 2
# From Forest to Plank House

One of the inescapable facts of life north of the Blue Mountain, which has long been taken as the line of demarcation between "up" and "down" in the Dutch Country, was the woods. Eastward into New Jersey, northward all the way to Canada, and westward to the prairie country stretched the endless miles of trees. Much of the time the forest, always a living presence, might appear to be indifferent to the invasion of the white man; at times it was hostile; seldom if ever could it be thought of as really friendly.

In the eighteenth century, the terms "woods" and "wilderness" could largely be considered synonymous —and there can be no doubt that the shape of life in the Poconos, from the most southerly foothills to the northernmost outposts, was determined by the forest environment in a way that the "deep" Dutch Country knew nothing about. In a later age it could be said with only minor reservations and perhaps only a small grain of salt that clothes made the man; in the beginning, the Pocono woods and their extensions and ramifications shaped not only the man but also his wife, children, domestic economy—and often death and burial.

From the first, unwanted trees and the shade they created—to say nothing of the enemies they sheltered —stood in the way of the venturer whose living had to come in large part from the soil. One could burn the trees, once they had been felled, or he could dispose of them in other ways. It is this matter of "other ways" that for a century gave northeastern Pennsylvania its distinctive, almost stereotyped character.

From the outset, too, it was clear that with some geographical sections little, if anything, could be done. On the top of the Poconos there were thousands of acres of scrub and marshland on which the harsh name of "Shades of Death" had been fastened, and for good reason. At the time of the Wyoming Massacre in 1778, when the white pioneers fled southward to escape the combined onslaught of the Indians and the Tories, so many of them met their death in the impassable morasses of the Poconos tableland that for years the mere mention of the place would produce a shudder in the sensitive. Some parts of the territory are almost as inaccessible today as they were nearly two centuries ago, but other sections have been cleared, drained, and transformed into summer —and more recently winter—resort areas.

Another "hopeless" section was the central wilderness of Pike County, where, it was said facetiously, only three constant factors, all bad, existed: rattlesnakes, bad whiskey, and Democrats. With the passing of time, some of this rugged terrain, too, has been subdued, but other portions have, on a "forever wild" stipulation, passed into the hands of the Commonwealth as game preserves or state forest. Perhaps, when the first snide stereotype was affixed to Pike County, things were not so utterly desperate as they sounded. For one thing, while the rattlesnakes were, during the warm weather, an ever-present menace, at least the country was free of the equally numerous and fully as dangerous copperheads which infested the neighborhood of Mt. Minsi. The whiskey, made secretly and circulated deviously, was undoubtedly bad, but probably no more lethal than the applejack of the Mt. Tammany section of nearby New Jersey. As for politics, it seems likely that the trio of woes attributed to Pike County must have been conceived by a Republican!

The trees had to be disposed of, as we have said,

*A broad ax, used for hewing, and its original wooden sheath.*

and so the sawmills came into being. It would be out of the question to list them in any really systematic chronology, since many of them operated for a short time and then moved elsewhere or changed hands or—only too frequently—burned down. Some were large operations and some were small. All were slow, but by turning logs into planks they enabled the pioneer to get started on his lifelong project of transforming the wilderness into a place of farms and homes.

One of the earliest mills on record was built in the Wallenpaupac territory, not far from Salem, between 1774 and 1779 by Jacob Kimble. This place was burned by hostile Indians in 1779. Another early mill was built not far away, and before 1798, in Paupac Township. Evidence of its primitive nature lies in the fact that it was a "spout" mill; that is, water was conveyed in hollow logs from its source to the millrace and the wheel. The simple superstructure of the mill and of the race was of hand-hewn

*Horseshoes are familiar to almost everyone, either as three-dimensional objects or as symbols. As for ox shoes, it has been suggested that hen's teeth are easier to find nowadays! The ox shoes shown here are from Kellersville.*

planks. The record does not indicate the owner. For every known mill of this type there were probably a dozen others, unrecorded and scattered throughout the wilderness in places which at the time could be identified only by the surnames of the hardy souls subsisting there.

The first sawmill in Dreher Township, Wayne County, is believed to have been established by Allen Megargle, in 1825. Megargle was also a gristmill operator. In nearby Greene Township, in Pike County, John R. Gilpin built a sawmill, said to have been the first in that township, about 1843. This enterprise, with modifications in its later years, was still operating in the early 1900s.

Lumber sawed at a mill had not yet become a standard building medium in 1843. In that year, one William Banks, a cabinet-maker, came from Yorkshire, England, and settled at what was first called Sugar Hill (from its groves of sugar maple trees), and later, Panther. His sons, William, Jr., James, and Samuel, helped him saw enough lumber by hand to build a plank house. Since the boards in this type of dwelling may be up to four or more inches thick, the construction is almost as close to that of a log house as to one of frame. The first Banks house burned, but was soon rebuilt. The second one is still standing, and has been occupied for five generations by members of the Banks family. A second house of this nature—the long-time residence of Emile Huguenin, a French-speaking emigrant from Travère, Switzerland—stood in Newfoundland until a mere decade ago. An earlier house of "hewn planks" in said to have been built on the so-called Wilderness Road in Blooming Grove, Pike County, before 1827.

Isaac I. Kipp operated a sawmill on East Branch Pond (Lake Paupac) in 1851. Many men in many other places followed Isaac's plan of operation: he set up a mill to turn into salable lumber the trees from the acreage he wanted for his farm, plus the trees from what would become the farms of near neighbors. When the little community had produced enough lumber for the buildings needed there, plus enough additional lumber to use in trade for hardware, equipment, etc., the mill was sold to another operator who repeated the process in a different location.

This procedure, systematic or unsystematic, according to one's point of view, left intact some very considerable stands of timber, with the result that a few lumbering operations are still going on in places which never developed into built-up areas. Present-day enterprises, though, often involve stands of second-growth—and once in a while third-growth—tim-

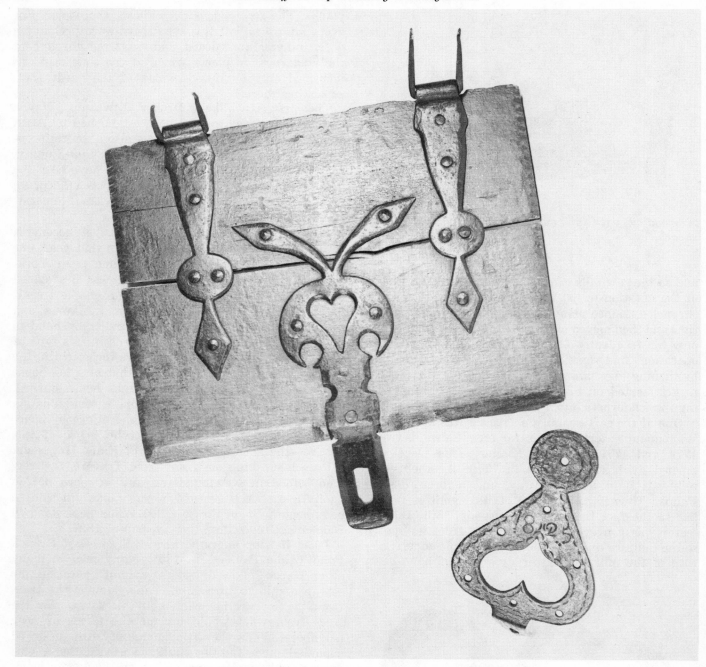

*The lid of a Conestoga wagon tool box with hand-forged decorative iron. The hasp of a similar lid, dated 1825, was found in the Delaware Water Gap.*

ber. Very few stands of virgin forest are to be found; those which do exist are in secluded places which have fortunately escaped the hazards of tropical storms, insect plagues, and forest fires.

While there was a wide variety in the tree species of the up-country—ash, oak, maple, hickory, birch, cherry, and beech predominating among the deciduous trees and spruce, pine, and hemlock in the evergreens —beech and hemlock were outstanding. As a matter of fact, beech trees were so numerous in the long reaches above Paradise, Cresco, and Canadensis that the usual name applied to the total area was "The

Beech." "The Beech" was noted—and is still noted—for the severity of its winters, a salient feature of which was the excessive depth of snow which accumulated in the woods. An early historian notes that William Stroud Reese, of Monroe County, went up to The Beech in 1836 to cut cherry for logs. (Cherry was the favorite cabinet wood of the time.) He was trapped in four and a half feet of snow near what is now Tobyhanna—four and a half feet on the level, presumably, since drifts assumed colossal proportions. The author recalls that one drift at a bend on Manhart's Hill in Panther was estimated to be 53 feet in depth at the time of the great blizzard of 1914.

Prices of commodities in times gone by are meaningless today, but can still be interesting. One notes that white pine, almost nonexistent now in clear or prime condition, commanded less than two cents a board foot back in 1813. An entry in John Turn's store ledger in Smithfield Township in that year indicates that Turn paid Gershom Bunnell $18.37 for 1100 feet. In the same ledger, but for the year 1836, Turn credited Moses Shoemaker with the following:

| | |
|---|---|
| 161 feet, chestnut posts | $ 1.46 |
| 279 feet, oak posts | 1.93 |
| 1552 feet, hemlock boards and scantlings | 12.41 |
| 1416 feet lath | 5.22 |
| 569 feet pine boards | 5.69 |

Lumbering was not always a family-owned business. Where it was profitable to do so, professional lumber outfits with skeleton crews would move into a locality, hire local labor, and remain as long as there were trees to cut. These companies built their own plank or corduroy roads, conveying the logs in winter by horse and bobsled either to the mill or to a stream which in the spring would be swollen sufficiently to float the timber to the river. The distant market was often Philadelphia.

Since in those days there was nothing like scientific forestry or a replanting program, raw, deforested tracts of land were so distressing to look at that an occasional family preferred the woods still standing to the wild tangle of cutover ground, and built its homestead there.

Many of the lumbering crews came up into Wayne and Pike counties from Monroe, where clearing had taken place earlier and under less rigorous circumstances. We are told, though, that in 1860 there were still 61 sawmills in Monroe. (Only 20 years earlier, the census of 1840 listed 107.) Recognizing that in Monroe by that time most of the forested land suitable for agricultural purposes had been turned into

farms, one gets some idea of the magnitude of the total lumbering operation in northeastern Pennsylvania.

Steam-operated mills had largely replaced those operated by water wheels by the end of the nineteenth century. They may have been less picturesque than the earlier mills, but they were undeniably more efficient. It might seem that they were also more dangerous, in the sense of fires started by flying sparks, but from the very beginning one of the commonest notations one finds in connection with an early mill, no matter how it was powered, is that it burned. Spontaneous combustion *could* take place in damp sawdust produced by whatever process, but the wind-borne spark from the smokestack in a sawmill could lead to deadly consequences in a matter of minutes.

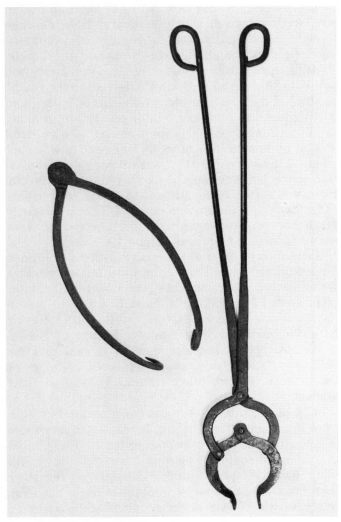

*A portable handle for a large kettle used in fireplace cookery and a pair of tongs also intended for fireplace use.*

An off-beat ramification of the usual lumbering operation was the production of props for the coal mines of Scranton and points near by. Since these timbers might be shorter than the standard twelve- or sixteen-foot length for boards, sections of damaged or flawed trees were often salvaged for the purpose. However, a ten-inch diameter—too small for profitable lumber production—was about right for mine props, and so young trees, especially hardwoods, were favorites. In western Monroe, at the village of Effort, where a spoke factory did a thriving business in the 1860s, only the perfectly straight-grained section at the butt of a tree trunk could be used for spokes. The rest of the tree was then utilized for mine timbers or for some purpose other than spokes.

After the railroads made their appearance, another by-product of the essential lumbering business was in great demand—the railroad tie. Ties, uniform in size, were cut from young hardwood trees as close to eight inches in diameter as possible, and flattened on two sides. The stunted scrub oaks of the Pocono Plateau, practically useless otherwise, were well suited to this purpose. For decades they were almost as staple a medium of exchange as eggs or butter, and cutting ties was a regular winter occupation in many families. Sometimes they were hauled to a railroad station by team and bobsled or team and wagon, but where it was feasible they were floated downstream to a convenient shipping point. In 1889, about 90,000 ties were rafted from Milford to Shawnee. Incidentally, "team" in the Pocono region did not necessarily mean horses; oxen were used for heavy-duty work up to—and in a few cases after—1900.

Some men made traffic in railroad ties a real business. At Dingman's Ferry, one Case McCarty was a well-known tie merchant. At North Water Gap, later rechristened Minisink Hills, Fred Eilenberger was in the business. George L. Nyce, at Bushkill; Harley Lamb, at Portland; and Andrew Yetter, at Blairstown, also bought and sold ties. It is said that the D. L. and W. Railroad was the favored customer of the tie men, though other railroads also used their product.

Mine sprags are all but unknown today, but once were in considerable demand. It may seem incredible to a generation which takes power brakes for granted that a loaded coal car speeding too rapidly down hill could have its pace suitably slowed by thrusting sharpened sticks of wood into the wheels, but such was the case. These sticks or clubs, called sprags, were cut from hardwood too small for ties. Their use called for real skill, but at best this method of slowing the wheels was a dangerous one. Sprags for use in the mines at Scranton were being cut in Panther as late as 1910.

Bobsleds as conveyances to get logs to the mill in the winter changed little over the years. The wagons —actually skeletal, bodiless structures for the most part rather than wagons in the usual sense—had little about them which could be changed except for the wheels. The wheels *did* change, and very early. In "The Minisink," which might mean any part of the Delaware River basin from Shawnee northward to Port Jervis, wagon wheels in 1800 were solid pieces made from cross sections of a large log, according to an early historian. There is no mention of tires that early—but unironed wheels of this kind could not long stand the grueling punishment to which vehicles would be subjected in the lumber woods.

Wagoning soon became an integral part of the lumbering industry, of course. Getting logs to the mill was one thing, but once they had been converted to planks or other sawed pieces, the product had to be taken away for the next step, whatever it was to be. Since the mills operated the year round, and since there was a limit to the amount of lumber which could be stacked at any one mill, teamsters and their conveyances were on the road from January to December.

## COLLECTORS LOOK FOR:

Seats used on early wagons

Whole sheep pelts used as cushions for wagon seats

Blankets, coverlets, or quilts once used as wagon seat covers

Wheel jacks (to raise wheels free of the ground, for repairs)

Wrenches used to remove nut from axle bolt

Handwrought brake blocks

Structural iron from early bobsleds

Iron ax sockets used on wagons and sleds—and, although they have seldom survived, wood sockets. It was a foolish woodsman who went anywhere without his ax.

Woodsmen's saws, hammers, and wedges—especially wedges with individual identifying marks. A balky tree, after it had been sawed across the base, could usually be toppled, even against a breeze, by a judiciously tapped wedge.

Ox shoes of iron—*eight* in a full set because oxen have cloven hoofs

Horseshoes and handwrought horseshoe nails

Horseshoeing equipment—carrying box, hammers, hoof-paring knives, etc.

Wooden yokes for oxen

Bentwood bows for yokes

*Jackpot:* Double wagon seat with original handwoven hickory splints for the seat itself

# 3
## Poling down the River

Rafting is a lost art so far as Dutchdom is concerned; if one wishes nowadays to see what a riverful of logs stretching from shore to shore and away to a vanishing point in the distance looks like he will have to go to the far Northwest or up to the St. Lawrence. Not only is the occupation lost; there is no more than an occasional peavey or cant hook left, since the last raft of any consequence was piloted down the Delaware about 1900. The incidence, growth, and decline of the activity paralleled those of the lumbering industry itself, but with the difference that enough cutting of trees still goes on, here and there, to keep the memory, if not actually green, at least alive, in the minds of descendants of old-time raftsmen. The activity was at its peak in the 1840s.

Men cut trees all winter long in the days when the country was being cleared for farm land. If there was no way of turning the lumber to account, it was burned, or dragged away and left to rot. Whenever and wherever possible, though, it went to market, even if the labor required to get it there would seem to us now to be out of all proportion to the ultimate gain. Roads were few and far between—Indian paths as often as not. Alone among arteries of travel, the Old Mine Road, following the course of the Delaware from below Kingston, New York, to the Water Gap, achieved importance as a thoroughfare in the 1700s—but it was on the wrong side of the river, so far as being of use to up-country lumbering was concerned.

One looks at the anemic-appearing creeks in the eastern part of the Commonwealth today and wonders how they could ever have had any importance as waterways; as for the Delaware, beautiful as it is, from the source as far south as Shawnee it is possible in many places to wade all the way across much of the year. Yet the creeks leading to the river ran full, in the days when the countryside was still for-

ested, and the Delaware, in consequence, was a mightier stream than it has ever been since. When in spring the water was high, the lack of roads was of little moment to the lumberman; in fact, it hardly mattered, except in areas where the distance from the slashing to the nearest navigable creek was considerable. It mattered, though, in the watersheds of such small creeks as Sugar Hill, Frühling, and Levis, up in the Poconos; they were so rocky, so winding, and so precipitous in their descent that any thought of utilizing them to float logs was ridiculous. Just the opposite in nature was the sluggish Wallenpaupac, which in its progress from South Sterling to Newfoundland and points beyond had so little current that there was a well-known quip to the effect that a local sluggard—the name would vary according to the occasion—had acquired his lethargic nature because in his childhood his mother had set him to prod the water forward with a stick now and then, lest it start to flow backwards.

The Lackawaxen was about the only tributary large enough to be significantly useful in floating logs to the Delaware; consequently, those who could not transport their logs directly to the river bank did the next best thing and got them to the Lackawaxen. The village of Lackawaxen, on the creek of the same name, was as far up in the watershed as it was practicable to construct a raft of any size. One should perhaps note that the stream beyond that point was not totally useless as an artery of transportation; dugouts, which could carry cargoes of three or four tons, had been in use way up stream even before the Durham boats came up the river in the 1750s. Two men using oars or pike poles for propulsion, according to need, could take a loaded dugout successfully into streams so narrow that one wonders how they did it.

So far as rafting is concerned, however, the "course" was from Lackawaxen to Easton, Trenton, or Philadelphia. A good deal of preliminary work had to be done in straightening out crooked spots, getting rid of dangerous boulders, and eliminating rapids on the Lackawaxen end of the waterway; even so, it was not an unknown occurrence for a raft to come to grief before it was well on its way. In the event of such an accident, the best that could be done was to seek out an eddy downstream and put

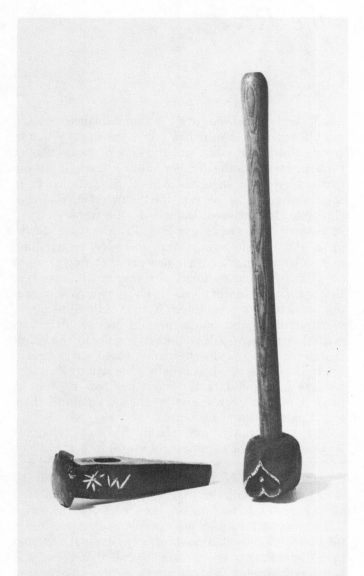

*Wedges which looked just like other wedges had a bad habit of disappearing; so distinguishing marks were used on valued ones. The logger's sledge was used to put the owner's insignia on logs which went to the mill or down the river.*

*The cant hook for turning or rolling logs is still used in lumbering operations, but the rafter's log dog—the sharp points driven into contiguous logs to hold them together—is now rarely found. Sharpened horseshoes joined by short sections of heavy chain often substituted for "real" log dogs.*

the pieces together again. Southward, after the river had grown broader and deeper, a different hazard presented itself—the sand or gravel bar, which could come into being after a single bad storm without giving any sign of its presence to the navigator. While

*A loggers' inn on the River Road east of Shawnee-on-Delaware, as rendered by artist Charles X. Carlson of Lancaster, Pa., in the 1960s. The front porch is a later addition.*

professional pilots tended to be a fearless and resourceful lot, they took few chances, especially when a large operation was under way; they made it their business not only to learn their territory, but to review it as frequently as possible, since it was never safe to assume that the current at any given point would be precisely where it had been the year before.

It was the young, inexperienced runner, not the pilot, whose performance had to be watched. Rafting was tricky and dangerous, and a single false move could throw a smooth operation into utter chaos. A man who ignored an order or who undertook to make a judgment on his own was not often given a second chance.

Rafts were not simply an aggregation of logs floating downriver at one time. They were entities built according to a thought-out plan. True, the logs of which they were composed might have been picked up at a dozen or more dumping spots along the river, but once a raft had been constructed it remained a unit, barring accidents, until it reached its destination. While there was some variation in over-all form and shape, the usual method was to mortise the ends of the logs, tying parallel ranks together with a cross member into which wooden pins would be driven, to hold them tight. These small units would then be combined to form larger ones, the fastening being done with chains or heavy rope. A short section of

chain with a sharpened horseshoe at each end, the
points driven deep into the outside logs of two contiguous units, allowed flexibility without a loss of
security. Rafts were usually large; the average size
would run from 70,000 to 125,000 board feet.

Once a raft had been completely assembled and
had been pushed away from the shore, it was steered
by means of oar stems set into stanchions, one at each
corner. Oar stems were usually 40 feet long. An extra
one was normally carried along on a trip—just in
case. The pilot took his stand at the rear right-hand
corner, and gave all his directions from that spot. His
word was both Law and Gospel throughout the trip.

On a river as broad and free as the Mississippi,
night navigation would have been assumed as a matter of course. On most parts of the Delaware it would
have been quixotic, and the raft was engineered into
an eddy before dark whenever it was possible. Accidents or unforseen problems which disrupted the
schedule were a cause for concern from pilot to lowliest
helper, especially on the upper stretches of the river,
because of the possibility that the vital operation of
docking might have to be done after dark—that is,
"blind."

The first raft of which there seems to be any record
was run by Daniel Skinner, of Damascus, Wayne
County, in 1764. A preliminary venture of his came
to grief, but so firmly convinced was he that the river
trip was feasible that he immediately tried again,
this time successfully. He took his raft all the way to
Philadelphia, earning the title "Lord High Admiral
of the Delaware" in the process. It is said that this
distinction was so great a source of satisfaction to him
that he constituted himself a kind of dictator over
river matters, and expected others to seek his permission and advice before undertaking expeditions of
their own. It is hinted, too, that if the petitioner presented a bottle of spirits as a more or less offhand
gesture the permission was likely to be immediately
forthcoming!

Other names are prominent in the history of rafting. The best forward oarsman in the days of the
Lord High Admiral was said to be Josiah Parkes. In
the years following, a number of men in the Parkes
family earned enviable reputations as raftsmen. John
Hornbeck of Dingmans Ferry was a leading river
pilot for many years. J. Depue Le Bar, who was born
at Pahaquarry in 1814, seems to have had a touch of
the Paul Bunyan in his makeup. He was a good
steersman and was thoroughly conscious of the fact,
boasting that he would successfully run the biggest
raft ever floated. He probably did; while no measurements were ever reported, the raft was so wide that

at some points it scraped both sides of the river!

The romance attaching to feats like that of Le
Bar's attracted to the river a following of young
men who were as much interested in the possible
achievement of glory as they were in the five to ten
dollars they could earn—the sum varying according
to where they started—in making the trip to Philadelphia. Usual starting places in the up-country, in
addition to Lackawaxen, were Port Jervis, Dingmans
Ferry, and Delaware Water Gap, but hands were
taken on at any place they might be needed.

The Water Gap was a particularly strategic point
in that it was here that a new steersman usually
came aboard. It was generally assumed that no one
man would have time to master the intricacies of the
entire length of the river because of the number of
changes that normally took place in a single year. The
steersman for the southerly part of the trip might
or might not wish to continue with the crew of his
upstream predecessor, and each spring a new crop of
young hopefuls flocked to the area on the chance that
they might be hired. Regular year-round hostelries
could not accommodate them all and so, on both sides
of the river, so-called loggers' hotels came into being. These places might actually be a good many miles
from the Water Gap, but in days when everyone
walked, a distance of five to ten miles did not appear
to be a stumbling block.

One such place was that of Valentin Weber, some
six miles east of the Water Gap, on the River Road.
Weber (his English neighbors translated the German
name, making it "Weaver") had lived in a small
house at the foot of a hill opposite Tocks Island, but
in 1867 he built an impressive stone dwelling at the
top, at least partly for the accommodation of river-
men. Two rooms on the second floor were connected
by folding doors which could be pushed back against
the walls when a considerable number were to be
bedded down for the night, and the entire third floor
and a loft were also guest quarters. Almost every
house of entertainment in those days had a bar, and
Weber planned to set up a tavern in the ell of his
house. However, since he was a known tippler he
was unable to secure a license and the tavern never
materialized. Like other "hotels" of the kind on both
sides of the river, including the justly famous and
much older Isaac Van Campen Inn, the place is now
within the National Park Area.

There were people other than those engaged in the
business of rafting who made the trip down the river
in the spring. When the water was both high and
turbulent the journey had less appeal than when it
was just high—but passengers under any circum-

stances were by no means unusual. Crude sleeping accommodations could be arranged; food was taken aboard at the starting point.

After the earliest years there were occasional rafts of sawed lumber, and in addition to passengers these rafts might also carry cargoes of split hoop poles, fence posts, and even flagstones. Passengers, like the raftsmen themselves, might return from port by stage or, according to their finances or desires, they might travel the entire distance on foot.

One small section of Pike County appears to have out-distanced all the rest of the up-country in the size and quality of its trees. This was Hemlock Hollow in Paupac Township. Much of the timber for the Philadelphia Navy Yard came from Hemlock Hollow, but the most celebrated achievement of the place was the providing of the masts for the good ship *Pennsylvania*. Enos Goodrich, of Salem (Wayne County), engineered the cutting and the delivery of the largest trees ever felled in the township—90 feet long, absolutely straight, and *two feet in diameter at the top end*. Such giants have rarely been seen at any time or place. The trees were drawn to Paupac Eddy, we are told, by 20 yokes of oxen, and eventually maneuvered to the Delaware.

Not a hazard, but often a vexation to the pilot was the place on the Delaware, south of Dingmans Ferry, known as Walpack Bend. The water was comparatively calm at this spot but, owing to the thrust of the mountains which rim the area, the river, which flows south, does a neat about-face and flows north again for a number of miles; then it makes another hairpin turn and heads south once more. Pilots could spend a day or more maneuvering through Walpack Bend, and at the end of the job see the same landmarks they had observed when they entered. A favorite local riddle was one which posed the question: "How can you shoot across the Delaware three times with the same bullet?" The answer was obvious to anyone who was familiar with the loops in the stream at Walpack Bend.

Partly in the nature of a riddle, too, was the identity of the Brodheads Creek colts—"How do you harness a Brodheads Creek colt?" The answer was,

*Three plates calling attention to the Delaware River and the Water Gap. Left to right: late specimen made in England by the Old Historical Blue Plate Company; German china marked "Made for Frank Nice, Stroudsburg, Pa."; English souvenir plate marked "Designed and imported by Houser's, Delaware Water Gap, Pa." Frank Nyce's store was well known in the Stroudsburgs; Houser's place of business was in the village of Delaware Water Gap.*

*A haunting and lovely melody of 1915, composed by a musician who has been a long-time resident in the West End. The cover is reproduced by permission of the composer, now Mrs. Henriette Hobbs.*

"With a chain." Only the initiate would know that very early in the history of rafting the Brodheads Creek, from a point south of Canadensis, could be used at times of freshets for floating short logs—logs, not rafts—to the bank of the river beyond Stroudsburg. As they arrived, these logs would be steered to shore and fastened together in small units—"colts"—according to the method described earlier. After enough units had been created to make a raft feasible, they were assembled in the usual manner and sent on their way.

Although rafting was a big spring-time activity, the river was busy, both across and up-and-down, throughout the year. It would be unthinkable that the enormously fertile valleys on the two shores of the Delaware should long remain unknown to each other. While we have no more than a few points of recorded reference for the earliest years, Aaron Dupuis was paying three shillings a day for "boating," according to a notation of 1745. Since the entry occurs in his ledger, with no further detail or elaboration, it is not improbable that it signified a routine operation connected with supplies for his store at Shawnee.

While we are not primarily concerned here with cross-river traffic, we should at least mention the names of some neighborhood ferries which, up to the time that motor traffic put them out of business, bonded the neighborhoods on the two sides of the river more closely than has been the case at any time since. The first was probably Nanatumam, which operated between Pahaquarry Township and Shawnee as far back as 1736, according to official New Jersey records. "Nanatumam" was an Indian name; the same crossing was known as Gould's Ferry when it was operated by James Gould; later still it was called Walker's Ferry. Most southerly in the up-country region we are considering would have been Dill's, about where the village of Portland now stands. A very early crossing was Decker's Ferry, farther up the river at Walpack Bend. This one was in operation in 1755. Rosencrans' and Dimmick's ferries were up-river from the Water Gap. Dimmick's, which operated until well into the present century, was known earlier as Shoemaker's. Still farther up-stream was Ding-

mans, the only one still getting people and vehicles across—but by bridge, now, not by ferry. Then, too, there were private operations, a well-known example being that of Adam Transue, where Karamac Inn once stood, not far from the village of Delaware Water Gap. A footbridge now spans the Delaware between Portland and Columbia, in the general neighborhood of the much earlier Dill's Ferry. This bridge was built where the long covered bridge between the two villages stood before it was destroyed in the flood of 1955.

While we tend to think of ferryboat crossings today as cumbersome, they were serviceable and expeditious in their time. They performed an economic function, of course, but were equally important as a means toward socializing. Jerseyites walked or, later, drove their horse-drawn conveyances to the ferry on Sunday, crossed the river, and then walked up the steep hill to Zion's Lutheran Church on the Pennsylvania side as a matter of course. Pennsylvanians visited their relatives—or went courting—on the Jersey side. And, of course, with recognition of the old saying about where the grass is greener, there were Pennsylvanians who bought top-quality molasses at the store in Calno, New Jersey, as consistently as Jersey-side residents came over to Shawnee to get top-quality vinegar at the store there!

### COLLECTORS LOOK FOR:

Loggers' chains, peavies, hammers, and cant hooks

Circular open-end links used to join chains

Hammers used to impress owners' initials or insignia in the ends of logs

Pilots' river charts

Postcard views of scenes along the routes taken by raftsmen

Memorabilia and ephemera from local hostelries catering to rafting crews

Photographs of rafts, crews, and places of overnight accommodation

*Jackpot:* Logger's hammer with initials identifying it as that of a known person

# 4
## Woodworking: Shoepegs to Ladderbacks

The variety of wooden products turned out in the nineteenth century is rather enlightening to a generation gradually learning how to get along without wood in the twentieth. It might require more than the traditional three guesses nowadays to elicit the right answer to a question like "What is a hoop pole?" However, there was a time—let us say a century ago—when even a backward child would have known that it was a lissome oak or hickory sapling, cut or stripped of its branches, which was shipped down the river on a lumber raft as auxiliary cargo destined to become hoops at a barrel factory. Hoop poles might well be termed an "ancient" commodity, relatively speaking; while the store ledger of Aaron Dupuis at Shawnee indicates that hoop poles were being cut in 1789, they were actually in use much earlier. For example, a hogshead of the kind purchased in Smithfield by James Hyndshaw on May 1, 1744, filled with 107 gallons of rum, would have been heavily bound with hoops made from poles. (The rum, incidentally, cost 12 pounds, nine shillings, and eight pence. Barrels, tierces, and hogsheads were "returnable.") Metal for this kind of container would have been prohibitively expensive in those days; the supply of wood was apparently inexhaustible.

No factory setup was needed for anything as uncomplicated as the hoops for a barrel. The barrel itself was a different matter, though, and called for skilled coopers and a proper place in which they could exercise their craft. Coopers seem always to have been included among the artisans when a planned colonization was to take place—and for the best of reasons: hollow containers were always needed; clay for pottery was not always present and, even when it was, clay vessels could be made only

in comparatively small sizes; work with metal, which had to come from a distance, presupposed complicated preparatory steps and fairly extensive equipment. The cooper needed good wood, simple tools, a roof over his head, and water near by—conditions met without great difficulty.

The Shawnee region in Smithfield Township, north of the Delaware Water Gap, apparently had the first coopers in the up-country. Flour barrels and hogsheads were in common use in 1744 at Aaron Dupuis's store. We do not know who made them. In 1783 Ichabod Grimes was producing pails, meat tubs, washing tubs, barrels, tierces, and hogsheads. John De Long specialized in the production of staves; a notation in 1791 indicates that he received one pound, nine shillings for 700 barrel staves, and six shillings for 50 pipe staves. The name of John Landers, cooper, appears on the tax list in Middle Smithfield Township in 1796. Melchior Heller, a cooper, who lived in the same neighborhood from 1828 to 1889, seems to have concentrated his efforts on the manufacture of flour barrels.

In 1845 there was a coopering setup at Saylorsburg, at that time a village of ten or twelve dwellings, plus a wagonmaker's shop, a tavern—and the cooper's establishment. One might observe that while flour barrels called for skill in the making, the labor required in their manufacture may have been less than what was called for in producing watertight and airtight barrels for cider, whiskey, molasses, vinegar —anything wet. One other name emerges in connection with coopering in this era, that of Joseph Buskirk. Members of this family came northward from Bucks County in very early times, settling mostly in the West End. The full original name was van Bus-

*Shaking forks to spread grain to dry after it had been cradled were a homemade commodity, as were threshing flails. The fork shown here was made and used on a farm at Panther not long after 1855. Later, with a member of the family, it made its way to the Pacific coast, but eventually returned to Pennsylvania.*

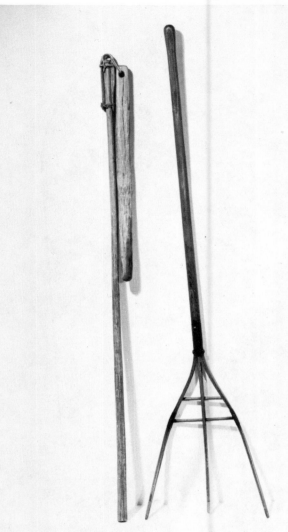

*Coffee and buns are served at the time of Love Feast —a special anniversary day in the Moravian Church calendar. The handmade serving tray is an old one from the church in Newfoundland; the ironstone mugs are of the kind used on these occasions.*

kirk, of Dutch origin and from Holland.

The planing mill was an important factor in taking the stigma of the backwoods off Upper Dutchdom. Rough slabs of lumber, often with bark still on the edges, have always been associated with shacks, shanties, and poverty. Once the pinch of meeting the absolute necessities of life could yield to some consideration for appearance, a community was on its way up. The planing mill, the *raison d'être* for which was making needed things look good, not only supplied the multitudinous wants of a rapidly growing young nation but also improved the situation on the home front.

The earliest of these mills in Wayne may have been that of Cornelius Hendricks, who in 1832 bought ten acres of land at Honesdale to establish a woodworking factory. The property changed hands a number of times, but was fitted for wood turning in 1857, when it was operated by Eliphalet Wood and Ten Eyck Depui. Up to 1880 it was run by water power, but after that time it became a steam mill, one of the first in the country.

Whatever the name of any woodworking factory, or of its special product, almost inevitably it was, first of all, a planing mill. The establishment of William Wallace on the McMichaels Creek, which meets Brodheads Creek at Stroudsburg, was both a sawmill and a planing mill in 1865. It turned out window sash, blinds, flooring, railing, siding, and ornamental brackets. This particular plant specialized in the use of oak, but other mills also owned and operated by Wallace handled other woods.

One of the intriguing phases of woodworking was the manufacture of clothespins. The Tobyhanna and Lehigh Lumber Company, which built a planing mill in 1858, was specializing in clothespins in 1865. The place was destroyed by fire in 1882, but was later rebuilt as a shoepeg factory. A similar retooling, but in reverse, took place in Mountainhome when in 1868 E. Dunbar and Company started a shoepeg factory and then sold it to C. W. Decker, who manufactured clothespins there in 1880. Fine grades of birch, beech, or maple were used for these small objects, and the factories were located close to the source of supply. Mountainhome was an ideal spot in which to set up the milling operation, since it was at the very gateway of the vast forested region known as The Beech. Tobyhanna and Pocono Lake, comparably located, also manufactured clothespins.

One of the special requirements of the shoepeg industry—now a thoroughly forgotten occupation—was that there be an adequate supply of soapstone (steatite) available. After shoepegs had been machined to

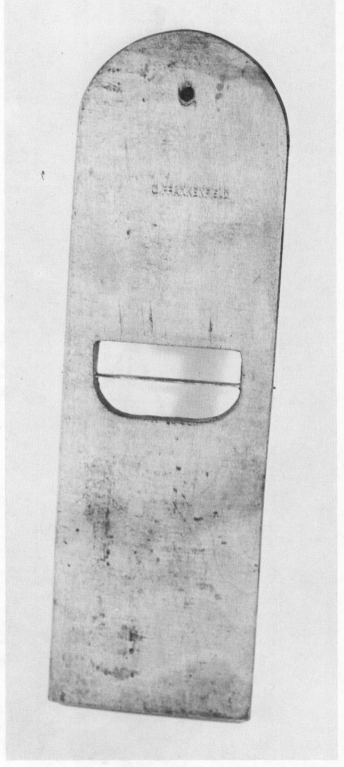

*Housewives in Monroe County a generation or two ago preferred a sweet corn grater by Frankenfield to almost any other they could secure.*

their proper shape, they still had to be smoothed or polished, and to achieve this end they were dumped into a revolving drum with a predetermined amount of the mineral. Prolonged contact with this slippery-textured talc rock gave the pegs a polish that could probably not have been achieved in any other way. Monroe County had a satisfactory supply of soapstone. As a matter of fact, the chances of picking up a soapstone pancake griddle or a footwarmer—two objects in common domestic use a century ago—are probably better in the up-country than almost anywhere else.

Another specialty at Mountainhome seems to have been the production of veneer for furniture. Our sources here are somewhat vague. One early historian speaks of the firm of Shafer and Rinehart, which in the second half of the nineteenth century produced veneer, barrel staves, split shingles, chair seat materials, and wild cherry frames for school slates. Another writer mentions only veneer, but credits its production to C. W. Decker, in a short-lived operation in 1881. There may be no contradiction here; as we have noted elsewhere, the phases of lumbering operations were subject to many changes, including changes of ownership. And, of course, there may really have been two veneer factories.

Still another venture at Mountainhome was the development of boxes for shipping butter. We do not know who produced these boxes—whether Shafer and Rinehart, Decker, or someone else, possibly in a separate establishment—but a Mr. Sperry is credited with developing a machine which put tin fastenings on the boxes. Before that time, the ends of the circular boxes were fastened ("sewed") with thongs.

The upper stretches of the Dutch Country still yield traces of another special kind of mill—that is, if one is given a clue or, better still, a guide. This lost enterprise was the stick factory, the "sticks" produced being dowel rods and umbrella handles. Quite obviously, a planing mill which could turn out these objects was using lathes or other wood-turning equipment, although the term "wood turning" seems not to have been used. The first one may have been the M. F. Van Kirk Stick Factory, established in Honesdale in 1832, actually not by Van Kirk but by L. T. Prescott. In addition to umbrella sticks, parasol handles, and dowel rods, this place produced cigar boxes.

In 1878 H. A. and George H. Lancaster operated an umbrella stick factory at German Valley. Information as to the exact location is in dispute. It may have been at what is still called the Mill Turn, but it is possible that ruins on what is inelegantly known as the Skunk's Misery Road, between Carlton Hill and German Valley, may mark the place. The factory burned in 1886. Another Lancaster enterprise was a stick factory established in 1882 in what is now LaAnna. Partners were H. A. Lancaster and Richard D. Jones, but the operator appears to have been George H. Lancaster.

A very late business, in terms of utilizing products of a primeval forest, was the one operated in Greentown, Pike County, by Samuel Hazleton. We are told that in the years 1897–1900 Hazleton sold $25,000 worth of dowel rods and that his place also turned out umbrella handles.

One of the shortest-lived enterprises—but one with an intriguing sound—was a match factory built in East Stroudsburg in 1882 and operated by W. E. Henry and Company. It sold its interest to a "match combination," according to the record, and closed its doors within the year.

The shaping of ax handles was a favorite leisure-time winter activity of many individuals—at least those who were good at it. Not everyone was, but there was evidently a great deal of satisfaction in fashioning a handle with just the right degree of curve for the individual who would use it, just the right thickness for the size of his hands, and just the right balance in weight between the handle and the metal head. Hammer handles, too, were often made at home, as were handles for shovels, hay forks, grain cradles, and so on, but they did not call for the virtuosity needed to produce a perfect ax handle.

Another implement produced at home, and fabricated with exceptional skill, was one for which there seems to be no name in English. The German is *Schüttelgabel*—a shaking fork. Comparable to a pitchfork but with three carefully braced flaring wooden prongs, it was used in a grain field for spreading newly cradled grain so that it would dry rapidly. Such implements, usually larger and frequently lacking the graceful curves which characterize the American product, were common in Europe. In recent years, metal-tipped forks with widely spreading prongs—a spread of as much as 18 inches, in some cases—have made their way into antique shops from Canada. For the person interested in the implements of the Pennsylvania Dutchland—*caveat emptor!*

From earliest times, most of the furniture in Upper Dutchdom was made right in the home community, not imported from outside. A one-room cabin in the forest could have only the most primitive of equipment, since food and shelter of necessity took precedence over such niceties as chairs and tables. It was

*Pine storage chest made by a local carpenter in the vicinity of what is now Cherry Lane in Monroe County. It is fastened throughout with wooden pegs.*

not long, however, before housewives were able to do away with the first clumsy, home-hewn pieces—and it is clear that they made a clean sweep. While bona fide "primitives" have come to light in New England and in the South, few objects of great age, although they once existed, have survived in up-country Pennsylvania. Just one of these pioneer survivals comes to mind: a four-legged stand-up desk with a slanting top and a number of small, crude drawers, in the possession of Omar Michaels, lately of Shawnee but now of Arizona. It has a record of continuous ownership in the Michaels family from the late eighteenth century. One bears in mind, to be sure, that there were settlements both in New England and in the South

that long antedated most of those in the up-country.

Most men were handy with tools; they had to be. While not all of them were skilled enough to make attractive or even acceptable furniture, it was a poor workman indeed who could not or did not turn out simple stools, benches, and perhaps storage cupboards —objects upon which the professional furniture maker would rather not spend his time.

Cherry was the favorite cabinet wood. Black walnut was well liked, but it grew only in limestone soil and, with only rare exceptions, no farther north than Monroe County. With a world of trees from which to choose, there was little reason to do much importing. Birch, tulip poplar, and maple followed cherry and

*A highly individual corner jelly cupboard, made to fit
an obtuse-angled spot in a German Valley kitchen.
The name of the first owner, born in 1799, may still
be seen on the inside of one of the doors. The gingerbread oak clock is of a type favored in many up-country kitchens.*

black walnut in popularity among the hardwoods. Soft wood, which would be painted, was best represented by white pine, although bull pine, spruce, and occasionally hemlock were utilized for kitchen pieces. Bird's-eye maple, which takes on a different appearance and is called tiger-striped maple when it is quarter-sawed, was frequently employed in combination with cherry. As there were comparatively few maple trees which boasted of the distinctive bird's-eye formation, the lumber was often converted to veneer so that it would go further.

Now and then a cabinetmaker who wanted to demonstrate just what he could do would, in a single piece of furniture, combine cherry, bird's-eye maple, regular maple, oak, and—to top it off—mahogany veneer. (By mid-nineteenth century, the vogue for mahogany was such that even the most remote furniture maker was called upon to use it.) One of these accomplished artists may have been John Jacoby, who in 1844 and 1845 was a member of the State legislature from Monroe County. We say "may have been," because the lone piece of evidence to make even a guess possible is the word "Jacoby" scrawled in pencil at the bottom of a large secretary-desk with the combination of woods mentioned above. We do not know who the first owner of the piece was, but James Wycliff Rinker of Sciota bought it at auction, presumably well before the end of the century. The piece went from him to his oldest daughter, Carrie, who married Van Orris Detrick and went to live in East Stroudsburg. Mrs. Detrick sold it to its present owner, who has returned it to its place of early ownership in Sciota.

Jacoby—if he really was the maker of the beautiful secretary-desk and not, perhaps, the first owner—would not necessarily have been the earliest among the numerous skilled cabinetmakers of the up-country. One of the earliest would have been David Hartson Carlton, who came from an unnamed place in New England in 1817 and set up a place for making chairs at what eventually came to be known as Carlton Hill, not far from the present village of South Sterling.

Another top-of-the-Poconos cabinetmaker was Samuel Banks (1824–1889) of Panther. While it is presumed that he was the maker of furniture used at Panther and other nearby hamlets, there is nothing beyond hearsay to substantiate the idea. He was also an early schoolmaster in the community.

In Wilsonville, the surrounding territory of which was later flooded, becoming Lake Wallenpaupac, lived a man of many affairs in 1843—one William Shouse (1787–1877). Not a native, he went to the place as a

young man and conducted a number of different mills. He may or may not, while there, also have followed his early training, which was that of chair and cabinetmaker. In 1870 he went to Easton to spend the rest of his days.

One of the hardest-working men ever to adopt the top of the Poconos as his chosen home was Nathan Houck, who is mentioned elsewhere. One of the things for which, as a woodturner, he is remembered, even today, is the fact that he made tent poles for the Union Army during the Civil War.

Farther south, in Middle Smithfield Township, a more accurate picture is possible. Hugh Pugh (Dupuis?) was a carpenter who made coffins as part of his trade as early as 1753. John Turn, Sr., first elder in the Middle Smithfield Church in 1814, purchased a farm which many years later became the Lutheran Ministerium Camp and which still later was acquired by the National Park Service as part of the Delaware Water Gap National Recreation Area.

*A slant-top schoolmaster-type desk credited to an early member of the Neyhart family in the Tannersville area. The interior is fitted wth chestnut compartments.*

*A Hamilton Township Fenner-Snyder ladderback which has remained in the family since the time of its making early in the nineteenth century.*

More significantly for us, we find that he made coffins, cases for grandfather clocks, tall-post and trundle beds, bureaus, desks, dough trays, rocking cradles, and chests. There is speculation that he may have made the remarkable wooden daybed which the Park Service acquired in 1970 for its Slateford Farm restoration. Other nearby cabinetmakers were John Clark (1813–1892) and his son Philip B. (1837–1906). Edward Walton, according to an advertisement in the Stroudsburg *Monroe Democrat* in 1837, made and sold chairs.

A claim to fame as a cabinetmaker was established by Nathan Wells, who was born at Milford in 1796. He was a man of more than ordinary ingenuity, and

it was he who created the Wells Fanning Mill—a device which separated chaff from threshed grain. Some of these mills—an over-simplification would be to call them antique wind tunnels—were beautifully decorated by the same painters who made horse-drawn carriages works of art. Wells was succeeded by his son Henry, born in 1837. When the present town of Milford was laid out it included ground which once was known as Wells Ferry, named for three Wells brothers of whom Nathan was one.

At Snydersville, the cabinetmaker par excellence was Levi Slutter. The graceful altar, altar railings, and pulpit in the church at Hamilton Square are Slutter's work. Although the church was established in 1775, it took its present form in 1829. Almost all, if not all, the pews installed then are still in use.

Who made the set of six ladderback chairs long in the possession of the Snyder-Fenner family of Hamilton is a moot point. It may have been Slutter, or Henry Miller, who will be mentioned later, but more probably was a member of the Snyder family. One by one, the chairs went to different members of the family in the course of time. They were so desired by Snyder descendants that it is probable all six are still in existence. Two definitely are—one in the house in which it is believed the set was first used.

Peter Williams was another mid-century cabinetmaker in Hamilton. Like many other skilled woodworkers, he was also a maker of coffins. He apparently did his own woodturning; a Kellersville store ledger for 1837 indicates that he was paid 30 cents for "turning" six boards. A ledger dated 1859 indicates that he turned two small bed "poasts" (15 cents); six tops for headboards on bedsteads (60 cents); and a small bedstead (15 cents). An Empire-style doll's bureau made in 1857 for his little daughter Frances is now in the possession of a great-grand-daughter. A magnificent solid walnut chest is owned by the same person and a small secretary-desk stands in the house in Sciota where Frances lived after she was married.

The most talked-about ladderbacks in Upper Dutchdom are probably those made by Henry Miller about this time. These chairs had handmade white oak splint seats, and were so tightly put together that the wood would splinter before the members could be pulled apart. The secret lay in Miller's method of gluing and in his simultaneous use of dry and of semi-cured wood. All the pieces to be glued had grooves cut into the tenons and glue was run into these grooves as well as on the tenons. The rungs of his chairs were made of dry wood; the posts were only half-dry, and shrank over the rungs with the passing of time. This

*In mid-nineteenth century tradition, this sofa is the
work of Peter Williams, cabinet and coffin maker of
Hamilton Township. For many years it was in the
possession of his daughter Frances (b. 1848) and is
now owned by one of Frances' grandchildren.*

shrinking process, together with the unusual gluing
method, produced a fit which has never been equaled
for tightness. Neither the posts nor the rungs of
Miller's chairs came from sawed lumber; only pieces
split by hand from straight-grained butt sections of
trees were used. There is a difference of opinion as to
whether Miller should be counted as a resident of
Snydersville or of Kellersville—both in Hamilton.

As was the case everywhere, stories grew up about
certain prominent individuals or places. One of these
has to do with a well-known coffin and cabinetmaker
in whose house the sound of hammering could be
heard at times when no one was actually at work.
Knowing from experience that he was being warned
of an impending death, the artisan would go out to
his shop and get his tools and materials in order.
Before long, word would come that his services were
needed to make a coffin!

An incomplete Hamilton Township ledger from a
place which might have been in Kellersville, Fennersville, or Snydersville presents an interesting picture

of millwork produced from 1856 to 1866, not only as
to the nature of the objects constructed but also as to
prices. One could buy, on order, a meal chest, a wood
box, a bedstead, a table, a bake tray, or a rolling
pin. Or he could secure a corner cupboard ($9.00),
a rocking cradle ($2.00), a teacher's school desk
($3.00), or a cabbage cutter (50 cents). "Pum buck-
its" (pump buckets) cost 75 cents in 1858. One could
have rockers added to a straight chair for 35 cents in
1862. He could have window shutters made, or secure
handles for farm tools.

Somewhat startling are the range and the degree
of services available at the time of a death. One could
order just a coffin, or a coffin and a rough box. The
coffin could be of pine or walnut or cherry, any one of
which might have a plain lining, a lining of velvet, or
one of velvet and lace. An added refinement (with a
corresponding increase in cost) was a coffin "with
glass." Moreover, for a fee, the coffinmaker would
also go to the cemetery at the time of the funeral.
The ultimate seems to have been reached when he—

the coffinmaker—was also paid to secure a "herst," drive it to the cemetery, and attend the funeral service there.

It would be difficult to say, in most fields of endeavor, that any enterprise was the best of its kind, especially since the criteria we might apply would not necessarily be those of the entrepreneur or of his customers. One of the last of a very good kind was the woodworking shop of Samuel B. Frankenfield in Stroudsburg. Frankenfield, a cabinetmaker, built and opened a shop on lower Main Street about 1895, operating it for about 30 years. He died in 1925. He did not create a stock and then dispose of it at retail; he took orders for—and apparently could make—almost anything the townspeople wanted in wooden gear. Treasured surviving specialties are ironing boards, weather vanes, bird cages, and wooden sweet corn graters stamped "Frankenfield." A man of great ingenuity, he is credited with having patented the early hatpin; he also secured a patent for an extension table. This latter achievement ultimately came to be a source of regret among people who remember him, since he sold the patent outright, feeling that there could actually not be much of a future for expansible tables!

## COLLECTORS LOOK FOR:

Hand woodworking tools, especially planes
Coopered objects, especially piggins and small or large tubs
Handmade and early factory-made clothespins. Although they were made by the million, it is almost impossible to find one today.
Shoepegs—these, too, have almost entirely disappeared.
Butter boxes
Wooden sweet corn graters
Round cheese boxes, especially those with covers
Early cigar boxes
Umbrella sticks
Finials and spool-turned members for beds or other furniture
"Shaking forks" of one-piece, hand-split construction
Corner cupboards. As is the case with all the items which follow, the emphasis is on locally made objects.
Jelly cupboards and other cupboards with solid doors
Dry sinks, with or without raised backs or "galleries"
Bucket benches
Dough boxes, either mounted on legs or unmounted
Cradles
Sofas
Tables
Beds—double, three-quarter size, or trundle. (A "twin-size" bed is almost always a larger bed cut down to please the customer.)
Daybeds
Blanket chests
Chairs—rocking, "angel"-back, arrowback, and ladderback
*Jackpot:* A set of six hand-decorated slantback bentback arrowback chairs

# 5
# Over the Hill: The Wagon Wheel

The very first conveyances—it would be somewhat anomalous to term them "vehicles"—in the up-country were probably what a later generation called stone sledges. The English and the Irish of Wayne County generally referred to them as stone boats—a term equally apt. They were usually made of two or three thick planks, set side by side and fastened together by means of cleats and bolts, and were used principally to haul rocks from fields being cleared.

The very first sledges seem to have been pulled by hand, but oxen were employed early in the nineteenth century, with horses or mules utilized a little later. While it is true that these conveyances were cumbersome, there was probably no later piece of equipment better suited to its particular function than was the stone sledge for its special job—transporting heavy objects without first lifting them. One made a depression at the side of a rock, drew the sledge up close, toppled the rock aboard with a crowbar, and drove away.

Farmers also used these sledges in later years to remove smaller stones from fields after plowing. Now and then, after a field had been seeded to grain, they would load the stone sledge lightly and drive back and forth over the field to firm the soil, much as one might use a lawn roller today. Actual rollers were sometimes used, for that matter, but it was only in a very dry year that a farmer needed to firm the soil at all.

The heavy farm wagon was a most versatile contrivance—one without which no farming venture could ever have gone beyond the most primitive stage. The very earliest ones were simply crude carts, made without iron; they served only until something better could be had. The real farm wagons are normally built in two sections, the high-wheeled rear being

bolted to a member which in turn was bolted to the short-wheeled front half. This arrangement, not usually necessary around the farm, made possible an extensible vehicle for hauling long logs or for comparable extraordinary chores. Front wheels were made shorter that the floor of the wagon body, in many cases, in order to permit a sharp turn. Construction was heavy; a wagon which would not last a man's lifetime was not regarded as much of a wagon—but since many of them were made by master craftsmen they often lasted through the lifetimes of several persons.

Wheels had to be greased at intervals to keep them from running hot. It is said that some blacksmiths or wheelwrights, who had the occasional job of tightening a heavy tire, could tell whose wagon was coming along the road, just by listening to the sound of the wheels. Even when an axle was newly greased, there

*Making spokes for wagon wheels is all but a lost art, so far as hand labor is concerned. The village of Effort is in Monroe County's West End. (From an early post card.)*

*The spoke-shave, used in reducing lengths of seasoned wood to wagon wheel spokes, is popular with collectors. This one, faced with a brass plate, has a razor-sharp cutting edge.*

was often a slight, not unmusical squeaking as the wheel revolved, and each had its own peculiar sound.

A somewhat comparable condition existed in the recognition of the identity of a driver who had passed unseen when roads were damp enough to retain the impression of a tire. Metal tires sometimes became scarred, and, in the case of the heaviest of the farm wagons, might have had bumps or irregularities on the surface; such flaws would leave a recognizable imprint on wet ground. Children often became peculiarly adept at this kind of identification.

Wagon grease with a mica base could be bought at the general store if one did not have the wherewithal to make his own. Any kind of fat would do, ranging from skunk's or bear's grease to lard which had become rancid by reason of being badly rendered or because it had been kept too long. Bear's grease seems always to have been popular, but became increasingly hard to get as years passed. Skunk's grease, it is said, forever and always smelled like skunk's grease, and women objected to its use on any conveyance in which they had to ride.

Greasing the wagon seemed to have a strange drawing-power for children, who would stand or sit patiently as each wheel in turn was raised from the ground on the homemade wheel jack, and the thick grease spread on the axle by means of a short paddle. Wagon grease was an anathema to housewives; it was dirty, odorous, and impossible to get out of clothes that had been stained by it. Whether there is an esoteric connection between the adjurations of the mothers as to children's keeping away from wagon grease and the fascination as the wheel was twirled in place on the smeared axle offers food for thought. Crocks and pots in which the grease was kept can not

be restored to a usable condition, as more than one antiques collector has discovered.

The basic structure over the wheels was a simple open box or "bed," which served normal hauling purposes. The depth of the bed could be increased by adding extensions which clamped down over the rest of the body. These boards were needed for such chores as hauling pumpkins or for transporting shocks of corn to the barn floor. For hay, or for sheaves of grain, a special rigging which extended past the width of the body and out over the wheels was required. One special piece of equipment went with a hay-rigging: the "gallows"—a ladder at the front of the load serving as a means of getting up or down and also as a place to fasten the lines. ("Lines" in the up-country was a term more frequently heard than "reins," be it noted.)

While the farmer minded the creaking and jolting of the farm wagon not at all, the story was different when it was his wife or feminine members of the family who were being transported—to church, to the store, to the home of relatives on the regular Sunday visit, or to any other place beyond reasonable walking distance. The four-wheeled spring wagon was a marked improvement over the farm wagon, not only because the springs, to some degree, at least, minimized the jolts, but because it was lighter, was free of the bits of litter which inevitably collected in the farm wagon, and most of all because it looked better. It looked better because it was not homemade, but had come from one of two far-off, mysterious-seeming places—up-country (usually from an establishment in New York State) or down-country (somewhere below the Blue Mountain and perhaps as far away as Lancaster).

*A superlative specimen of the Conestoga wagon wheel
jack, dated 1830.*

The spring wagon automatically took second place, though, to the surrey, with or without fringe on the top. The family in the spring wagon, caught in a sudden shower on the way to church, might actually get no wetter than the family in the surrey, all according to how the wind was blowing—but the discomfort was more than mere wetness; there was status in riding in a surrey, even if one got soaked.

Horse-drawn conveyances in the up-country differed little if at all from those elsewhere in rural areas, but some of them came into use later, as might be expected. A young man going courting would have as good a horse and as fine a four-wheeled buggy as his means would allow. The polish of the harness would match the expert grooming of the horse, and there would be some shining patent leather in the buggy itself—perhaps on the inside of the dashboard. The whipstock and the whip would be new, and the heavy winter laprobe—or the light summer duster—would be the best he could buy. The buggy would

*Farrier's box and butterises (butterises were used for paring the horse's hoofs during the shoeing operation) from the barn of the late Harry Kautz, Shawnee-on-Delaware.*

*A simple object, but one calling for considerable skill on the part of the blacksmith, was the rein hold—a device into which the driver could fasten the reins of his team and thus temporarily free his hands. The sharp point of the rein hold was driven into a log. The skill came in making the two sides perfectly symmetrical.*

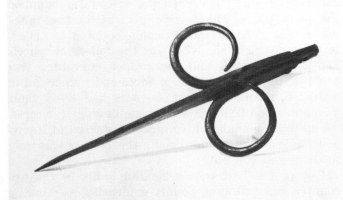

have side curtains, even though they would seldom be used, and sometimes a top which could be pushed back like that of a motor convertible. In all these respects he would differ but little from his counterpart in Berks or Lancaster except for the fact that what was new and prestigious to him had probably become old hat to his southward counterpart a generation earlier. That some of the buggy-type conveyances used in Wayne or Pike had actually originated in Mennonite or Amish communities seems clear; they had the same foursquare construction, though up-country blacksmiths and wheelwrights had a way of making adaptations to suit local tastes, particularly as to dashboards and curtains.

Without either prestige or pretension was the buckboard, a four-wheeled, topless conveyance for which the best that can be said is that it was handier than walking when one needed to make a trip in a hurry. The seat was separated from what we should now call the chassis by a kind of V-spring which absorbed some of the road shock. The buckboard was often thought of as a poor man's vehicle; consolidating the impression was the fact that it was not infrequently drawn by mules, which were less expensive than horses . . . and less manageable, too.

Past the farm wagon stage, all horse-drawn vehicles represent a step into a new era. A farmer might well undertake the construction of a hay-rigging, complicated as it was, but it would not occur to him that it might be possible to make any part of a buggy; that was a job for the specialist. In the same way, while he would have undertaken almost any job of home painting one could name, he would not attempt even to touch up the stenciling or striping which graced an expensive buggy.

Somewhere between the pioneer attitude and the feeling that certain jobs were only for highly skilled or trained specialists there is a territory of significance to us—the time when the up-country supplied the plain parts which were utilized in the fancy whole. The bending factory could be cited as an enterprise of this kind. Wood for the felloes of wheels had to be curved, and the proper curvature was achieved by a combination of force and immersion in water. Evidently the first farmers had tried their hands at wood bending, with some degree of success. As soon as persons with a greater degree of know-how came on the scene, though, the farmer was only too happy to bow out.

One of the best-known bending mills in the up-country was a Monroe County enterprise operated by Mershon and Eilenberger in 1870. For their establishment they took over a tanning factory which had been built by George McEwing, and their curved-wood products of all kinds were not only used locally but were exported to carriage-making factories.

A wheelwright's shop at Snydersville, owned by Sanford Hagerman, assumed much importance in the second half of the nineteenth century. This was, in a sense, a cooperative enterprise. After the carriages, wagons, sleds, and farm implements (especially corn shellers, which appear to have been a specialty) had been completed as to their wooden components they were taken across the way to John Stackhouse, who "ironed" them; that is, he supplied the necessary rims, runners, gears, etc., to complete them. Marsh's Foundry, near by, was a source on which Stackhouse could draw, so that the total business was a close-in community affair. It was no ordinary affair, either; the workers, we are told, were meticulous and the quality of the finished work unimpeachable. One instance of Hagerman's exacting standards is to be found in his curing of the oak and hickory he used. No piece which had not been "dried"—that is, cured—by immersion in water for a full year was considered fit for use!

For sheer quality and astronomically high standards, however, nothing could match the wagon spoke factory at Effort. The place was conducted first by Samuel Arnold and later by his son-in-law, Simon Shupp. Its heyday was in the 1860s and 1870s, the years of the very finest in horse-drawn carriages. Arnold started out by making yokes (for oxen), whippletrees, and handles for all kinds of farm tools and implements, but as his reputation spread, first locally, then state-wide, and finally nationally, he limited his production to wheel spokes and wagon accessories.

Only the first thirty inches at the butt of any tree were considered suitable for wheel spokes, because only that length was so completely straight-grained that it could be split with geometrical perfection. In the beginning, every spoke was actually split by hand and then also shaved smooth by hand. The shaving took place at a bench which farther south would have been called a schnitzelbank but which in Monroe was oftener dubbed a shaving horse. Such a time-consuming process could not long be continued, however, and when Shupp took over he introduced machinery to do much of the job. We have noted that in the Snydersville wheelwright's shop the appropriate curing period for lumber was a year. At Arnold's the drying process was more elaborate (it did not involve immersion in water) and took up to three years— first outdoors and then under a roof.

The steps following the cutting of the spokes and

*Heavy velour-type lap robe of the kind regarded as* de rigueur *for winter driving, either by buggy or by sleigh.*

preceding their sale were five in number: turning (this of course was after Shupp took over), sanding, grading (there were five qualities), packing, and storing. Even these did not include the final painting, varnishing, and decorating. A full set for a wagon comprised 52 spokes—24 for the front and 28 for the rear wheels.

There were, of course, other spoke factories, in-cluding one just west of Stroudsburg operated by a Mr. Klaer, but none which enjoyed the kudos of the enterprise at Effort. Time eventually did away with horse-drawn carriages, the need for their component parts, and the business which produced them—but as late as the turn of the century the Effort Spoke Factory achieved a kind of immortality: it was pho-tographed for use on a new-fangled idea just coming into prominence—the penny postal card. While we should not today find anything particularly attractive about a veritable forest of chunks of split wood standing on end, we can not help being impressed by the sheer number the photographer was able to include in the picture.

The wagon wheel has become an antique, now—a collectible of interest to the person who finds in it a symbol, however slight, of a bygone way of life. What to do with an old wheel, once the collector has acquired it, becomes a purely personal problem, as is the case with any acquired antique. Some persons use wheels as gates; some use them as backdrops for tall flowers or as trellises on which vines may climb. Some cut them in half and set them up as markers or edgers for driveways. The occasional groaning one hears when they are sawed in two is not a throwback to the noise made by an ungreased axle; it is the sound of the distressed wheelwright turning over in his grave.

### COLLECTORS LOOK FOR:

Wagon wheels

Schnitzelbanks

Hubs of wheels, remade into lamps or other objects

Buggy whips

Mule whips (The stocks were shorter than those of horse whips.)

Lap robes

Whip sockets

Bridle rosettes

Fly nets—leather strings arranged in a kind of blanket shape and worn over the harness in summer (The motion of the strings helped to keep insects away.)

Ear caps—homemade covers which kept insects or bees away from the sensitive ears of horses

Horse blankets

Singletrees—or the full complement, for a team, of a doubletree and a pair of singletrees

Handwrought hardware from wagons, including tires

Postcard pictures or photographs of wagoning enterprises

*Jackpot:* A lap robe in superior condition

# 6
# Mills and Millers

"Flouring mills," they were called. The unfamiliar term makes as good sense as does the more common "gristmill" and in terms of phonetics is perhaps more euphonious. Euphony had nothing to do with mills, of course; what mattered was that each succeeding venture, by putting the pioneer a little further ahead, also pushed the wilderness a little farther back.

There seems to be a relationship, not entirely fortuitous, between the circumstances of living at a given time and the quality of bread eaten at the same period. The Indians prepared a cake made from crushed grain, its primitive character in keeping with the conditions under which it was produced. Our earliest colonists not only learned about grain from the Indians but also borrowed their simple bread-making techniques. The flat cakes baked on hot stones helped to keep starvation away—but nobody pretended that they were very good eating, and so the march toward better bread and better living went forward simultaneously.

In the up-country, so far as records give any indication, few persons ever had to live under conditions quite so primitive as those in which the Indians lived, but there were those who, for lack of better facilities, were compelled to grind their grain as the Indians did, in hollowed-out chunks of wood or in stones made concave by the action of water. Indian "mills" of rock of this kind stood along a roadside in Middle Smithfield Township as late as 1935 when a highway-widening operation did away with them. Portable Indian mills were found on the farm of a man in the same area. He attributed their making to a period earlier than the late 1700s, with convincing reasons for so doing. No such stone mill known positively to have been used by the white man has survived.

Mills were built where there was a strong enough flow of water to turn the millwheel which set the grinding machinery in motion. In early times, when the forest floor and the unturned soil of open spaces held enough water to keep the flow of a stream constant the year round, there was little difficulty in finding a good mill brook. About the only real problem then was making sure that the drop between the start of the raceway and the point at which the water hit the millwheel was neither too gradual nor too abrupt—and any good miller could adequately assess and control that kind of situation. No particular attention was paid, in earliest times, to the convenience of patrons; it was the problem of the grain grower to get to the miller, not the miller to the grain grower.

At first, the water wheel-operated mills ground both flour and feed—flour for human consumption and feed for the farm animals. As time passed, some mill owners had to choose between flour and feed, since changing over the machinery from one operation to the other was cumbersome and time-consuming. It was at this point that some became feed mills and others, flouring mills. The grinding stones, after the earliest years, were seldom of native stones, as is often assumed; many of them originated in France, and came over as ballast in sailing vessels.

Probably the earliest mill north of the Blue Mountain was the one erected at Shawnee-on-Delaware by Nicholas Dupuis in 1735. Since Dupuis is credited with being the first "permanent" white settler in the up-country, having established a residence and a place of entertainment at Shawnee as early as 1727, the attribution seems safe. ("Nonpermanent" settlers, it may be noted, included trappers and such venturers as the Dutch who came down the river looking for

Hand-whittled meal or flour scoops used by the miller in dealing with small quantities of his product. The iron-bound half-peck measure stands about midway between similarly constructed containers holding as little as a quart or as much as a half bushel.

minerals in the 1600s, but who for the most part returned to the places from which they had come.) Practically every traveler who wrote about his trip up or down the river in those days mentions the hospitality of Dupuis. Store records of the time show that buckwheat and rye ("rie") were the grains most generally grown.

Another mill of pre-Revolutionary days was one established between 1750 and 1760, at what is now Sciota, by Jacob Brinker. Brinker was listed on the Hamilton Township tax assessment rolls by 1772. That much is definite, but there are two schools of thought as to the exact location of his mill. One faction has it that the site was on property lately owned by Mrs. Harry Hobbs. Traces of an early structure— as well as traces of an obviously later building—are to be found there.

The second theory is that Brinker's Mill stood where the stone mill at the corner of Business Route 209 and the Neola Road now stands, antedating the present structure. Both the disputed locations are on the McMichaels Creek. A commemorative plaque along the highway, placed by the Monroe County Historical Society, indicates only that "Brinker's Mill was the storehouse and advance post for the Sullivan Expedition, which left Easton June 18, 1779, to attack the hostile Iroquois Indians."

Some time after 1790, the estate of Jacob Brinker sold the property to John George Keller, who in turn sold it in 1796 to Barnet Fenner. This property included a mill at the crossroads—the corner of what eventually became Business Route 209 and the Neola Road. The mill had originally been a log structure, but was replaced in 1800 by the stone building now standing. The miller's stone house near by, built in 1805, according to tax records in Stroudsburg, is now separated from the mill by the highway.

Since the history of the mill at the crossroads, whether or not Jacob Brinker's eighteenth century structure stood at this particular spot, is reasonably well documented, and since the enterprise is also a good example of a flourishing milling operation of the nineteenth century, let us trace it briefly down to the twentieth and its present boarded-up but still solid condition.

As rebuilt by the Fenners—Barnet and his sons— it was an impressive structure, two and a half stories high. The gable date stone proclaimed it a Fenner enterprise. Since it had a strategic location at the center of a good farming district, it was sizable enough to keep two operations going simultaneously, one miller grinding feed and another, flour. After Barnet's time, it was operated for many years by

*The owner of this two-bushel homespun bag apparently wanted no misunderstanding as to whose grain was whose. Few bags were so thoroughly marked.*

Henrich Fenner and members of his family. They were followed by George and Christopher Bittenbender. These men in turn were succeeded by William Haney, who came up from Northampton County shortly before the Civil War. At about this time, or perhaps a bit later, the little community about the mill came to be known colloquially as Fishville because of the excellent trout fishing both above and below the mill. The miller's house and the extensive surrounding property were dubbed Fishville Manor.

The name of Fenner ceased to be associated with the mill when a Fenner daughter married George Snyder and the property passed to the couple. Their son William inherited it, but country milling operations everywhere were coming to an end by that time and the mill, with all its gear intact, finally closed its doors like the rest. Limited operations were going on in the first half of this century.

That competition was entering the picture as early as 1844 and that it seemed necessary to do something to protect personal interests are indicated in a transfer of farming land from Henrich Fenner to his son Joseph. The deed specifically stated that "[The recipient of this property] shall not at any time to come build or erect a flouring or gristmill on the hereby granted premises or to use or in any way dispose of the water of the McMichaels Creek, as far as the same passes through the property." The stipulation seems not to have stemmed from any lack of fatherly confidence in a son but rather to have been a sensible precaution in the event that changing times might bring changing circumstances.

Up-country mills ground what was brought to them, and what was brought varied from place to place. In the broad fields of the West End, in flat river lands in Smithfield, and in some stretches in

*Homemade bag stretcher, used to hold the top of a grain bag open while it was being filled. The small stamp with the initials* PB *was inked and then applied to identify it for the owner.*

Wayne wheat would flourish. In sections where fall-sown wheat stood but a poor chance of surviving the winter or where the soil was unsuited to its growth, the big crops were rye and oats instead of wheat. To compensate in some degree for the lack of wheat, great quantities of buckwheat were produced in Pike and Wayne. Buckwheat, although its uses were limited largely to the making of pancakes and to chicken feed, required only a short growing season. Rye was grown over the entire area, as was flint corn.

Each kind of grain posed its own problems, with the greatest degree of refinement called for in the processing of wheat. Buckwheat, each grain encased in its hard little shell, had to be hulled before it could be ground. Corn was shelled at home before it was taken to the mill. A device consisting of a strong metal hook—sometimes a sharpened oak peg—attached to a thong and fastened to the hand of the worker helped to expedite the process. The development of hand-propelled shellers, into which ears of corn were dropped as the wheel was turned, was a boon to the country farmer—but was still hard work for the boys or women to whom this chore was usually assigned.

A circumstance which frequently became a bone of contention between farmer and miller was the length of the drying period between harvesting and milling. For the best results, grain had to be thoroughly dry; if it were not, it might clog the mill wheels. On the other hand, many farmers were in actual need by the time a new crop was ready for harvest, and waiting for any length of time became unendurable.

Some mills remained enterprises catering to local patrons only, either because the miller lacked helpers or because of the remoteness of his operation. Others quickly attained major importance, especially those in Monroe. The Keller mill at Kellersville in Hamilton Township is a good example of the larger milling operation. Christopher Keller, for whom the village was named, built his mill shortly after 1765. A man of boundless energy, he also undertook a sawmill and a carding factory for wool. On his death the property went to his son John George (1774–1833), who expanded the family interests and enterprises and in 1815 built a stone tavern, still standing but now used as a private dwelling.

John George felt that the mill stood too far from the road to Easton, and since a steadily increasing portion of his output was being shipped south, he relocated the gristmill so that it stood right by the road. This removal took place between 1815 and 1820. The mill burned in 1847 but was rebuilt. The Kellers, John George and his son Joseph, left little to chance.

When the Easton market proved to be too limited, they purchased teams and wagons of the Conestoga type and set up regular traffic between Kellersville and Philadelphia. Then, from Philadelphia, they extended their route to Pittsburgh.

The trip from Hamilton Township to Philadelphia, a distance of 75 miles, began on Monday morning and ended Friday evening. So that the long return trip would not be devoid of profit, they regularly did jobs of hauling, especially of merchandise for country stores—including one which they established. The total enterprise did so much to promote the growth of the village that in 1836, when the choice of a spot for the county seat was being put before the voters, Kellersville was considered by many to be the logical place. In an election which we should today call outrageously rigged—on both sides—Stroudsburg won over Kellersville.

From Joseph Keller, the mill with its auxiliary buildings and adjuncts passed, in 1870, to Levi and David Slutter, after which, in turn, it went to Samuel Fabel and Joseph Metzgar. Like other local milling operations it came to an end when enterprises in the West assumed a magnitude which made small operations everywhere unprofitable. The decline of Kellersville, once perhaps the busiest spot in a busy county, began to set in after 1836 in inverse proportion to the growth in importance of Stroudsburg. Today, only a highway marker on a side road indicates that the remaining stone houses and a few accompanying auxiliary buildings constitute a village—perhaps less a village than a wide spot on a very pleasant country road.

There were comparatively few Quakers in Monroe, but one enterprise was founded with Quaker capital —Experiment Mills, at what is now Minisink Hills. James Bell in 1810 built a gristmill there, branching out as years passed with a sawmill and a paper pulp factory. By 1815, the firm was known as Bell and Thomas, and was shipping milled products to Philadelphia, not overland as the Kellers of Kellersville were doing, but by Durham boats on the Delaware. Bell and Thomas did not devise this means of transportation; John Van Campen, who had a mill at Shawnee, was sending his flour downriver in 1780—and Durham boats had actually been in use since 1758. Three operators of these long, narrow vessels—not necessarily operators for Bell and Thomas or for Van Campen; the records do not say—whose names are preserved in the archives were David Bogert, Jacob Lamb, and Cornelius Coolbaugh.

Other nearby feed and flouring operations met the needs of local residents and helped boost the economy

*Wooden "meal" chests with two compartments were sometimes used in the out-kitchen to hold wheat and rye flour when families were large. Chests used in the barn for horse or cattle feed were larger and ordinarily had three or four compartments.*

of the county. Among these, one should certainly mention the Zimmerman activities. George had a mill at Minisink Hills in 1815, and Peter built one not far away on the Silver Lake road shortly afterwards. Two important places to the east were the plants at Marshalls Creek of Dr. Philip Bush and of William Brown. In the Bushkill region, James Hyndshaw, for whom Fort Hyndshaw was named, had a mill some time before the 1800s. In Stroudsburg, a mill on the McMichaels Creek, burned by the Indians in 1755 before Jacob Stroud lent his name to the place, was

rebuilt four times between then and 1889. It was known affectionately as "Ab Heller's Mill" when it finally stopped functioning in 1941.

Farther afield, where a broad-scale commercial angle was of lesser concern, there were mills which operated largely on the basis of local service. Above Marshalls Creek, the hamlet of Egypt Mills took its name from a gristmill built by the Nyce family some time before 1800. In its earliest days, this mill was the only place short of Kingston, New York, where farmers along the upper Delaware could take their grain for grinding. Because of the length of the trip, the farmers, familiar with the Biblical account of Joseph and his brethren, came to refer to mill-going as a "journey to Egypt." The name caught on and lingers to this day, though the mill has long since disappeared.

In Greene Township, in the Poconos, Allen Megargle was the first to establish a mill, in 1825— the same year Moses Kellam started his enterprise in Palmyra Township. At Honesdale, J. C. Gunn was grinding wheat in 1839. A native of Connecticut, he had been invited to come to Honesdale because of his reputation as an outstandingly competent miller.

The Poconos had a "Gold Rush" miller, one John Haag, who had left Germany in 1853 to make his fortune in the California gold fields. He arrived in the United States with insufficient funds to get to the West Coast and worked at various jobs in Dreher Township, Wayne County, until he had saved enough money to move on. According to an early historian, he was "quite" successful in California, but the big days of the rush were over and he returned about 1856 to establish a gristmill between Owl Hoot (later, Angels) and Newfoundland. A son, A. L. Haag, followed his father as operator of the mill. A. L. Haag was in turn succeeded by his brother Maurice. The mill discontinued operations in the early 1900s, and was totally destroyed in the disastrous flood of 1955.

"Old" mills have for years been favorite subjects for restoration or remodeling, with subsequent use as taverns or restaurants frequently the goal. In some cases, as much of the working gear as possible, even including the race and the wheel, is put in order, or restored, if missing. In others, "atmosphere" is achieved in less thorough-going fashion. Notable in charm, even after the long passage of time and a wide variety of uses, is the building called simply "The Old Mill," at the heart of the village in Bushkill, Pike County. Restoration, while not complete, has been careful. Not far away are the remains of a probably earlier mill, but much research needs to be done—and conflicting theories will have to be resolved—before an authoritative statement can be made as to when or by whom it was built. It is the hope of many that "The Old Mill" can be moved by the National Park Service to higher ground when the Bushkill region becomes part of the Delaware Water Gap National Recreation Area. The earlier structure —if, indeed, it is earlier—would appear to be beyond salvation—or salvage.

Working gear in old mills, while often missing and presumed defunct, is not always completely lost. For example: not far from Plymouth, in eastern Massa-

chusetts, there is a thorough-going mill restoration . . . made possible by the incorporation of working parts from an early flouring mill in up-country Pennsylvania. Proper credit has been given. Now that it is too late to do anything about it, there are those who wish that the restoration might have been effected at home!

There seems always to have been a feeling in the up-country that millers were, if not actually wealthy, at least well-to-do. Some of them were undoubtedly well off, in the sense that they seldom had to go long

*Up to three bushels of flour could be stored in this kind of heavy tin drum, which was normally kept in the out-kitchen.*

without work, and that, unlike most of the men who patronized them, their pay was immediately forthcoming. Most of them operated on a tithe system, but alternative financial arrangements, sometimes including barter, could often be made. Since grain frequently had to be left at the mill to await its turn to be ground, most farmers developed a means of identifying their own grists. Because grain bags, either the homespun ones of earliest times or the heavy cotton or linen ones of later years, looked pretty much alike, the owner's initials were often stamped in ink on each bag. Farther south, bag stamps of elaborate designs were not uncommon. One particularly fine linen bag, dated 1828, is marked, in indelible ink, with a flat Dutch heart, a horse, and the owner's full name. Another, dated 1863, has a spray of tulips and the owner's name. In the up-country, the identifying marks seem more often merely to have been initials. If the miller had the farmer's complete confidence, no marks at all were used; the farmer assumed as a matter of course that the miller would remember whose grain was whose.

## COLLECTORS LOOK FOR:

Millstones

Measuring containers used by millers, usually of bent-wood, metal-bound

Grain bags stamped with owners' name or initials

Wooden bag stretchers—to hold bags open during the filling process

Flour drums, especially those with stenciled designs

Bag stamps—usually wood, rarely metal

Flour and meal scoops—wood, metal, and wood-and-metal. Copper rivets lend importance and desirability.

Grain shovels, especially those made by hand

Toolboxes from Conestoga wagons

Fancy ironwork from Conestoga wagon toolboxes

Strap devices for hand-shelling corn

Mechanized corn shellers

Fanning mills

Hoppers and bins from flouring mills

Compartmented meal or flour chests

*Jackpot:* Handmade wooden grain shovel with date and name or initials

# 7

# *Forge and Foundry*

Most of the iron needed in getting the economy established in the northeastern counties was brought in from a distance, the obvious reason being that, while a little bog iron existed in Monroe, there were no deposits of any significance. When one has occasion, therefore, to look for sources of up-country iron, he will find them elsewhere, notably at Durham Furnace, below Easton, or across the river at Oxford, New Jersey.

Early records tell of only one iron-ore operation in the up-country. Its original name is uncertain, but in 1841 it was called the Analomink Iron Works. It was located at Forge Cut, on the Brodheads Creek (once known as Analomink Creek in its upper basin) between Stroudsburg and Minisink Hills, and appears to have been an outgrowth of operations going on over in Jersey at Oxford Furnace. It was established in or about 1830 by William Henry and John Jordan, Jr., of Philadelphia, at a spot where the normally peaceful creek takes a sharp drop between two precipitous rocky rises with almost the proportions of mountains. The "peaceful" Brodheads can be very deceptive, however, and has carried violent destruction to everything in its path on a number of occasions—one during torrential rains in 1903; much later, following two hurricane storms in close succession in 1955; and, of more significance here, in 1841. While the plant was badly crippled by the flood of 1841, it was rebuilt and continued operations until about 1850. Its specialty was car wheels for the railroads then coming into prominence.

Early names associated with the immediate region of the furnace were Croasdale, Thomas, Jordan, and Bell. The present towering bridge across the creek, on a relocated highway route, is still referred to as Bell's Bridge by old-timers, and the railroad crossing was long known as Bell's Crossing. The Bells remained in Monroe and became prominent, as did the Croasdales. The record on the Thomases is confused, but apparently all the Jordans returned to Philadelphia in the course of time. The furnace turned out "bar" iron, more commonly called pig iron.

That local enterprises using pig iron were not wholly dependent on the Forge Cut furnace seems indicated by the fact that at the village of Bushkill, less than 20 miles away, Benjamin Schoonover built a foundry in 1824. According to early history, this was the first such operation between Newburgh, New York, and "Lehigh." We do not know where he got his iron. It would be comforting to know just what place the historian had in mind by "Lehigh"—but any place along the Lehigh River would have lain to the west or south of Monroe. An early name for Lehigh was "Lecha" and while there were several different settlements which at one time or another were known locally as "Lechastettel" (Lehigh Village) there is no indication of an iron enterprise nearer than Bethlehem—and Bethlehem has been called Bethlehem since 1741. Perhaps "Lehigh" simply meant "Lehigh County."

Schoonover's establishment must have been more than welcome, since one of its products was wagon tires. Up to that time most wagon wheels were without metal of any kind, the sections of the felloes being fastened together with wooden pins. It is not surprising that, with the rough terrain of the time, the wheels did not last long.

By far the most ambitious foundry in Monroe was one in Hamilton Township on Pensyl Creek at a place known now as Sand Hill, between Snydersville and

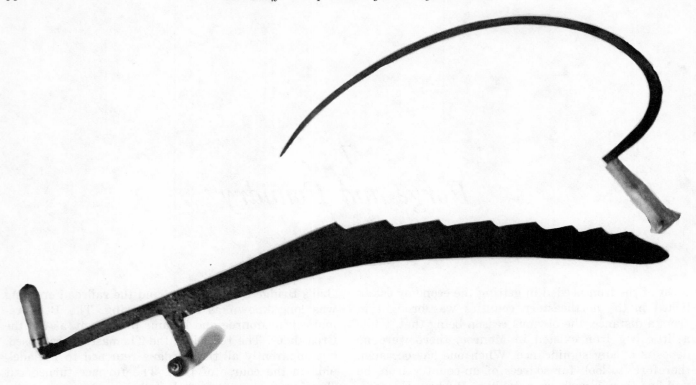

*Familiar to farmers a generation or two ago: the reaper's hook and the hay knife. The hook shown here, die-stamped "I. Christ," was found in a long-unused barn in Sciota. Hay knives were used to cut through heavy piles of hay or to even up the edges of the haymow facing the barn floor.*

Sciota. No documentation exists as to who carried on the very first operation there, but the first on record is that of the Marsh family. Abraham Marsh (1791–1863) moved to the area from down-country with his family. His son Isaac, who had mastered his trade before coming to Monroe, was an iron moulder, and it was apparently he who established the first plant. Abraham's grandsons, Isaac and John, were operating a foundry and machine shop in 1848. As years passed, changes in management occurred. In the 1870s, Levi M. Slutter became a partner and the plant was enlarged, finally becoming known as E. B. Marsh and Brother. The business interests were transferred to Stroudsburg in 1903, and the plant at Sand Hill, like so many country enterprises before there was adequate fire protection, later burned to the ground. Traces of foundations and bits of wall still remain. A resident some years ago, trying to landscape his property, declared that wherever he tried to dig a hole for his evergreens he ran into a piece of subterranean foundry wall.

The lift given to the agricultural development of the area by Marsh's Foundry was tremendous. Up to this time, most plows were of wood; most harrows were improvised from sections of trees on which short, stubby branches had been left; the usual threshing implements were flails. In only rare instances were the farmers able to own the better machinery which had come into existence below the Blue Mountain. The Marsh Foundry, often referred to as the Hamilton Foundry, changed all that. Practically all kinds of farm implements known to agriculture at the time were made at Marsh's. Carpenters, mill workers, and cabinet makers were at hand to carry through a job from start to finish. The business expanded, expanded again, and branched out into the manufacture of mill gearings, stoves, wood saws and sawmills, tread mills, and threshing machines. One item from early years long remained in production, simply because small farmers wanted it and not because it was a bona fide foundry product. This was the so-called wedge plow—an ingenious device fastened together by wooden wedges instead of nuts and bolts. Eventually, of course, it had to yield to more up-to-date implements.

The age was, of course, the time of the horse and buggy, and the blacksmith-wheelwright shop came to be as nearly ubiquitous as has the automobile service station today. The Monroe County census of 1860 indicates that there were nine establishments in the county, but historians note that there were many more than that—some of them overlooked by the census takers and others which chose not to be counted. McIlhaney, McMichael's, Effort, Pleasant Valley, Snydersville, Fennersville, and Kunkletown—all of these communities in a fairly concentrated area in the West End alone—had their own blacksmith shops, and to the list must be added those in the rest of the county. Pike had fewer, but it appears that Wayne, with about the same degree of doubt as to the accuracy of census figures, had at least as many.

While minor demands on the blacksmith were legion—and only too frequently the trade was less than lucrative—there were two which stood out in importance: the shoeing of horses and either the actual ironing of the wagon wheels or the tightening of the tires. Getting the horses shod was a time-consuming operation, but it had to be done at frequent

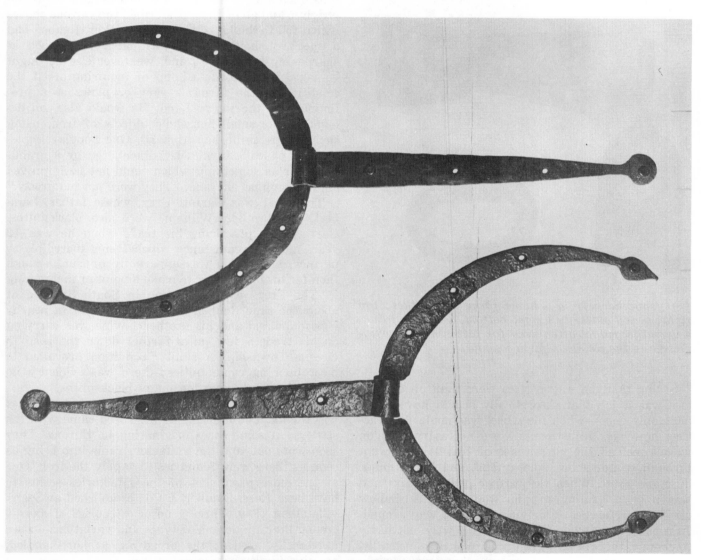

*Massive hand-wrought door hinges could be turned out by most good blacksmiths, the designs depending on what was currently popular or on what the artisan could do best. These are 21 inches long.*

intervals, and in the late fall an additional trip to the shop was made to have caulks put into the shoes so that the horse would not slip on ice. Placing the caulks was a precise operation; each horse had its individual length of stride, and the caulks had to be matched to it. Hind-leg caulks either too long or incorrectly angled would injure the animal's forelegs, and the job would have to be done over. In early years, each smith had to make horseshoes from scratch, but eventually he could purchase stock shoes, which would then be altered to fit the individual horse.

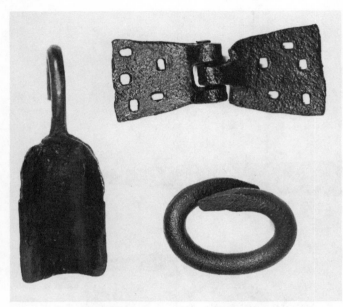

*Left, shoe horn from a home forge in Panther; top right, heavy butterfly hinge; bottom, a coupling link, a versatile gadget often used for fastening the whippletree to the clevis on farm wagons.*

Seeing that the wagon tires were tight on the felloes was a job that theoretically should have to be done only once—when the wheel was made. In practice, however, adjustments were necessary. Wagon wheels met all the vicissitudes of travel; they went through winter snow, spring mud, and hot summer dust and sand. When the farmer had his team and wagon on a hauling trip he would ford a shallow creek in preference to driving the long way around. In consequence, while the metal tires were not likely to change, the wheels were prone to shrink just a little, or perhaps lose their perfect alignment. Shrinking a wagon tire to fit a wheel was not a job for an amateur—but the blacksmith-wheelwright took it in stride.

A mere recital of the names of up-country blacksmiths could have little point except in a history of blacksmithing. (Perhaps we should observe here that for all practical purposes there was little if any distinction in the up-country between the services of the blacksmith and the wheelwright; a man who did the work of one would ordinarily do the work of the other, too, except that an occasional wheelwright would have nothing to do with horses.) We might make a note on two, however, who should not go unrecorded. One was Reuben Sieg (1844–1933), son of one Jacob Sieg, who emigrated from Germany in 1838 and eventually settled in Newfoundland. A number of Jacob's sons, including Reuben, became blacksmiths or wheelwrights, and all of them performed the various chores which fell to the lot of the metal worker. Reuben had a specialty, however; he was particularly good at sharpening plowshares, and, whatever else he might be asked to do, made a point of inquiring about the condition of the farmer's plow or plows as a preliminary to the job at hand. He would also, on demand, make small household objects of iron, using such scraps as he had at hand. One popular implement, a pancake turner, is remembered by a granddaughter as something which could not be improved on, although, as she said, "They were not too pretty."

The other was Garrett Frey, whose father, Lambert, and brother, William, were also blacksmiths. Garrett was practicing his trade when he was 12 years old, a circumstance which seems incredible to us now, and which was apparently unusual enough then for his biographer to make a point of mentioning it. The Freys were operating in South Sterling at about the time Reuben Sieg was working in nearby Newfoundland and his brother Lavine was carrying on his trade a few miles farther down the road in Greene Township. A similar condition prevailed in most farming communities; there was evidently no such thing as having too many blacksmiths.

An object of iron vitally needed from earliest times was the ax. The implements first used came with the settlers, in some cases originating in Europe. They soon wore out, and the ax factory came into being as soon as there were foundries to supply the iron. One of the more prominent of these factories seems to have been Ross, Baldwin & Co., established at Seelyville about 1830. Three general categories of axes— among literally dozens of types and variations—were universally needed: the broad ax, a short-handled, massive implement used for hewing at close range; and the poll (single edge) and double-bitted longhandled axes used for two-hand cutting and chopping operations. The specialty of Ross, Baldwin was the

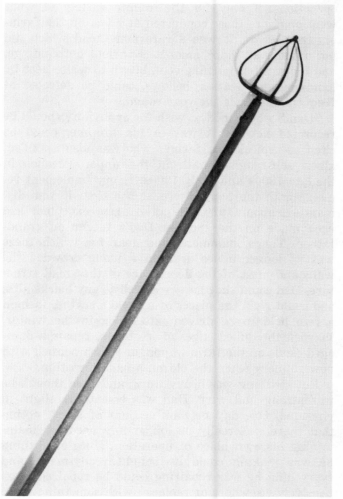

The turtle hook is a highly individual creation—a long-handled pitchfork with the prongs neatly welded together at their tips. This contrivance, according to a long-time resident of the West End, was used to bring snapping turtles out of their hiding places at the bottom of shallow ponds when snapper soup was desired. Only part of the seven-foot-long handle is shown.

Locally made ornamental objects in cast iron are scarce in the up-country—but in the second half of the nineteenth century Fred Wagner of Effort liked working with iron so well that he carved his own molds for this eagle and then walked all the way to Stroudsburg (fifteen to twenty miles) to have the casting done.

broad ax. The enterprise seems to have started in a building first used for something else, but Col. R. L. Seely is credited with having erected a new tool shop in the year mentioned. Helves, or handles, for axes were not ordinarily considered as part of the transaction when one bought an ax; the purchaser either made his own or, if he was lucky, could get one at the country store, where skillfully made handles for various implements often constituted articles of barter.

John Bangs started an ax and scythe shop at Traceyville, close to Honesdale, in 1832, but the venture was short-lived. Like axes, scythes had specialized uses, and like axes they had to be kept sharp. A sharpening device not reported north of the West End was the *dengelstock*—a small anvil on which the blade was laid and the edge was pounded smooth with a hammer. Only the best of steel could long stand such treatment. Early Pennsylvania Dutch dialect writers —the poets in particular—have noted the musical sound of the *dengelstock* in action. Elsewhere, the grindstone served the purpose. Like millstones, grindstones were ordinarily imported, frequently serving as ballast on early America-bound sailing vessels.

If one judges by such fragmentary records as exist, not many blacksmiths liked to make scythe blades. According to John Turn's store ledger, Henry Shoemaker was credited with $1.75 for making a "Dutch sithe" in 1812—but a single reference is not enough for us to assume that Shoemaker was a professional blacksmith. He lived in Smithfield Township. One may hazard a guess that the reluctance was owing to the difficulty of tempering the blade so that it would hold an edge. An ax blade could be tempered by a calculated plunge into a handy bucket of water —but the long, curving scythe blade demanded a number of immersions and, since only a few degrees in the hot metal meant the difference between a good job and a poor one, the result only too often left something to be desired. To be sure, the whetstone had to be employed frequently to keep a cutting edge sharp, but no amount of whetting could make up for a poorly tempered blade. As time passed, methods of manufacture improved, in close proportion to improvement in the steel itself.

One of the earliest records having to do with the scythe is an entry in Aaron Dupuis's store ledger in Shawnee-on-Delaware in 1753—"one sith, 6 shillings." A scythe *handle*, however, was purchased for nine pence in 1745. We do not know where these items originated; one would guess that the blade was imported and that the snath was made locally.

Probably most interesting of all the blacksmithing operations, if only for the infinite variety of what went on, were those conducted at home by the farmers themselves. It was a rare homestead which did not number a "shop" among its various outbuildings, and the smell of burning coal, blown to white heat by hand-operated leather bellows, could be detected at frequent intervals the year round.

"Dad," whose modest wish for anonymity should be respected now as it was in his lifetime, could be cited as typical of a farmer who was also a skilled, albeit self-taught, smith in the upper Poconos in the late 1800s and early 1900s. Every implement remaining in the home forge at the time it was dismantled, about 1920, the anvil alone excepted, had been made on the spot by Dad's father or grandfather. Tongs, hammers, and gear for which there was no longer a use or even a name crowded the walls and most of the floor space of the small structure. Dad could shoe horses as well as any blacksmith, and could weld the pieces of a broken scythe, fashion a rein hold to be driven into a log in the winter, sharpen the dulled edges of ice tongs, repair a damaged clevis on the farm wagon, or refit a bobsled with new runners when the old ones had worn thin.

But smithing was heavy work, and even though he was strong and wiry, Dad was essentially slight in physique. One day he took account of stock, noting that there was really no longer any need for maintaining his own place of operation, since everything he was making could be bought ready-made, and everything he was repairing could be repaired inexpensively elsewhere or replaced with something more up to date. There was a swamp just beyond the edge of one of his fields—a horrendous place which had been all but impenetrable since the time a tornado had turned it into a mass of uprooted trees, roots, and rhododendron snarls some years before. Along the very edge was a stretch of quicksand; he knew, because "Cherry," a cow beloved for her gentleness by the children of the family, had been rescued there just in the nick of time when she had reached too far for a tempting clump of marsh marigolds, and began to sink into the morass. Dad hitched his team to the low sledge he used for carrying away stones after plowing a field, and load by load removed everything in the shop, transporting it to the swamp and throwing it into the quicksand. Then he demolished the shop and replaced it with a different building—about the time he acquired his first Model T.

At the time, while members of Dad's family may privately have found the action a little quixotic, they could completely sympathize with his solution to a problem which was becoming increasingly onerous

*Every housewife liked to have at least a few cooky cutter patterns no one else possessed. The central figure of Uncle Sam, here, is flanked, left, by a wanderer with a cane; right, by a fireman; below, by an unusual tulip, a fearsome cat, a turkey, and an ice saw.*

and distasteful. Now, they are prone to look back with regret on the loss of the handmade artifacts which can never be recovered. Like Dad, they know—for they have explored the quicksand. There is a difference, though, between thrusting planks into the ooze to rescue a cow, and fishing up heavy iron tongs which must long since have reached a stopping place somewhere short of China.

One of the old-time skilled specialists using iron as his medium was the gunsmith—but most of these operated south of the up-country. There is a degree of éclat attaching to the ownership of a weapon made at Henry's gun factory, for instance, and up-country gun collectors like to think of such possessions as locally made. For the record, though, the Henry manufactory was over the line in Northampton County. The state historical marker at Belfast, Pa., bears the following inscription: "Here rifles and other firearms were made for use in the War of 1812. Built by William Henry, 2nd, about 1800, the famous Henry shotgun was made here as late as 1904."

At the same time, in the operation of the Henry

*Jointed "walking" toys, usually made by blacksmiths or tinsmiths in off moments for the amusement of children. There is no record that such objects were actually made up-country; they may have come with the itinerant peddler.*

factory there is a note of considerable significance to Monroe Countians. One Nicholas Hawk (1782–1844) of the village of Gilbert was a gunsmith noted for the all-around excellence and beauty of his flint-lock long rifles. According to an early county historian, he received his training at the Henry factory—and then returned to Gilbert, where he combined farming and gunsmithing. How many rifles he made, we do not know—but a Hawk rifle is considered a gem in any collection. All his guns were individually made—to order, according to the wishes of the prospective buyer. Some were inlaid; some of the stocks were of curly maple. A particularly choice specimen in the collection of the late Asher Odenwelder of Easton was inscribed with the name of the person for whom it had been made—C. B. Heller of Easton. Hawk is buried close to the entrance of the cemetery at Gilbert. He and his wife, Catherine Shupp, had one son, Peter, who died in 1892.

Another early establishment existed in Kunkletown. It was founded in 1812 by one Philip Hess and operated to 1830, but details beyond that point are lacking. Later, in Greene Township, Pike County, a gunsmith from County Armagh in Ireland took up residence. This was Samuel Hopps, who had emigrated in 1850. He died in 1881. Again, details which might help to bring to life this facet of the past are missing.

A sideline of some blacksmiths was traffic in tinware, generally for such purposes as stove pipes, repairs to farm machinery, and the like. It seems to have been a usual assumption that if a man were skilled at one phase of metalcraft he could also acquit himself creditably at another. Much of the small tinware used about the house in earliest times came from the itinerant peddlers' carts; later it could be purchased at the general store. Not all of it originated commercially, however. The sturdy evaporating pans and iron-bound carrying buckets used at maple-sugaring time were products either of the home artisan or the local blacksmith. Locally made, too, were many of the tin cooky cutters which have skyrocketed both in desirability and in price in recent years. Itinerant tinsmiths carrying their soldering gear and a number of samples sometimes utilized worn-out household containers of tin in turning out cooky designs for the delight of children and the satisfaction of the housewife. Other cutters, it is said, were made at local blacksmith shops but, once more, proof of the fact seems to be lacking.

It is difficult to find more than a few marked objects made by men for the use of women. Whether a skilled maker of iron wedges felt it beneath his dignity to create a tin sponge cake pan for his wife—although he would do it—or whether he felt that indoor domestic operations were of minor importance we may never know. We do know that if he applied a characteristic mark, or his name or initials, it was to something likely to be seen by other men rather than by women. Heavy tin jointed "walking" toys for children fall into this same unmarked category; while they turn up now and then, we do not know who made them.

COLLECTORS LOOK FOR:

Reaping hooks, especially those with impressed name of maker

Scythes, either the blades alone or the complete scythe-and-snath unit

*Dengelstocks* (Pennsylvania Dutch hand-anvils)

Handmade hinges of all kinds

Hasps (used as door fasteners)

Jamb hooks of all sizes

Portable meat hooks, single or in clusters

Hand-forged nails and bolts

Hatchets

Hewing axes, single- or double-bitted

Broad axes. While handmade specimens are considerably more valuable, factory-made ones are also in demand.

Iron rein holds

Pans, pails, coffeepots and other articles of tin made by country blacksmiths

Handmade tin cooky cutters

Jointed tin walking toys

Early long rifles and other firearms

*Jackpot:* Authenticated Nicholas Hawk rifle

# 8

# Glassworks and Glass

Residents of the up-country were glass-conscious from very early times. It seems to be the case that some of this feeling was generated by a widely known auctioneer, one Jacob Fries, who lived in Northampton County, not far from Bethlehem, but whose occupation took him far afield. Fries was not exactly a friendly or popular man; indeed, the records tell us that his only real friend was a yellow dog—and, in the end, even his dog betrayed him. However, what he may have lacked in personal popularity was more than offset by his forcefully reiterated convictions that the new Federal government had no right to assess property and collect taxes.

In particular, Fries was bitter over what he considered the flagrant injustice of levying taxes on window panes. Things came to a showdown one time when he was crying a sale and, as usual, inveighing against the unfairness of government practices. Federal marshals moved in to pick him up, but he fled to a nearby swamp and might have made good his escape except for the barking of his canine friend. He was tried for and convicted of treason, but was later pardoned by President John Adams.

Rebellion against taxation—or at least the methods of taxation in effect during the eighteenth century—spread throughout Hamilton and Chestnuthill townships in Monroe County, we are told, with at least as much bitterness as there was elsewhere. Whether or not the surprising number of up-country glass-making establishments constitutes a gesture traceable to Fries Rebellion is probably destined to remain an open question, and one of little importance now—but certain it is that a great deal of money and a great many persons were involved in the glass industry throughout the nineteenth century.

One of the first was a Philadelphia-based establishment headed by Mathew Ridgway. Fuel to operate a glassworks, in the pre-anthracite year of 1800, was prohibitively expensive in Philadelphia, and Ridgway's company poled sand and other raw materials necessary to make glass up the Delaware, by Durham boat, to Matamoras. There, firewood was plentiful and cheap enough that the venture was profitable, and remained so until the widespread availability of coal put an end to it. Blown window glass appears to have been the principal—perhaps the only—product of the Ridgway enterprise. The glass was shipped to Philadelphia, not by boat but by teams of horses.

More extensive than the Matamoras establishment was one considerably farther down the Delaware at Columbia, New Jersey. Columbia, across the river from the village of Portland, is just a few miles south of the Delaware Water Gap. One of its attractions for many years was its long covered bridge, which was lost in the flood of 1955. The Columbia Glass Works was established in 1813 "by Germans"—there seems to be no record of the names—who had earlier operated similar works in South Jersey. In fact, the Columbia plant, according to tradition, was like the parent South Jersey plant in every detail.

While the Columbia venture operated with some success until about 1832, it never wholly met the expectations of its founders. The first big problem was the matter of quality of the sand, which turned out to be inferior. In consequence, sand had to be brought up-river from places farther south. The Germans built their own flat-bottomed Durham-type boats for the purpose, and also built a small harbor or cove along the shore to anchor them. Great iron hoops five inches thick were embedded in rock, and to these the boats were tied up. Fragments of these hoops are still in place.

Window glass, the staple product of most early glass enterprises, was made at Columbia. Windows in one of the churches in the nearby village of Hope have panes made at the Columbia works, and there are dwellings in Columbia which can make the same boast. What else was manufactured is less a matter of record than of conjecture. An important vase in a private collection in Portland purports to have been made across the river. A demijohn in a museum in Hope is also believed to have been made locally. The story goes that this piece was a gift to a little girl whose grandfather had contracted to supply rocks for a wagon bridge to be used as an adjunct to the glass works. The bridge was never completed. An ironical touch to the Columbia project is that, had the operators but known it, there was an all but inexhaustible supply of sand over in Monroe County in Pennsylvania—a minor fraction of the distance to the source in southern Jersey.

Farther north, in Wayne County, venturesome entrepreneurs who set up their establishments in the wilderness also encountered difficulties. One company which made a reasonably promising start was established in 1816 near Bethany, not far from Honesdale. From the outset it was an inter-family affair, the members being emigrant glassworkers from Frankfurt am Main. Those of the original company were Christopher Faatz, Sr., Adam and Nicholas Greiner, Jacob and Christopher Hines, and Christian Faatz. Christian was a glassblower for his father (Christopher) as long as that gentleman remained in the glass business. Christopher died in 1868. ("Christopher" Faatz may actually also have been "Christian"; the record is very unclear.) The glassworks suffered the fate of only too many country enterprises of that day, burning to the ground in 1848. By that time there was considerable competition and the plant at Bethany was not rebuilt. We have very little information about this project beyond the statement of an early county historian that the product was good. Unfortunately for the gratification of our curiosity, he gives no clue as to the kinds of wares made.

Evidently some of the good will, if not of the physical establishment, remained, for Jacob Faatz, son of Christian, reestablished the business in nearby Traceyville, where eighteen to twenty thousand boxes of window glass were produced per year. Vicissitudes and misfortunes followed. Then, in 1871, the Honesdale Glass Works, which made both bottle and window glass, was established and operated successfully.

It is in the '80s that the famous cut glass of Honesdale was made. Two companies in particular appear to be outstanding: T. B. Clark, who established his place in 1884, and N. A. Ray and Company, in 1885. For all the popularity of cut glass when it was at the peak of production, there is very little either implicit in the pieces themselves or available by way of documentation, to distinguish one Honesdale product from another. In consequence, only someone who has actual records to substantiate his statement can say with authority that a given unmarked piece is of Clark, Ray, or Honesdale Glass Works provenance.

*Two media for the protection of easily broken glass containers—wood pulp and wicker. The carboy shown was covered at the Catlin works in East Stroudsburg; the wicker-covered bottles were found locally, but their origin is undocumented.*

An interesting footnote to a consideration of cut glass is the matter of bottle stoppers. It may be a little ironic that while few names of cutters or engravers have survived, we are in possession of that of an expert stopper maker—one Joseph Halter, Sr., who worked for the Honesdale Glass Works. Halter later became a cutter, but not at Honesdale.

Known worldwide are the products of the Dorflinger Glass Works, established in White Mills, Wayne County, in 1852 by Christian Dorflinger.

*Bottles bearing the names of Burt or Mervine, familiar to most Stroudsburg residents a generation or two ago, grow scarcer as the number of collectors increases. "Mervine" is also recorded as "Merwin" or "Mervine."*

Dorflinger, born in Alsace in 1828, came to America in 1845. At 17 he was already an accomplished glass blower. In the years that followed, he established, in addition to the plant at White Mills—perhaps the largest of its kind in the world—the Long Island Flint Glass Works and the Green Point Glass Works in Brooklyn.

Earlier glass factories in America had for the most part been established to meet the need for window glass and for simple glass containers. Dorflinger's intent was different; to him, glass was first of all a medium for the creation of beauty, and while the pieces he made also served utilitarian purposes, Dorflinger glass a century ago and now evokes first a thought of loveliness and then of usefulness.

Blown glass was made at White Mills from the outset; glass cutting and engraving followed shortly.

After 1881, Christian's sons William, Louis J., and Charles were in partnership with their father. Although the plant has ceased to be active, and little remains of the vast complex of buildings, an educational and historical collection maintained by the family is still in existence.

A major impetus to fame came in 1861 when Mary Todd Lincoln ordered a set of Dorflinger glass for the White House. The invoice reads "One set of glassware, rich cut and engraved with the U.S. Coat of Arms." The charge was $1500.00. Unlike much cut glass, the set designed expressly for the Lincolns is exceptionally thin and delicate. Included in the service were goblets, champagnes, and wines in various sizes, in clear, green, and ruby; and finger bowls and plates, butter dishes and covers, decanters, and celery holders.

As the years went on, succeeding presidents down to Woodrow Wilson augmented the service, in some cases adding new patterns. In 1902, Teddy Roosevelt had the Lincoln service copied, substituting the initial "R" for the coat of arms, paying for it out of his personal funds. He was thus permitted to remove it to his home in Oyster Bay when his term expired. Incidentally, Mr. Roosevelt was the first to add highball glasses to the collection.

Original factory working samples of all the presidential glass were kept at White Mills as a part of a permanent display. One requirement was made at the outset for every order which went to the White House: the original samples, sent for inspection, must be returned before work on the order was begun. It is not impossible to pick up a piece of Dorflinger glass at an antique shop today—but neither is it easy to do so.

A story is told of a novice in the world of antiques collecting. This young man was in his physician's waiting room, a place tastefully furnished in early American pieces. As he stood, admiring the frame of a courting mirror, the doctor entered abruptly and then, noting the rapt look on his patient's face, went to a closed cabinet, took out a blue wine glass, and demanded, "Tell me what that is!"

The young man was nonplussed. Glass was not one of his major interests; in fact, he could hardly have been less informed on the subject than he was. But from somewhere in the depths of his subconscious a name emerged. He had no idea when, where, or how he had heard it, or whether it was good or bad—but desperation may have qualities of which the possessor knows nothing.

"Dorflinger," he said, with what conviction he could muster.

"Right!" said the doctor, with quick respect. "Not many people would have recognized it. How did you know?"

"It's beautiful, isn't it?" asked the young man, cagily changing the subject.

Dorflinger interests went beyond the immediate family. In 1882 the Hawley Glass-Works was established as a limited partnership, the members of which were William F. Dorflinger, Samuel W. Weiss, Henry Z. Russell, F. C. White, and Joseph Atkinson. The plant, which cost $100,000, stood on a 20-acre tract of land on Middle Creek. Green and amber glass were manufactured there. The partnership was dissolved in 1885, but a reorganization took place and the business continued.

A number of glass operations contributed to the growth and importance of the towns of Stroudsburg and East Stroudsburg during the second half of the nineteenth century. Outstanding among these was the East Stroudsburg Glass Company, established as a stock company in 1876 for the manufacture of window glass and of glass containers. In 1879 William Burrows and Milton Yetter purchased the stock and the interest of the company. In 1886, according to the records, the daily output was 3600 bottles of various kinds, and a hundred men and boys were on the payroll. The interests of the company expanded, and a second plant was established at Binghamton, New York. Sand of excellent quality for the factory at East Stroudsburg came from the vicinity of Saylorsburg and Kunkletown, in the West End. A still fairly new product of any glassworks at this time was the fruit or preserving jar, and the East Stroudsburg Glass Company produced many. Housewives did not yet buy them by dozens, however, as they would in a few years—dozens and hundreds. Store ledgers of the '60s indicate piece-buying—at 25 cents each.

As might be expected, "offhand" pieces of ornamental nature were made by individual blowers or other artisans, and it is these—glass beads, toys, stocking darners, pieces of tableware—which are treasured today by descendants of the makers. A number of pieces of this sort are in the collection of the Monroe County Historical Society.

Beer bottles might seem to be unlikely objects for antiques collectors, but at least one name attached to an East Stroudsburg product has achieved status—"Burt." The Burt Bottling Works was established in 1868 and over the years the word "Burt" on a bottle seemed a natural, inevitable state of affairs.

William Valentine Kautz operated a bottling works at Eighth and Monroe streets in Stroudsburg as late as 1902. Some of his bottles were of blue glass and were marked "Wm. V. Kautz." Kautz was descended from Abraham Kautz, who was born in Germany in 1772 and was one of the early settlers in Monroe.

Fruit jars, as indicated above, were just beginning to become a significant commodity in the 1800s. Those made earliest were blown, and often exhibit bubbles and lines or flaws. Such marks are found less frequently on later molded wares. The superficial resemblance is often close, and the collector can not always be sure, until he has actually handled his supposedly individually made jar, that it is what he had hoped it would be.

Three local names have achieved a kind of fame in the present-day fad of collecting fruit jars—Star; Lyon and Bossard; and Van Vliet. Family recollections here do not always completely tally, either with one another or with presumed actual facts, as to who

*As the old saying has it, "Just for fancy"—a twenty-inch perfect glass sphere blown at the East Stroudsburg Glass Company. The scraps used for decoration were applied on the inside through the small opening left when the glass was detached from the blower's rod. The final step was to fill the globe with plaster of Paris. (Courtesy of the Monroe County Historical Society)*

*Ruby-stained souvenir glass probably exists for al-
most every place visited by summer tourists—and
many places that were not. Up-country pieces sometimes traveled far afield; specimens from distant
points fraternize comfortably with those which never
got far from home.*

built or owned what in 1881, but perhaps one may
say, with fingers crossed, that the Star Glass Works
was built in 1881 and that it operated for little more
than a year. Since the total output was limited, one
of the conditions which establish collectibility in any
commodity was automatically present—rarity. There
are persons today who can remember digging up
pieces of rejected glass from the ruins on the pur-
ported site near the old State bridge over the Brodheads Creek between the Stroudsburgs. The factory
was built by a stock company the members of which
were George E. Stauffer, C. L. Rhodes, and Joseph
Westcott.

The Lyon and Bossard company's plant stood in
East Stroudsburg near the junction of Crystal and
North Courtland streets. Philip Lyon, one of the part-

ners, was mayor of East Stroudsburg from 1875 to
1876. Joseph Bossard, the other partner, was evidently also a man of affairs. He had a stove store in
East Stroudsburg at that time, according to the census of 1880, and was mayor of the town from 1883
to 1884.

Lyon and Bossard fruit jars are not commonly
found, but perhaps they are not so rare as collectors
like to think. Since the advent of the food freezer,
preserving jars of all sizes, shapes, and ages have
been relegated in great numbers to cellars, sheds,
and attics. Some of them are indubitably old—and
some of them are clearly marked "Lyon and Bossard."
By now, a good many of these glass jar caches have
been gone over by their owners, who, hearing of occasional astronomical prices realized at auction by

Lyon and Bossard jars, have investigated to see just what potential wealth is theirs. And since in just a few years such a jar has risen in value from a few cents to a handful of bills, the likelihood is that many of them will remain exactly where they are now, awaiting what will happen next.

More thoroughly publicized than either the Star or the Lyon and Bossard jar is the metal-bound product of the Van Vliet factory. (Was this enterprise actually *on* the site of the short-lived Star plant—or very near it? There are those who believe so.) The date of 1858 on a Mason fruit jar means only that the company was established in that year—in spite of a popular belief that the jar was made then. (Some jars undoubtedly were.) However, "1881" on a Van Vliet jar is said to mean just what it appears to: it was

made in 1881. There may conceivably be room for argument, since the company remained in operation for a number of years and no date other than 1881 has appeared. However, the tradition is that Van Vliet jars were made in 1881, period.

Van Vliet is an old name in the Stroudsburgs. The first of the family appears to have been Derrick ("Dirk"?) Van Vliet, who was born in Amsterdam in 1699, emigrated to Esopus (Kingston), New York, in 1728, and removed to Pennsylvania in 1734. He lived in Stroudsburg for 40 years, dying in 1774. Now, at the end of the long span of years following his death, conflicting claims have arisen as to just which member or members of the family established the glassworks. Perhaps it was Warren. If it was, the works were established before 1881, according

*Cut glass pieces made in Stroudsburg. The final cutting or engraving process took place on pressed blanks.*

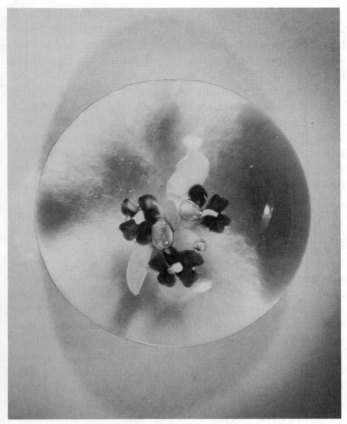

*Dorflinger glass from the plant at White Mills, Wayne County. Left, a cut glass salt cellar, the silver top marked "Dorflinger, Sterling"; right, a blown-glass paperweight by Nicholas Lutz, who worked at Dorflinger's from 1867 to 1869.*

to family tradition, though fruit jars may not have been made in the beginning. The plant was still operating in 1900; the records indicate that Jackson Lantz, a dentist in East Stroudsburg, owned a half interest in the enterprise then. One thing is certain: the sloping Van Vliet jar, wide at the bottom and narrow at the top, with its vertical metal hoop closely encircling it, is a very interesting specimen among the fraternity of glass objects intended to be utilitarian rather than beautiful.

Two plants in East Stroudsburg provided an added service for their customers by equipping their products with protective coverings—one establishment with wicker, the other with pulp. The East Stroudsburg Glass Works had an auxiliary plant which covered the larger vessels (some were intended to hold as much as five gallons—molasses, vinegar, acid, etc.) with a kind of basketwork of willow or oak. This wickerwork was applied wet. When it dried it made a snug and often attractive covering for the

glass containers, which could then be handled with a degree of safety not otherwise possible. Sadly enough for the antiques collector, most of these coverings have long since moldered away in damp cellars and comparatively few specimens remain in sound condition.

The Catlin bottling plant on King Street in East Stroudsburg not only made its own bottles but covered them with a pulp mixture which hardened quickly and became tough with age. Less attractive to collectors than wicker-covered objects, these bottles, usually in large or carboy sizes, have an appeal more historical than aesthetic.

So accustomed were the two towns to the manufacture of glass that a cut glass operation was still going on in Stroudsburg during the first quarter of the twentieth century. The vogue for cut glass had by then largely run its course, however, and the plant went out of existence—not, it should be observed, before many local householders acquired, and packed away, some resplendent pieces. As cut glass becomes fashionable again—and it would seem that the wheel has gone almost full circle—some Stroudsburgers will be way out ahead if they choose to display their treasures.

A glass factory many people still remember is the Scott-Warman plant, which operated from 1916 to some time in the 1920s. At this place perhaps the most interesting product was the great hand-blown carboy. Several processes of hardening, shaping the neck, and molding still had to follow after the gaffers had performed the initial step of blowing. It was hot, physically demanding work—and dangerous.

Glass telephone-wire insulators have joined the list of collectibles within the past decade or two. There are more sizes, shapes, and colors than the noninitiate might expect, and some are of peculiar interest to the up-country specialist. Among these are the Hawley-made product, with patent dates of 1899, 1901, and 1902. Some are marked "H. I. Co.,"; some "Harloe's Pat.,"; and some with an insignia of the intertwined initials "H. I. Co." The third one in this group has a peculiar appeal for collectors: one batch, in aqua-colored glass, bore the inscription "Hawley, Pa., U.S.A." below the insignia—with the "S" of "U.S.A." *reversed*. It is said that all the defective ones were shipped north of Hawley—presumably by accident.

Another insulator with a particular appeal is the Hawley "pigtail" specimen, of which apparently not many were made. The name came from a set of three curving glass protuberances at the top, around which the wire was anchored. One might hazard the guess that this variety was especially subject to breakage.

### COLLECTORS LOOK FOR:

Blown bottles—clear, aqua, blue, green, amber, in any size or shape

Fruit jars, especially those marked Lyon and Bossard, Star, or Van Vliet

Pieces made by the East Stroudsburg Glass Company, including green or amber flasks; carboys, druggists' bottles; beer bottles; and porcelain-topped fruit jars. "Porcelain" here is actually glass.

Bottles made at the Burt Brothers plant

Bottles marked "Mervine" for a bottling works in the Stroudsburgs

Any glass known to have been made at the Columbia Glass Works

Off-hand blown or ornamental objects of any kind made in local plants

Window glass which with the passing of time has become iridescent—in particular, amethyst-tinged

Blown window glass—single panes or a complete sash —in which bubbles are prominent

Wide-mouthed preserving jars of any vintage

Dorflinger glass pieces—old or recent. All are collectible.

Cut glass made by any of the Honesdale houses

Stroudsburg cut glass (late)

Ruby-stained souvenir glass with local names

Wicker-covered bottles and pulp-encased carboys

Telephone-wire insulators

*Jackpot:* Signed piece of Dorflinger cut glass

# 9

# *Droving and "Droviers"*

The name droving is so unfamiliar today that one who sees it in print as a free-standing word with no explanatory context is likely to assume that it is a misprint for something else.

A drove was a herd of cattle on the move, the aggregate including calves, yearlings, and occasionally two-year-olds—the youngsters, so to speak, both steers and heifers—along with dry cattle. Cows to be milked were kept close at home. The others were kept at home, too, in the cold months and in the spring for as long as there was adequate green pasturage for all.

In the southern and western portions of Pike County—the only part, really, which had passed from wilderness into anything resembling a state of cultivation—and in southern Wayne the grass was green all summer long. Moreover, the condition extended northward all the way up-country and into New York. Grass was the most satisfactory crop in the entire region, the production easily out-stripping that of wheat, corn, oats, rye, or buckwheat.

On the other hand, while grass grew just as well in Monroe as it did farther north, grain grew a great deal better. The question arose, then, as to which phase of the economy was the smart one to tackle. It was hardly possible, in a day when rural areas had to be more or less self-sustaining, to get along without cattle, as a source of milk and butter and also of edible beef. It was irksome, though, to devote to the needs of the nonproducing segments of the herd, good grazing land which could be much more lucrative if put to grain. Now, if there were only a way of meeting the needs of the young animals without sacrificing the grain which would be needed in their maintenance later . . .

There was a way: droving. For years—from the mid-nineteenth century until its close—the practice of driving hungry, slab-sided young cattle north in the spring, pasturing them by arrangement with farmers in Wayne and Pike, and driving them south again in the fall, this time sleek and in fine condition, was almost if not quite a major industry. Boys trained themselves to become drovers; men became specialists in the techniques called for in getting great numbers of excitable young animals safely from a nearby spot to another far distant; way stations, "homes," and hotels came into being to cater to their needs. While it lasted, it was both profitable and picturesque.

For all practical purposes one may say that the northward droving activity started at gaps in the Blue Mountain—Wind Gap, Tott's (in earlier times known as Tatemy's) Gap, Little Gap, and the Delaware Water Gap. North from these points went the cattle, with their mounted custodians and outriders, over dusty, crooked roads that the hoofs of the cattle and the horses helped to beat down finally into highways. Not many miles could be traversed in a day—and the total distance to cover might be considerably more than a hundred miles. It was slow business.

Perhaps the most notable of the various arteries used by the drovers, for all that today it is impossible to retrace accurately more than a few sections of it, was "The Great North and South" (Turnpike). This road started at Wind Gap—"started" in the sense that it was here that cattle from contributing farms were first brought together—proceeded to Saylorsburg, and then continued through good farmland territory northward and upward to Tannersville. From

The ever-popular cow—in tin (De Laval cream separator advertisement); in copper (weather vane); and in flocked paper (toy).

The product of the cooper was in demand from earliest times. There seems to have been a keg or cask of a size appropriate for any liquid needing storage, from molasses to vinegar or rum.

Tannersville it went into more rugged territory up to Mt. Pocono. Drinker's Turnpike began at Mt. Pocono, continued to the Dutch Flats (now Newfoundland), to Sterling, and on to Scranton.

Mt. Pocono, it may be observed, not only marked the beginning of Drinker's Turnpike but served as the focal point of a long-lasting controversy. There were those who said that the entire length of the road, from Wind Gap to Scranton, was properly called The Great North and South—and that dubbing any part of it "Drinker's" was a mere affectation. The opposing faction argued just as vehemently that, while the portion in Monroe might with some trifling degree of sanity be called The Great North and South, what belonged to Wayne was properly termed Drinker's, and nothing else. While many a nose was bloodied and an occasional bone broken over the matter, the controversy was never settled. It was not forgotten, though, nor was it wholly dropped until straightened-out curves and relaid portions made the old road all but unrecognizable and the argument ridiculous.

The cattlemen did not slavishly follow the turnpike, whatever its proper name. Especially where there were steep grades, they would take side trails, if any were available. Up to the Half-way House (halfway between Wind Gap and Scranton), a celebrated hostelry north of Mt. Pocono, the drove remained essentially intact. Past that point, groups of animals would be siphoned off here and there and conducted to the farmsteads where they would spend the summer. The great bulk, however, which might run into the thousands, went on into Wayne County, spreading out fan-wise into their destined grazing places, after passing Newfoundland or Sterling. Some of the men then returned to their homes, where they would busy themselves at a different occupation until fall. Others, however, still had considerable business to transact by way of making payment, settling claims, checking arrangements for the fall, and establishing contacts for the following year.

A drover had to be good at his work. If he lost too many animals on the trip, whether to an occasional poacher or for any other reason, he would not be invited to participate next time. He might, and sometimes did, make a practice of getting drunk and disorderly at the inns where the men spent the night when possible, and that without prejudice. If he let even the most wayward calf break a leg, however, in a wrongly calculated endeavor to get it back to the herd from which it had strayed, he became a marked man and would be under observation from that point on. (A broken leg meant a lost animal; on the northern trip the creature would probably be too lean for slaughtering and would have to be shot, since the leg could rarely be set.)

The inns seem to have matched their patrons in rough and ready quality. It was a rare place that did not serve liquor; alcoholic beverages were taken for granted wherever there were overnight accommodations. Before the comparatively innocuous present-day euphemistic tags of "taproom" or "tavern" achieved currency, the less pleasant term of "saloon" was widely used—and in the minds of most people "hotel" was synonymous with "saloon" and any thought of overnight accommodations in connection with either was merely incidental. This stereotype has not entirely disappeared in the up-country, even now.

A few names and places persist in memory. Perhaps most highly thought of was one which long antedated the practice of droving—John McMichaels' place at Mt. Paul, some two miles west of Stroudsburg. McMichaels, whose name has been perpetuated by a village and a stream, was less than universally popular. In fact, when his inn was established in 1762, the license was applied for and received by his wife, since a request on his part, as he well knew, might be denied. It was a good inn, for all that—and remained a good inn for many, many years. There is no longer a trace of it, however; the land on which it stood now forms part of a locally well-known real estate development.

We have mentioned the Half-way House, which, in addition to its convenience, was celebrated for its pulchritudinous and compliant waitresses. It is said there were mothers who put their feet down in complete finality when a boy let it be known that he had been offered a job as an apprentice drover. Perhaps, knowing what they knew about the Half-way House, they had good reason. If anyone today, however, actually knows whether the place was or was not—in addition to its being an inn—a house of assignation, he is not telling. Indeed, there are those who maintain that the idea was pure fiction, created by certain sadistic husbands as a means of tormenting their suspicious wives. The building was torn down, long ago.

Deubler's was a well-known stopping place, a long day's (cattle day's) journey over the mountain from the Half-way House. It continued to operate into the present century. One of its claims to remembrance is that of its ballroom. There were those who thought of a ballroom—any ballroom—as a place of sin, or, at the very best, of potential evil, as well as those who did not. At a time when the sentimental ballad "After the Ball" was at its peak of popularity, someone in the up-country did a clever bit of musical interpolation, including the incorporation of "Deubler's" as part of a refrain in the well-known song. The phrase caught on at once, producing contrary reactions. One group made an association of "Deubler's" with "hotel," and "hotel" with "ball" and denounced the place as immoral. Another group, however, whole-heartedly adopted the new line and seemingly forgot the original. "After the ball was over" became "After the ball at Deubler's" and so remained.

Another inn which persisted into the present century was situated in Newfoundland. It, too, had the stigma attached to other hostelries: it had a bar. Once called "Correll's," after its founder, it was known over the years by a number of names, "Newfoundland House" probably being familiar to more people than any other.

Drover's Home—for whatever reason widely mispronounced as "Drovier's" Home—was a name applied to a number of establishments in widely separated places. There was one "under the mountain," apparently at or near Stockertown, south of Wind Gap. It is said that there was one in Paradise Valley, north of Analomink. And there was one between the top of the Pocono Plateau and LaAnna. All have long since disappeared.

The high degree of skill of most of the drovers has long been forgotten except as it may have lingered in the memories of their families. Most of them, as might be determined from the mere fact that they were able to do an almost impossibly complicated job, were obviously resourceful, tenacious, and dedicated. Two names, however, have come down to us out of the anonymity of the total as being those of exceptionally able men: Aaron Bittenbender, first of Monroe County but later of Northampton; and George Hagerman, also of Monroe and later associated with Palmer Butchers in Stroudsburg.

The return trip in the fall was more likely to be full of tension that the trip north had been, and was considerably busier. True, in the spring the cattle were nervous and jumpy. The calves were hare-brained— calf-brained?—and skittish, easily frightened, and prone to set up a miniature stampede over something as slight as the chattering of a squirrel.

There were more serious hazards than squirrels, though. The returning herds were headed for one or two destinations—the slaughter house or the dairy barn. Accustomed to good grazing for the summer, they could not subsist alone on the sketchy roadside pickings they encountered on the return trip, and, unless they could be provided with decent pasturage at a number of places, would lose some of their brand-new embonpoint. One of the drover's summer jobs, of

course, was to arrange for these periodic stops—and another was to make sure that the cattle got to them at the time stipulated. If any unfortunate delay occurred, and the drover arrived even a day late, he might find the fields for which he had bargained occupied by a herd which had been scheduled to follow him. Since any one calf looks pretty much like any other calf, the ensuing mix-up could assume frightful dimensions. "Losing" an animal then ceased to be a joking matter. The only way the drover could successfully survive such a crisis was to take with him, when he left, exactly the same *number* of animals he had had when he arrived. Somehow, he usually managed.

His problem grew greater the farther he went. On this trip, his journey would not end at one of the Gaps, but at Easton or Bethlehem or even Philadelphia. The reason was that, in order to make his summer financially profitable, he would buy stock from farmers along the way, add animals to the herd of which he was the acting custodian, and sell them at the distant market, wherever it was. Thus, his array of creatures changed in size and appearance with each passing day until ultimately he could rid himself of them all. Let us pause to observe that the word "creature" was probably totally nonexistent in the up-country. An animal past calfhood but short of adulthood, whether male or female, was a *critter*—no more, no less.

The successful drover was usually one who had learned that there were three prime aids available to him, if he was fortunate enough to secure them: a boy seemingly without nerves, a dog which could think like a calf, only faster, and a good lead cow. The boy, as a kind of rear guard, had to be able to prod stragglers without frightening them or causing them to break into a run. The dog had to be on hand at the moment a calf felt an uncontrollable urge to hightail it for the woods—and nip the attempt in the bud.

Discovering and making a pet of the lead cow was a matter first of keen observation and then of preferential treatment. Nobody knows just how it happens, but in any herd of cattle, large or small, the so-called pecking order will produce one tacitly acknowledged leader. When she eats, the others eat; when she gives the signal, they lie down; when they move, she sets the direction. With a good lead cow, well petted, at the head of the procession, a dog attuned to the vagaries of the flighty adolescents, and an equally watchful boy bringing up the rear, the drover could perhaps not take it easy but could at least breathe easily—now and then.

*Hand-blown bottles of the kind found not only at drovers' hotels but at most country taverns. The colors used are pale green, very dark olive, and amber. Note the three types of lips.*

*Every barroom was equipped with spittoons. This flint enamel specimen, from an up-country house of entertainment, has a special distinction; it is marked and dated—Etruria Works, East Liverpool (Ohio), 1852. (The year 1852 is reputedly the first in which flint enamel was made at the Etruria Works.)*

*Just about everything at the County Fair seems to have appeared larger than life, whether livestock, vegetables, or the blue ribbons awarded to first-prize winners.*

The seasoned drover had one more conspicuous element in his makeup: he was psychic in the matter of estimating the weight of the animals he purchased. When he got them, he bought them by the head—but with a mentally adduced figure, since no scales were available, as to their poundage. When he sold them in the city, however, where scales were available, he was paid by the pound. Experience, of course, was a big help in the long run, but a man could have gone bankrupt before he gained the experience unless he had something supersensory about him—or unless he was a better guesser than the farmer from whom he made his purchase.

Droving ended with neither a bang nor a whimper. It simply came to a stop when the overall economy had reached the point at which a man no longer had to produce everything he consumed. Once he was able to purchase his meat from the butcher and his milk from the store or the creamery—and pay for them with cash—there was no longer a need for either droves or drovers, and so they both disappeared. For years, up-country cattle in custody have ordinarily been seen only on dairy farms or at county fairs.

COLLECTORS LOOK FOR:

Old-time highway finger-posts
Inn signs
Weather vanes showing cows
Advertising objects bearing the names of old inns
Barroom and dining room furniture from inns
Tableware marked with the names of inns
Bar mirrors, shelves, foot rails, etc.
Spittoons—brass, pottery, or wood. (Wooden spittoons were usually square, and were intended to be filled part-way with sawdust.)
Liquor bottles and flasks
Casks, kegs, barrels—even hogsheads
Powder horns
Drinking vessels, spoons, combs, etc., of horn
Cowbells
Metal or flocked-paper figures of cows (toys)
Old veterinary kits
Containers for patented nostrums for animals
Saddle gear and blankets
Horse collars, bits, and bridles
Ledgers used by innkeepers
Books of treatments and cures for ailing animals
County fair posters
*Jackpot:* A copy of Johann Georg Hohmann's *Der lang verborgenen Schatz und Haus-Freund* (*The Long-Lost Friend*) of 1819 or 1820. This is one of a number of the so-called "forbidden" powwow or magic books filled with "cures" for the ailments of man and beast. Powwowing, while not completely unknown, was much less common in the up-country than it was farther south. Source: a rare book dealer or store.

# 10
# Tanning Their Hides

Today, the chances are perhaps no more than 50–50 that the shoes one wears are of leather, or even partly of leather. So many synthetics are available that one can by no means be sure of what is between his bare feet and the ground. This condition is a far cry from the one prevailing in the 1800s; shoes were made of leather then, and no nonsense about it. The leather might be stiff and unyielding, but it had started as cowhide—good, durable cowhide with at least a year's daily wear in it.

Cowhide, to be sure, was not the very first animal skin to be used on this side of the Atlantic for foot covering. The Indians taught the early colonists how to treat animal skins—usually deer, but others also—so that they could be used for personal gear after clothing brought from Europe had worn out. Whether or not the technique of processing woodchuck skins can be attributed to the Indians is debatable; there may be a trace of burgeoning Yankee ingenuity in it. Woodchuck skins were not employed in the making of shoes, but they met a dozen other everyday needs for which we should now use a length of twine or a piece of wire. Shoestrings were normally made of thin strips of woodchuck hide as were the tough pieces necessary to hold the component parts of the grain flail together, and the longer strips which, with the aid of an awl, were needed for the mending of harnesses.

Curing—the word "tanning" did not really apply here—woodchuck skins took a little time, but not so much as was later required for the curing of heavy animal hides. The first step was to bury the skin in a pit filled with wood ashes and then pour in water until the ashes were soaked. By the time the ashes had dried out, the hair could be scraped off the skin

without difficulty. Several skins were processed at a time; the supply of woodchucks seems always to have been an abundant one.

The second step—and one the Indians could not have taken—was to immerse the cleaned skins in a keg of homemade soft soap. This soap was rather powerful stuff, and a week's immersion would shrink and close all the pores of the skin. A thorough washing came next, and then a pounding and beating exercise which brought about a satisfactory degree of pliability. Once the skins had been thus worked over, they were stretched across a board framework and hung up out of direct sunlight to cure. The curing might take months, and if the drying-out process had been too speedy the skins were taken down and given a second going-over. In the end they were cut into thin strips, the width varying according to their intended purpose. Eel skins were subjected to much the same procedure—the first step, of course, not being necessary!

The deficiencies of skins as light as those of wild animals served to point up the pressing need for something better; and the something better came as a by-product of the big gun of the whole upper region —the conversion of trees to lumber. Among all the trees in Wayne, Pike, and Monroe, there were two which had a special quality at first regarded as a mere nuisance but soon recognized as a revenue-producing asset. These were the oak, which grew as far north as the foothills of the Poconos, and the hemlock, which started about where the oaks left off and continued all the way north through Pennsylvania and into New York State. Like other straight, tall-growing specimens, they made good lumber; unlike the others, their thick bark was loaded with a powerful acid—

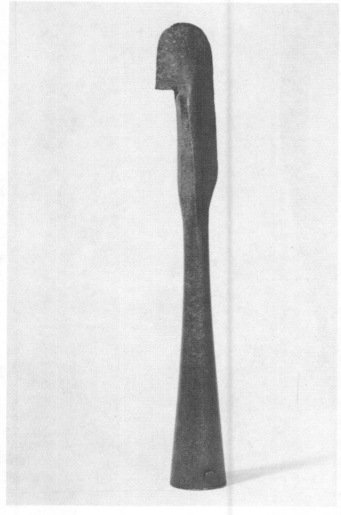

*On its way to joining the carrier pigeon is the hand-forged bark spud—the implement used to strip bark from felled hemlock or oak trees for tanning purposes. The three-foot wooden handle is missing from the specimen shown here.*

tannic acid.

Ordinarily, the bark which accumulated at sawmills was a problem, and if the planks were not trimmed at the mill the bark became an even greater problem whenever the lumber was shipped. Both oak and hemlock trees could be peeled, however, if they were felled when the sap was running, the bark coming off in large sheets which were stacked up in the same way cordwood was. As a matter of fact, bark was measured by the cord. Logs which went to the sawmill could thus go "clean," with the handling and processing of the bark a completely separate operation.

Tannic acid was the best known agent for effecting the transition between rawhide and leather. If the only needs to be met had been those of the immediate community, or even of the commonwealth of Pennsylvania, the wholesale harvesting of hemlock and oak in the 1800s would never have been so speedily prosecuted. However, with the population of the New World steadily growing, it appeared that everybody, everywhere needed leather, partly for shoes, of course, but even more for harnesses, and all at the same time. Once a few tentative establishments had been created and their products tested, capital for larger operations became available. Investors from foreign countries got a finger in the pie—and an industry was born. There were periods of boom and bust, but tanning pyramided into an outstanding operation in the up-country and remained so for three quarters of a century. At the time of the 1860 census in Monroe County, 19 major tanning enterprises were under way.

Happily enough, the big operations did not put small, individual ones out of business. Long before the first tannery had begun to operate, farmers were curing animal hides in vats on their own homesteads. (Incidentally, while the skin from a calf was simply a *skin,* that from a full-grown animal was a *hide.*) The farmer seldom had time to make shoes, even if he possessed the skill; itinerant shoemakers took care of families about once a year in the "circuits" they established for their operations. But the farmer was expected to supply the leather.

The farmer also provided the metal lasts—many of which, in a complete range of sizes, seem still to be in existence. One reason they were not thrown away after the 1870s, about the time store-bought shoes became a possibility, was that repair jobs fell to the head of the household. The shoemaker would not ordinarily waste his talents on anything less than a total job. The man of the house, while he might not like the job, could often sole a pair of shoes as well as the professional. The leather was at hand, as were the wooden shoe pegs and the woodchuck leather strings. The size of the family might conceivably have been a factor in the rather general distaste for cobbling shoes; after all, ten to fifteen children could wear out shoe soles—even the heavy leather ones of the day—faster than a man felt like repairing them!

Perhaps it is unnecessary to observe that the low-cut shoes so commonly worn today had not yet come into use. Shoes were actually boots—heavy and high. Men's boots were so stiff and clumsy that special devices known as bootjacks had to be employed to get them off the feet.

Early store ledgers give us some bare bones of fact

Tender, loving care was sometimes lavished on even such lowly objects as the bootjacks needed to remove the stiff leather footgear of an earlier era. "Kicking" one's shoes off at the end of the day was a luxury unknown to our up-country ancestors.

*Wooden shoe-trees of the nineteenth century were as carefully shaped as the shoes themselves. This kind of gear was not limited to Pennsylvania.*

on leather and shoemaking. Aaron Dupuis, in Shawnee, was buying raw animal hides as early as 1743, an ordinary cow's hide or a deerskin "in the hair" commanding six shillings. A ledger entry for 1744 indicates that Mathew Brantum paid Aaron one pound, three shillings, and sixpence for an elk skin. While there is no notation as to whether the elk hide was tanned, the price might seem to indicate that it was. Benjamin Schoonmaker was buying tanned leather at Shawnee in 1746. Between 1781 and 1787, John DeLong, in the same community, was making shoes professionally, with an interesting scale of prices: shoes, two shillings, sixpence; women's shoes, three shillings; and moccasins, three shillings, twopence. He resoled shoes for one shilling.

A little later, between 1823 and 1825, we find Jacob Buss as a maker of shoes. We do not know what he charged, but in 1835 Ezra Kennedy made a pair in January for 50 cents—and in March for 62½ cents. Presumably they were different types of shoes.

A 39-page ledger for 1827–1830 in the possession of the Monroe County Historical Society is that of another local shoemaker—possibly Joseph Anderson but not indisputably so. Shoes cost from 37 to 50 cents a pair then. These were presumably everyday shoes; "lais" (laced) boots cost 62 cents. Cash transactions were less common than those involving barter. Tallow for barter was accepted at the rate of ten cents a pound; a bushel of rye was worth 40 cents. Henry Smith, mentioned elsewhere, received credit for weaving when he purchased shoes. The shoemaker probably had an immediate use for tallow; homemade shoes could be made supple—to a degree, at least—with it, as well as comparatively watertight.

One could no more establish an accurate chronol-

ogy of professional tanning operations than he could of sawmills, but it is possible to call attention to those outstanding enough to have been noted by early historians. In 1822, Charles and Jacob Stroud, grandsons of the founder of Stroudsburg, operated a tannery on what is now Ann Street in Stroudsburg. From the first, it did a considerable business; in fact, so many loads of bark made their way daily to the plant that residents called the road "Bark Street." The Strouds sold the business to Depue S. Miller in 1833; later still it was owned and operated by James and Gershom Hull.

While this establishment was achieving importance in Stroudsburg, another was shaping up in Smithfield Township, at Buttermilk Falls, under the management of Francis Erwin. Although the tannery has long since disappeared, the falls remain—as breathtaking in their beauty at the time of spring freshets as they ever were. These falls enjoy a kind of reflected glory in that, at the time of the catastrophic flood of 1955, the Buttermilk Falls Bridge was the only one for miles around not seriously damaged or affected by the high water. A second tannery was built there by George McEwing, shortly after Erwin's venture. It continued to operate to about 1870. John Heller is mentioned as a tanner in the community in 1838.

Tanbark operations appear to have approached a peak by 1860. Early newspapers were widely used to recruit workers in various fields, for the most part with considerable success. Even the best efforts of advertisers, however, in a territory of the size served by a local paper, could hardly produce satisfactory results for such demands as "200 men needed at once in Tannersville; spuds supplied; 62½ cents a day." The spud was the long-handled curving-bladed implement used in stripping bark from the log, and was usually provided by the company. The pay rate was standard. There simply were not that many men available, however—and this deficiency in manpower, more than a lack of capital or a market, proved to be the limiting factor in many enterprises.

In 1841, Joseph Singmaster operated the Stroudsburg Tannery. One of the biggest demands on the whole industry was for leather to be used for harnesses and saddles. The tannery did not ordinarily go beyond the actual production of the leather, though a few had harness-making establishments as auxiliary operations. Singmaster went a step beyond many others; according to the record, while he made harness, he also produced gloves and fine "calf"—a thin, flexible leather of superior quality usually used for the uppers of "Sunday" rather than work-a-day shoes.

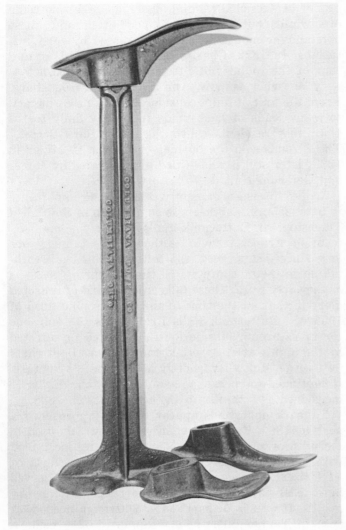

*A shoe-soling outfit was a needed but not especially popular unit of equipment in most farm homes. Commercially manufactured lasts enabled the man of the family to repair shoes of any size. More primitive, homemade lasts exist, but are now seldom seen outside museums.*

In 1850, Joseph Fenner built a tannery at what was then called Fennersville, in Hamilton Township. Subsequently enlarged, it eventually took on impressive proportions. The smokestack—important in dissipating noxious fumes—was 87 feet high and so big around that 1000 bricks were needed for a single tier at the base. From Fenner it went to Melchior Bossard, who kept it only a short time before selling it to Charles E. Kistler of Tannersville.

The Kistlers were a tanning family; many of the men were engaged in separate or joint operations in a number of places in and out of the up-country.

Stephen Kistler, father of Charles, purchased an ongoing venture in Tannersville in 1852. The business prospered and in time the management passed to Charles, who in 1867 purchased the plant which Joseph Fenner had built in Hamilton Township earlier. Confusion followed. "Fennersville" and "Tannersville" sounded alike—and "Kistler's in Fennersville" and "Kistler's in Tannersville" helped but little to ease the embarrassment of patrons or decrease the complications in the two business offices.

In 1867 Kistler moved to Fennersville, where he built a fine Victorian mansion, still standing, for his personal residence. In the same year the name of the village was officially changed to Sciota.

Jay Gould, the financier for whom the village of Gouldsboro was named, was involved in up-country tanning. With a partner, he had established the firm of Zadok Pratt & Jay Gould in Luzerne County, but was so impressed with the potential in Wayne that he invested heavily. In 1859 or thereabouts, faced with the alternatives of getting an enormous quantity of bark out of the swamp immediately or going bankrupt, he spent $10,000 in building a plank road from the wilderness to the plant he established at Gouldsboro. The road was completed in time, but there were so many complications in ownership transfers, road-building, and contracts and subcontracts that eventually he abandoned the tanning business completely and moved on to greener, less rugged pastures.

*A homemade device which provided a storage place for a man's shoe-shining equipment as well as a convenient surface to carry on the polishing operation.*

Peter Kester at Hamilton; Palen and Northrop at Canadensis; Dowing and Company at Knipesville; Miller and Mackey at Resaca; Burger and Bleckler at Kunkletown—all these engaged in tanning in 1860. In 1869, White's Tannery at Mountainhome assumed importance, as did the Oak Valley Tannery (Mountainhome) and the Oak Valley Branch Tannery at Spragueville (Analomink). George L. Adams managed both the Oak Valley enterprises.

Largest—and last—of the giants was the Elk Horn Tannery, built in East Stroudsburg in 1869 by Stephen Kistler. The place covered six acres of ground, the main building itself being 267 feet long. In 1885, when George L. Adams, previously mentioned, acquired it, about 175 hides were processed daily. It discontinued operations in 1927, recently enough that many people remember it distinctly, although there is no remaining trace of it today.

Curiously enough, while tanning is one of the most malodorous of enterprises, there is nothing in the records to indicate that people objected to the industry. Out in the country, of course, there might be few people living near enough to be bothered by the noisome fumes. In town, apparently the operation was well enough controlled that it did not become a public nuisance.

The process of turning hides into leather is fairly simple, but there were several well-defined steps. Hides first had to be soaked in a mixture of lime and water and then scraped on one side to remove the hair and the other to get rid of any bits of animal tissue overlooked at the time the creature was skinned. (The hair was often sold for use by plasterers.) The hides were then returned for a second soaking—this time in a sulfuric acid solution. When these preparatory steps had been taken, the real tanning process could begin. The tanyard was filled with oblong pits of any length or width convenient, but always six to eight feet deep. These pits were heavily lined with clay to keep the tanning mixture from draining into the ground. The tanbark was shredded, and the pits were partly filled with it. Water was added, the hides were put in, and the tanning operation was underway.

A three-month soaking was considered minimal; a year's time was better—and a year and a half was considered about right for top-quality leather. During this period the hides were moved or stirred from time to time, and water was added as needed. Long hooks somewhat suggesting those used on ice ponds were utilized to push the hides back and forth, the idea of course being that every inch should be subjected to the tannic acid.

The job was not done when the hides finally came out of the pit, so stiff that they were stood up to dry.

The process of softening still had to take place, and for this purpose a number of manipulations, sometimes including an oil treatment, were involved. What was done with the leather at this point depended on the purchaser's needs; the maker of women's gloves and the producer of harness would have completely different sets of requirements.

The up-country tanners did not depend to any extent on local sources for the skins or hides they processed. They went into business primarily because an inexpensive supply of tanbark was at hand; the skins had to come to them—from local farms, from country storekeepers far and wide who had taken calf skins in barter, from down-country sources, from nearby New Jersey, and from counties to the west. After the D. L. and W. Railroad reached the Stroudsburgs in 1856, hides were secured from places even farther afield and the industry continued to expand.

The horseless carriage was largely responsible for the eventual decline of the industry. People still needed shoes, of course, but tastes were changing, and heavy leather boots were less and less commonly worn. The leather in shoes for dress wear grew thinner, and gloves of fabric instead of leather came into common use. It all added up to a greatly reduced need for leather in personal apparel. So far as horses, saddles, and harness were concerned, as soon as mechanized farming became possible the horse gradually disappeared—taking with him the harness, the tannery and one of the distinctive occupations of the region.

COLLECTORS LOOK FOR:

Sets of cast-iron shoe lasts

Iron stands for shoe lasts

Shoe lasts of wood with sizes (and half sizes) indicated

Bootjacks of wood or of iron

Bootblack equipment

Fancy iron footrests used on bootblack stands

Shoemakers' implements—hammers, awls, knives, etc.

Cobblers' benches

Wooden stretchers for small animal hides

Sheets of tanned and processed unused leather

Harness straps which can be adapted to a present-day use

Leather fly nets for horses

Vintage leather footwear

Colored advertisements and advertising posters

Bark spuds

*Jackpot:* Hand-carved bootjack with name and/or date

# 11
## Butter for Barter

The earliest medium of exchange in North America, at least as we know it, appears to have been wampum. The Eskimos and the pre-Columbian Indians may have traded with something different; we do not know for sure—but we do know about wampum. For a time, the Spanish real and pieces of eight were dependably standard. Pieces of silver are mentioned in Aaron Dupuis's store ledger in Smithfield Township in 1745, and a doubloon was taken in exchange at the store not much later. Pine tree shillings—or any shillings—were equally sound, and for a longer time. In fact, mention is made as late as our grandfathers' day of the cost of something in terms of shillings and pence.

But in the up-country the standard trading medium was not wampum, nor was it pieces of eight or shillings. It was butter. Railroad ties, sometimes; animal pelts, to the 1860s; eggs, seasonally and in many places—but butter, always. We might note in passing that in 1753 butter commanded sixpence a pound at Dupuis's store; Daniel Crely was credited with 17 shillings for 34 pounds on May 11 of that year. If one assumes that the figure remained stable, a quart of timothy seed was worth twice as much as a pound of butter in 1756, when John McDowell received one pound sterling and 16 shillings for 36 quarts.

Prices on animal skins did not remain stable; they varied according to condition, color, demand, and availability. The ledger just mentioned lists a bear skin as worth one pound and five shillings in 1743; two fox and two muskrat skins in 1744, as a lot, six shillings and sixpence; an otter skin, in 1745, five shillings. Such figures must be accepted as variables; bigger, better, or less desirable pelts would be subject to a different evaluation.

Let us bypass the traffic in railroad ties, timothy seed, animal hides, and eggs, for the time being at least, and discover, if we can, what was so special about butter. The up-country, in the beginning, from the West End in what is now Monroe to the rapids at Shohola in Pike, and across the wastes to the northern tip of Wayne, was largely a place of individual, widely scattered homesteads. In villages and hamlets, and later on in towns, people saw their fellowmen daily, but out in the country each family lived essentially unto itself unless a conscious effort was made to establish contact with the rest of the world. Since pioneering people were busy from dawn to dark, there had to be a good excuse for leaving the farm for a day or even part of a day. Doing one's trading offered just such an opportunity—and though probably no one would have made an open statement on the subject, trading was as much a social matter as a business occasion.

Money—cash money—was not really needed, although it was handy to have around. Youngsters needed pennies for the collection plate at Sunday School and, if one had a letter to write, the stamp had to be paid for with coins. Beyond that, one could do well enough with butter or eggs, and occasionally both.

Making butter required a lot more effort than gathering the eggs once a day or taking them to the store when several dozen had accumulated, but it was usually worth it in the long run. In the summer, when the hens laid well, the price of eggs was so low that it was a source of discouragement rather than of satisfaction. In the winter, when the price was high, the hens were usually on vacation—likewise a discouraging circumstance. Butter, however, while there

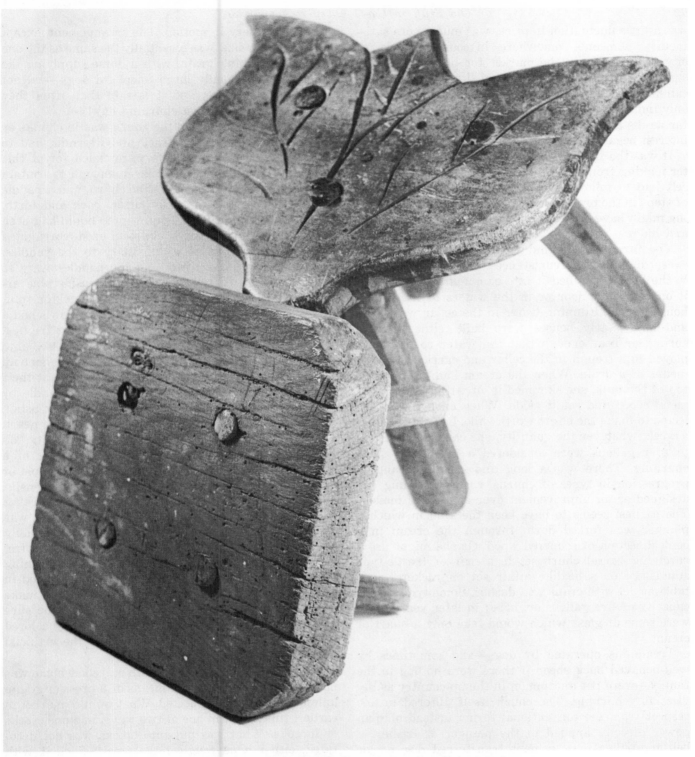

*Plain and fancy in milking stools. The legs of the four-square, four-legged specimen have been worn short from long use. The tulip-shaped, three-legged stool is in more solid condition—and considerably more ornate than is usual for such lowly objects; someone was apparently trying to see how handsome a milking stool could be made.*

was a little fluctuation in price, was much more satisfactory; someone, somewhere, in country, town, or city, was always in the market for butter. The consumption of butter was a fact of life to a degree we can hardly believe, today. The farmer, of course, was only indirectly concerned with supply and demand so far as distant urban consumers were concerned; his interest began and ended at the local general store.

It was the farmer's wife who was involved in butter making from start to finish. Had the farmer himself had to follow through with the long succession of steps in the processing, perhaps all the family trading might have been achieved by the exchange of eggs and hides!

The farmer's wife did the milking, twice a day, except in unusual circumstances. She carried the milk to the house, strained it into cans and pans, and set it on the cellar floor or in the waters of the spring house to cool. Running water in the cellar was ideal, and many early houses were built, either over a spring, or near enough that the water could be deployed to a trough in the cellar and carried away by means of a drain. When the cream had risen to the top of the milk, she skimmed it off with a wooden or metal scoop and set it aside. When enough had collected to make the effort worthwhile, but at least once a week, whatever the quantity, she churned it. Three to four gallons were considered a reasonably sized churning. There was a long and steadily changing progression in types of churns, each succeeding one designed as an improvement over all earlier models. The earliest seems to have been the kind in which a plunger was forced down through the cream in a conical section of coopered wood. Or she might use a revolving barrel churn set in a pair of trestle-type standards, or a boxlike affair set on rockers, or a table model with crank and dasher. Some types had a capacity of five gallons or more; in later years there were some of glass which would take only a quart of cream.

Treadmills operated by dogs—and sometimes by well-behaved buck sheep if there were no dog in the family—were not uncommon in the up-country as devices for churning. The churn itself differed in one respect from the conventional form: instead of man power directly applied to the plunger or dasher, a belt-and-pulley arrangement transferred dog power from the treadmill to the churn. The animal was harnessed in place on a slanting conveyor of sliding blocks; the blocks would move downward and backward as soon as the brake was released, and the animal had to start walking in order to keep its balance. The continued movement, of course, set the belt-and-

pulley machinery in motion. The arrangement, except for its smaller size, was essentially the same as the one used for threshing grain, with a horse supplying the power. Dogs—usually large Shepherd dogs—did not much like the chore, and it is said that often they would go into hiding on churning day!

Butter as it came from the churn was in chunks or globs, from which every trace of buttermilk had to be expelled. Two implements were called for at this point: a round or oval bowl large enough to contain all the butter as it came from the churn, and a paddle which was plunged into the butter, back and forth, back and forth, until all the unwanted liquid had been expelled. In some places, women used corrugated wooden rolling pins as an auxiliary to the paddles. Frequently both the bowls and the paddles were so carefully made that they possessed considerable artistic merit. A burl bowl would seldom crack or split, and was preferred over any other. Round bowls had a greater capacity than pointed oval ones, but the oval ones were ideal if the butter was to be tossed into elongated rolls. Not only were the paddles as smooth as the craftsman could make them; they had, at their most ordinary, a knob at the end of the handle by which the implement could be hung up after using, or at their best a finial or fancy shape, often a heart. One most unusual specimen in a Monroe County collection has a finial, painted red, in the shape of a rooster's head. A tightly grained wood like maple or birch made the most desirable butter-making utensils.

Salting took place just before the last working over in the bowl. In the dead of winter, butter was prone to be pale in color and a coloring agent, usually saffron, was added. If the saffron was in liquid form, it would be put into the cream before the churning took place, but a powdered form would be applied in the bowl and then thoroughly worked over to make certain that there were no streaks. One of the sure signs of slovenly housekeeping was unevenly colored butter. There was no prejudice against the artificial color—but it did have to be uniform.

In the up-country, butter which stayed at home was not ordinarily decorated by means of a press or stamp unless company was expected. What went to market in earliest time, went in one of two ways, in stone crocks or in rolls. What was put into crocks was not decorated, either. One weighed the crock; filled it with butter and weighed it again, substracting the weight of the crock; spread cheesecloth over the butter; sprinkled a half inch of fine salt over the cheesecloth; tied a paper cover over the top of the jar—and it was ready to go. This was the method ordinarily used in warm weather, when butter would not easily retain its firm shape. Let it not be thought that any old stone crock would serve the purpose, either; to to-day's collector, gray stone jars may look pretty much

*An up-country butter churn with its original wooden plunger. This churn was actually constructed in two separately coopered sections, the portion between the two upper hoops having its own flare.*

alike—but only those with *straight* sides were properly used for butter. Slant-sided vessels were reserved for lard! (Butter, which went to the table, could be neatly cut from a straight-sided jar. A neat job was much more difficult when the container had slanting sides.)

In cold weather the butter was simply patted or tossed into rolls weighing perhaps three pounds. These were then stamped with small geometric or floral designs, both "for pretty" and as a kind of trademark to identify the maker. Rolls of butter were wrapped in cheesecloth and placed in a basket before they went to the store.

The wooden butter stamps which have been so popular with antiques collectors because of their designs —sheaf of wheat, cow, eagle, heart, whirling swastika, and tulip, among others—were often designed for molds which would hold exactly one or two pounds of butter, either for home consumption or for the market. Less widely used in the up-country than they were farther south, they still enjoyed limited popularity, and some families had their own special patterns. One very interesting device, acquired by the National Park Service for its Slateford Farm restoration near Portland, Pa., in 1970, smacks of assembly-line production, though it bears a date in the 1860s. There are two different double (that is, side-by-side) designs, one floral, the other a sheaf of wheat. The pattern desired is attached to a plunger, and a pound-size box is placed below it. As fast as the box can be packed, the plunger is lowered, and the design impressed on the butter.

There was enormous variation in the quality of farm-produced butter. In some households, it was admittedly no more than a commodity which could be traded for something more desirable. In others, it was a prized symbol of quality and was recognized as such more widely than just by members of the family. Storekeepers who had a local sale for what they took in trade would be on the alert for butter from a particular farm, for a favored customer. Seldom if ever would they reject butter brought in for trading, but there was some which was not put back into circulation in the immediate community—and some, it is said, which was privately destroyed as an alternative to risking the storekeeper's reputation. Good butter tasted good; its qualities were hard to define except by negative definition. Using this negative approach, one would say that it had no aftertaste from any container in which the cream or the butter had been kept; it had no taint coming from something the cows might have discovered in an out-of-the-way place— wild garlic, for instance; there was no suggestion of staleness or rancidity either in odor or in flavor; it was pleasingly colored and uniformly salted.

Butter was, and is, peculiarly prone to absorb odors or flavors. A story still told in a top-of-the-mountain Pocono family is that of a cow, something of a pet but also a kind of renegade in the herd, which had an overweening curiosity about matters which were not really a cow's business. On her way from barn to pasture, while the rest of the herd ambled sedately along, "Stub" would dash out of line, seize a garment which was being hung on the clothesline, and carry it off. A rose bush well off her path would get her full and devastating attention; a bag of cottage cheese, draining at its place at the corner of the grape arbor, would be snatched or butted, according to her mood. Her greatest hour, however, as a miscreant came on the day she seized a bar of strong yellow soap from an outdoor bench where carpet was being scrubbed, and swallowed it. It was almost too nasty to get down, but Stub braced all four feet and managed somehow— and then kicked up her heels and went on her way. A

full family council was called, to determine the length of time her milk would have to be destroyed, since obviously it would be unfit for use. The decision was that a week should be enough. No one offered to lessen the period by tasting the milk.

Some women, perhaps more knowledgeable than others, recognized the fact that they were exceptionally good butter makers, and unobtrusively capitalized on the matter. One such was Christina Sieg, of German Valley. In 1870, Christina was, by the standards of her time, no longer a young woman. The mother of 11 children, she had her hands full, as the saying goes, looking after the family, keeping her house in order, minding her garden, and helping her husband, Frederic, with the farm work. There were few so-called conveniences to ease her daily chores. She rose at four in the morning, carried water from the spring down in the meadow for cooking, drinking, and washing, and by six o'clock had her day well organized.

But there was an exception to the routine. Once every two weeks, from early spring to late fall, she arose at two instead of at four, and prepared meals ahead for the day. Then she went to the cellar and brought up two stone crocks of butter, topped with cheesecloth, salt, and a paper cover neatly scalloped and tied on tight with a string. Shortly after six she said goodbye to Frederic, took a crock under each arm, and set out for the railroad station at Cresco, nine miles away. The walk became easier after the sun rose, since the rutted dirt road led through dense woods the first six miles of the trip, and it was hard to make much progress in the dark.

She got to Cresco in time to catch the train to Stroudsburg, 15 miles down the line. Once in town, she tramped from store to store to see where she could get the best in trade for the 12 to 15 pounds of butter she had brought with her. We do not know the price of butter in Stroudsburg at that time, but at the general store in nearby Stormsville the going rate was 40 cents a pound in March; 30 in June. When Christina had achieved this part of her comparison shopping, she made her transaction with the favored storekeeper, accepting in exchange for the butter the grocery staples, calico, and other necessities which would keep her family going until the next excursion to town. Late in the afternoon, with two empty butter jars of the same size as those she had carried in the morning, and with her purchases of the day she set out again for German Valley, arriving after dark.

Evidently she did not regard the performance as extraordinary, nor did her husband, whose working day was fully as long as hers. He could not have been spared from the farm to do the trading, but Christina,

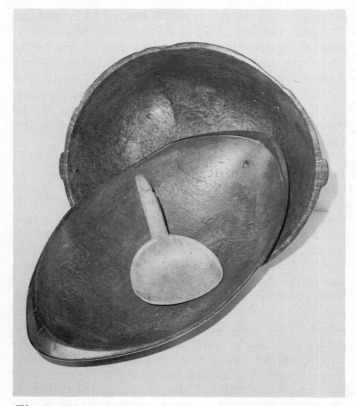

*Elm-burl butter bowl with ears, from Newfoundland; oval bowl pierced for hanging, from German Valley; paddle, from Monroe County. Oval bowls were widely popular in the up-country for tossing rolls of butter into shape. They were also used as chopping bowls.*

*Some of the most "wanted" patterns in butter stamps, with the strawberry and the fish rating as scarce. Designs were widely copied and adapted, with the result that now one can point to few if any purely regional characteristics.*

with only woman's work to do day after day, could take the chore in stride. That the performance actually was somewhat exceptional we might deduce from the fact that her family would sometimes mention it admiringly in her later years. She could, of course, have disposed of her surplus locally, but she just happened to live in an area where a number of women prided themselves on their butter-making prowess. In Stroudsburg, where she came to be well known, she was without competitors—and for that reason her butter commanded a higher price than it could have done at home.

Gradually, of course, times changed. The day eventually came when few persons consumed much butter at the table, or expected it as a major constituent of practically all cooked or baked food. Gone was the time when, in sets of glass tableware, the covered butter dish was designed to hold a pound—and a fresh pound was "broken on" at every meal. Nowadays it is not alone the competition of lower-priced spreads, as the advertising slogans intimated only a short time back, which has reduced the demand; a number of factors are operative—among them medical opinion, calorie-consciousness, and the simple fact that almost no one now thinks of bread and butter as a diet staple.

Barter as a major factor in a way of life has all but

disappeared except, perhaps, among children—and antiques collectors. Whether the circumstance should be considered cause or effect in the up-country is a good question, albeit not a very important one. Each of the three counties, possibly by coincidence, possibly not, embarked on a different economic path, beginning about the time that the last butter and eggs were taken in trade in the early 1900s. The excellent meadowlands of Wayne, ill suited to agriculture except on a minimal scale, were ideal for grazing, and the great dairy farms of the county began to take shape at this time, gradually absorbing smaller operations. Blooded herds of Holsteins, Ayrshires, Guernseys, and Herefords replaced the scrub stock of earlier days. As long as half a century ago, many of the operations were mechanized—and if there are any dasher churns or butter molds in the area today they are in the hands of antiques dealers or collectors.

Monroe, or at least the part of it far enough from the mountains to be free of thin, rocky, acid soil, headed in the direction of big-time agriculture. Its grain production even fifty years ago would have entitled it to the appellation of the "bread basket" of the Northeast. If the term were bestowed now, one might have a legitimate argument on his hands to the effect that it could just as logically be called the "fresh

vegetable basket," with recognition of its acres of
sweet corn, tomatoes, and cabbage, as well as vegetables of lesser abundance. There are dairy farms,
too, and creameries for the manufacture of butter.
Monroe Countians, however, like most other people,
buy their butter at the supermarket.

Perhaps Pike Countians, from the first, by the very
nature of their rocky acres, had to toil longer and
harder than most others. What one acquires by the
sweat of his brow he is not likely to relinquish easily
—and Pike County farmers were reluctant to accept
the fact that as families became smaller, men grew
older, and standards of living changed, it made sense
to give up the subsistence farms and find another
way of making a living. The county was picturesque
in a rugged, uncontrolled way that Wayne and Monroe were not. Boarding houses came into being to accommodate the city folk who were eager to purchase
a week's or a month's or a summer's worth of this
picturesqueness. Sons who succeeded to their fathers'
ownership of small farms for the most part declined
to continue farming operations. A state forest came
into being. Hunting and fishing preserves spread far
and wide, and—irony of ironies—land that once
knew little but toil became a place noted for little but
recreation.

Like their peers elsewhere, Pike Countians these
days buy their butter—and their eggs, for that matter—at the supermarket.

## COLLECTORS LOOK FOR:

Butter churns
Stoneware butter jars
Wooden bowls—large, small, round, oval
Paddles and rolling pins for "working" butter
Carved butter molds
Wooden saffron cups
Old saffron bottles
Wooden butter pails (for shipping butter), especially
    those made in local wood-turning factories
Pressed or cut glass butter dishes
Butter knives (often made as presentation pieces)
Swiss-type and other cowbells
Milking stools
Milk cans
Triangular wooden guards fastened around the cows'
    necks to prevent their breaking through a fence
Store ledgers listing current prices of items of barter
*Jackpot:* a fine burl bowl of local provenance

# 12
# The Egg Economy

"What are eggs?"—one of the most frequently postulated inquiries throughout Dutchdom in the days of butter-and-egg barter—was by no means a philosophical question; it was an instantly understood way of finding out what the storekeeper was paying, per dozen, at that particular time. The figure was subject to the law of supply and demand; farmers grumbled mildly when the price dropped to 10 or 12 cents a dozen in summer when hens were laying their heads off, as the saying went, and they grumbled again at the lack of cooperation on the part of the hens in the dead of winter when the price was high. At the same time, everyone—not including the hens—knew and understood the situation.

Rare indeed was the farmstead which did not include a flock of poultry as at least a minimum requirement in its operation. There might be as few as a dozen hens or as many as 50 or more, but a chickenless, eggless farm would have been unthinkable. The actual size of the flock generally bore a relationship to the amount of time the woman of the family had available, since chicken culture was taken for granted as women's work. Some women found it distasteful, but the unpleasant aspects of the job were partly offset by another generally accepted arrangement: any profit realized after the running expenses of the household had been satisfied by "egg money" belonged to the woman of the house. Here there was a bit of a catch, however; little actual money changed hands. Eggs were essentially a medium of exchange, and the storekeeper preferred to establish credit for any leftover amount due the trader at the time of the weekly trip to the store. At the same time, he could hardly refuse an occasional request for cash in hand; he was as well aware as anybody that the only cash money

many farm women ever had was the revenue from eggs and butter.

It would seem that, since the price was set for a dozen, eggs would arrive at the store in units of 12. Country store ledgers give a contrary indication; it seems that, while a few methodical souls made a point of taking 12—or 24, 36, or 48—to the store at a time, there were some who simply put into the basket whatever they had on hand at the moment, and the storekeeper did his figuring in terms of twelfths of a dozen.

Assuring the family of a supply of eggs for the winter, when the hens were producing little if anything, was not a wholly insurmountable problem. The usual method was "putting down" eggs in fine salt. The process was simple. Eggs stored in salt would remain usable for two to three months. While the hens were still laying well, but as late in the fall as possible, women would start the salting-down process, using a big stone crock for the purpose. An inch of fine table salt was spread over the bottom of the jar. Eggs were carefully set on end—the large end—as they became available, with at least a half inch of space separating each egg from its neighbor. When one layer was completed, a covering of salt was applied and the layering process started over again at the next higher level. While eggs preserved in salt could be used for baking purposes, they were seldom consumed in any other way.

By the time of the early 1900s, a water glass (sodium or potassium silicate) solution was substituted for salt as a preservative. It was just as effective, but eggs which had very thin shells or shells with minute cracks or flaws were likely to come out of the solution badly discolored. The most objectionable feature to

*There is enormous variety in the decorations of
Easter eggs and of blown egg shells. Those shown
here have been incised through a previously applied
coat of dye. The one outside the bowl is dated April
16, 1793.*

*Easter egg decoration, in itself an old art, becomes
increasingly elaborate on artificial eggs of glass,
marble, or pasteboard.*

most housewives, however—and to antiques collectors today—was the fact that the interior of a vessel containing water glass could never thereafter be used for anything else. The disfiguring white rings of the silicate deposit, from the top of the jar all the way to the bottom, could never be completely scrubbed away—apparently bonding with the silicon in the jar itself.

Many chickens were just chickens—a mixture of various breeds. Since a flock would deteriorate from inbreeding in a matter of a few years, rooster trading went on as a regular yearly procedure, and in consequence a flock might soon lose its major distinguishing characteristics unless one could be sure of the purity of the breed at the time of trading. Probably the best known breed at the end of the nineteenth century was what was affectionately called the "Dommyneck" throughout the up-country—the single-combed gray-feathered Dominique, which far outnumbered all other breeds. The Dominique was an all-purpose bird, as was the not dissimilar gray Barred Rock or Plymouth Rock; all were of good size for the table, and they were also good layers.

Beyond these, however, the farmer had to make a choice. Certain breeds were good egg producers, but small for the pot; others were big fowls, but they laid few eggs. The Leghorns, either brown or white, were small, nervous creatures, but wonderful egg producers. There was no better breed to fill the egg basket —but they had a bad habit of flying over the highest fence and heading straight for a newly seeded grain field. Their vigorous scratching habits could reduce a kitchen garden to shambles in no time flat. The Cochins, on the other hand, while they could not be beaten as pot fillers, laid so few eggs that the farmer's wife sometimes had to borrow from a neighbor to get enough for a setting—13 to 15 eggs.

Rhode Island Reds and White Wyandottes were good compromise fowl, as were Buff Orpingtons —average-sized birds which were also reasonably good layers. Most women liked to have a few iridescent-feathered Bantams about the place, "just for pretty." Even prettier, but not always breeding true to type, were the Silver Spangled Hamburgs—spectacular in their checkerboard feathers of black and white, albeit too small to eat and inconsequential as egg producers.

As important to the housewife as the size of the hen was the size of the egg. One who purchases store eggs today ordinarily has two sizes from which to choose—the "extra large" ones, which the farm woman of yesterday would have termed "little," and the "large" size—so small that a self-respecting housewife in days gone by would have been ashamed to serve it fried or boiled. For marketing purposes, uniformity in size is needed nowadays. Really big eggs, including those with double yolks, very rarely reach the market. It is equally true that very small ones—sometimes called "pullet" eggs—are not packaged for the general consumer. Perhaps it is only a trick of memory, but were not *most* "farmers" eggs, years ago, nearly twice the size of what we buy today?

A hen which felt impelled toward motherhood would, if the flock was allowed to range at will during the day, choose a secluded spot and lay an egg there each day until she had as many as her wings would cover, usually 15. She might or might not return to quarters at night once she had started the incubation period of 21 days. Sometimes she was lucky enough to bring a brood home, but the number of predators made such an occurrence a rare one; foxes, weasels, hawks, crows, even wandering dogs would not infrequently thwart her intent. In the spring, when hens were prone to turn ill-tempered—"clooky"—when disturbed, children were often set to follow hens which wandered away from the others, since they were probably heading toward concealed caches of eggs. Generally speaking, several brooding hens were set on clutches of eggs at one time for the convenience of the housewife in taking care of the "peeps" after they were hatched. By the twentieth century, incubators replaced the brooding hens, which were only too likely to lose interest in their projects and abandon the clutches of eggs unless they were kept in confinement for the full three-week incubation period.

By present-day standards, nineteenth century chicken coops frequently left much to be desired, both as to cleanliness and as to the comfort of the hens. There can be little doubt that in some cases hens stopped laying in the winter as much because they were badly housed as for any other reason. An ingenious makeshift hen house which in some parts of the up-country achieved semi-permanent status was the wooden box in which upright pianos were shipped from the factory. Piano boxes were of sturdy construction, and with the addition of a door, a window, and a tar paper roof they served the purpose fairly well. Moreover, they could be moved, if one changed his mind about the location—probably the first mobile homes in all Dutchdom! A pair of them was sometimes set back to back on a raised foundation. Worn-out wagon wheels served as roosts in many country chicken coops, and soap boxes, each filled with straw and supplied with a "china" nest egg as a starter gave hens an indication as to where the

*Opaque and clear glass mustard containers, back row,
were popular in and out of Pennsylvania. The smaller
specimens may be found in a variety of colors. Those
shown here are blue.*

housewife expected to find the eggs.

Odd as it may seem in theory, the idea of the nest
egg worked in practice. A hen would make the rounds
from box to box, depositing her egg when she found
a place to her liking—but a box without a nest egg
would remain empty all day. Nest eggs, bought at the
country store, were normally of glass, realistically colored. Very early ones were blown; some from Victorian times were of milk glass. In the Poconos late
in the nineteenth century, eggs of turned wood,
painted white, were tried out, but the hens, apparently under some misapprehension as to the purpose
of such extraneous objects, pecked at the paint and
were poisoned. That was the end of *that* experiment.
Eggs of marble or even of alabaster were used now
and then, but hens seemed to like the glass ones best.

In the summer, chickens were ordinarily allowed
to roam at will but were also given a supplementary
feeding late in the afternoon, usually a mixture of
oats, wheat, buckwheat, and a little cracked corn. Too
much corn would fatten the birds—and more than a
little wheat would give them too much protein. Winter
diet was augmented by "something green" when possible—a large mangel-wurzel or a head of cabbage
being hung in the coop each day where the chickens

could get at it easily. A box of crushed oyster shells
was kept in the coop the year round.

The practice of coloring hard-boiled eggs at Easter
time, and attributing them to the mysterious *Oschter
Haas*—Easter rabbit—for the delight of children is
generally accepted as of Pennsylvania Dutch origin.
One of the all-time favorites in egg colors was the
deep, rich red-brown achieved by putting the eggs
into an iron pot with an equal volume of dried onion
skins, filling the vessel with water, covering it,
bringing it to a boil, and then letting it stand for
hours at the back of the stove. Special effects could
be attained by applying dabs of wax—or initials or
names, if one were deft at manipulating a sharpened
candle stub—to the eggs before they were boiled; the
waxed areas would remain in the natural color of the
shell. Some persons believe, even today, that a delicate flavor is imparted to eggs boiled in onion skins.

Vegetable egg dyes were on the market very early,
and were used freely in most homes. Dyes used for
yarn or fabric were less frequently used for eggs—
indigo, madder, and chips which produced tones of
yellow and brown. Housewives were not always sure
that these dyes were safe if, as sometimes happened,
the color would go through the shell and touch the

egg itself. A preliminary step taken long ago in egg dyeing, and just as effective today in securing a completely uniform color coat, is that of immersing the eggs in an alum-water solution and then letting them dry before putting them into a color bath.

For some weeks preceding Easter Sunday, youngsters often made a practice of filching eggs from the chicken coop, trying to outdo one another in the number they could bring in on Easter Day. According to family circumstances at the time, they might be allowed to market these eggs as a personal enterprise. Boys would sometimes choose to eat them instead. A common kind of competition in Newfoundland, Greentown, and other places was to see who could consume the greatest number at Easter breakfast. Notes were

usually compared before church! Filching took place, too, at the time of maple sap boiling in early spring, when boys who had to spend the evening at the sugar works in order to finish a batch of syrup were likely to get hungry. Eggs boiled in hot syrup were believed to taste better than those cooked in any other way.

Up to this point we have been talking about eggs intended to be eaten. Some, however, were intended only for show—and any kind of dye might be used. Requiring considerable time but creating a spectacular effect was the practice of cutting such shapes as stars or birds out of dark-colored calico, dampening them, and laying them on a raw egg. Over each of these would be laid a larger pattern of a lighter color. The practice would continue as long as there was

*Single-block folk carving of superlative caliber: an Aaron Mounts rooster and a polychrome-painted specimen of which only a few examples are known. Collectors should be on the alert for such pieces, which may come to light almost anywhere.*

room on the egg. Finally, the whole egg would be encased firmly in cloth of the lightest tone available, after which the egg would be boiled in the usual way. A favorite progression of colors was red at the base; then pink; and finally, yellow.

For weeks or even months before Easter, eggs used for cooking were pierced at each end and the contents blown out. The shells were then dried, and eventually were given dye baths and used for decorating purposes. The simplest use was probably to string the shells on twine and use them as festoons. Calling for greater skill was the creating of birds, fish, or animals by adding appropriate heads, wings, fins, legs, tails, and so on of adroitly folded paper. Birds were most effective when suspended where currents of warm air would keep them in motion, after the fashion of today's mobiles. Now and then someone, trying to outdo an inventive relative or neighbor, would create a doll of an egg or an egg shell. In early times a blown shell with the top neatly cut off would be transformed into a play pitcher by the addition of a fold or two of calico and a loop for a handle.

Below the Blue Mountain, the careful incising of boiled eggs, dyed black or any very dark color, became something of an art. Specimens from the late 1700s to a point past the mid-1800s have been preserved privately and in museums. Abroad, where egg decoration was far more widely practiced than in America, fancy Easter eggs have long constituted a recognized form of folk art. Polish, Ukrainian, Czechoslovakian, and Hungarian eggs in particular show beautifully detailed colored decorations, for the most part geometrical in nature. These eggs, however, normally rely on decoration applied to the surface rather than on ornamentation attained by cutting in to the shell. While both paint-decorated and incised ("carved") eggs are found in America, such decoration seems to have been more widely favored below the Blue Mountain than above it. Incised decorations appear to have been impromptu rather than studied; motifs include flowers, hearts, houses, birds, trees, beehives, initials, names, and dates.

Easter egg trees appeared at various places in the up-country before the beginning of the present century, and the practice—albeit no longer with folk overtones—continues today. Like Christmas trees, the egg trees may be set up either in the house or outdoors. For an outdoor display, ordinarily only shells dyed a solid color are used. Indoors, where there are no sudden winds or storms to wreak havoc with the project, the finished tree may demonstrate a high degree of artistic virtuosity, with water color, tempera, oil, and textile dye techniques all being used, in addition to the most difficult one of all—carving.

Carving a hard-boiled egg is a ticklish process, as anyone who has tried it will agree. Carving the dried *shell* is more than ticklish: it can be nerve-wracking, frustrating—or stimulating, according to the point of view. The chosen design is roughly sketched with chalk as a preliminary in only exceptional cases; the carver is more likely to think things out as he goes along. A major handicap for beginners is the difficulty of adapting a flat pattern to a curved surface, and preconceived designs often have to go by the board. A sharp-edged instrument—anything from a pen knife or single-edged razor blade to a discarded dentist's tool—is used to cut through the dark surface and into the white of the shell. The egg must be carefully cupped in one's hand throughout the process in order to equalize the pressure of the cutting edge. Even so, accidents will happen. Contemporary egg carvers aver that from two to five hours are required for a good carving job on one egg.

The egg tree, whether up-country or down-country, as a colorful custom appears to be a kind of wayward departure from ancient rites of the kind practiced to win the favor of Ostra, goddess of fertility. The word "Easter" seems to have originated from "Ostra." Eggs placed on sheaves of wheat in some parts of the Ukraine as late as the nineteenth century indicated that faith in the goddess of fertility had not entirely disappeared—or perhaps, as is the case with those who have a lingering half-belief in folk medicine, the practitioners figured that nothing could be lost, while something might be gained. So far as records are concerned, we have no notion of what Pennsylvanians of an earlier day may have had in mind when they decorated small trees with colored eggs or egg shells; no reference or notation has thus far been reported. It is probably safe to say, however, that esoteric fertility rites have been farthest from the thoughts of the persons who have erected egg trees in the twentieth century.

The art of egg decoration is far from dead; in fact, it is in a distinctly flourishing condition, with two diametrically opposed schools of thought operating side by side. The first is that of the traditionalists, who attempt to reproduce the old designs and the old methods, at least to the extent that the methods are known. These traditionalists include the *binsa grawss* artist, who winds the eggs with the pith extruded from a kind of fresh-water reed (the *binsa grawss*) growing in the Dutch Country. North of the Blue Mountain, this pith has to be imported, since the reed does not grow there. Decorations are applied to the wrapped egg: sequins, beads, flowers of yarn, fancy

*John Haney, Saylorsburg artist, had he been born in
an earlier day, might now be called a "primitive"
painter. There is nothing primitive, however, in the
way he depicted his favorite subjects—chickens. It is
maintained locally that Haney chickens look more like
chickens than chickens do!*

stitchery—anything, in fact, which is colorful or will sparkle. The contemporary school operates as it would in such media as textiles or pottery—by creating designs deemed appropriate for our time, without necessary dependence on the past.

Possibly an offshoot of the egg tree idea, but equally an artistic development in its own right, is the bird tree. Egg trees are thickly branched, bare-limbed trees of wild apple, beech, white birch, spice bush, or dogwood—seldom evergreens. Bird trees are contrived or simulated trees, not necessarily realistic, on which carved and painted birds perch. One or two superlative specimens of this genre are privately owned in Monroe County. One hears now and then of others, but investigation usually reveals that the report was only hearsay. Occasionally, trees with carved birds which seem to have been made for use in a different connection are found, but most appealing as to their folk touch are those in which tree and bird were carved at the same time, by the same hand.

More than three centuries ago, Shakespeare used

the term "the harmless, necessary cat," a characterization of cats perhaps not entirely accurate, but one which it is comfortable to accept in principle. Had he lived in the up-country, where cats were probably fewer than they were in England because mice were also fewer, he might have applied his adjectives to the hen—in which case the characterization might also have left room for occasional variation. One thing is indisputable: the lowly hen, in spite of her unpredictable, addle-pated qualities, probably did as much to promote the economic progress of the up-country as anything else one could name.

She also, in innocent unawareness, set in motion an argument as endless as the dispute between the Big-endians and the Little-endians in Swift's satire, or as frustrating as the old chestnut, "Which came first—the hen or the egg?" This argument has to do with the presumed difference in flavor between brown-shelled and white-shelled eggs. *Is* there a difference? Certain breeds lay eggs with brown shells; others, with white. In some of the country stores of

*Squeak toys, once regarded merely as minor collect-
ibles, have joined the ranks of the near-inaccessible.
Of brightly painted pasteboard or papier mâché, most
were imported from Germany during the nineteenth
century.*

yesteryear, white-shelled eggs commanded a cent or
two a dozen more than the brown ones. Some pur-
chasers would buy only those with white shells. The
cook who prided herself on the quality of her angel
food cake would scorn the idea of anything but white
eggs.

On the other hand, the baker of sponge cake would
generally prefer brown-shelled eggs, which, she was
likely to maintain, were richer in flavor as well as
fuller in color. She believed there was a difference—
and would all but do battle in defense of her belief.
Science has been of little help in the matter; the
flavor of eggs can be influenced by the nature of the

hen's diet, we are told, and the statement makes
sense. As for brownness *vs* whiteness, is it perhaps
time to bury the hatchet and, at the grocery, institute
a search for a carton which, whether the contents be
brown or white, contains a full dozen—none broken
and none cracked?

COLLECTORS LOOK FOR:

Nest eggs, especially blown-glass specimens
Enameled or other decorated glass Easter eggs
Fancy Easter egg containers, usually egg-shaped, of
    paper

Brown or gray flocked-paper animal toys, especially rabbits

Milk glass hen-on-nest mustard containers in blue, white, or blue-and-white

Gillinder "Just Out" chick-and-egg camphor glass ornaments

Tin two-piece candy molds in Easter egg and animal shapes

Squeak toys including hens, roosters, and roosters-in-coops with spring doors

Egg birds (shells with paper accoutrements)

Early incised eggs

Contemporary pottery eggs in sgraffito technique

Egg pitchers, animals, fish, dolls

Storekeepers' ledgers

Early farm periodicals, books, catalogues

Paper or metal containers for poultry powders, medicines, etc.

Bags which served as containers for cracked corn, mash, etc., especially those with printed advertising matter

*Jackpot:* a hand-carved hen or rooster by Wilhelm Schimmel or his "pupil," Aaron Mounts

*Jackpot of jackpots:* a polychrome-decorated hand-carved wooden rooster with full tail spread, usually attributed to the Scoharie valley (New York). Only five are known to exist.

# 13

# The Peripatetic Trader

Nowadays one goes shopping, paying for his purchases with coin of the realm or with a card which permits him to pay at a later date. A hundred years ago, in the up-country, he was more likely to go trading, shops for the most part existing only in cities or good-sized towns—and if the term "shopping" had been invented, not many knew about it. Trading meant just what the basic denotation of the word indicated—the direct exchange of one commodity for another. One "traded out" a jar of butter, a basket of eggs, or possibly a load of corn. If money changed hands, that was fine, but until the nineteenth century was well advanced, it happened only now and then. The exchange of kinds of goods, rather than of goods and money, was deep-rooted, and its persistence may quite possibly be attributed to the tight control exercised on early Colonial affairs by England, as she dispensed her own manufactured wares in return for fish, furs, and lumber. Cash money was less a medium of exchange than a status symbol.

By mid-nineteenth century, most up-country settlements large enough to be considered communities had at least one general store. Frequently the store was a large room in a dwelling house, fitted out with a counter, a stove with a number of chairs about it, and shelves reaching to the ceiling. Here the housewives or members of their families brought their butter and eggs to exchange for salt, sugar, window panes, coal oil (kerosene), plain dress goods, and other necessary but unexciting commodities. Sometimes there would be a penny or two—in credit—left over for peppermint or wintergreen lozenges for the children.

For all the convenience that store transactions represented, as compared with the wilderness hardships some customers could remember, there was little of romance about it. Romance was supplied by the itinerant, whose visits were likely to be irregular but whose stock, in the aggregate, represented just about everything known to or desired by the consumer.

Too much has been written, and too ably, to make it necessary here to give an extended treatise on peddling as a commercial activity—from the tin pans and pails of earliest times to the patent medicines which marked an end, in the twentieth century, of almost all peddling practices. We should bear in mind though that, far from being regarded as a nuisance, peddlers were eagerly welcomed over a long period of time—for the goods they had to sell, the news they brought from the outer world, and the break they created in the monotony of day-by-day toil.

Some of the earliest peddling activities had passed into history before the up-country became a recognized market. The very first tin-peddlers' carts made their way down along the seaboard from Connecticut, all the way to Georgia. As they increased in number, of course, they began to move inland, too, but by the time they had become a familiar sight in the Pennsylvania hills there were stores here and there which had begun to feature articles which only the peddlers had carried earlier. Since the peddlers included some of the most shrewd and enterprising characters to be found anywhere, they immediately updated the nature of the goods they carried; sales depended almost as much upon the novelty of what they could display as upon actual need—especially if the customer could be made to feel that a given purchase might put him a step ahead of the Joneses.

One should probably draw a line somewhere between the local entrepreneurs who established trading routes as a regular business matter and those who

*Ornately decorated tin containers seem to be gaining
a firm grip on the tastes of collectors, one of the rarities being the "Red Indian Cut Plug" tobacco can.
This specimen is from an old home in Pike County.*

were actually outsiders engaging in wandering mercantile expeditions before settling down somewhere
to become solid citizens. Such a line is a little difficult
to draw, however. A great many people were on the
move in a great many places; enterprises opened,
prospered—or failed—and closed in a matter of a
year or two, sometimes with a repetition of the process only a short time later in a place not far away.

The idea of security in the way one earned his livelihood seems to have been less firmly rooted than the
idea that one might do better by pulling up stakes
and moving somewhere else—perhaps to Ohio or
Illinois or Kansas or points beyond. Early county
histories which specialize in biographical data are
studded, to a degree startling to the uninitiated, with
such expressions as "-----removed to Iowa (or

wherever) where he engaged successfully in (whatever) to the time of his death in -----." Everyone
knows in a general way, of course, that the West was
settled in large part by Easterners, but the fact comes
home to him poignantly when he undertakes a study
of nineteenth century personalities, family by family.

A near-perfect representative of the business enterprise which outgrew its local origins by consistent
travel to more remote points is that of Christopher
Keller of Kellersville, whom we have mentioned elsewhere in connection with milling operations. The
Keller product was milled grain, principally wheat
flour; the market at home could not absorb more than
a fraction of the finished product—any more than in
an earlier day the environs of Berlin in Connecticut
could make use of all the tinware produced by the

Pattison boys. The Pattisons moved out from the center with their jingling, horse-drawn tin wagons; the Kellers drove to Philadelphia with their six-horse Conestoga wagons and then to points beyond.

The Pattisons—it would be more nearly accurate to say the *travelers* for the Pattisons—traded their tin for corn, the corn for chickens, chickens for mules, and so on, aiming always to return to base with cash if possible. The Kellers—or their travelers—did much the same thing; in the course of a single round trip they might have handled a dozen widely varying commodities. One is reminded, in this succession of swapping, of old folktales recorded by the brothers Grimm. What concerns us most closely is not what they transported en route but, as in the case of the folktale trader, what they brought back. They seem regularly to have loaded at Philadelphia for the return trip to the up-country, bringing with them almost everything that was sold in the country stores. This was

the way the stores got the bulk of their stock: shoes, clothing, groceries, medicines, household and farm necessities—all the things the farmer either could not make or did not have time to make for himself.

Not included were items which stores took in trade and could resell on the spot—dried apples, homemade soap, knitted mittens, plowshares made at a local foundry, ax handles, corn brooms, and so on. Any surplus of these items at the stores—or any concentration of unsold goods, for that matter—could go along on the next outward-bound trip, together with the inevitable freight of butter and eggs and, when the weather was favorable, dressed fowl and veal.

Some trading enterprises started on a less specialized basis than others. (One remembers that the business built up by the Kellers grew out of their need for selling their flour.) A typical instance is that of Jacob and Daniel Wyckoff, who moved to Pennsylvania from Mendham, New Jersey, in 1851. Daniel,

*Majolica pieces were popular tea-wagon premiums.*
*Many, including these, were made at Phoenixville,*
*Pa., and are marked "Etruscan."*

according to the record, established routes throughout the country in the vicinity of Stroudsburg, buying produce from farmers who otherwise might not have had any market for it. Jacob conveyed the produce to New York in covered wagons, and traded or sold it there. For the return trip, he secured, through trade or purchase, merchandise to supply local retail and wholesale customers. Before long, according to the historians, he regularly had a number of six-horse wagons on the road and became a popular supplier of country stores.

This method of operating helps to explain otherwise puzzling items in store ledgers like the one kept by the Metzgars in Stormsville in 1868. In the ledger, David Wyckoff is credited on February 15 with a barrel of crackers and on March 11 by four pounds of candies. If we did not know that he was a wholesaler, we might, as a matter of fact, be more than puzzled at finding crackers and candy in the column normally listing credit in terms of butter and eggs. A puzzle comparable to that of the Wyckoff crackers and candy would exist in the case of B. Dongan and Son, with credit at the Stormsville store for shoes at $1.80 per pair. (Either these shoes or others like them retailed at $2.00 and up, per pair.)

Jacob Wyckoff's son Amzi established a store in Stroudsburg in 1875, for years known as The New York Store of A. B. Wyckoff. It continued to expand and is still owned and operated by members of the family.

For the person who has accepted, without any reason for doing otherwise, the stereotype of butter and eggs as "the" media of barter, there is a degree of surprise in the wide variety of items taken in trade at country stores—taken because they would be as good as cash at the places the storekeepers themselves patronized. Some have already been mentioned. Others include onions, dry beans, shelled corn, elderberries, tobacco, tobacco "shorts" (fragments and scraps of tobacco), chestnuts, pitted cherries, pheasants and quail, beeswax, and wool. Farmers killed off their surplus of fowls in the fall to avoid the expense of keeping them over winter. Chickens were not very special; a typical going-rate in the 1860s was 37½ cents apiece. Ducks, less usual, brought 80 cents apiece; turkeys commanded 15 cents a pound.

Seemingly, there was always a market for scrap iron, and old castings and broken pieces were taken in trade at a penny a pound—a rate that held for many years. There was also a perennial market for old rags, which were used for the manufacture of paper of high quality. There were men who traveled widely, buying nothing but old rags, which for the most part they sold directly to wholesalers but occasionally also to country stores which disposed of them to wholesalers. In later years a kind of stigma came to be attached to rag gatherers, possibly through no fault of their own. Up-country women got the last possible degree of service out of worn-out garments by utilizing them in carpet rags. What was left for the ragman was a pretty hopeless agglomeration, and some of the distastefulness of soiled and dirty rags seems to have become attached to those who dealt in them.

A roughly comparable stigma sometimes attached to the pack peddler, and for no better reason, apparently, than that he was assumed to be too poor to own a horse and conveyance. His stock, while widely varied, almost always included the small items like pins, buttons, combs, and so on which we call notions today. Often a pack peddler was a man of mature years; less frequently he was a young man on the way up. One of these young men in Monroe was Nicholas Ruster, who came from Reinfeld, Germany, in 1853. Starting as a pack peddler, he soon took over a store at Craig's Meadows, and from there moved to Stroudsburg, where he established a clothing store.

Wandering tinkers have frequently been called peddlers, and vice versa. Essentially, a tinker performs a service on something already owned, whereas a peddler makes an original sale. In practice, it is not quite that simple: an itinerant drives up to a farmstead with a load of miscellaneous objects—none of which he offers for sale. After an appropriate period devoted to the exchange of amenities, he produces a soldering iron and asks whether the housewife has any tinware needing repairs. She usually has, but whether she does or not it usually develops that on his wagon he just happens to have a number of repaired objects which he would dispose of for almost nothing rather than continue to carry them around with him. Obviously he is both tinker and peddler, but if a person had to choose one term and reject the other he would be on the horns of a dilemma.

The conveyances used by peddlers were less varied than the objects they sold, but there was an amazing variety. Simplest was probably the two-wheeled, one-horse cart which could traverse country lanes where no other vehicle could go, but which lacked practicality because of its limited carrying capacity. The old-fashioned buggy was a little more capacious, but its principal virtue was that its contents could be protected from the rain. One peddler in the Sterling-Newfoundland-Canadensis area who specialized in making photographic enlargements either from conventional photographs or from earlier daguerreotypes used a buggy in preference to any other vehicle because, as he said, he could carry all the frames on end without the likelihood of breakage. (Neither tinker nor peddler in the usual sense, he should probably have a title all his own . . . though there were those who would not have found fault with "tinker.")

Probably most widely used was a small spring wagon with side and back curtains which could be rolled up or down, according to need. If the load was light, one horse would draw the vehicle; otherwise a team was called for. A number of today's great superstores had their humble beginnings as wagon enterprises serving customers both in villages and in sparsely settled countrysides. One of them had tea as its specialty, and many persons came to think of any carriage with its side curtains down as a tea wagon, no matter what the use to which it was put. Flavorings and extracts (especially vanilla), coffee, scented soap, and assorted toiletries were popular specialties, too. An interesting side angle of one of these enterprises was its giving of "premiums" when purchases reached a satisfying figure. Often, the premiums were pieces of colorful majolica from a Phoenixville, Pennsylvania, pottery and have become

*Steel-bladed knives and forks are collected more for the designs on their handles than for utility, since they have to be scoured after each using. Blades and tines are usually of English steel. Three-tined forks are usually considered older than those with four tines.*

widely sought collectibles. It is to be doubted that all majolica collectors are aware of the humble origin of some of their prized pieces.

One of the last of the so-called tea-wagon merchants or operations was the George F. Hellick Company of Easton. The specialty of this importing house, which discontinued operations only a matter of decades ago, was coffee—professionally selected, expertly blended, and test-brewed by a taste specialist before it was released for sale. There are still persons in the far-ranging upland areas once served by Hellick wagons (actually trucks, by this time) who maintain that no coffee can ever again approach the quality of Hellick's.

Let us move back, however, and see if we can determine what charisma gave the itinerant peddler the firm hold he had on the imagination of so much of the rural American world. He tended to be young and agreeable, for one thing—young because only a physically vigorous man could take in stride the multitudinous problems of travel in those days, and agreeable because the total amount of his sales was likely to depend directly upon his personality. Too, he tended to be honest, although now and then there were shysters, of course. Perhaps his greatest appeal lay in the fact that he seemed always to have with him something the potential customer had not thought about but which he—oftener "she"—craved upon sight. Having something completely new at each visit might have posed a problem for some merchants—but not for the wandering Yankee, whose mixture of intuition and inventiveness was proverbial.

Spectacles, for instance: ophthalmologists today might justifiably go into a state of shock over the methods used by the peddlers to dispense their optical aids. The peddler who had a boxful of eyeglasses in his cart would make a point of observing the mature woman of the family as she examined a piece of colorful dress goods, one of the favored articles for sale. If her vision seemed to be entirely normal, he might forget about the spectacles. If, however, she held the bolt a little too close or a little too far off as she examined it, he soon found an adroit way of getting her to try on the spectacles he had. The glass was not ground to correct astigmatism or any other aberration of sight, but it existed in anywhere from three to five or more degrees of magnification. If one of these happened to enable her to see more clearly, the peddler's sales were likely to go up in proportion to her degree of pleasure. Spectacle fitting did not long remain a prerogative of the peddler, however; the opportunity for sales in the kerosene-illumination era was a broad one, and boxes of spectacles soon ap-

*Connecticut-made shelf clocks were enormously popular in Pennsylvania. The veneer pattern in this specimen (Waterbury Clock Works) is unusual.*

peared in most country stores. History does not record the fact, but one wonders whether these, too, were not supplied by the peddlers!

From the time the mid-century vogue for fancification came into being, pretty ribbon was desired, from city house to remote farmstead. Country stores could produce the "staple" kinds of drygoods, as we intimated earlier, but that was about all. When the peddler unveiled his remnants—so-called—of bright ribbons, gay brocades, pieces of fancy velvet and lace, lengths of braid and insertions, he could almost always be sure of a sale. Most women did the sewing for themselves and for all the members of the family, and whatever kind of trimmings or buttons or other embellishments could help to create the special occasion dress every woman desired was eagerly welcomed.

Probably more pocket knives were sold by peddlers than ever came from a country store. Although the fashion was eventually to change, no man or boy for perhaps a century felt that he was completely dressed unless he carried a pocket knife with him. The English Barlow knife was universally popular, but any knife with steel good enough to take and hold a keen edge would do. The peddlers supplied steel-bladed table knives and forks, too. Many of the knife blades bore the stamps of English makers, but the steel components of both knives and forks were fitted out with American bone or horn before they embarked on their travels in the cart. Straight razors, too, were almost exclusively a peddler's product.

From the first, clocks were a popular item. Most of the vast output of Connecticut clocks made its way throughout the country via the peddler's cart. Only the fact that they were so well made as to be practically foolproof can explain why a peddler could jolt over the tree stumps, rocks, and potholes which characterized even the "good" country roads, take a clock out of the wagon, set it up in the country kitchen, and have it start on a course of ticking which might last for sixty to a hundred years. Connecticut-type clocks, so-called, whether by Seth Thomas, Chauncey Jerome, Eli Terry, Silas Hoadley, Elisha Manross, J. E. Brown, or any of a dozen other clock makers, in and out of Connecticut, were one item accepted without question and without competition everywhere in the Dutch Country—up or down. True, the tall-case clocks were grander and far more expensive. The inexpensive, good-looking, dependable shelf clocks could hardly have been better received than they were.

Many small articles of the kind which became the stock-in-trade of the five-and-ten-cent stores could be secured only from peddlers—small brushes, hairpins, thread, dyes, pins and needles, shoestrings, and the like. Just as the jingling tin coffee pots, pails, and pans of an earlier day gave notice of the arrival of the cart, the sound of brass bells for sheep, for cattle, and for the hames of harnesses in a later day served as an announcement. There might be dolls for small children, and sometimes there were watch chains and fobs, plug tobacco, and cigar cutters for the men, and white metal filigree jewelry for the women.

In the beginning, the young peddlers working out of New England secured most of their stock directly from sailors on incoming English vessels. As soon as New England manufacturing operations got under way, American rather than foreign products were sold. In the end, almost all the peddlers' items could be secured at stores at any time one desired, and the once- or twice-a-year visits of the itinerants trickled to an end. One exception, though, should be noted; the vendors of "patented" nostrums of dubious virtue gave up the battle very slowly. Snake oil for various ailments and magic cures for rheumatism, falling hair, and toothache persisted well into the present century. Many of them were eventually ridiculed out of existence, but it is possible that some, with only a minor metamorphosis in content or label, are now being sold over a counter.

COLLECTORS LOOK FOR:

Old store ledgers
Country store furniture and articles of the kind sold
    in the stores of a hundred years ago
Old spectacles, spectacle cases, and lorgnettes
Old pocket knives, cutlery, and razors
"Etruscan" majolica (From Phoenixville, Pa.)
Tin containers for tea, coffee, and other commodities
    sold from tea company wagons
Any containers marked "Hellick" or "George F. Hellick"
Shelf clocks by Connecticut makers
Plug tobacco and cigar cutters
Patent medicine bottles, especially those with labels
    intact
*Jackpot:* Any very early sales ledger or daybook

# 14
# The Death and Reincarnation of Slate

Historically, slate has seldom been regarded as aesthetically important far from its place of origin. To residents of Wayne or Pike, it was something which came from down-country, somewhere, and there were those who knew that the term "Bangor," applied to slate, signified Bangor, Pennsylvania, and not Bangor, Maine. As for Pen Argyl, where the quarries were equally productive—well, Pen Argyl was the place where the people were so much interested in singing, wasn't it? Or *was* it?

Bangor and Pen Argyl are in Northampton County, much of which was strongly Germanic, but the population of the two towns, with exceptions, of course, tended to be as Welsh as the names of the settlements themselves. As for the music, who but a Welshman could possibly pronounce something like *eisteddfod,* the word for the music festivals? The combination of letters, *not* pronounced EYE-sted-fod, as one might expect from its appearance in print, was as incomprehensible as the rest of the language heard on the streets when Welshman met Welshman. Thus, this end of the county, rugged and unproductive for all that it was picturesque in an uncompromising way, for years remained in a state of limbo in the thinking of much of the up-country.

All the while, of course, Bangor, Pen Argyl, and smaller places to the north, on both sides of the Delaware, were supplying the roofs of houses far and near with some excellent slate. The quarries went steadily deeper and the slag piles grew higher as year followed year. Now and then a man plunged to his death, or a quarry was flooded, could not be pumped dry, and had to be abandoned, but the industry went on. Quarrying was physically demanding, with long hours, dubious working conditions, and less than munificent pay as constant factors, and only the number of incoming orders as variables.

Eventually the variables took over, as cheaper roofing became easily available, as the costs of production rose, and as later generations seemed less eager to risk their necks, daily, than their forebears had been. The industry slowed down, almost to the stopping point, it seemed to many. It never ceased entirely but, unless a miracle occurs, the great days of the slate industry are in the past. Bear in mind that we are speaking of the northeasternmost fringe of the Slate Belt, and not of larger sections farther south.

Not until, in our own time, when it became next to impossible to get good slate for a roofing job did the layman look around and for the first time make an assessment of this hitherto largely unstudied industry. The picture is a revealing one, with a number of surprises for those who had not been particularly history-conscious up to that point. The Lenape Indians, they discovered, knew about slate; in fact, they shaped pieces of it into digging blades for some of their primitive agricultural tools. The first white man's quarry of which there seems to be any record is the Pennsylvania Slate Company, in Upper Mt. Bethel Township, only a few miles southwest of Stroudsburg as the crow flies. This enterprise, founded in 1806, produced roof slates, floor tiles, flagging, cistern liners, window sills, mantels, counters, and billiard table tops. It is to be doubted that many specimens of the objects made by this company have survived—and only the merest handful of people can remember what some of them looked like, or even that such objects had ever been made. Too heavy and too frangible to ship great distances in early times,

*Memorabilia from the Slate Country are less than easy to come by, but this napkin-size cloth from Bangor records the surnames of a great many of the families in the town in 1899.*

they were largely confined to local use, at least so far as we can determine.

Joseph Kerr, who emigrated from Ireland to America during the War of 1812, spent a brief period in Philadelphia, after which he became a superintendent of slate quarries at Slatington, Pennsylvania. He lived in Stroud Township in Monroe.

When the Zion's Lutheran Church was built at Smithfield, in 1850–1851, we find that John Morey and Thomas Mack, slaters, were paid $78.39 for slate for the roof of the church. (There was a separate bill for their labor.) The record does not show where they secured their material, but a Kellersville store ledger for September, 1853, contains a notation, "Bringing a load of slate from the Water Gap." Morey and Mack may have utilized the same source, but we shall probably never know.

Bangor slate, like the product of towns and communities farther south in the Slate Belt, was excellent for roofing, as we have noted. As one goes north, however, the geological strata change with a marked difference in the nature of what was produced at Slatington or Walnutport and what came from the Wind Gap area. By the time one reaches Monroe County, native slate of roofing quality becomes all but nonexistent. We discover, however, that as early as 1826 Samuel Snyder built and operated a school slate factory in Smithfield Township. After the death of Snyder the factory was run until about 1890 by Amos Le Bar. It is said that the bulk of all the slates and slate pencils used in American schools originated here. A notable contribution made to the industry by Snyder, in addition to the slate, of course, was his invention for sawing and shaving it mechanically. Up to that time, all the processes had been manual. Presumably the framing operation was a normal part of the manufacturing process, but a notation in the Kellersville store ledger for November 14, 1855, indicates that Mathias Stecher paid ten cents to have a slate framed. Perhaps this was a repair rather than an original process.

Edward Hawk opened a slate quarry in Polk Township, near Kresgeville, in 1855. He discovered that, while his product was unsatisfactory for roofing, it made good school slates. A local historian, writing later on Hawk's venture, advanced the opinion that had there been better railroad facilities the plant "would still be profitable." That was in 1886.

Tourists traveling west of Stroudsburg or going south from Tannersville often comment on the oily appearing slatelike fragments which constitute the embankments along the road bed in spots. These actually are slate, of a quality not suited to quarrying but good for the bedding of roads. In fact, slate "gravel" was dug for that very purpose at Snydersville at least as early as 1884.

One of the most northerly slating operations was located high up on precipitous Mt. Minsi, on the Pennsylvania side of the Delaware Water Gap, facing the rather frightening rock falls on the slopes of Mt. Tammany, across the river. Here, in or after 1789, Samuel Pipher, Jr., took title to 1200 acres of unimproved land. In the course of time he built a cabin and then other structures, including a ten-room farmhouse of substantial proportions. While neither the cabin nor the house bears a date stone, the initials "P P" (for Peter Pipher, son of Samuel) and the date of 1827 are cut into a smooth stone in what was once the spring house. The farmhouse was built before 1840, when the property, "with improvements," changed hands. ("Improvements" nowadays ordinarily has a connotation different from the early meaning: "buildings.")

It would seem that Pipher acquired the property in order to engage in farming. As the years passed, parts of the acreage were sold, and various farms were created. Then, in the 1860s, someone decided

*A framed three-part slate of the school type; a slate bound to resemble a book; and slate pencils in their original red, white, and blue container. The squeaking of these pencils as slate met slate, we are told, destroyed the composure of many a rural teacher.*

to take a flier in slate, and the New York-Delaware Water Gap Slate Company was formed. After a few years the place reverted to Samuel Pipher II, son of Peter. After that, farming appears gradually to have receded in favor of the production of slate until, early in the twentieth century, the quarry was flooded and the fraction left of the original 1200 acres became a mere adjunct to the house, which was then used only

as a summer residence. It was still being used as a summer residence when the National Park Service acquired it, in the 1960s, for Park purposes, and named it Slateford Farm.

Even though the chain of ownership has been rather thoroughly traced, there is apparently no record of quarry products. Only one object of slate is known positively to have been made at Slateford

riod of time, and then vanished from the scene—and eventually from the memories of men.

Household objects of slate have seemed for the most part to be so elementary, even uninteresting, in nature that until very recently they were ignored by the rank and file of collectors. By the time local interest in indigenous creations began to mount, however, it became obvious that other, more astute individuals had been on the scene earlier, and many desirable collectibles were no longer to be had.

Over-mantels for fireplaces constituted one of the more ambitious manifestations of slate as an *objet d'art*. The heavy gray slab was cut to the desired size and then scribed or grooved according to a stencil or other pattern placed on the surface. The pattern areas thus created were painted to please the artist or the customer. At its best, a slate mantel piece of this kind may have been very good—or it may have proved less attractive than a mirror or an ancestral portrait; we

*Fancy-shaped kneading "boards" of slate. Except for the piece at the top, these would seem to be too small to serve as actual kneading boards and may have been used as pot covers. From the Mt. Bethel–Delaware Water Gap area.*

Farm: slate pencils. A former resident of nearby Portland recalls that her father, as a youth, was a slate pencil polisher there. Other, more elderly residents remember that the farmhouse and the cabin served to shelter some of the workers while the quarry was still in operation, but do not recall any particular kind of objects made there. Piles of broken and discarded slate seem to indicate that fairly extensive quarrying must have been done—but the record is as mute as the stones lying under the hot sun. Did the roof slates for the church at Smithfield come from *this* quarry? The guess may or may not be a reasonable one; they might have come across the river from Knowlton Township, New Jersey—or even farther up in Pahaquarry Township. Slate for school purposes was produced at Pahaquarry in 1835; perhaps roofing slate was produced there, too. Incredible as it may seem to us now, slate quarries, like other businesses, came into being, operated for a variable pe-

*Hand-gouged (or chipped or carved) decoration on slate is little known away from the Slate Belt, which extends into the up-country. Was the model for this Indian a coin? If anyone knows, he is not telling.*

are told that many of them were simply covered over with something else or torn out when fireplaces were closed up in favor of space heaters.

In the same artistic vein as the over-mantels are the checker and chess "boards" which skilled slaters created in their spare time. Such a checkerboard came to auction in the village of Neola as recently as 1969, but so determined was the bidding among antiques dealers that the usual local collector would have had little chance to acquire it. Similar boards are to be found in private collections, as often because the owners are descended from early slaters or just happen to take pride in local history as because they regard slate decorations with favor. The usual ornamentation, in addition to the geometrical layout of squares of red and black, is a border featuring running vines and floral motifs. This territory of collectibles is only partly explored, however, and it is entirely possible that other different pieces may come to light. One attractive specimen is decorated on both sides. On one side, a conventional checkerboard has been expertly laid out and framed with well-conceived geometrical creations; on the reverse, a parcheesi board layout has been executed with equal care. It is said that a retired slater in the Bangor area, skilled in the making of these game boards but no longer active, is passing on his knowledge of the craft to younger family members, in the hope that the art may not be lost.

Decorated slate was subjected, toward the end of the 1800s, to a typically Victorian conceit—"marbleizing." The marbled effect, a more or less successful attempt at reproducing the veinings of real marble, was achieved in some instances by pouring paint of the desired colors into a vessel of water. The paint would rise to the surface; the object to be decorated was immersed in the liquid and then rotated as it was withdrawn so that the paint would cling in a streaked effect difficult to secure with a brush. This method was satisfactory for small objects, such as book ends, picture frames, or ornamental plaques. Paint stores in our own times occasionally stock marbleizing kits, not necessarily for slate decorating.

Perhaps one should observe that the Victorian idea of making an object look like something foreign to its essential nature was so successful in the case of slate that it is quite possible to pass over, in a crowded antique shop, a piece which looks like wood or iron, heavily painted, but which is slate underneath. A glance at the base is usually all that is needed to make a determination; Victorian decoration did not, as a rule, extend to a part which would not be seen.

*Marbleizing slate was a way of making a severely plain object look glamorous—or, if not actually glamorous, pretty. Many of these dressed-up creations go unrecognized as slate.*

Interesting and highly individual is a representation of an Indian head, complete with eagle headdress, in carved bas-relief. The slate itself measures about ten inches by twelve, and is nearly three-quarters of an inch thick. The carving is skillful. One wonders whether pieces of this nature were not more frequently made than the dearth of information on the subject would seem to indicate. Sand-blasted plaques of slate are on the souvenir market in up-country Pennsylvania, but could hardly be confused with real carving. A template or stencil is used in the creation of the deeply grooved sand-blasted design. Two patterns noted recently are an eagle and a horse.

Typically Victorian is a three-piece fireplace "screen"—perhaps more properly called a shield, since the slate slabs are solid—given to the Slateford Farm restoration. The slates have been drilled so that a cord can be run through to fasten the separate pieces into a unit, and the oil-paint decorations are suggestive of the flower clusters found on hand-painted china and glass of the period. A little less than 18 inches high, this shield, according to tradition, was intended to conceal the yawning fireplace opening during the summer.

Since slate is susceptible to cracking and can not stand sharp blows of any kind, it is hardly surprising that few floor tiles can be found today. There are collectors, though, who watch assiduously for them when they visit nineteenth century houses in the Slate Belt. The same condition is true of the solid quarried blocks used for lintels over doors and windows, and also for sills at entrances. Fireplace mantels of slate are known.

Were there chessmen made of slate? An occasional old-timer thinks so but is not sure. Such carving would be a real find for a collector, whether he likes slate or not. What he will probably have to be contented with is a simple household object—a brick-shaped door stop; a circular slab used either as a hot pad or a pot cover; a slate member in a metal trivet or flatiron stand; a cutting board. The cutting or kneading boards are interesting not only because of their shapes (circular, hexagonal, octagonal, or just polygonal) but for the shape of their handles. A kneading board was normally hung on the wall when not in use. Sometimes a hole was drilled so that it could be slipped over a nail; sometimes, especially in smaller pieces, the body of the object was extended or elongated so that it could be grasped easily, and the nail hole was placed in the extension.

As always, when one deals with an undocumented facet of the past, questions arise for which there seem to be no answers. Slate as a kneading board for

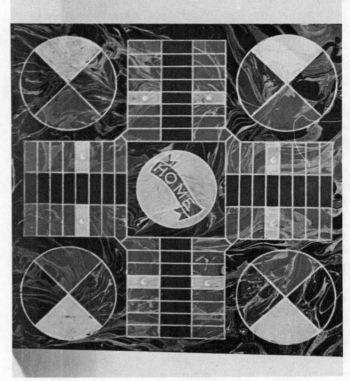

*The game of parcheesi, ordinarily played on a portable, folding board, may have been more fun when played on marbleized slate. The reverse side of this piece is laid out as a checkerboard.*

bread, buns, biscuits, etc., seems entirely reasonable since it was both clean and impervious to moisture—but what about slate as a *cutting* board? Slate is so soft that a piece could be completely marred in a short time by the application of a knife blade, to say nothing of what would happen to the knife and the dough. In actuality, no deeply incised or hacked piece has come to the attention of the writer. Moreover, most of the smaller pieces said to have been used for kneading bread are actually too small for such a purpose. What then? Perhaps, unlikely as it seems, geometrically shaped slate slabs came into existence just because a slater wanted to see what he could do, without any thought of utilitarian purpose. Such a statement could hardly be made for slate sink tops, which are still found in houses in or near Bangor; it would be hard to think of anything more thoroughly utilitarian!

School slates offer a reasonably comprehensive field for the collector. The broad slabs which lined the front, and frequently the side walls of most country schools would not necessarily be intriguing, but every youngster had his portable slate, too, the practice persisting into the present century. (Wall slates are a casualty, now, but as late as the tag end of the nineteenth century there were men who still saw a future in the school slate business. The Stroudsburg *Monroe Democrat* for February 2, 1894, notes that one Henry Fulmer purchased machinery to set up a school slate factory in Portland, with William Roberts to act as foreman.) Very rarely found, but in existence, is a long, slender blackboard pointer, perhaps more interesting than practical. Individual school slates were probably more economical than paper tablet-pads, but they may well have disappeared as early as they did because they were unsanitary, children finding various unacceptable methods for erasing and keeping them clean.

A single slate, framed in beech or maple and bound with red twine, would break no collector's piggy bank; a hinged pair might come closer, but since there seem to be few in existence not many collectors—or banks—would need to suffer. A hinged unit of *three* exists and is something to watch for, though without much real hope. Rare, and therefore greatly desired, are those which have been hinged and then covered with paper simulating a book binding.

COLLECTORS LOOK FOR:

Slaters' tools (a collection in themselves)

Fancy roof slates, curved or pointed at the exposed edge. These were put on roofs in narrow tiers extending the length of the roof, to relieve the monotony of ordinary slates

Kneading boards of various sizes and shapes (another collection in their own right)

Pot covers and hot plates

Flatiron holders with slate insets

Door stops (occasionally covered with carpet)

Pieces of sawed and polished architectural molding

Ornamental over-mantel slabs

Book ends

Picture frames

Fireplace mantels

Fireplace screens or shields

Single, double, and triple school slates

Slate pencils and the red, white and blue paper boxes in which they were sometimes sold

Small table tops and tea wagon tops or shelves

Marbled slate clocks

Marbled slate picture frames

Marbled checker and game boards

Carved slate—animals, human profiles, etc.

*Jackpot:* Any authentic slate artifact not reported in these pages!

# 15
## Brick? Brick!

The traveler who for the first time comes upon the city of Reading, far south in the Dutch Country, may jump to a quick conclusion that the whole city must have been engaged in the making of brick ever since brick was first thought of. It isn't so, of course—but there is a lot of brick in Reading.

There is a great deal of it as one starts northward through the Dutchland, too, but by the time he approaches the up-country there is less—and in the Pocono region only a little, at least by comparison with what he saw in Reading. This condition was partly a matter of taste in those who did the building, of course, but also a matter of the availability of the right kind of clay for brick making.

It would seem that there must have been brick-making enterprises in Pike and Wayne, but the extant records—and the memories operating—point to Monroe as the place of origin of much of the old brick found throughout the region. In the demolition or the renovation of stone houses of the vintage of 1800–1830, one occasionally comes upon brick used over a doorway and around windows, perhaps to ensure sharper right angles than would be possible with stone as the only construction material. Chimneys built at this time were more likely to be made of brick than of stone, and at least partly for the same reason.

In a stone house at Sciota, the original bake-oven was constructed against the outside wall at an end of the house, with the principal fireplace just inside. Access to the oven was by means of a small inside opening at one side of the fireplace, and this aperture, as well as the baking surface itself, was lined with brick. The beehive dome was of brick, plastered over. When the outside oven was removed, many years ago, some of the brick was used, instead of stones which might match those in the rest of the house, to close up the hole left in the wall. The chimney of the massive fireplace in an adjacent out-kitchen is of brick, stuccoed over at some time in the past. Similar conditions prevail in other stone houses of comparable age—the point being that brick, wherever it was made, was available if one wanted to go to the trouble—or expense—of getting it.

A seeming explanation for the paucity of brick structures in some up-country areas may well be the fact that brick transported for considerable distances was bound to be so costly that its use was impractical. Much of it stood a strong chance of being broken in transit over the roads which then existed—and brick burned in small home kilns was not always of good quality. Within memory, when brick was being hauled in town by horse and wagon, the tiers in the wagon body were separated by straw to absorb some of the road-shock. Probably no amount of straw in wagons transporting bricks over many of the back roads in Pike could have assured anything like safe delivery.

A small local operation existed on the River Road, not far from Shawnee, on the Samuel Michaels property, in the 1850's. Two structures known to have been made from bricks burned there are the little Zion's Lutheran Church on the hillside, and Michaels' dwelling house, a short distance up the road. The church was built in 1851 and the house at about the same time. Construction of the church was a matter of considerable local pride, as well it might have been, but in the course of time the brick tended to crumble. Two receipts signed by Cornelius Starner, the brick burner, are on record for brick needed in the con-

Brick Works, Saylorsburg, Pa.

*The making of "fancy" light-colored brick was the specialty of the Blue Ridge factory—and a major West End industry.*

struction of the church: $50.00 on October 12, 1850, and $37.50 on October 19.

Although specific operations have long since been forgotten, probably the leading early figure in the industry in Monroe was William S. Wintermute, who was born in Stillwater, New Jersey, in 1810. He moved to a location west of Stroudsburg in 1836. He was unmarried at that time and his sister Esther kept house for him, presumably to the time of his marriage in 1841. He was a farmer as well as a brick burner until 1843, when he moved to Stroudsburg and made the manufacture of brick his life's vocation. It is said that practically all the early brick houses in Stroudsburg and East Stroudsburg were of materials of his making, including those used in the old court house. Some of the streets and sidewalks of Stroudsburg were brick-paved at one time, but there seems to be no record as to whether or not the materials were of Wintermute origin.

Wintermute's town house was built on the site of

a Revolutionary War fort—Fort Penn, on what is now Main Street in Stroudsburg. In a bad freshet in 1869 it was undermined and destroyed. To make sure that a similar catastrophe could not happen again, when he rebuilt the house he started the foundation at the bottom of a washout—23 feet below the level of the pavement.

Less accurately recorded than the vital statistics of Wintermute are those of Oliver D. Stone, a farmer and brickyard owner. One early account gives his birth and death dates as 1808–1885, noting his birthplace as the Van Buskirk farm in Stroud Township. Another source, however, says that, like Wintermute, he came to Stroudsburg from New Jersey. Whatever his birthplace, his son William, who worked in the brickyard in his youth, was born in Stroudsburg in 1836. Oliver's name and occupation appear on both the 1850 and 1860 census lists of Stroudsburg.

Samuel Smiley, who was born in 1844, had a brickyard near what later came to be known as Phillips

*Single specimens of some of the faced bricks and tiles
made at the Blue Ridge factory at Saylorsburg.*

*The up-country door stop was often a brick—either
a real brick or a piece of brick-shaped slate, but one
could go a step further and encase it in carpet to
match the floor covering of the room in which it was
used. (Courtesy of the National Park Service)*

Street—at that time outside the borough limits, but now within the boundaries of Stroudsburg. This area, largely open country at the time Smiley knew it, has been built up to such an extent that it is difficult now to pinpoint exactly any old-time location. Thus, depressions pointed to as the places where the clay was once dug and where the kilns operated may or may not be the original locations in fact. Phillips Street may have been named for another brickyard operator—S. P. Phillips, who had a place of business not far from the juncture of Eighth Street at Phillips. There was also a brickyard on Fifth Street, in the neighborhood of a handsome stone house long called the R. C. Cramer house, still standing. The business was operated by S. Shug and C. G. Ramsey. The last two enterprises named are indicated on a map of Monroe County by F. W. Beers, dated 1875. We should allow here for the possibility of overlapping in identity or succession of ownership, and not assume, in the absence of satisfactory documentation, that all the businesses in this area were separate entities . . . though, of course, they may have been.

Familiar to many who have forgotten or lost track of earlier operations is the family name of Zacharias. According to the record, Joseph Zacharias, who had earlier worked for an unnamed brick manufacturer, purchased property in East Stroudsburg and opened a brickyard there in or about 1878. So many of the houses on North Courtland Street, north of the Milford Crossing, were built of Zacharias's bricks that the place came to be called "Bricktown." Later he also had a brick kiln just outside Stroudsburg. Clay for his operations was dug in East Stroudsburg.

An advertisement in the *Monroe Democrat* (Stroudsburg) for November 29, 1888, reads as follows: "For sale: 300,000 bricks of all grades, hard, soft, salmon for sale at the East Stroudsburg Brick Yards at the lowest cash prices. Orders by mail will be promptly filled. Jos. H. Zacharias." (A "salmon" brick was one which was under-burned.) Zacharias was succeeded in the business, which still continues, although without a kiln, by a son and later by a grandson.

Brick gets its reddish tone, after it is fired, from traces of iron or iron oxide present in the raw material. "Common" brick, the kind used for most non-decorative purposes, was made almost entirely of clay; "face" brick, which normally had a smoother surface and a fancier appearance, had a mixture of sand and limestone added to the clay. Since appearance was a significant factor in face brick, this type was ordinarily used only where it would be seen.

The brick which achieved a kind of fame for itself

and which brought reflected credit to the up-country was an elaboration of face brick made at Saylorsburg about the turn of the century. It was known as enamel (or "enameled") brick, the term applying to its highly glossy surface. The company producing it was the Blue Ridge Enamel Brick Company, which utilized for its product the exceptionally fine white clay found on Summer Hill Ridge. While most of the brick was white-faced, colors were used, too, in limited degree and perhaps as much by way of experiment as because of any conviction that colors would prove popular. One tone was buff; it is believed that the last house of buff-colored enamel brick was built on Normal Hill in East Stroudsburg by Victor Dimmick in 1912. At least two tones of green were also made, according to the mute evidence of surviving marked specimens of the brick. Perhaps most attractive was a clear sky blue. When the Indian Queen Hotel on Main Street in Stroudsburg was razed in the 1960s, a fireplace of white enamel brick with this blue trim came to light.

In general, enamel bricks looked like other bricks of yellowish rather than reddish cast, except for the heavy coating of glassy-looking enamel on the surface exposed to the weather—or the viewer. For jobs in which no actual construction was involved, and only the matter of decoration was under consideration, surface tiles of various sizes, and in the colors mentioned, were manufactured.

Enamel brick, for whatever reason, never entirely caught popular fancy, at least to the extent of displacing either common or face brick. One reason may have been its sun-reflecting qualities; a dwelling house of shiny white brick, in strong sunlight, was too pronounced in effect for many tastes. It was remarkably waterproof, never needed painting, was impervious to most of the ills which beset other building media—but, as we have said, it achieved only limited popularity. The Castle Inn at Delaware Water Gap, built between 1904 and 1906, still standing although now not used for its original purpose, may have been the largest up-country building to utilize enamel brick, although other important structures in the Gap also made use of it. A number of dwellings of more nearly "average" size, some in the village and others along Route 209, may be spotted by the tourist who is on the alert for them.

The Blue Ridge company closed its doors about 1910. One of the problems of an extensive business in which heat or dangerous fumes are a necessary part or a by-product of the operation is what to do about the smokestack when the enterprise becomes defunct. Since the Saylorsburg operation was a large

*Bricks used for lining hearths in early fireplaces were
often larger than the size now considered standard.
(The hearth here is in the living room of a stone house
built in Sciota in 1805.)*

one, there were *four* smokestacks, all of which
eventually had to come down to make way for a
highway or for some equally pressing purpose. The
first three stacks—90, 110, and 125 feet high, re-
spectively—were dynamited in the early 1930s, with
several thousand persons in attendance to watch
the demise. The remaining stack was the real problem, though; it stood 185 feet tall. The words "Blue
Ridge" were spelled out vertically in great colored
brick letters on the light stack, and the combination
was a striking one, constituting in its total effect a
landmark visible for many miles. Demolition of this

stack raised the inevitable question: how to get the
thing down without damaging nearby property. It
was finally safely dynamited in February, 1960. The
brick was salvaged for making alterations or repairs
in houses, mostly at distant points, which had used
the same kind of material originally; but local residents liked—and still like—to search out attractive
single bricks to use for door stops . . . or, in some
cases, to have around just for old times' sake.

For all its rather extensive importation of Saylorsburg enamel brick, Delaware Water Gap—the village,
that is—had at least one kiln and one brickyard of

its own as early as 1875. This was the enterprise of P. Frederick, not far from Lake Lenape on what is known as Mountain Avenue. Additional details seem to be lacking, although the brick in the Water Gap Presbyterian Church is said to have come from this yard.

"Weathered" brick has for years been popular as a material for such new constructions as sidewalks, fireplaces, and occasionally floors, in places in which an antique atmosphere, so called, is being attempted. Many have been the antiques buffs who have followed the progress of demolition of old buildings in the hope of salvaging materials for a patio, a wide fireplace hearth, or a wall. When old mortar has to be painstakingly cleaned off each brick, the labor can reach awesome proportions, but there is no denying the fact that there is a mellowness to old brick that is found nowhere else. Old brick for modern pur-poses is likely to do better indoors than out, since it has often become very porous.

COLLECTORS LOOK FOR:

Old bricks for use in restorations or in new construc-tion in which an old look is desired

Structures which utilized enamel brick (to photo-graph)

Single enamel bricks impressed with "Blue Ridge"

Colored enamel bricks—buff, green, blue, and, of course, the basic white

Enamel bricks with rounded corners or edges (used for architectural facings and moldings)

Pieces of Blue Ridge tile

Postcards and photographs in which the Blue Ridge factory plays a part

# 16
# *Potter and Pot*

If the first white arrivals in Upper Dutchdom had not known how to make vessels of clay, the usually friendly Indians would have taught them; clay pots for cooking or just for keeping food in storage seem to have been known to aborigines the world over. Smithfield Township in Monroe County would have been one of the best places in the East to pick up fine points on how Indian artifacts were created. Evidence strongly points to the fact that right along the Delaware, perhaps on the farm owned by the late Harry E. Kautz, perhaps farther east, there was a kind of historically unrecorded manufactory of Indian artifacts—arrowheads in particular, but other weapons and implements as well. Parts of what is believed to have been an Indian village have been excavated and removed for scientific university study—but any small boy in Shawnee-on-Delaware, trailing the plow behind his father, well toward the end of the nineteenth century, could pick up a treasure trove of newly exposed artifacts. The late Arthur Kroll, of the Hollow Road leading east of Shawnee, acquired much of his fine collection by tramping newly plowed fields, particularly after a rain.

The whites knew about pottery, however, and had no interest in arrow making. They were well past the Robinson Crusoe stages of experimentation in this regard—and just as there were carpenters and metal workers and weavers in the early colonizing groups, there were potters of considerable skill.

Monroe County has one outstanding name in the annals of early potting and pottery—Rudolph Drach. According to the worn headstone in the churchyard at Hamilton Square, Rudolph was born in 1770 and died in 1842. The stone of his first wife, Magdalena, is also there, but a little distance away. (A common early practice in burying the dead was to inter each person next to the one who had last been buried, without regard to keeping family members together. Such niceties or amenities as burying in family plots, while observed in some congregations, were by no means universal.)

"Drach" is generally considered the original spelling, but in early references it may be "Traugh," and since it was a German name and as such subject to phonetic rather than historic treatment in a largely English-oriented world, other forms appeared. "Trach" is one; "Druck" is a second; it may be that "Trux" is another. A West End village called Trachsville might well be the English equivalent of what, in an earlier day, would have been called "Drachstettel."

This potter was not a native Monroe Countian; indeed, the county had not yet been created as a governmental or political unit when in 1763 Thomas and John Penn deeded one Rudolph Traugh a 300-acre tract in Bedminster Township, Bucks County. This land was divided between Rudolph's two sons, Henry and Adam, when Rudolph died in 1770. A *second* Rudolph, son of Henry, received his father's portion of the land in 1787. This grandson of the first Rudolph appears to be our potter. Just when he left Bedminster, went north, and established himself not far from Saylorsburg in Monroe's West End we do not know—but we do know that he and Magdalena were baptismal sponsors for Lea(h) Roth in Hamilton Township in 1809. We might note in passing that the name Daniel Druch, with an accompanying date of 1842, appears on a small, handmade footstool now in the possession of a great-great-granddaughter of Rudolph—the second Rudolph. Under the top of the

*The probable work of Rudolph Drach, eighteenth
century potter who moved from Bedminster, Bucks
County, to the up-country about 1800. All these pieces
have come down in direct line—but since Drach apparently signed only his sgraffito ware, absolute documentation is lacking.*

*Brown-glazed, mica-flecked jars found in and pre-
sumed to be native to Hamilton Township. The only
positively identified early potter in Hamilton thus
far is Rudolph Drach—but no mica-flecked pieces by
Drach have been reported.*

stool appear the initials H. D. and the date 1843; just beyond this date are the initials A. D. . . . for Henry and Adam? One refrains from jumping to conclusions—an all-too-easy exercise but, recognizing the repetition of names in families generation after generation, one does have food for speculation.

Drach's massive stone house is still standing, but has long since ceased to be known by the family name. There is no sign at all of the pottery, which stood across the road in what is now grown-up meadow land, and any shards which might have survived had the pottery been abandoned instead of torn down have gone to earth, if one may apply the term in this connection. The road is now little traveled; once it was a convenient route from the crossroads at Hamilton to Saylorsburg, but today it comes to a dead end because of a superhighway just ahead.

We know that Rudolph was making sgraffito pottery deep dishes before he came to Monroe; one of his pie plates is marked "Rudolph Drach, Bedminster Taunschib, 1792." But another plate, also marked, and now at a nationally known museum, was found and presumably made in Monroe. It went through the usual vicissitudes of descending from one owner to another until finally it became merely something old and unwanted and was sold from its shelf at Minisink Hills to an antiques dealer.

It was at the time of this sale that the existence of other pieces, made by the same hand, became known. None of those which have been run down are sgraffito-decorated—with the exception of the plates mentioned above—but some are of well-exe-

*A jug (minus its handle) and a pudding bowl for which strong claims of Monroe County provenance have been advanced. Pottery with spatter decoration is rarely found north of the Blue Mountain; as a matter of fact, it seems to be scarce anywhere.*

*The cover of a Monroe County Vorschrift or specimen copybook. Much of the early fraktur of Monroe County includes the words "Hamilton Township School," as does the piece shown here.*

*Hooked rug with interestingly conceived and well-laid-out original design, in wool strips pulled through burlap.*

*Not many potters attempted the difficult gray and blue tones found in this incised up-country plate. It was made as a presentation piece for a member of the Getz family, but the name of the potter has not been recorded.*

*The woven coverlets of Jacob Setzer (Jackson Township), with their red, white, blue, and faded green tones, are considered a prize among collectors, both for their beauty and because of their rarity. (The green yarn was not always included.)*

*Show towels, similar but not an actual pair, bearing the name of Elisabeth Rinker. The Rinker family was well known in Monroe County.*

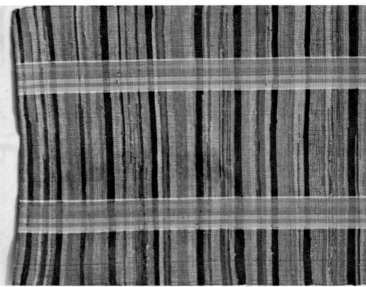

*Rag carpet may be dull or lively, according to the colors of the warp. It is not difficult to see why this type is called "rainbow" carpet. From Kunkletown, Monroe County.*

*Wool embroidery, comparable with but not identical to crewel work, on woolen homespun blanket. From Kresgeville, Monroe County.*

*Quilt in a formalized tulip design—or, according to the nomenclature of some communities, a variant of the Bear's Claw pattern.*

cuted slipware. There is no positive documentation for the slipware, but for years, when certain pieces have been discovered—or displayed—in the county the accompanying comment has been, "This pottery was made right around here—out Saylorsburg way." With the disappearance of association with the family name, the demolition of the kiln, and the dispersal of the pieces made there, it is perhaps not surprising that few facts are available. Equally lacking in surprise may be the circumstance that surviving objects to which a "near-Saylorsburg" provenance is so unhesitatingly attributed bear a strong resemblance to one another in three ways—a massiveness in proportion beyond what may be considered usual; a high orange glaze; and a rhythmic under-glaze black sponged decoration, strongly applied.

There might, of course, have been other early potteries near Saylorsburg; if there were, they have vanished so completely as to leave not even the elusive but at least existing evidence attaching to the work of Rudolph Drach.

There is a more or less prevalent belief among neophyte collectors that the calligraphically blue-decorated heavy gray stoneware pots, crocks, and heavy jugs so much in demand in recent years were made at the place indicated in the flowing script which constitutes the decoration. Well known in up-country Dutchdom are the butter jars and other pieces on which the words "Joseph Wallace and Sons, Stroudsburg, Pa." appear. The fact is that such lettering was an advertising device, and it would seem that much of it was done, in any given pottery, by the same man. The merchant ordered his crockery for the coming season from the supply house, and the supply house provided whatever lettering was desired. (We are talking here simply of handwriting—"brush" writing would be more nearly accurate—and not of bird, floral, or other decoration.) Now and then pieces from farther north are found: Lynch, Olyphant, Pa.; Whyte, Scranton, Pa. There is reason to suppose that much script-decorated pottery came from the Trenton, New Jersey, area, where much of the supply of utilitarian ceramics originated.

Be that as it may, Wallace pots and jars are thought of in up-country territory as "our own" and are collectible on that count. They are not really very old—sixty to seventy-five years would probably be a fair estimate—but it is in antique shops that one is most likely to see them. The Wallace hardware store in Stroudsburg is still an active, ongoing concern—although it no longer handles the blue-decorated ware. It occurred to a collector not long ago that just possibly there might be an all-but-forgotten supply of jars in proof condition in one of the cellars of the giant store, but the proprietor, who bears the name of the founder, stated unequivocally that for many years none had been either bought or sold, and that there were no jars in the cellar. That should settle the question.

A number of other pieces known to have been decorated for local use have been seen. One marked "Loder" is in the hands of a Minisink Hills collector-dealer. A store operated by the Loders in East Stroudsburg persisted well into the present century. One marked "Gillette, Newfoundland, Pa." has defied all attempts to establish a place of business in which the name "Gillette" figured. A Gillette-operated store in Newfoundland would have had to operate rather far back in the 1800s; families with other names have had all but a monopoly on mercantile operations there for nearly a century.

Names of stoneware pottery makers are usually impressed in the wet clay below the top rim, when they appear at all. Often the impression is irregular because of unequally applied pressure, and therefore partly or totally illegible. The capacity of the container, either in quarts or gallons (it is apparently taken for granted that the purchaser will know which), will appear, if it is supplied, just below the name. Collectors do not look for stoneware pieces on the strength of makers' or other names alone, although any marked object is considered more desirable than an unmarked one. The decorators who wielded the cobalt brush could do more than write a good hand; they applied leaves, sprays, roses, tulips, and other flowers with considerable abandon, and when in the mood would create birds, bees, butterflies, and tree-like creations as well. However, there seems to be no up-country record of the dogs, human figures, and man-in-the-moon decoration found farther afield.

Two potters and places in or near the northern fringe of the up-country are Weston (Honesdale) and Jones (Pittston). Horace Weston, who had earlier been a minister, started the manufacture of stoneware at Ellenville, New York, in 1829. The Delaware and Hudson Canal, which started operations the same year, proved to be such a stimulus to trade throughout the entire region that he made plans for a branch plant at Honesdale, Pa., in 1848. He died the same year, however, and his son William W. Weston completed the plant in 1849 and took charge of it. William's brother, the second Horace Weston, at first looked after the Ellenville plant, but took over the operation of the one in Honesdale in 1854. The firm was dissolved in 1857. Weston

*Typical up-country salt-glazed stoneware: jug with
pomegranate by H. (Horace) Weston, Honesdale;
preserving jar with so-called butterfly decoration,
Hawley area, perhaps Phillipsburg (Paupac).*

pieces may be marked H. Weston, W. Weston, or
W. W. Weston.

What collectors especially like about the Honesdale
product is the elaborate freehand scroll and pomegranate design used on many pieces. The Westons
used brown clays as well as gray, and their salt glazes
vary from thin to heavy. An eccentricity found in a
few pieces occurs in their method of abbreviating
the word Pennsylvania—"P.A" rather than "PA"
or "PA." This circumstance seems to operate as with
postage stamps: collectors may bypass perfect speci-

mens in favor of those with an aberration, and therefore rare.

Evan (one bibliographer makes it "Evans") Jones
was working in the town of Pittston about 1880. His
output must have been very considerable; one is
likely to find marked specimens in many places in
eastern Pennsylvania. It consists of the major pieces
needed for country living—jugs for holding liquids;
preserving jars of various sizes; handled batter pots,
some of which at one time had tin lids; butter crocks
and lard jars. Jones would seem, by his name, to

have been of Welsh extraction, but whatever his ethnic origin he was one of the most prolific producers of pottery for the up-country.

While Weston stoneware seems not to have been so abundant as that of Jones, it is interesting to note that on some pieces from the Cowden-Wilcox pottery in Harrisburg the distinctive pomegranate motif of Weston appears. Whether the design in one place was "borrowed" from the other or whether, as is not unlikely, the same decorator operated at the two plants at different times remains a matter of speculation.

An interesting pottery survival is a piece purporting to have been made at or near the town of Bangor, a short distance from Stroudsburg. There is no record of a working pottery there, at least as far as we know, but this pie plate has been in up-country Dutchdom for something like a century. It had been in the possession of one member or another of the same family from the time it was made as a presentation piece for a man who in the course of years came to be known as "Old Man Getz," and remained there until Mr. Getz's grandson, himself eventually "Old Man Kuhnsman," died and his household effects were put up at auction. This was in 1969.

The Getz plate, as it is called, is of redware with an unusual tone of cream-colored slip on the upper surface and geometrically regular sgraffito decorations, among which the ornately lettered word GETZ plays the major part. Blue decoration of any kind, common on stoneware, is very rare in sgraffito redware, but it was used among the earliest potters, then abandoned, and eventually used again, sparingly. Blue dots have been utilized effectively as decoration on this plate. It is the opinion of the writer that the distinctive color tone of the cream slip is owing to a slight escaping flow of blue in the kiln. Admittedly, a differing opinion on the subject is one which can not be flouted completely: the bluish tinge, suggests an observer, comes from the fact that the plate had been used many times, here in the thick of huckleberry country, for the baking of huckleberry pie! One thing is indisputable: the plate has been used oftener than any piece on which so much care has been lavished should have been.

It is said that the wind which blows no one any good is indeed an evil one. What kind of wind was blowing on the hot summer day on which the Getz plate went to the block is of no great importance—but there were two persons present, not including the auctioneer, who recognized the plate for what it is: a little-publicized kind of sgraffito. One of the two men was dubious about the bluish-toned glaze and said as much to his auction-frequenting friend, adding that he would not bid if the friend wanted it. He kept his word. The auctioneer, little interested in old pottery and assuming that he had before him a discolored dish which should probably have been discarded before the sale, paired it with a late, commercially made plate and insisted that the buyer would have to take both. The buyer did!

"Baffling" is the word for three seemingly different types of redware found in the up-country—baffling in that they appear to have come to light nowhere else, and that no person questioned seems to have any recollection of a pottery or a kiln which might have produced them. "They were made around here; I've always heard that" is the less-than-helpful suggestion—and the only suggestion—which has thus far been forthcoming.

One type is an exceptionally heavy jug with a bulbous body, in a thick, very dark red glaze. Long ago, the two specimens reported had ceased to be used for something like vinegar or molasses, and were filled with machine oil. One of the two has responded to attempts to clean it up, but the other still oozes oil at unexpected times. These jugs, from Newfoundland, are as heavy as the heaviest stoneware; yet the body

*The woman with the hat: was she a conscious creation, or did she come into being unbeknownst to the wielder of the brush?*

*Wallace and Loder—two names long known and respected in Stroudsburg and East Stroudsburg merchandising. The grocery store of McFall and Warne gave away, as souvenirs, rolling pins of the kind shown.*

has all the appearance of redware. When discovered, they were heavily encrusted with layers of paint. The handles of both have been broken. One could not state with finality either that they are natively up-country pieces or that they are not. The only certainties are that they are different from conventional pottery, either stoneware or redware, and that they had been in the place in which they were discovered since some time in the 1880s.

A second type—and again only two specimens have been reported, one well up in the Poconos and one at the West End village of Neola—has a spattered under-glaze decoration as its distinguishing quality. The body of the vessel is in a yellowish rather than a reddish tone, although it is redware, and dots of dark pigment have been scattered irregularly and thickly over the surface. The effect is striking and attractive. One piece is a pudding dish or bowl about four inches deep and seven in diameter. The other is a jug which approaches the globular in shape and has a capacity of about six quarts. The flattened lip of this piece suggests the similarly shaped lips of the

heavy red pieces mentioned above, but is not identical.

The third type has a very dark brown, almost black, glaze in which mica flakes figure prominently and effectively. As is the case with the types first mentioned, just two specimens have appeared, both in the Sciota-Neola section of the West End. They are somewhat thin-walled jars or pots, flaring gracefully out and up from the bottom and then curving inward again toward the top. For each of these, the owner adduced the information that they had definitely been locally made, but stopped short of even a tentative attribution to a known potter or pottery. For that matter, they do not closely resemble other pottery found in the up-country.

A forgotten or nearly forgotten up-country pottery venture, short-lived, was one conducted near Ledgedale (Paupac) by Cross and Burns in the early 1870s. Abram Cross, who was born in County Tyrone, Ireland, in 1828, was brought to this country when he was four, and spent his childhood in Wayne County. When he grew up, he went to Easton to work on "the" canal—presumably the Lehigh. He carved out a career on the canals, with time served on the Lehigh, the Delaware and Raritan, and the Morris and Essex, eventually becoming a captain. He returned to Wayne in his later years, living first in Dreher Township but later in Greene, in Pike County. For two years he engaged in pottery making, taking a partner whom we know only by his surname, Burns.

The Burns family, of north-of-Ireland stock, was a prominent one. A long hill in the general neighborhood of Wilsonville was named to honor the family. The Cross and Burns Pottery was in existence for only two years; it was destroyed by fire and never rebuilt. A surviving bill of sale which came to light in a general store in Monroe a few years ago is dated 1873; the pottery, therefore, must be placed in a two-year time span somewhere between 1871 and 1875. Evidently its location was a well known one, since I. C. White, a geologist for the Commonwealth of Pennsylvania, used the pottery site as a point of elevation in 1882, locating it eight miles southwest of Wilsonville. This territory was also known as Phillipsburg at one time.

It would appear from the bill of sale mentioned that Cross and Burns produced utilitarian pieces largely unrelieved by attempts at decoration. One piece said to be from this area has been tentatively attributed to the pottery—a large, two-handled preserving or pickling jar in grayware with a cobalt butterfly as a decorative device and the name S. Phillips on each side. The evidence is too meager to make an attribution seem stronger than a mere possibility.

One needs to bear in mind that, over all, surviving pottery, either grayware or redware, is much less common in the northern up-country than it is farther south, for the simple reason that there never was a great deal of it. Both types were early products, and had begun to yield ground to more satisfactory kinds of containers while great reaches of Pocono territory were still wilderness. When claims of unusual antiquity are made for a Pocono-area piece, therefore, one would do well to consider all the evidence before making a judgment.

### COLLECTORS LOOK FOR:

Redware pottery—apple butter pots, jars, pie plates, drinking mugs, pudding dishes, etc.

Sgraffito pieces (no harm in looking!)

Blue-decorated stoneware (grayware)—jugs, crocks, jars, pitchers, batter pots, flasks, ink wells, spittoons, water coolers, fruitcake brandying jars or crocks

Stoneware with place names—Stroudsburg, Newfoundland, Honesdale, Jubilee, Easton, Shickshinny, etc.

Stoneware with makers' names—Weston, Jones, Moyer, Cowden, Cowden-Wilcox, Daub (Easton), etc.

Stoneware with sellers' names—Loder, Wallace, Gillette, etc.

*Jackpot:* Any piece of local sgraffito

*Jackpot of jackpots:* A signed piece of Rudolph Drach sgraffito

# 17
# Schnitzelbank—and Other—Basketry

Whereas a number of the crafts of earlier times have disappeared from the face of the earth or, if they have not disappeared, have been metamorphosed into something hardly recognizable, basket making lingers on—a patient too tough to succumb, especially if the right kind of transfusion takes place now and then. The actual *need* for the traditional types of up-country baskets has almost entirely disappeared; it would be hard to state a requirement for which a wooden or straw basket would be more satisfactory than a present-day container in some medium other than wood or straw. A *desire* obviously exists, however, and it is this desire which keeps the craft going.

Allowing for individual variations and vagaries which might swell the list, there are four basic types of up-country basket work: white oak or splint; willow; slat or tacked; and rye straw.

Of these, it is the white oak, melon-shaped basket which generally comes to mind first. In the early 1930s, on a quiet stretch of country road not far from Wind Gap, there was a typical white oak setup, complete from the piles of split tree sections and the *schnitzelbank* to a modest collection of baskets offered for sale to the occasional passerby at prices low even for Depression times. The road has since been wiped out by a highway so crowded on Sunday afternoon that the traffic jam seems endless. The farm buildings and the brook, too, have disappeared—and if the Philadelphia-bound tourists are taking country eggs or vegetables or fruit home with them, they would no more know about woven baskets as conveyors for food than the basket maker of the '30s would have known about traffic jams.

The demise of one such operation, while admittedly it is indicative of a general condition—and probably prophetic, for that matter—did not mean the immediate end of the craft. In Palmerton, an operation of very similar nature was going on only a year or two ago. Farther south, and away from the territory with which we are immediately concerned, baskets are still being made in a few remote spots. But to the north, through much of Monroe and practically all of Wayne and Pike, if white oak baskets are being constructed, news is also being made, since white oak now grows there but sparsely and what is grown is seldom free enough from blemishes to be suitable for the straight-grain demands of basketry. Straight-grained trees developed in forests where the trees shot up to considerable heights to get the sun—and such forests have long since disappeared.

Melon-shaped baskets, while not really complicated in construction, call for strong hands and a sure eye. Both the framework of the basket, which includes the handle, and the splints woven into it are made from flawlessly grained young oak trees, five to ten inches in diameter. One exception might be noted; infrequently one comes upon a frame of hickory. The trees are felled and then cut into sections of varying lengths, according to the size of the projected basket. Six-foot sections would be about right for a bushel basket. Perhaps only one such section could be cut from a tree, but a number of shorter ones could be secured, for baskets of smaller size, before one reached the first limb—and the usual end of the potential for that particular tree.

Methods of working a solid log down to strips pliable enough for weaving varied from person to person, but up-country procedure usually started with splitting the log into quarters. If the grain did not run perfectly straight, there was no point in going fur-

*White-oak splint baskets. The flat-bottomed specimen at the back was used to hold seed for broad-cast hand sowing; the melon-shaped example is often called an egg basket. The third might be regarded as just a utility container.*

ther. If the grain was straight, the splitting continued with each quarter until finally the strips were almost fine enough for weaving. The last step in this phase was to shave the strips thin and smooth by means of a two-handled drawknife and the peculiar kind of homemade wooden clamp device called the *schnitzelbank* or cutting bench. Since wood became unworkable as soon as it began to dry out, it had to be processed shortly after it was cut or else be immersed in water, often a nearby brook.

The frame of the melon-shaped basket was constructed first. After it had been completed, the weaving often started at the handle and proceeded downward on each side toward the center. (For flat-bot-

tomed baskets, weaving usually started at the bottom.) When the worker approached the bottom center of the basket, he hung the incomplete object up to dry and shrink before filling in the last inch or so. In this way he managed to secure a fairly close weave. The touch of the expert appeared in the tightness of the weave, the regularity in size of the splints, the deftness of the fancy diamond-shaped joining at the handle, and the even balance of the basket when it was set down. Since many baskets of this kind were used for gathering and carrying eggs, a lopsided creation could prove disastrous. One wonders why round-bottomed baskets were made in such numbers, since by their very nature they invited trouble. Sometimes, parallel cleats were attached to the bottom to assure an even keel, but these cleats seem not to have been a part of the original construction. Incised names or initials on the handle might be those of a maker who felt that he had done an unusually good job, but in some cases they are said to be those of the purchaser. Identification of the makers of old baskets thus comes to be a difficult matter.

A county historian notes that one Nelson K. Detrick of Spragueville (later Analomink) made baskets of all kinds professionally as late as the 1890s. The chances are perhaps just fair that among his stock there were white oak baskets, since by that time the local supply of white oak was beginning to run out. Cicero George, an octogenarian of Stroudsburg, remembers making melon-shaped baskets in his youth, and Alfred Hawk, at the western extremity of the up-country, still practices the skills he learned from his wife's family, some of whom were basket makers. A West End enterprise familiar to motorists driving from Stroudsburg to Lehighton advertises a great variety of baskets, some of which are in the tradition of the old oak-splint method of construction, but most of which are imported.

Baskets are frequently named according to their originally intended use. Among them are large flat grain baskets, sometimes in the shape of a squared oval, once used by farmers in spring for hand-seeding their fields. These called for a strap fastening, so that the weight of the loaded basket was borne on the shoulders. The farmer thus had one hand free to steady the basket and one to scatter the grain. Another type is a tall, heavy basket in bushel size used for measuring grain, apples, or other heavy commodities. In some cases both the seeding and the measuring baskets have handholds or grips instead of attached handles. Similar in appearance are smaller ones which range downward from half-bushel size to those which hold no more than a pint. Missing in the up-country is the graceful, divided creation known

*Fancy rye straw baskets with oak splint binding.
Such containers were often used for decorated Easter
eggs.*

colloquially farther south as the *arsch-backe korrup*. The name is not translated in polite society.

Willow baskets were much lighter in weight and have survived less well than the sturdy, seemingly ageless creations of oak. While they are still being made and sold in some Dutch Country strongholds, the last reported enterprise in the Poconos came to an end at some time before 1910. This was a small operation, a family affair, carried on in German Valley by Raymond and Sabina Lauffer. Mr. Lauffer died in 1918. The specialty of the Lauffers was wash baskets —outward-flaring oval hampers, one of which seems to have been needed in every rural household. The prevailing sentiment was that a Lauffer basket would outlast two of the kind available at the general store.

The manufacture of willow baskets, which called for peeled willow whips not more than a quarter inch in diameter, was feasible only in marshy places or along streams where the willows would grow quickly. In a single year the basket maker, unless he had a long-range plan for his operation or unless his reserve of growing willow was very extensive, might exhaust his resources. An outstanding virtue of the willow clothes hamper was its light weight, a significant factor for the housewife. Not necessarily a virtue but a pleasing asset was that it was almost white. Moreover, willow baskets tended to bleach with use, whereas oak baskets gradually darkened. Willows could be planted along any stream, though they grew best where the water was all but motionless. A continuing supply could be assured by sticking crooked or unusable but live whips into the mud or along the bank. They would root at once, and might produce usable basket material in as short a time as four years.

A source of comment or amusement or wonder in the village of Newfoundland a few decades ago was a willow stockade completely surrounding a bungalow built at the edge of a creek. The owner had cut willow posts for the fence enclosing his property, not anticipating what might happen; after all, they were just ordinary fence posts. But every one took root in the rich soil and shoots were put out in profusion. Instead of uprooting them at once, the owner trimmed them for a number of years as one might trim a catalpa tree. Soon, however, each tree became a hydra-headed monster, with dozens upon dozens of young, lush branches completely shutting out the sun. In the end they had to be destroyed, of course, but for years there were sly references to the "Robinson Crusoe" house.

The making of slat or tacked baskets inevitably came to be important in wood-minded Upper Dutch-dom. Such baskets may not always have been objects of beauty, but they did meet a need. How early these baskets—principally peach baskets—were produced there is no way of knowing; like veneer or clothespin factories the places of manufacture seem to have operated for a year or two and then, the marketing possibilities being exhausted, the owner converted his business to something different or moved away.

In East Stroudsburg, the Van Vliet family, which established its own glassworks and which later became celebrated for its fruit and garden produce, had a peach basket factory at Eagle Valley Corners in 1880. The operators were W. R. and W. E. Van Vliet. In 1897 a novelty basket factory was operated by Daniel Van Why, but details as to the kinds of baskets made are unavailable.

About 1915 a noncommercial basket-making activity was introduced in Shawnee at what was later to become part of a well-known inn and country club. The civic-minded patroness undertook to teach interested women of the community the techniques of making various kinds of ornamental baskets and, over all, a high degree of competence was achieved. Neither native to the region nor traditional in any usual sense, they serve as a kind of postscript to the art of local basket making. Surviving Shawnee Inn baskets, as they are familiarly called, constituted part of a historical display in 1970, when the Delaware Water Gap National Recreation Area of the National Park Service staged its first annual crafts fair at Peters Valley, in nearby New Jersey.

Rye-straw baskets were and are widely known north of the Blue Mountain, but for a reason the originators could hardly have foreseen: for years upon years they have served as egg baskets for children at Easter. Of long, straight rye straw bound into tight coils—in earlier years by white oak fibers and later by raffia imported from Madagascar—their prototypes were the celebrated bread-raising baskets of the Pennsylvania Dutch Country—the part below the mountain. There, the housewife lined her baskets with clean white cloth, put the kneaded bread dough into them, covered the dough with another cloth, and set the baskets in a warm place for the dough to rise. Most such baskets are round; a few are elongated or oval.

The artistic quality of these rye-straw creations was discovered long ago, with the result that even in the practical-minded down-country they were finally moved from the kitchen to the living room corner cupboard. Some—but only a very few—were obviously woven "for fancy" in the beginning, since one of the upper coils is looped in the assembling stage,

*Old-time willow hamper of about one-bushel capacity. Such containers were used for dry storage of all kinds, from dried apples to carpet rag balls.*

*A quarter-bushel "tacked" fruit basket of Monroe County origin. Larger tacked baskets, widely used for peaches, were loosely referred to as half-bushel baskets, although the capacity was actually five-eighths of a bushel.*

with a pleasing resultant open-work effect. It is a fortunate collector, indeed, who comes upon one of these. Another method of embellishment was the use of a dyed binding splint at the rim of a basket. Baskets woven by the Indians frequently have colored splints or other decoration, and it is possible that non-Indian basket makers borrowed the idea.

How the rye-straw containers came to be used so widely for dyed "rabbit eggs" in the up-country may always remain a mystery—as much a mystery as a companion puzzle: who made them? There seems to be no record, whether journal, diary, log book, or bill of sale, which mentions the subject or gives any indication of local manufacture. The best guess is that they must have been homemade. Some old-timers maintain that they came from the general stores in the community, but can offer no suggestion as to where the stores got them. Their Topsy-like quality in no way invalidates them as antiques or collectibles; they were performing, in their own homemade way, their Easter duty at least as early as the 1880s.

Also used in the up-country are occasional goose-feather, carpet-rag, or dried-apple *schnitz* baskets with capacities up to considerably more than a bushel. These rye-straw containers for the most part seem to have come from down-country—as gifts, as part of a dowry, or possibly as antique shop purchases. Nowadays they may be minus their flat covers, but their owners treasure them, nonetheless. In spite of all the rye grown in the up-country counties, none of the straw appears to have been used in the making of baskets there—or, if it was used, the matter has been a masterfully kept secret.

The would-be restorer of a soiled, frayed rye-straw basket should heed a bit of advice: *don't!* Any moist cleaning agent will speed the disintegration of straw which has been subject to years of slow desiccation, and a dry cleaning agent will merely fill in the interstices in the straw and increase the dinginess of the object. Skillful work with linen thread of neutral tone will sometimes help to keep frayed ends in place, and now and then a strip of raffia can be cut to perform a minor repair job. Generally speaking, the collector does best to ignore inferior specimens and search out those which can be used just as they are.

### COLLECTORS LOOK FOR:

White oak baskets—all sizes and shapes

Drawshaves or drawknives. These are larger and often less finely detailed than spokeshaves, which were used on wagon wheel spokes.

*Schnitzelbanks* (working benches with foot-operated clamps)

Willow baskets, including occasional novelties such as handbags or bureau boxes

Tacked baskets of small size, especially those with local histories

Late oak or raffia baskets in novel shapes—pitcher, canoe, duck, etc.

Rye-straw bread baskets and Easter egg baskets

Large *schnitz* (or feather or carpet-rag) baskets

*Jackpot:* Loop-topped rye-straw basket in prime condition

# 18
# Fraktur

Peculiarly "Dutch" are early documents of various kinds combining print or script with fanciful colored decorations. These are known as *fraktur*, a word which stems from the Latin *fracturus*, meaning "broken." Since many of the larger or more ornate letters of the documents were done in a manner suggestive of what, in type, we call Gothic or Old English, the term is an apt one.

The subject of fraktur writing, of the kinds of decoration employed, and of the scriveners who produced it has been handled ably by writers who have made exhaustive studies in the field and whose publications have justly become famous. About the only reason for picking up the subject again is the fact that for the most part they stopped short of the up-country—and the up-country has its fraktur, too, as well as its scriveners and perhaps a few special touches not found elsewhere. In the impact of the Germanic and English-Irish cultures upon each other, the fraktur documents of the German-speaking element seem to have gone underground. Now, after years of forgetfulness or neglect, as they gradually come to light again, they have much of the charm of novelty, and "up-country fraktur" has almost the force of a brand-new term.

At this writing, it appears that there were fraktur writers only in Monroe County. One can not say flatly that none existed in Wayne or Pike, but in view of the fact that a great deal of all the fraktur we know was done by teachers in German-language schools, and that German-language schools existed in Monroe but not in Wayne or Pike, the chances seem remote. In cases in which the documents were not created by the schoolmaster, they were ordinarily done by the minister. As time went on, the efforts of the teacher and the minister were augmented, to a small degree, by those of others.

Fraktur writing must be counted as an art—a primitive or a pioneer art or, if one qualifies the term somewhat, a folk art—but an art, none the less, just as handwriting with flourishing has come to enjoy the status of an art. It derives from the manuscript illumination practiced in the monasteries in the Middle Ages—though there are those who give it even greater antiquity by bypassing the Middle Ages and insisting that it springs from the illumination found in the ancient Book of Kells. Whatever its origin, reduced to simplest terms it is almost always an attempt to beautify, usually with embellishments in color, an important vital record. In America, fraktur writing came over with the German immigrants and was practiced in the 1700s and 1800s; the "good" years—those in which the finest pieces were created—are considered to be from the 1770s to perhaps 1830, although fine pieces both earlier and later are known.

Just what records were important? There were a number: the combined birth-and-baptismal certificate, with its complete record of name, place, date, parents, sign of the zodiac, religious denomination, baptismal witnesses and officiating minister; the name plate in one's Bible, Testament, prayer book, or singing-school book; the elaborate copy of the alphabet—upper and lower case, both print and script—prepared by the teacher for a promising handwriting student; the title page (which was often the cover) of an important ledger or book; the house blessing; and the reward of merit, prepared by school or Sunday School teacher. In toto, these account for perhaps 80 percent of all the pieces of fraktur (loosely, one

*Title page of the general church book of the Zion's Lutheran and Reformed Church in Lower Smithfield Township done by the scrivener known as the Easton Bible Artist. Records in this church book start with the year 1798, but births as early as 1787 are recorded. (Courtesy of the Monroe County Historical Society)*

complicated initial capitals, first of all . . . and then scrolls, leaves, vines, angels, hearts, tulips, stars, the sun, human figures, clocks, buildings, and so on. Some are masterly in execution; others have been done by practitioners whose good intentions surpassed their skill.

It is not safe to state without qualification that an unsigned fraktur was written in a given place by a given person. Only a fraction of the scriveners ever signed their names; moreover, both teachers and preachers traveled widely during their careers, and a piece credited to a given village or county may actually have been done in a spot far removed. The difficulty of identification is accentuated when one recognizes that some writers apparently imitated the style of an earlier person whose work was much admired.

Fraktur writing has gone by the board now, but it died a slow death. In the beginning it was possible to have a hand-written birth-and-baptismal certificate for each child whose parents wanted one. (Not all religious groups and not all communities interested themselves in this kind of record. There is, for instance, no known piece of fraktur that may fairly be termed Moravian.) As time went on, however, and births multiplied, preprinted forms with blanks to be filled in with the appropriate vital statistics when the time came became available. To these were added a degree of handwork commensurate with the time someone—perhaps a member of the family—had to spend in adding embellishments in color. Eventually, even these "late" certificates gave way to colored lithographs, and finally to the strictly functional certificates we know today.

*The cover of a challenging little book—challenging in that the handwriting has been done by a number of persons. Members of the Youngken (Jungchen) family still live in Monroe County. Abraham, whose name appears in the illustration, is buried in the Delaware Water Gap cemetery. (Courtesy of the Monroe County Historical Society)*

just calls them "frakturs") known today. There are others—confirmation and marriage certificates; presentation pieces which have a minimum of wording or perhaps no wording at all; impromptu pieces, often done by children; family registers; book marks for hymnals or prayer books; and lesser pieces which frequently defy classification.

Originally, when one spoke of fraktur he had in mind the actual "broken" letters first of all, and the ornamental additions secondarily. It is seldom now that such a distinction is made; the total work is the fraktur. Cursive writing in exquisite early German script gives some pieces much of their charm, and frequently either takes the place of "printed" words or supplements them. The embellishing devices employed are as widely varied as the artistic inspirations of the men who created them. There are fancy,

*An outstandingly competent* Vorschrift *or specimen copybook bearing the name Georg Adam Roth and dated 1808. The Roths were a well-known family in Hamilton Township.*

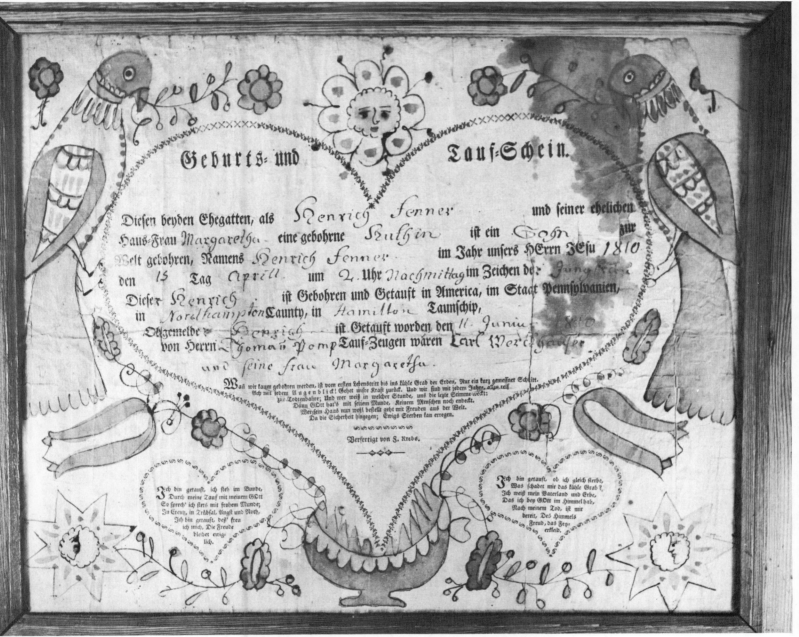

*Early birth certificate done by F. Krebs of Reading for Henrich Fenner, Hamilton Township, in the days when Hamilton was still in Northampton County. (Monroe County was created from Northampton in 1836.)*

Other forms of fraktur writing vanished, too, many of them before the birth-baptismal certificate. After the School Law of 1834, which made English the required language of instruction in the Commonwealth, there was no longer a need for the copybook model—the *Vorschrift*. Illuminated flyleaves serving as book plates in Bibles and New Testaments disappeared about the same time. Printed cards replaced the hand-drawn, hand-colored Rewards of Merit. (The words "reward" and "award" were used interchangeably.) The house blessing, a religious invocation ordinarily used as a wall hanging, was packed away and no new ones seem to have been created. Family registers as such were seldom kept in later years.

Not every type or subdivision of fraktur was created in the up-country—although perhaps one should not make a statement so positive, since only a few years ago it was assumed that there was no native fraktur of any kind north of the Blue Mountain. Most spectacular among the pieces which have now come to light are the *Vorschriften*. One of these, privately owned near East Stroudsburg, is not a mere page, as is often the case, but a complete booklet of eight pages. There are highly individual touches on the cover—tiny, leaflike insets in the broad members of the decoration, and six-pointed stars with one side of each point shaded. The remainder of the booklet is devoted to the letters, numerals, religious precepts, and quotations usually crowded together on a single-page *Vorschrift*. It was made for George "Schlotter" —originally undoubtedly spelled "Schlatter"—in 1820, according to the information set in the fraktur medallion on the cover. A comparable piece, but in less fine condition, owned by a collector in the West End, was made for Johan (John) Angelmeyer in 1816. An earlier one-page specimen, also privately owned, marked Georg Adam Roth, is dated 1805. All bear the words "Hamilton School" or "Hamilton Township."

The cover of a fourth *Vorschrift*, dated 1809 and made for Henrich Werckheuser, is in the possession of the Monroe County Historical Society. Most elaborate of the group in its ornamentation, it is distinguished by partial representations of Adam and Eve at upper left and right, by a lightly sketched quill pen and ink bottle at one side of the base, and by a hand holding a pen at the other. (A pen is held in the hand of a completely drawn male figure in eighteenth century costume, in the Angelmeyer fraktur.)

There is a feeling that all these pieces were created by George Adam Roth, whose name appears on one as a *Schreib-Schuler* ("writing student" or "writing school student") in Hamilton. "Roth" was a familiar name in Hamilton, and a Georg Adam Roth and his wife Catarina (Biesecker) were listed in the 1810 census. Eight of their children were baptized in the Hamilton Church between 1805 and 1820. Had Roth used the word *Lehrer* ("teacher") instead of *Schuler* ("student") the nagging question of authorship would have been settled long ago—but *Schuler*, used locally to mean anyone going to school, whether teacher or student, keeps the question of authorship open.

A very early schoolmaster in Hamilton noted for his fraktur writing was John Eyer (the name is sometimes given as "Oyer"), who lived from 1755 to 1837. Eyer is as much a legend, in a sense, as an historical personage; only two specimens in his handwriting are extant. One is an Award of Merit made for Catherine Arnold in 1804 and is privately owned. The other is a transcription of the Articles of the Hamilton Church and was placed in the cornerstone at the time of the rebuilding of the church in 1829. Eyer taught at Mt. Bethel before going to Hamilton Township, where he is buried.

In an entirely different technique is the title page of the Lower Smithfield Lutheran and Reformed General Church Book, the records of which start in 1798. Here, the floral decorations are blocky flowers set on short, heavy, curving stems, and the lettering is in careful but slightly irregular print. (Apparently the writer dispensed with guide lines.) At this writing, no one seems to know the identity of the scrivener, who a number of years ago earned the appellation of the Easton Bible Artist because of the double title page in the Michael Schlatter Bible in the First Reformed Church in Easton. The two performances are the unmistakable work of the same person, whoever he was. One by one, during the past few years, pieces by the Easton Bible Artist have been recognized, so that at the present time about twenty have been identified—but only one of them is in the up-country. Characteristic touches in these frakturs, in addition to the flowers, are corpulent trumpet-blowing heralds in knee breeches.

Of more than passing interest are the fragments of an arithmetic book done for Abraham Youngken in 1788 and 1789. In these early years, it was not uncommon for a zealous student to copy the contents of an entire textbook—for whatever reason, almost always an arithmetic—and thus create his own personal book. We do not know how extensive or how nearly complete Abraham's book was, or for that matter who did the beautiful lettering on the two partial pages which have come down to us. One guess might be that it was Abraham's own work, since practice

One of the rarities in fraktur: a piece printed in
Stroudsburg—and in English rather than in German.
The decorations are hand-done. The Henry and
Margaret Fenner whose (Anglicized) names appear
here are the Henrich and Margaretha of the 1810
fraktur shown elsewhere.

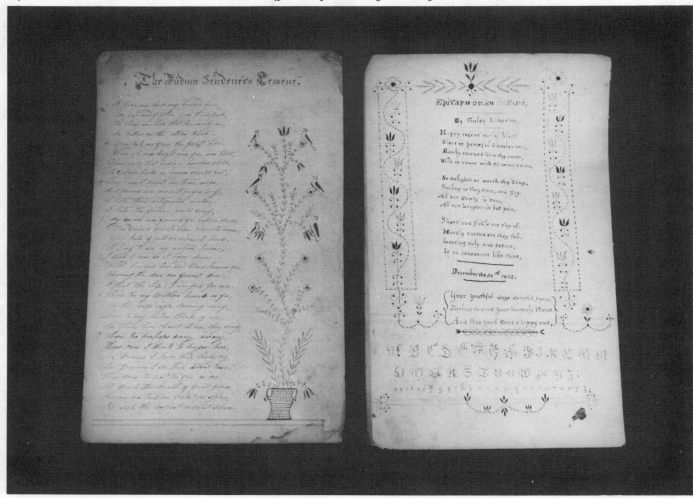

*An unusual combination—fraktur motifs with verse
of the so-called Graveyard School. The date, 1852, is
later than the time when most fraktur came into being.*

lines and finished copy appear on the same page. On
the other hand, there is a curious half-resemblance,
in the execution of the fractured letters "Abrah —,"
to the work of the Easton Bible artist. One is forced
to wonder . . . could Abraham, or another member
of the Jungchen (or Young) family—possibly John
Young—be the scrivener whose identity has been hidden all these years? Younken (from the German
*Jungchen*) is a name still familiar in the up-country
and in the neighborhood of the Stroudsburgs. Abraham (1775–1850) is buried in the cemetery at Delaware Water Gap. His arithmetic book—what remains of it—is in the possession of the Monroe
County Historical Society.*

* Since the above was written, a signed birth-baptismal
certificate of apparent Easton Bible Artist creation has been
discovered. The signature on this piece is that of a schoolmaster, one Johannes Spangenburg ( ? -1814).

A number of early pieces from the Fenner family
in Hamilton Township are in private hands. They include completely hand-done awards of merit, two of
which are especially noteworthy because of the eagle
which figures prominently in their decoration, and a
Friedrich Krebs certificate of 1810, recording the
birth and baptism of one of the Henrich Fenners. (A
Henrich John and a John Henrich Fenner appear in
each generation for a century and a half, to the perennial confusion or despair of the genealogist.) Friedrich Krebs was an early fraktur decorator in Reading.

Many birth-and-baptismal certificates of the preprinted or partly preprinted type are cherished in the
up-country. Like such certificates farther south, any
one bears a marked resemblance to any other in decoration, with a pair of angels and two pairs of birds
constituting the major ornamentation. The handwrit-

ing, cursive or "printed," ranges from the competent to the unquestionably beautiful. In this classification of fraktur, one certificate deserves particular mention—that of Simpson Angelmeyer (son of John, previously mentioned), who was born "March 30, 1836, in Pocono Township, Monroe County" at or near Tannersville. The certificate itself is not especially striking; what is noteworthy is the fact that Monroe County as such did not exist on March 30, 1836; it was not separated from its parent, Northampton, until April 1, 1836. It would not call for the services of a super-sleuth to explain that Simpson's certificate was purchased and filled in at some time after his birth—and of course after Monroe County had become an actuality.

Most of the certificates used in Monroe seem, by the evidence, to have been printed outside the county, with Reading, Allentown, Easton, Nazareth, and Bath well represented. A certificate printed in Stroudsburg is a rarity, and therefore, as one might expect, is considered especially desirable. Probably not many were printed. The job was done by the press of the leading local newspaper at the time, the *Monroe Democrat,* and the wording, while it followed the traditional formula, was in English rather than in German—not a popular touch. The single copy known to the writer, bearing the date of 1829, is in a private collection.

Over the years, many of the fraktur records which once formed a significant part of the memorabilia in old families of German extraction have been destroyed. To the uninitiated, only too often there appeared to be nothing of moment in the often amusing, frequently stained and damaged pieces, frequently folded and folded again until they came apart in the handling. By now, the situation has largely been subject to an about-face, and possessors of old papers often believe that they have a potential gold mine in something which is actually of little or no value. Lacking reliable information, they can hardly be blamed, and the situation is not remedied by saying that the person who, knowingly or unwittingly, once threw away a piece of John Eyer's fraktur might better have thrown away a fistful of ten-dollar bills. A naïve little drawing, with names and dates, may be just a little drawing with names and dates—but when it is old and genuine it may also be an historical document, a primary source; as such it is unique, invaluable, and perhaps beyond price.

### COLLECTORS LOOK FOR:

*Vorschriften* (handwritten, hand-colored copybooks, copybook covers, or single "master" sheets)

Detached pages, segments, or even fragments of *Vorschriften*

Hand-drawn and -lettered birth-and-baptismal certificates, whether or not they come from the up-country region. The wording usually begins *"Diesen beiden Ehegatten —"*; that is, "To this honorably married couple. . . ."

Printed birth-and-baptismal certificates. The wording usually begins as indicated above, but there is a heading: *Geburts- und Taufschein* ("Birth-baptismal certificate").

Marriage certificates (*Trauscheine*)

Confirmation certificates

Awards of Merit

House blessings (Look for the heading *Haus Segen.*)

*Geddelsbriefe*—usually of Catholic, European-German origin, these are hand-decorated sheets of paper used as wrappings for coins given by sponsors as baptismal gifts.

Bibles or Testaments with handwritten book plates, or the plates alone

Bookmarks

Hand-drawn and hand-decorated singing-school books (but although they are found south of the Blue Mountain, none has thus far been reported in the up-country).

Sunday School presentation pieces—often fanciful floral sketches

Lithographed birth certificates, including those of N. Currier or Currier and Ives

Family registers. Very often these were done on a blank page in the family Bible. A favorite spot was the sheet just before or just after the Apocrypha, between the two Testaments.

Any fraktur piece of any description, of Wayne or Pike County origin. (They may not be nonexistent, after all. Who knows?)

*Jackpot: Vorschrift* by Georg Adam Roth or John Eyer

# 19
# A World of Apples

A prospective buyer looks at a property in the sub-urbs, with the support of his wife and the advice of family and friends. If there is a tree on the place, it may tip the scales in favor of the sale. If, per-chance, this particular real estate development is one which has been created from an old farm, and if the tree should be a good-sized apple tree—well, our friend hasn't a chance. The broker will mention the shade; the wife will think of pies made from cost-free apples; Grandma will recall the ineffable fragrance of spring apple blossoms; the youngsters will talk of a swing—and the prospect, willy-nilly, will reach for his checkbook. There is something very special about an apple tree.

The probability is, however, that in a few years, while the shade, the blossoms, and maybe the swing will still have an appeal, our homeowner will stop one day in early spring at his garden-supply place, and buy spray and a sprayer—not to aid in the production of fine fruit, but to prevent the formation of any fruit at all. He will have taken this step because there is, in all truth, something very special about a lone fruit-producing apple tree in a suburban development: it is, oftener than not, an overwhelming nuisance. The fruit is edible in only very exceptional cases; the apples fall to the ground and rot before they are ripe; on the ground they attract, not the good old bumble-bee favored by the poets, but a myriad of unwanted and in some cases deadly stinging creatures; the leaves of the tree turn black and start falling in July or August; and the smelly, messy combination of dead leaves and trampled apples has to be raked up before every use of the lawn mower.

The chances of buying a lot with a good apple tree are not, of course, totally nonexistent; they are just very dim. Most "good" apple trees reached their ma-turity and then their old age years ago, were cut down and burned, and if replaced were replaced with newer "improved" strains—not where the original orchard was located. There is nothing wrong with a good new variety; that is, if one can duplicate the conditions which produced the good old variety. Even the complete amateur, however, knows that contem-porary patterns of storm sewers and drainage, the differing air current patterns produced by streetfuls of houses, and air and soil pollution of various kinds make the duplication of original conditions completely out of the question. (We are still talking of apple trees in a town or city—not making generalizations about all apple trees!)

The up-country once produced some of the best apples in the world—many of them. It still produces some, but not in the myriads of home orchards which once constituted a major asset of every home place. More are now produced south of the Blue Mountain, in the "real" Dutch Country, than north of it. Both north and south of this point of demarcation, more-over, the production is done in scientifically planned, operated, and controlled enterprises, on a scale which would have staggered our grandfathers. About the only phase of apple culture requiring the human hand is to hold the fruit if it is being eaten raw; the spray-ing, trimming, fertilizing, cultivating, picking, trans-porting, grading, and packaging are partly or wholly mechanized. There are eye-opening fruit operations at Mt. Bethel in the up-country which can be matched in skill and efficiency only by similar operations out-side Allentown or over in New York in Slate Hill territory. Fantastic quantities of beautiful, delectable fruit are processed and sold each year to satisfied customers, but . . . the present-day apple enterprise replaces a world of apples, of production, and of conditions vastly unlike our own—the days when the up-country had thirty to fifty varieties of apples, all flavorful, good to look at, and wanted, on even the most rocky, unprogressive farm.

To use a term which our forbears never knew, one would say that the up-country was apple-oriented. The thirty to fifty varieties just mentioned did not by any means represent all which would grow well in this particular area. As a matter of fact, S. A. Beach, in *The Apples of New York*, a study published in 1903 by the Department of Agriculture of the State of New York, noted that there were more than 700 varieties known to the experiment station of the Department in 1900. The territory covered in the study included not only New York but northeastern Pennsylvania, northwestern New Jersey, and sections of New England and southern Canada—a region of homogeneous climatic and ecological conditions. When one recognizes that for many of these varieties there were anywhere from five to a dozen additional designations by which the fruit was known, one begins to understand how a place could be apple-oriented.

Of the 700-plus names listed by Mr. Beach and his associates, there are probably fewer than half a dozen which would be recognized by the layman today—and even then he would probably not recognize the fruit. A person familiar with the farm and orchard operations of a half century ago might do considerably better, with at least a nodding acquaintance with forty varieties. Ironically, the kinds he can ordinarily buy at a wayside fruit stand today—Macintosh, Cortland, Red or Yellow Delicious—would not be included, since they had not yet been developed or had barely reached commercial production.

Trees in the home orchard were normally set out in straight rows, twenty feet apart in either direction—with allowance made for buildings which got in the way, or perhaps a spring, or a stone wall, or a winding lane. As often as not, only about three trees of each variety were planted, and those three did not necessarily stand next to one another. In consequence, the orchard, so called, comprised a rather scattered aggregation of trees—around the house and barn, in the pasture, in cultivated fields, and sometimes along the road. It should perhaps be noted that while much stock had been grafted before it came from the nursery, many farmers—or, at the very least, one or two in a community—were adept at grafting scions from the desired variety on young seedling stock.

A variety known to be "tender," like the Early Strawberry (one of the most spectacular-looking of

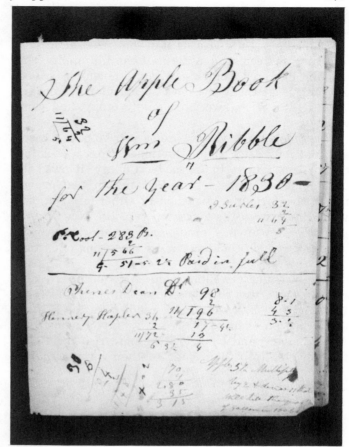

William Ribble, a man of many activities, had a cider mill in 1830 in Pahaquarry Township, on the New Jersey side of the Delaware. His little account book constitutes a typical record of apple sales and cider making. (Courtesy of the National Park Service)

all apples ever grown, with its pointed "strawberry" shape and vivid red-and-yellow striping) would probably be given a sheltered location. The Early Harvest, Red Astrachan, and Yellow Transparent would be planted close to the house for the convenience of the housewife who wanted an apronful in a hurry for apple sauce. These early maturing apples were rarely good for pie, since they tended to be sweet and rather soft. The Transparent was a notable exception; it was crisply textured and mildly acid—ideal for cooking or baking.

Once the August fruit had passed its prime, one kept his eye on such varieties as Vandevere, a small, flat, lightly striped green-and-red variety best eaten out of hand; the Early Bellflower, a tangy yellow variety which may eventually have been dropped from the roster because the variation in size of the fruit on a single tree was extreme; the Jersey Sweet, a large, juicy, unusually sweet but comparatively tasteless kind; and the Striped Rambo (or Seek-No-Further), which had a slightly viscous skin somewhat adversely affecting its keeping qualities. Of the fall apples, the brilliant dark red Tompkins King, oftener just called the King, was easily the most spectacular in appearance. It was crisp, sweet but mildly tangy, and very widely popular.

The Smokehouse variety seems to have been a casualty not long after 1900. Developed from a seedling on an Amish farm in Lancaster County, it owed its unimaginative name to the fact that it had grown up by the farmer's smokehouse! Other good apples which lost out in the long run were the Newtown—properly Newtown Pippin—and the Butter Apple, neither of which could survive a succession of bitter-cold winters.

An unfortunate-seeming name for a peculiarly distinctive apple was the Sheepnose—an elongated fruit with an over-sized core and a reddish purple skin so dark that one can easily see why farther north in New England and Ontario it is known as the Black Gilliflower. Aptly named as to their size were the enormous Pumpkin Apple, the Twenty-ounce Apple, and the Pound Sweet, all of them tending to retain a pale greenish color after they ripened.

Remembered pleasantly are the Fallowater, locally pronounced in a number of ways, including (at the top of the Poconos) "Foldy-Wolder"; the Rhode Island Greening; the Winter Banana (not quite the same as the fruit of the same name today); the Gravenstein; and the York Imperial, which came up from the Dutch Country. The York Imperial, incidentally, is probably the only apple in the country to have a monument erected in its honor. This monument stands south of the city of York, Pennsylvania, and calls attention to the importance of the variety—probably more widely grown than any other for commercial purposes.

Celebrated for their ability to survive winter storage were the Baldwin, the Northern Spy (but not the Northern Spy as we know it today), and several subvarieties of Russet. Equally good keepers but less widely popular in texture and flavor were the Ben Davis, Smith's Cider, and Jonathan. Farmers who disliked the Jonathan sometimes said disparagingly

*Three types of funnels: hand-spun pewter, with the top shown toward the reader; copper measuring funnel with one-quart capacity; and a machine-turned wooden specimen.*

that it made almost as good sawdust as a hemlock tree did.

Some varieties had been known for at least a century before Beach catalogued them. Dr. James Mease, whose *Domestic Encyclopedia* was published in Philadelphia in 1804, listed the Rambo, the Vandevere (known to him as Van de Vere), the Winesap, and the Newtown Pippin as being fine varieties. One wonders what kinds were grown in Smithfield Township back in 1727, when Nicholas Dupuis first set out his trees.

It is not always remembered that some varieties may reach a peak of perfection in one locality but fail to achieve more than mediocrity in another— often a matter of the length of the growing season. A point suggested by present-day pomologists to account for the fact that the quality of fruit on a given tree may decline as the tree grows older is that flavor is influenced by "trace" minerals in the soil. As these minerals are exhausted, the flavor of the fruit changes. Trace minerals, some known and some unknown, exist in infinitesimal amounts, and up to the present have not been very successfully provided by artificial fertilizer.

Farm families learned by experience which of their varieties would best suit specific needs. In many homes a bowlful of apples was brought up from the cellar during the evening in winter and consumed while the man of the house perused the almanac, Mother took up her unfinished sewing, and the children concentrated on—or wriggled out of—their homework. One bears in mind that apples were the only fresh fruit that many families would have, all winter long. While each family member was likely to have his own favorite, Fallowaters, Kings, Bellflowers, and Seek-No-Furthers were strong preferences as long as they lasted, while among the leftovers, if any, in April or May, Ben Davis and Smith's Cider would probably be found.

For making apple butter, varieties were chosen according to well established criteria: part should be sweet; part should be tart; all must cook completely soft as quickly as possible. Ideally, the cooked-down, concentrated cider in which they were processed, while it, too, was made from both sweet and tart apples, did not repeat any of the varieties put into it for cooking. Familiar combinations of apples were Kings and Pound Sweets; Bellflowers and Jersey Sweets; Fallowaters and Vandeveres. Sometimes a great many varieties were used, as long as the sweet-sour combination was kept in mind, both for the sauce and for the cider.

Cider mills came into existence in communities of any size as soon as apple trees reached bearing age. One of the more important early cider mill operations was the one conducted by William Ribble in Pahaquarry Township, across the Delaware from Shawnee. His little account book, entitled "The Apple Book of William Ribble, for the Year 1830," now preserved in a museum collection, details on the cover the amount of cider a farmer could expect from a given number of bushels of apples.

A widely known steam-powered mill was operated by Frederick W. Eilenberger in the Smithfield territory on the property of his father-in-law, Melchior Heller, Sr., in the 1890s. For the most part, cider mills tended to be in operation for only a few years— sometimes, it is hinted, by men with a fondness for their own product—and then to go out of business, usually leaving no records for posterity. Thus we have no accurate notion as to how many of the enterprises there really were.

Apples were cheap in early times. The going rate was 15 cents a bushel in 1813 for eating apples at John Turn's store in Smithfield Township; we do not know the variety—they were just "appels." Pippins, however, must have been rather special; Jacob Buss paid 30 cents for a bushel and a half of them. A barrel of "winegar" sold for $1.25 at the same store in 1830. Even young trees were inexpensive, by our standards; George Michael bought 20 trees at Turn's for $2.50 in 1828.

But to return to making apple butter: boiling down freshly pressed cider to the consistency of a very thin syrup in advance of the actual cooking of the apples lessened the amount of sugar which had to be added— if one chose the apples wisely. It was at apple butter time, too, that the housewife boiled down the cider she would need later in the year for mincemeat. The mincemeat cider was a little more concentrated than apple butter cider. It was bottled and corked while hot and would not, even after long storage, develop an alcoholic content.

Sweet cider which was intended for drinking purposes was never submitted to its recent indignity of an infusion of sodium benzoate. For "regular" cider, when the juice began to ferment it was allowed to develop its latent powers without outside aid. Not everyone liked hard cider, but among farmers there was a stated conviction carrying all the force of a folk proverb: "At the end of a day's threshing, there is nothing like a glass of cider to cut the dust in a man's throat."

Cider wanted for vinegar got a slightly special treatment. Only sweet apples were used, and sometimes a very little sugar was added in order to bring

*A time-ravaged transformer used to reduce the size of the bunghole in a barrel, to accommodate a spigot of smaller diameter; a bung starter, or heavy burl mallet with the wooden bung, still encased in its burlap lining, it was intended to dislodge.*

about an early fermentation. Once the fermenting period was over, the bungs were pounded tightly into the kegs or barrels and the whole matter was put into escrow, so to speak, for a year or two. Pound Sweets were a favorite vinegar apple.

A well-kept secret in the village of Shawnee was the particular combination of apples used for vinegar long sold in the village store under the facetious name of Shawnee champagne. The proprietor boasted that this special concoction was good enough to be served across a bar, and there were those of his customers who agreed with him.

While there is nothing to indicate that anyone ever became inebriated by the use of Shawnee champagne, there was an apple beverage, made privately throughout the length and breadth of the up-country, which had considerable potency. This was Cider Royal, which became a super-hard cider if one knew just when to add the extra ingredients called for, but which had to be thrown away if one guessed wrong. The extra ingredients were sugar, raisins, and whisky. They were put into the barrel after fermentation had begun, but before it had stopped. The barrel was then tightly closed and its contents allowed to meditate. It took longer to bring Cider Royal to maturity than it did just ordinary hard cider. This

specialty was considerably more expensive than ordinary cider—possibly depending upon the amount of whisky added. Jacob Buss paid $5.25 for a barrel of "cideroile" in 1829 at Turn's store.

The ultimate in an alcoholic drink made with apples was the liquid fire called White Lightning, Jersey Lightning, or something similar. This was a beverage distilled from hard cider and then distilled again to be sure that all the microbes were out, as the saying had it. While ordinary applejack could be sold legitimately, White Lightning changed hands privately and without the preliminary formality of revenue stamps. Its manufacture, oftener than not, was a family affair, with both the copper still and the esoteric formulas being passed from father to son. Some of it was made in little-frequented places in Pike County —though one wonders just how the entrepreneurs managed to convey the sizable quantities of hard cider they needed, through trackless woods to the site of the stills. The ancient mine holes at Pahaquarry, on the Old Mine Road along the Delaware in New Jersey, are said to have housed Jersey Lightning operations at one time.

Weird and wild are the stories told concerning the potency of "apple," as applejack is usually called locally. According to legend, apple rather than ether

*From Hamilton Township: a receptacle to hasten the drying of apple "schnitz" (sections) by placing it so that warm air could rise through the perforations in the tin bottom. The name of the owner, E. Berry, is clear, but the message "2 per day as long as I stay" seems somewhat cryptic.*

was used by early surgeons to anesthetize patients before an amputation; an open bottle of apple set on the threshing floor of a barn would do away with all the rats in the place; a half pint of apple poured into the Delaware at a time of high water would reverse the current; a swallow of apple would neutralize a copperhead bite—and two swallows would not only neutralize the bite but kill the snake.

One remembers the distinctive flavors and the aroma of apples of an earlier time with pleasure that is tinged with a little sadness. At the same time, he is compelled to recognize that the apples which have disappeared have disappeared for good reason. Some, as climatic conditions slowly changed over the years, could not adjust. Many of them could not develop an immunity to scale and other pests. Some would rot so early in the storage period that their marketability was jeopardized. An over-riding major consideration, of course, was the fact that some of them would not ship well. When the consumer was only a day's journey from the producer and the road

was rough, the juiciness of the apple and the thinness of its skin might matter only a little. But when repeated handling and a lengthy journey were involved, apples which had left home in prime condition might —and often did—arrive at their destination bruised beyond usability. The upshot of it all is that apples in the market now are first of all tough-skinned and reasonably immune to the rigors of transit; after that, they must look attractive. If, in addition, they taste good, so much the better.

As long ago as the 1870s orchardists concerned with developing hardy strains were importing varieties from abroad for experimental purposes. Some kinds at first seemed promising, but in the long run proved no more satisfactory than the others. Two Russian varieties persisted for a time. One was the Duchess of Oldenburgh, now no longer heard of. The other was the Red Astrachan, occasionally found up-country but as a rule only when someone, for auld lang syne, privately perpetuated a favorite old-timer by means of a graft on new stock.

COLLECTORS LOOK FOR:

Handmade apple pickers
Cider mill equipment
Bung starters (heavy wooden mallets)
Spigots
Funnels—wood, pewter, copper, or tin
Hand-whittled barrel stoppers
Kegs and casks with coopered staves
Handled, narrow-mouthed pottery jugs
Glass or pottery flasks, especially those with local labels
Cider pitchers of pressed glass
Cider tumblers—heavy, pressed-glass pieces, each with its equally heavy hand-grip
Copper implements or equipment from old distilleries
Horticultural books and fruit growers' catalogues and manuals, especially those with colored illustrations
Early grafting tools and equipment
Ornamental apples of painted wood or pottery
*Jackpot:* At a roadside stand off the beaten track, a gallon of cider made from local apples—and no added preservative!

# 20
## Sap Bucket to Maple Sugar

Almost everyone has a sweet tooth, and almost everyone does something about it. In degree, the gratification of the yearning for sweets may range from out-and-out indulgence to complete control, but in both extremes there is an acknowledgment of an innate craving, perhaps a need. From earliest times, in America, the settlers from Europe exercised their ingenuity or their skill in trying to provide something which would compensate for the sweetening agents they had left behind. They did their best to find honey; they boiled down the fruit of their apple trees to create a confection which could be used to sweeten other food. In the course of the years they were able to get sugar from the West Indies, but at the outset those islands might as well have been where they had originally been sought—at the other side of the world.

It was the American Indians who at some long-ago point in time discovered that maple sap, sweet in itself, became sweeter the longer it was boiled, and that an epitome of sweetness could be reached by evaporating all the water in the sap. This discovery they passed on to the colonists from Europe, along with other priceless information which kept the newcomers from starvation in their first years here.

With their meager equipment and primitive gear, the Indians could make but very little sugar. The colonists did better once they could settle down to serious production. Today it is northern New England which has the reputation for volume in maple syrup production, but boiling maple sap was a major spring occupation throughout the northern stretches of up-country Dutchdom for much of the nineteenth century and at least part of the twentieth.

As a matter of fact, a section of rough terrain in the Poconos looking down on Newfoundland or German Valley, according to where one is standing, has long been called Sugar Hill, from its extensive sugar bush. One of the first mentions of maple sugaring in the Poconos has to do with the time in 1779 when five young men in a settlement on the Wallenpaupac Creek went out into the wilderness to boil maple sap and were attacked by Indians. These men were Ephraim, Jephthah, and Silas Killam and Ephraim and Walter Kimble. Killam (now "Kellam") and Kimble are still familiar names in the vicinity.

In the 1790s, residents of what was to become Manchester Township in Wayne County sent President George Washington a gift of maple sugar. His polite letter of appreciation suggested that perhaps in maple sugar there might be a profitable business possibility which ought to be explored.

The first-growth maple trees of our ancestors have long since disappeared, and with the steady decline in extent of once far-reaching maple groves in Wayne and Pike counties, the annual flow of syrup has dwindled to a comparative trickle. Even so, there are a few sugar groves where great evaporators still operate, and where it is possible to buy syrup as good as Granddad's—and one hundred percent maple.

Not just any maple tree is good for producing sugar. "Soft" or swamp maples, with their silver-gray bark and fragrant clusters of tiny red blossoms in earliest spring, will yield sap, but only a little, and that little will not really be sweet. Farmers do not care much about soft maples in spite of their beauty; the wood is soft and branches are subject to much storm damage. Moreover, they rot easily, even saplings three to four inches in diameter often being rotten at the core. Nor are the ornamental maples good sugar producers. The gooseleaf or cut-leaf maples; the red-leafed maples; the popular Norway and other European varieties—all these have their virtues, but producing sweet sap is not one of them.

The hard maple is the sugar-producing tree, and among its sub-varieties the one known as the rock or sugar maple (*Acer Saccharum*) has no equal. Any forestry expert will tell one so . . . but he can not tell it to a Pocono Plateau farmer, who from long experience has formed his own opinion. North of Canadensis—in German Valley, Newfoundland, Greentown, Roemerville, LaAnna, Sterling, Paupac—the best

*Wooden sap bucket combining expert coopering with some equally competent whittling in the handle attached to the two elongated staves.*

*Shoulder yoke hand carved in German Valley in mid-nineteenth century. The sixteen-quart sap bucket, one of a pair, was made at a home forge about the same time. The sumac spiles are from Shawnee-on-Delaware.*

variety is the black maple (*Acer Nigrum*), which produces more and sweeter sap over a longer period of time than any other. Black maples seem to have a kind of gregarious tendency in that one may find a pronounced stand of them in a given locality, but none at all in places only a short distance removed. An entire sugar bush of black maple would be a rare possession indeed, but if any landowner presently has such a stand, he is not telling.

It is still possible to tap a maple tree on one's property by boring a three-inch-deep hole with brace and bit, angled upward, driving in a metal spile purchased at a country hardware store, and hanging a bucket on a hook attached to the spile. In fact, many people do it. Some even go so far as to tap a number of trees, collect the sap, and boil it down to the desired

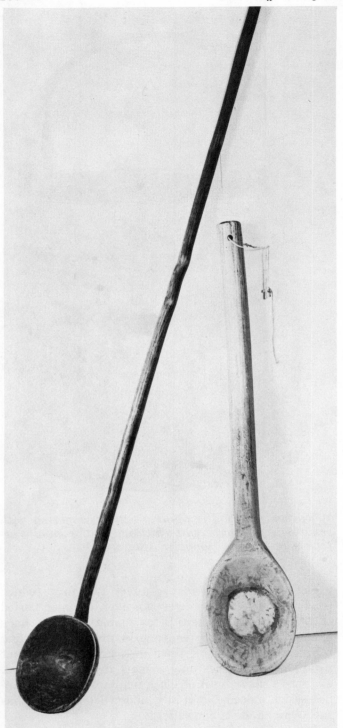

*Ladles for stirring maple sap during the boiling-down process. Each is whittled from a single piece of wood —curly maple in the case of the four-foot-long specimen at the left. Men good with a pocket knife sometimes worked on such ladles at night in the sugar works during the long hours of boiling-down.*

consistency on the kitchen stove. It is a long, slow process, though, and many are the backsliding enthusiasts who have sacrificed nostalgia in favor of a low-calorie synthetic purchased at the supermarket.

There is one exactly right time of the year to tap maple trees, and neither the farmer's almanac nor the signs of the zodiac, so useful in some other enterprises, can help in determining it. In the Poconos, there will be a warm day in late February or early March, following a hard freeze the night before, when the sun will start the sap running in the maples. One can not tell that it is running, just by looking at the trees, nor can he tell whether one day of warmth will be sufficient to start a steady flow of sap from root to outermost bud. A single warm day could be and often is followed by a real blizzard at this time of year—but the sugar maker gets his gear ready just the same. When the sap begins to run in earnest, it runs in flood tide, and the person who has dilly-dallied or guessed wrong is out of luck. Most often it is only the rank beginner who is unlucky; the experienced farmer has learned just about what to expect of his trees, and when.

Now and then a newspaper columnist makes a nomination for the meanest man in the world, usually after some reprehensible incident which gets wide publicity. In a hamlet in the Poconos, the pupils in a now long-gone one-room school would have had their perennial candidate for this title—the man who tapped the maples along the road in front of the school, a whole row of trees marching down the road all the way to his house. They were not his trees; they were on the right-of-way of the dirt road—but the sap buckets and spiles were his, and he claimed the sap. More than that, he made a point of complaining to the teacher whenever the wind detached a bucket or when it seemed to him that there was less sap than he had a right to expect. The pupils were not, to be sure, above taking a drink of the sap when they could do it undetected. At the same time, they felt that they were being victimized, and only the end of the sugaring season and the removal of the pails stopped the bickering that went on.

Today's mechanized, large-scale sugar-making operations, in which few functions any longer are performed by hand, have little charm for the person whose concern is the concentration on bygone procedures. The one-man or one-family operations of the up-country, however, along with the equipment used, have a considerable appeal for the researcher—and the collector of antiques. Let us see what was peculiar to the situation, starting at the tree. Nowadays, as we said before, short metal spiles are used, but traditionally the sugarworks tapper used foot-long sections of sumac, from a half to three-quarters of an inch in diameter, the pithy interior being burned out with a metal rod heated in the stove or at the forge. The channel thus created accommodated the sap, but tended to become clogged quickly. This difficulty was alleviated by exposing about half the channel to the air, through judicious whittling. The spiles were sharpened on the end to be driven into the tree, either with a drawshave or a pocket knife, and then firmly tapped into place. Sumac (often pronounced "shoemake") spiles lasted for about two years and then had to be replaced, since they tended to split once they had dried out.

Galvanized tin sap pails without handles but with circular cutouts so that they could be hung on hooks attached to metal spiles were commonplace after the beginning of the twentieth century. In earlier days, the sugar maker had a choice of two kinds of vessels —heavy homemade tin pails with capacities varying from ten to fourteen quarts, or coopered buckets made expressly for the purpose. These containers were not always hung from the tree but were mounted on flat stones just a little above the ground. Heavy in themselves, they were much heavier still when filled with sap, and would often pull a fastener right out of the tree. If there was any likelihood that they might be disturbed by curious wild animals, or even by cattle, protection had to be provided.

Sap was conveyed from the trees to the boiling place either by the use of a neckyoke and a pair of buckets as large as could be managed—twelve to sixteen quarts—or by means of a barrel. Since the terrain was ordinarily very rough, it was not always practical to utilize horses or oxen, but now and then a homemade device consisting of a covered barrel mounted on a stone sledge and drawn by a horse could be seen in the Poconos.

The neckyokes—more properly "shoulder yokes"— were expertly hollowed out of choice dry wood, by hand, and lasted for generations. If there is such a thing as up-country folk sculpture, some of these beautifully executed neckyokes would approach it rather closely. It could hardly be expected that the perfectly fitting yoke made by a man for himself would fit his son or grandson equally well; in consequence, some shoulder padding occasionally took place. As a general rule, though, it was a matter of pride for a man to wear the yoke "just so," no matter how uncomfortable he might privately find it.

The best carrying buckets had their own peculiar shape—wider at the bottom than at the top, for stability. Of very heavy tinned sheet iron, and reinforced

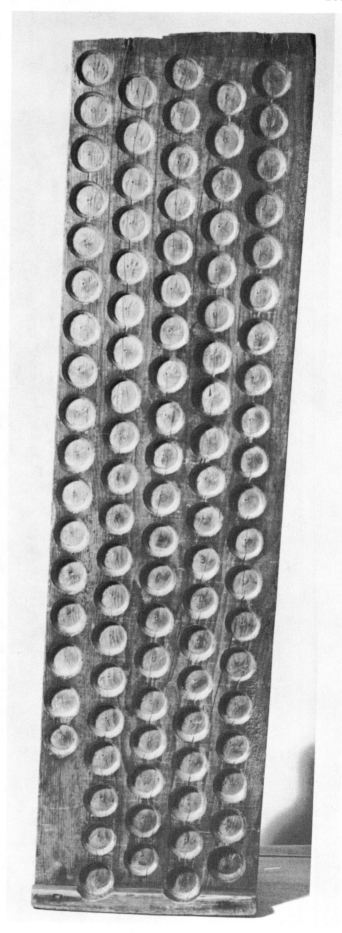

*Heavy slab with shallow depressions for molding maple sugar. (One wonders why the maker stopped at 96 instead of going on to 100.) Found at Trachsville, but not necessarily indigenous there. Two similar slabs are known, both in a down-country museum.*

*Fancy containers for individual cakes of maple sugar,
of wood blocks in northern New England and Canada,
were oftener of tin in the up-country. These tin containers were also used for baking.*

at the bottom with iron strapwork, they frequently represented the best efforts of the local smith, and, like the yokes with which they were used, were practically indestructible. The neckyokes were fitted with short sections of rope to which stout hickory hooks were attached. The heavy bails of the buckets were slipped over these hooks—and the carrier was in business. A degree of skill was called for in emptying the containers at the trees into the carrying buckets, since the buckets had to be kept in careful balance. Novices stopped being novices at the art of sap gathering when they were able successfully to work around the injunction of their elders: "Remember: It takes three hands to do the job—two to hold, one to empty."

The boiling place itself ranged from the primitive to the almost-comfortable in nature. The bare essentials were a supporting structure of stone or brick on which were mounted the sap pans—perhaps eight inches deep, three feet wide, and six feet long—and, like the carrying buckets, handmade; a supply of firewood; and barrels to hold the sap as it was brought in from the grove. Refinements were drafts, flues, and covers of some kind for the fireplace, and a shelter for the operator. Since the boiling lasted all day and well into the night when the sap was running well, lanterns were needed, too.

The normal procedure was to keep the pans boiling steadily, fresh sap being added as soon as there was room for it. Eventually, of course, the increasingly fragrant liquid in the pans began to take on the nature of syrup. At this point the fire was reduced somewhat and a long stirring spoon or paddle was put into operation to prevent burning. The final steps did not usually take place at the sugar grove. When the syrupy mixture had diminished to the point at which it could be put into the carrying buckets it was usually taken home, where the housewife completed the boiling-down on the kitchen stove the following day.

If the syrup was to be consumed at home, it could be cooked down to any desired consistency. If it was to go to market, however, it had to meet the standard weight of eleven and three-quarters pounds per gallon. In either case, if the syrup was to be clear and sparkling as it was poured over the morning buckwheat cakes, a clarifying process was needed. Usually a couple of eggs, broken into the kettle towards the end of the boiling period, shells and all, would attract any sediment which might have accumulated. The earlier in the season, the clearer the syrup would be, without artificial assistance. According to the degree of sweetness in the sap, anywhere from thirty to sixty gallons of sap were needed to produce a gallon of syrup.

The whole business might stop when syrup of the desired consistency had been achieved, or one could go a little further and turn the syrup into pale brown sugar. Maple sugar had to be made in small quantities at a time. With a little experience, the housewife could tell by the bubbling in her heavy iron skillet when the syrup was about to solidify. It had to be poured swiftly—into tin, iron, wooden, or pottery molds either especially designed for the purpose or normally used in some other capacity. Youngsters in the family were especially fond of a soft confection made by pouring over a bowlful of snow a large spoonful of syrup in the final sugaring stage. This glob of sweetness, in the Poconos, went by the inelegant name of bellywax. Equally loved by children were the hard crystals which would develop at the bottom of a container of syrup if it stood open for any length of time. Crystals would develop, too, if the syrup had cooked a little too long—but not long enough to become sugar.

For the antiques collector, the paraphernalia used in the total operation seems to have a fascination in which nostalgia can hardly play a part, since few persons now remember an operation which for the most part was going into a decline half a century ago. It would seem that sumac spiles, sap buckets, and neckyokes would have little charm for today's decorator-collector, but demands at antiques emporiums indicate that such is obviously not the case. It is easier to understand the charm of four-foot-long stirring spoons, skillfully carved from a single piece of wood and whitened from immersion in boiling syrup, and of the iron-bound buckets, the finest of which had covers with a raised decorative motif—a favorite being a star.

The attractiveness of maple sugar molds needs neither apologist nor spokesman. Molds made for maple sugar and nothing else are usually carved out of blocks of close-grained wood, either singly or in tandem; that is, a number of differently shaped depressions in a single slab of wood. It would be romantic to call attention to the heart-shaped wooden molds presently found in antique shops as typical of Dutch Country artistry—romantic but probably not true; most of them come from Canada, as do those of tin with a wooden base. Of foreign provenance also, so far as we can tell, are the "house" molds which one sees rarely. Other wooden molds were used for maple sugar, too, but they were usually borrowed from such operations as candy and pastry making. Often they were European in origin—Dutch and Belgian, in particular.

"Real" maple sugar molds in the up-country were the heart-shaped so-called Moravian mint tins; small individual tin molds with ornamental figures of flowers, fruit, animals, etc.; sets of fancy muffin tins in shapes of hearts, stars, butterflies, and others; cast iron gem pans; and, for larger units, pudding molds and fancy-shaped cake tins.

It may be that the attractive bite-size maple sugar candy so temptingly packaged and sold as a regional specialty today is as good as the kind once ladled from a heavy iron skillet at the back of a wood-burning kitchen stove into a row of battered small receptacles. It may be. It may be—but if nostalgia has anything to do with flavor there is just no comparison at all.

COLLECTORS LOOK FOR:

Handmade sap-boiling pans

Iron-bound heavy tin sap-carrying buckets

Wooden (coopered) sap buckets. Some of the oldest of these have one elongated stave, with a hole bored near the top so that the receptacle could be hung on the tree.

Long-handled one-piece wooden sap pan ladles—two to four feet in length

Handmade wooden spiles

Neckyokes

Individual maple sugar molds in pottery. Some of these may originally have been used for marzipan.

Cast iron gem pans

Muffin pans

Moravian mint tins, heart-shaped tins, and patty pans

Wooden molds in fancy shapes. These are often of Canadian origin, especially if they have a cross carved in the bottom.

"Tree" books which have a section devoted to maples. Especially sought for: *Pennsylvania Trees*, Joseph S. Illick, Pennsylvania Department of Forestry, 1923.

*Jackpot:* Maple-sugar slab—a single short plank with auger-started hand-cut depressions—up to a hundred in one plank

*Highly desirable in this type of spatterware (variously known as stick spatter, kitchen spatter, sponge spatter, and design spatter) is the bowknot design. The so-called Adams rose supplies the finishing touch.*

*Pipsqueaks, generally termed squeak toys. Some were imported from Germany, but many, including these, appear to be of American origin.*

*A "primitive" portrait of Bertha Solt as a little girl, done by a family member, a West End artist.*

*Seldom do Chinese ("Chinee") rice straw baskets receive the special touch of wool embroidery seen here. Ribbon decorations were not unusual, but have seldom survived.*

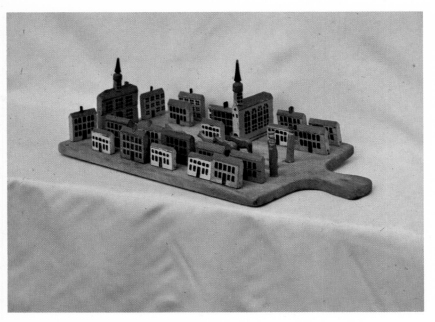

*Watercolor "painted" components of a toy village. Similar buildings are now being imported from Europe—and others are being made in down-country Pennsylvania.*

*Sunflower decoration on a butter crock probably made in Easton, perhaps at the Daub pottery, which occasionally used this design. The sunflower may be considered rare.*

*Lacking an actual signature, little slipware can be attributed beyond cavil to a particular potter. What evidence there is, however, strongly points to these pieces as being the work of Rudolph Drach.*

*This curly maple bureau box, colorfully ornamented in the Victorian tradition, bears the name of Harriet D. Fenner. The Fenners have long been a well-known family in Monroe County.*

# 21
# *The Honey and the Comb*

In the correspondence of the Reverend Mr. John Heckewelder, the Moravian missionary, there is a letter, dated 1811, written by his friend, John Arndt, of Easton. Arndt had something extraordinary to relate: it seems that four men—John Place, Barnet Walter, Henry Shoemaker, and Joseph Michaels (Michaels was only 14) had gone out on an expedition to try to find honey. Their quest took them to the top of the mountain at the Delaware Water Gap. The letter says nothing more about honey, but we assume that the search was abandoned for the time being because of the discovery of an unusual cairn of stones. Closer investigation revealed a skeleton and a number of artifacts which seemed to indicate that the exposed burial place was that of an Indian.

Heckewelder was a friend of man—and man included Indians. Arndt was conveying information he knew would be of interest to his friend; the mention of honey was incidental. We are concerned with the honey at this point, and *Indians* are incidental. It has frequently been said that there were no honey bees in America before the white man brought them; in fact, an Indian designation for honey bees was "the white man's fly." Had the white man brought honey bees to America and to the Delaware Water Gap this early—and had a swarm or more of them taken to the wilds, as bees will do? Or were there honey-making bees here, despite what the early chronicles tell us? Almost certainly there were, but it might be difficult to prove it.

There are stories—and they could hardly all be apocryphal—about hollow trees and wild honey, from very early times. It has been suggested that it was the Indians who taught the white man how to find a bee tree, survey it well by day to ascertain the open-

ings used by the bees, and then, stopping up all but one hole or fissure by night, smoke the bees to a state of asphyxiation or death, usually the latter. Then the tree would be cut down and the honey removed. Sometimes, it is said, the tree was cut down first—but that was after the colonists used a saw for the purpose. History does not tell us how the colonists eluded the bees while the tree was being sawed down—nor does it mention the fact that wild honey often has little to recommend it beyond the bare fact that it is sweet.

The need for sweets, to be sure, was something ever present among the pioneers. In the early 1700s, in the settlement in Smithfield, one of the surprises awaiting visitors coming up from Bucks County was the presence of apple trees, much larger, it was averred, than those in the Philadelphia area. (Had the visitors but known it, the Smithfield area was settled before Penn's Commonwealth took shape. There was no communication between these settlers, who had ventured down the river from Kingston, and the Quakers of Philadelphia. Largely Dutch in extraction, the Smithfielders neither knew nor cared what lay to the south of them; the English were equally unconcerned about what lay to the north.) The presence of apple trees did not mean that the Dutch were unusually fond of apples; it did mean that they had, in apple juice and in cooked-down fruit, something to satisfy their sweet tooth.

Visionaries among westward-moving pioneers in Pennsylvania and Ohio planted apple seeds, and often followed up by transplanting the apple seedlings later, so that those who came after them might have, if not sugar, at least something sweet. A thick paste of boiled-down fruit, often plums, in Europe, was once known by its Latin name, *electuarium*. Some linguists believe that the Pennsylvania Dutch term for apple butter, phonetically spelled "latwaerrick," or sometimes "latwerg," derives from *electuarium*. Not only the word but the article itself suggests the European confection. It might be noted that apple butter made from very sweet apples and cider would be over-saccharine for most tastes today.

The sugar trade with the West Indies began to meet the needs of the seaboard colonists very early—but in the backwoods the principal evidence of that trade for many years was rum, which is made from sugar cane. Whoever imported bees from abroad—or domesticated native bees, an achievement which seems somewhat debatable—then performed a notable service.

In Monroe County, Philip Miller was evidently marketing honey as early as 1819; the store ledger of John Turn in Smithfield Township credits him with 50 cents for a half gallon in that year. The same ledger records a transaction in 1833 in which Jonathan Mann bought a bee skep and hive for 50 cents. (A "skep" might mean either a swarm of bees or a hive for a swarm; here it appears to have been the swarm.)

We have little evidence as to when honey was first

*Honey is now normally marketed in clear glass containers—but light was once thought to jeopardize both the keeping qualities and the attractiveness of all kinds of sweets. Opaque jars like these were therefore pressed into service whenever possible.*

*A never-used rye-straw and oak-splint beehive. A hive of this type, less durable than those of wood, would be set on a low table.*

produced farther north in Pocono territory, but Daniel Schoonover (1796–1880) was among the early beekeepers. He "kept bees and had honey" in what later was to become Honesdale. We pass from such offhand notations to fact in the case of Sidney Coons. In 1857, Coons (probably originally "Kuhns," since he was of German stock) and his four sons were in the honey business—not producing just a little for home use, but enough that the endeavor took a considerable amount of their time. The apiaries of the Coons family were near Honesdale, and the honey was shipped to Philadelphia and New York. In 1855, they sold 35 tons—70,000 pounds.

Bees at first were sheltered in log or conically shaped hand-wound straw hives. The straw hives were picturesque but not very durable, soon giving way to box hives. Honey produced in box hives was known as cap or box honey. To get the honey out, the producers stupefied the bees with sulphur smoke—often, unfortunately, with high mortality for the bees. Two different men are credited with improvements which may actually have been identical: Coons, who "invented hives from which honey could be removed without disturbing the bees," according to the record, and George W. Leonard, who perfected a "movable comb hive" in 1867. It was Leonard who imported Italian bees—smaller and less even-tempered than other honey bees of the time.

The producers of honey knew to the day when a given variety of honey—named for the plants or trees

*The proverbial industry of the honey bee was as popular a theme in Pennsylvania as it was elsewhere—even in chapbooks like this hand-colored specimen from the attic of an old farmhouse in Hamilton Township.*

from which it was gathered—would be ready for the bees to harvest. In the northern up-country, the chronological progression in bloom was as follows: willow, the alders, soft maple, hard maple, wild cherry, cultivated fruit (pears first, then cherries and apples), dandelion, wild gooseberry, sorrel, and raspberry. These were light-colored honeys. They were followed by sumac, milkweed, basswood (linden), buckwheat, goldenrod, and aster—the dark and more full-flavored honeys. There was little overlapping; the bees took the flowers as they came, storing each new flavor in cells adjacent to what had gone before. (Knowledgeable farmers today will not plant sweet corn and cantaloupes in close proximity; they flower at the same time, and bees will pollinate one and ignore the other. It is usually the cantaloupes which suffer; the sweet corn, being taller, is likely to get first attention.)

Incidentally, two presently well-known flowers or flavors are conspicuously missing from the north-county list—clover and alfalfa. Clover, one of the mainstays in Monroe County, was grown but little in the sections to the north at the time the name "Coons" was all but synonymous with "honey." Alfalfa came even later. It is interesting to note that the honey from sweet clover, which somewhat resembles alfalfa in growth but is completely unlike ordinary red clover in appearance, is markedly similar to alfalfa honey in taste and appearance. There may well be specialists in the flavors of honey today; in fact, it would be strange if there were not. It is doubtful, though, in the very nature of things, that there are many who can tell, at a single taste, just what flowers gave a given honey comb its distinctive flavor. Among our ancestors, however, there were those who could, either from long experience or because of an extraordinary set of taste buds. The professional taster of coffee or tea, at least as we hear it from old-timers, had nothing on the skill of the expert in honey flavors.

For the average buyer, honey is honey; he is seldom likely, especially with today's commercially prepared product, to know one kind from another. In rural areas, though, and not very long ago, buyers were likely to specify the flavor they wanted, and it was up to the producer to get that particular variety, before the bees began adding what came next in the progression. We are speaking of comb honey, here, and comb honey is less popular now than it used to be. Rendered or extracted honey, attractive in appearance and easy to handle, seems to have comparatively few nuances in flavor.

Honey production, with the single exception of the

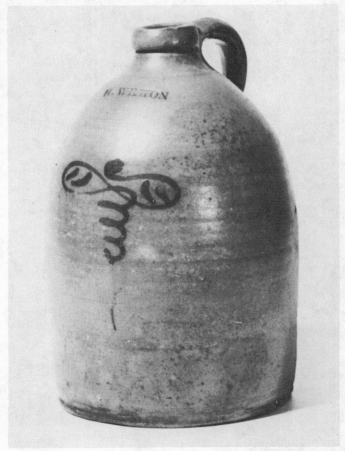

*The bee was used variously as a decorative device—even on gray stone pottery. Would it be too far-fetched to suggest that this design would be appropriate to identify a jug containing metheglin?*

Coons family, was for the most part a small, home operation. Many, perhaps most, homesteads at one time had a hive or two of bees, especially if the owner happened to have an extensive fruit orchard or—in much of Pike County, where the growing season was short—large plantings of buckwheat.

According to an early historian, while the bees, generally speaking, could harvest about all the honey the various flowers produced, there was one plant with which they could not cope—the wild raspberry, which grew in such profusion in the far-flung clearings or slashings which resulted from lumbering operations that the nectar simply dripped on the ground and "tons of it yearly went to waste."

Wherever honey was produced, its accompanying product, beeswax, also found a ready sale. As early as 1868, Abel Staples, in Monroe County's Cherry Valley, was receiving 37½ cents a pound for his wax.

*Scratch-carved Easter egg with beehive decoration, dated (on reverse) 1864. Bees in the swarm about the hive do not show clearly in the illustration.*

*The beehive design on a spatterware cup. Up-country spatterware is rare, but does exist.*

The store ledger which records the fact makes no mention of honey. Wax was widely used in the processing of leather goods, including harness and shoes. Even today there are those who maintain that for household cleaning or polishing there is no commercial product which can equal beeswax dissolved in turpentine.

Farther south, in the Dutch Country proper, yet another by-product of honey once enjoyed considerable popularity. This was mead, made from fermented honey and water. One does not exempt the up-country from the possibility of mead production; there just seems to be no record, either of its making or its use. Almost the same statement can be made of distilled mead—metheglin; almost, but not quite: there is a single, isolated reference which should probably be noted. Aaron Dupuis's ledger of 1783 credits an unnamed person with a pint of "mathiglen," taken in exchange. Generally speaking, this was a rum-drinking age; there are more notations of sales of rum in Aaron's ledger than for any other single commodity. How the metheglin came to be there is at best a matter of conjecture. Perhaps someone had put a supply of wild honey to this use; or perhaps, in spite of the fact that available records are so silent on the subject, there really was an abundance of honey in Smithfield all the while!

### COLLECTORS LOOK FOR:

Wooden beehive models of various types, especially those of apparently early date
Coiled straw beehives
Pottery honey jars with wax-sealing tops
Blue-decorated stoneware with bee or beehive design
Pressed glass honey dishes
Cut glass honey dishes and jars
Cakes of beeswax. Country auctions are sometimes a source of beeswax.
Old commercial honey containers
Buttons with bee motifs
Nineteenth century hand-colored chapbooks having to do with bees, flowers, birds, etc.
Spatter, stick spatter, and other tableware with beehive pattern
*Jackpot:* Yellow spatterware cup and saucer with beehive decoration

# 22
## Berrying: Pail to Preserve

Just as there was a closely observed progression in the times when flowering plants, shrubs, and trees came into bloom—a matter of importance to the honey producer—there was a progression in the maturation time of wild berries—a matter of comparable significance to the housewife. It was not a case alone of preferring wild strawberries or raspberries to cultivated cherries or pears, which were introduced to the up-country very early; it seems to have been the fact that the berries were there, free for the taking, and a goodly supply of the fruit, at first dried in the sun but later preserved in pottery or glass jars, was an indication of thriftiness understood by every woman in the community.

If a woman canned a hundred quarts of cherries, it was because there happened to be some very productive cherry trees on the place, and the credit to her was no more than normal approval like that accruing from having a clean house and a neat dooryard. If she "put up" a hundred quarts of wild strawberries, however, the accomplishment was of interest to the entire negibhorhood; an unusual degree of industry and of patience went into such an achievement. The fact that the strawberry plants either grew or did not grow in a given location and that, as in the case of the cherries, one had the raw materials handy or he did not, was not especially significant. It was the effort expended on the unusual which was important.

Children did much of the picking of berries. It goes without saying that the greater the number of children of berry-picking age in any one family, the greater the advantage in the annual race to see who would emerge as berry-picker-of-the-year. Since early families tended to be large, the handicaps were usually minor although, if there were a mere two or three youngsters to tackle the problem, the adults would usually help. The larger the family, the greater the quantity of food needed, of course; so perhaps everything came out even in the end. Actually everyone physically able to do so would "go after" especially desired wild berries. To say "I hear Margaret—or Alice, or Catharine—isn't picking raspberries this year" was a less than completely subtle way of saying that the lady was expecting, that the confinement was imminent, and that she therefore had a good reason for not joining in the berry-canning marathon. A merely minor indisposition of course would not keep one away from the berry harvest.

Earliest were the strawberries, which seemed to thrive best on gentle slopes facing south or southwest. Often, as a farmer increased his acreage, fields cleared in the past but less productive than had been expected were allowed to become grassy pasture. For the first two or three years, normally, the grass might still be mowed; after that, the field became a part of the permanent cattle or sheep pasture. Whether or not strawberry plants started to grow in the undisturbed ground would depend on whether or not seeds were carried and dropped by the birds. Once a good stand had been established, however, the plants would spread like wildfire into adjacent hayfields—and many an irate farmer had to choose between having his growing hay tramped down so that the scythe could hardly pick it up, or have his wife lose her chance at the strawberry championship for the year.

This matter of fantastically yielding fields of strawberries, or a complete dearth of them, defies prediction and appears to elude reason. It still goes on—in Monroe, in Wayne, and in Pike. One year an aban-

*Jams and jellies were often put into preserving jars like the dark-glazed redware pots on the outside or the one of stone in the center. The usual seal was melted paraffin, poured around the lid.*

doned field or an unused pasture will have nothing at all or nothing to speak of; then, for several years, it will be knee-deep in berries, so to speak. Similarly, a long-abandoned tract partly grown up with sumac and poison ivy will suddenly come into lush productivity. The irony of the whole matter is that few persons are concerned with gathering wild berries now. If they are interested in berries at all, they rely on cultivated varieties. As for canning—one wonders what even the largest, hungriest family today would do with a hundred quarts of canned strawberries; and if there is any competition it may lie in seeing who can boast of the largest and most up-to-date deep-freeze unit.

Perhaps it is unnecessary to observe that wild strawberries have a piquancy of flavor which few if any of the cultivated strains can match. Even so, among wild berries there are innumerable variations, not only in flavor but in shape and size, to say nothing of the fact that some will separate easily from the stem while others are unusable because the berry is destroyed in the stemming process. Seemingly peculiar to the cooler sections of the up-country—German Valley, Sterling, and points north—is a small white alpine-type strawberry which grows in the shade. Farmers who first observed its conical shape called it the sheep's-teat strawberry. It tastes unlike any other of the strawberry family, including the cultivated

White Bunting which once was a specialty, we are told, in the vicinity of Bethany. The Bethany berry, incidentally, is not native to its Wayne County habitat; it was imported from New Jersey in 1803 by a Mrs. John Bunting.

One might say that strawberries—preserved, in jam, or in pies—have enjoyed almost universal popularity. An exception to the rule comes to mind in the case of a Hamilton Township matron who would use the berries only if they were raw; heating, she maintained, not only destroyed their flavor but made them inedible!

Another ground-hugging berry of considerable popularity where it grew well was the dewberry. Something like the blackberry in shape, it grew on runners or vines which in a few years choked out almost all other growth in the fields in which it took hold. Farmers were prone to let it grow around rail fences or stone walls and in rocky places. Elsewhere it became a pest hard to eradicate. Dewberries grew luxuriantly in Monroe, and still do if they are given a chance. Farther north, while the vines will grow, they seldom produce edible fruit. Dewberries were canned or used for pie.

Cranberries demanded one particular kind of growing condition and would flourish in no other. What they needed was a sandy marsh, slowly evolving into dry land. The soil had to be acid, and the berries would grow best in a condition somewhere between actual sunshine and light shade. The upland bogs in and about the Pocono Plateau were well suited to the purpose. Many were accessible only around the edges, since tilting grass hummocks and lurking quicksand were an ever-present menace to the picker who found the biggest berries just beyond his grasp. Farmers and others averse to the idea of making a trip into the cranberry barrens were prone to point out that this terrain also produced the biggest and most dangerous snakes to be found in Pennsylvania.

Cranberries were not ordinarily picked by hand. A deep scoop with a comb-like edge was used to strip the berries from the low bushes into a large container. Of course, a considerable quantity of rubbish was gathered at the same time, but since cranberries were firmer than any other kind it was easy to remove the dirt and leaves afterward. Cranberries did not achieve popularity in earliest times because of their sourness; if there were no available sweetening agent, they might be hard to market today. It seems safe to say that most of the cranberry crop in Pennsylvania came from the upland area north, east, south, and west of what we have noted elsewhere as the Shades of Death country, territory known locally simply as "The Cranberry."

*Tin pie peel; a slip-decorated redware pie plate; and a pair of wooden tongs used to remove a hot pie from the oven. (Wooden tongs were probably used oftener for pies baked in tin plates than those baked in pottery. Pottery and pie made a heavy combination.)*

So early in the spring that its almost formless white flowers stand out sharply against the stark winter brownness of other trees, the bush called Juneberry, June cherry, or shad bush demands attention. It is not really a tree, although it may reach a height of 20 feet and a circumference of three or four inches, any more than it is a bush, since it has one recognizable bole and a minimum of shoots or suckers. Its fruit is sweet and mild-flavored—pink when it is at its first stage of edibility and a dull red or purple at its best, about three days later. It will grow on rocky, exposed elevations, but produces better fruit when it is found in better soil. Few people nowadays have a chance to learn to know the Juneberry, since the wild birds leave little or nothing for them to taste. It was never a very important fruit but, in Pike County, children gathering the earliest low blueberries liked to go home with the tops of their pails crowned with pink Juneberries.

Like cranberries, blueberries (almost universally called huckleberries in the up-country) started out as a product of the wet wasteland at the top of the mountain. One went to the barrens to pick them, and "barrens" is an apt name. Under foot was the bog; hip-high were the cranberry bushes or other low growth; at shoulder level and on up to a distance of eight feet or so were the huckleberry bushes; at widely spaced intervals stood the stunted pines which grew to a height of ten or twelve feet and then died, and the equally stunted scrub oaks at which one sometimes took a second look to determine whether they were alive or dead. For mile upon mile, this unchanging prospect was what the berry picker faced, and unless his sense of orientation was perfect he blazed a trail as he went into the barrens, in order to find his way out again.

In the course of time, huckleberry bushes spread to pasture fields, the edges of cultivated areas, and any abandoned place which had more than a trace of moisture. Elderly men unable to do a thorough job of farming in their later years and without sons or other help to carry on, soon found their acres becoming, whether they liked it or not, a huckleberry preserve. For a few years they would be able to capitalize on the fruit if there were enough people willing to pick it for a modest fee per quart, but it was only a matter of time before the forest once more moved in to crowd out the berries and claim its own.

There is undoubtedly a wider range of flavor, color, and size to be found in huckleberries than in any other wild fruit. The picker who found a "good" place —that is, one with many bushes from which to choose, would often have his criteria in mind and make a sortie from bush to bush, tasting as he went, before getting down to the business of filling his ten- or twelve-quart pails. A typical set of qualities might be the following: color, pale blue; size, approaching that of a small cherry; shape, flattened rather than round or pointed; flower-end tip, completely smooth; flavor, sweet but mildly acid. Add to these the fact that only heavily loaded bushes would be touched; that the berries must grow on the outside of the bush rather than within it; that they be so situated that one needed neither to stretch nor to stoop: that they come from the bush completely free of their individual stems; and that all the berries in a single cluster be equally ripe—all this, and one had a "good" picking situation.

Young pickers were often advised to find a good bush and eat their fill before they started the serious business of filling their pails. The advice seems to have been sound. Another admonition was that they should fill one of the pails with water, since the prospect of finding drinking water in the barrens was nil. Those who ignored the advice were usually sorry, since huckleberry-picking weather is hot weather.

Losing one's pail was said to be a beginner's fault— not the two-quart pail suspended from a strap around the shoulders or the waist but the larger vessel into which the smaller one would be emptied. One had to keep both hands free in order to pick at all, and a suspended small pail was a necessity since there was seldom a place to set it down. However, grown-ups not too sure of their sense of direction lost pails sometimes, and one of the most painful experiences a berry picker could have was to face—empty-handed—the almost certain derision of his companions.

Competition became inevitable. It was always a matter of pride to have one's own pail or pails filled first. Sometimes a loyal younger brother or sister who could not hope personally to excel would surreptitiously add to the level in the "big" pail. On the other hand, one of the most abysmal sins anyone could commit was to steal from a competitor, even if he saved the berries and restored them later.

The journey from inside the barrens back to the place which would mark the beginning of the homeward trek was fraught with peril. While one liked to return with pails heaped high, the path was nonexistent or rocky or boggy—one condition as bad as another—and one good stumble . . . well, both pride and berries would go with the fall.

Raspberries grew wild over the top of the Poconos and down their slopes largely according to activities of the lumbermen. The first year following a lumbering operation, what grew in the slashings was principally the seedling crop of whatever trees had been cut. The second year, however, the first berries came in, the seeds of course carried by birds. The third year marked the beginning of about a five-year period in which berries grew in almost unbelievable quantities, the rank canes, often ten to fifteen feet long, crowding out everything but their own exuberant growth.

The black variety, oftener called blackcaps than raspberries—and actually thought of as a variety independent of the raspberry family in many cases—were of enormous size, at least as compared with the berries of today. They were often dried. They would normally be spread out one-deep on trays and exposed to the sun. A preferred place was the top of the grape arbor near the back door. Dried blackcaps were used for pies in the winter time, alone or in combination with dried apples.

Red raspberries seem always to have been highly esteemed except, perhaps, by the children who picked them. More than any other wild fruit, raspberries tend to crush easily, and the berries which youngsters found so beautiful at the time of picking often became

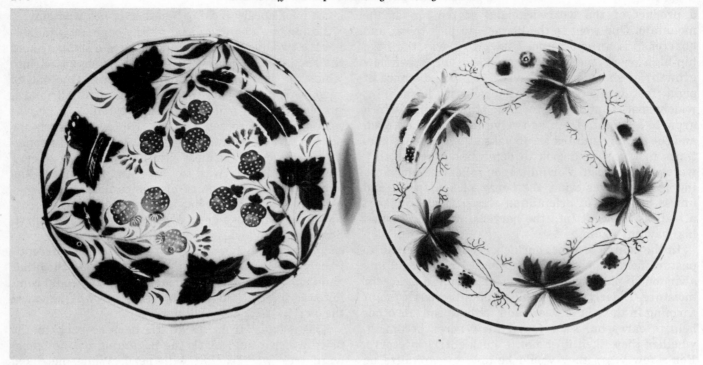

*The blackberry and the strawberry as depicted on
Gaudy Ironstone plates—used, as one might suppose,
only on very special occasions.*

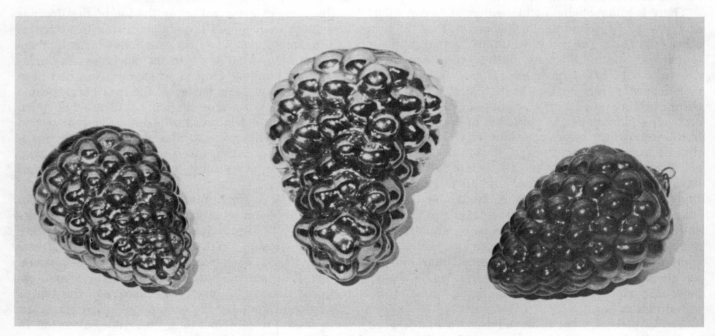

*Bunches of grapes have long been popular as art
motifs. In heavy molded glass of green, gold, and
blue, they made well-liked Christmas tree ornaments.
They are being reproduced today, oftener in pale colors than in the deep jewel tones of the old glass.*

a sodden red mass during the rough trip home. Red raspberries were preserved in jars if possible, since there was so little fiber in them that they could not be dried successfully. This very fact made them ideal for preserving in the form of juice boiled down to the consistency of light syrup.

Ending the berry-picking activities of the year were the blackberries, which started to ripen in July in sunny places and would continue until late August or even early September. Two factors operated in determining the length of the season—the wetness or dryness of the summer, and the amount of shade in the spot where the berries grew. In a dry year, berries would be sweeter than usual, but the vines would produce for only a few days, after which the remaining berries would dry up.

Blackberries would grow well and mature later in semi-shaded locations, and often would move into lumber clearings which had grown up sufficiently to choke out the sun-loving raspberries. There was enormous variation in the size, flavor, and sweetness of blackberries, and in a good year the picker would be able to bypass seemingly choice stands of fruit, knowing from experience that the berries were sour or bitter. Because of their size, juiciness, and sweetness, blackberries were popular for brandy making among the few who engaged in this activity. Perhaps the most popular product, however, was spiced blackberry jam. Only a minimal quantity of sweetening agent need be used, if the picker had done a good job of tasting as he went along, and had ignored the vines which yielded sour fruit. The sweetness and flavor of blackberries tended to remain constant as long as the canes produced fruit. New canes from the old roots could be counted on to produce the same kind of fruit their predecessors had.

There were other berries, too, but none of great importance or so widely used that they could be stereotyped as characteristic of the up-country. One liked by children was the flowering raspberry, so called, with viscous stems, widely spreading leaves and a broad, flat fruit. Sometimes known as thimbleberries, they grew in sunny fence corners, along country roads, and occasionally in pasture fields. Since they matured when raspberries did, if they were gathered at all they usually went into the pail at raspberry time.

Another was the gooseberry, which was probably originally an escapee from an English-Irish kitchen garden. In a favorable location, gooseberries multiplied so fast that farmers had to grub the bushes out to keep them from taking over needed pasture space. Gooseberries would reproduce from seed, but the berries of the seedlings were often too full of spines to use for anything except juice. Currants, too, tended to escape from gardens and become established in places not likely to be disturbed by the plow. Usually the fruit was smaller and even more sour than that of the parent plant. One exception was the black currant, the fruit of which was insipidly sweet. Elderberries and choke-cherries made good jelly, albeit not always a clear one, and there were occasional families who used elderberries for pie. Wild grapes were popular for jelly and conserve.

### COLLECTORS LOOK FOR:

Pottery and stoneware preserving jars

Pottery and tin pie plates

Glass fruit jars (See chapter on glass)

Tin mouth-guards for fruit jars (to prevent spilling while jars were being filled with boiling-hot fruit)

Pressed glass jelly jars. The beaded grape pattern was probably the all-time up-country favorite.

Jelly paddles and stirring sticks of wood

Sugar bins or other containers

Tin or wooden sugar scoops

Tin or wooden lifters to remove hot pies from the oven

Cranberry scoops (to strip berries from the bushes)

Tin dinner horns (used to call distant pickers home to dinner)

Granite-ware pails, oftenest in mottled green, blue, or gray tones, with capacities from a pint to twelve quarts

Old recipe ("receipt") books, especially handwritten ones

Hanging brass scales. Many recipes for jelly or preserves were in terms of pounds rather than quarts or pints.

Old seed-house and nursery catalogues

*Jackpot:* Marked pottery preserving jar with its original tin top intact

# 23
# Kitchens—Down and Out

The term *Out-kitchen* has a sound less than entirely pleasant; there is something derogatory about it—or, if not actually derogatory, faintly belittling.

Whatever the sound of the term—perhaps one would do better to substitute "connotation" for "sound"—the out-kitchen played an important role in the economy of rural America, especially during the 1800s. Essentially, it was an extra kitchen, but one in which special kinds of work took place. Up-country, the chances are that it was not referred to as an out-kitchen at all, unless the speaker was of English or English-Irish background; one was more likely to hear of a "cellar" kitchen—which stood at ground level but not necessarily in a cellar—or a summer kitchen, which was probably used the year round and could be located almost anywhere . . . including the cellar.

To clarify this confusing situation, let us indulge in a bit of retrospection, with particular reference to Monroe and Pike Counties rather than to the Commonwealth at large. The very first dwelling of the pioneer family—and we are not now talking about the influx from Europe in the nineteenth century, but of the early eighteenth century immigrants—was ordinarily a simple cabin containing one or two rooms, a massive fireplace, and a loft reached by a ladder or by the most primitive of staircases. As soon as the family managed to get on its feet, economically speaking, the cabin was abandoned in favor of a house both larger and of better construction.

This abandonment did not mean that the original dwelling was no longer used—far from it. If the original construction had been of stone, the cabin was not infrequently incorporated in the newer structure, and its identity was lost. (In Pike, the cabin was almost always of logs; in Monroe and farther south it was more likely to be of stone.) Usually, the new building was ambitious enough in construction that the cabin would not fit into the scheme of things —but it was allowed to stand, anyway. It was ordinarily so close to the new structure that it could be reached by a short, covered walkway. It has been said that a bona fide Pennsylvania Dutchman never discarded *anything;* the up-countryman certainly never discarded a structure that could be kept in use, even though it might no longer be exactly an object of beauty.

An honest-to-goodness cellar kitchen was an integral part of a larger dwelling, and was properly located at ground level, as we have indicated. Bank *barns* were built so that the broader dimension of the building was partly underground; bank *houses* were so constructed that while one end, or most of it, was set against and into the bank, the other end, with a full complement of windows and outside door, appeared to be the first floor. The cellar kitchen was a large room, usually the entire width of the house, and could be reached not only from the outside but by an inside stairway from above. It had its own fireplace; there was easy access to the basement storage space under the rest of the house; it was, in essence, almost a self-contained dwelling. For many and many an elderly couple, it served as home when management of the farm devolved upon a son, who moved his family into the house proper. Below the Blue Mountain, where the bank house was less common than it was in the hillier country to the north, separate but attached living quarters for the old folks, so called, were sometimes known as the "Dawdy Haus"—Dad's house.

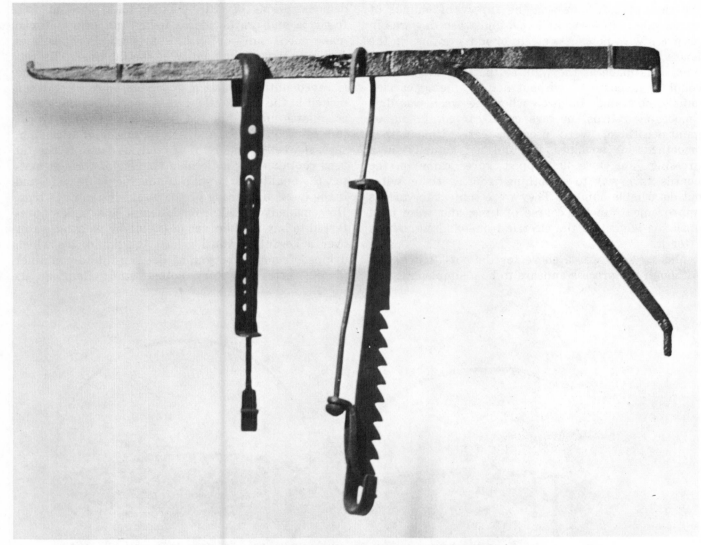

*Fireplace crane from the out-kitchen of a logger's inn on the River Road east of Shawnee-on-Delaware. Sawtooth and "straight" trammels in great variety were used to suspend heavy pots from the crane.*

Thus we have two types of extra or spare working units on the nineteenth century farm—the built-in ground floor housekeeping arrangement and the detached or semi-detached unit. Occasionally there was a third—the summer kitchen—but we shall come to that.

Once the first two types had passed beyond the point at which they were needed for dwellings, they performed a number of ancillary purposes, many or most of which centered upon the use of the fireplace. Many home buyers today insist that a fireplace is a Must, and for a year or two it is in frequent use. As time passes, however, there often seems to be less and less of romance in an open fire, and the expensive equipment stands idle oftener than it is used. Not so the great stone structure of earlier years; too many of the processes directly concerned with the domestic economy were overly cumbersome for the kitchen ranges coming into use, and the fireplace was pressed into frequent service.

Getting the laundry done was one of these chores. Two massive cast iron kettles hung on the crane in most out-kitchens, and fires were started under them early in the morning—as soon as they had been filled with bucketfuls of water carried from the well or spring. Wooden tubs were set up on sturdy benches;

the cask of soft soap—or the supply of chunks of homemade soap—was at hand, and wash day was in progress with no excess steam or muss or fuss in the house itself. Sometimes a trough-and-drain arrangement was made at the wall, so that the wash water could be disposed of without actually being carried out. "Smoothing" followed when the wash was dry. Smoothing boards, in rare cases carved, inlaid, or paint-decorated, were used in early times; they smoothed out wrinkles, but did not actually do a pressing job. Once flat-topped stoves came in, the boards gave way to smoothing irons, with or without detachable handles. They were subject to various improvements in the course of time, and were used until the advent of the electric iron—and sometimes after it.

Making soap was a chore for the out-kitchen, too. Although the process appears to be a simple one, and demonstrations of soap making take place at folk festivals and crafts affairs today, not everyone can make good soap—or so it is averred. Perhaps it is just a matter of the quality of the fat used. Theoretically, all excess or waste animal fat of whatever kind is saved until there is a gallon or more of it when melted in the iron kettle. Lye is poured in; the grease coagulates and is allowed to harden. Then it is cut into cakes or chunks and, after a period of seasoning, several weeks or more, it is ready for use. If the fat used contains any noticeable amount of foreign matter, the quality of the soap is adversely affected—and if the lye is too strong or too weak, the same is true. Homemade lye could be made (most soap makers preferred to buy it whenever possible) by pouring water over a kegful of wood ashes; the liquid fire which dripped from the bottom of the keg into a container placed there was very potent stuff. Gauging its

*A brazier in which cooking was actually done by placing the grid over hot coals and setting a pot or pan on it, and the more familiar three-legged iron kettle for either fireplace or cookstove use.*

strength was largely a matter of experience—or, for the inexperienced, simply trial-and-error. Lye and oil would produce soft soap.

Making apple butter, a process described elsewhere in these pages, was normally an outdoor task, but in the event of bad weather it could take place in the out-kitchen. Similarly, if the weather turned bad on butchering day, the out-kitchen was pressed into service. Frequently the heavy trestles and butchering slabs were stored in the out-kitchen and could be set up quickly if or when the need arose.

One phase of the butchering operation was usually reserved for the out-kitchen anyway—that of processing ("rendering") the lard. The job almost always fell to the women of the household, and a considerable number of them dreaded the chore; they simply could not, they said, make good lard. ("Good" lard would remain sweet-tasting and odorless for a full year.) As one looks back from the practically lardless present to the refrigeratorless past, he marvels that it was possible to make a product which, without benefit of an additive or chemical or special processing, could remain in pristine condition for so long a time.

The secret, it was maintained, lay in rendering separately the fat which came from different parts of the animal. Some raw fat was completely free of either taste or odor; fat from a different part had a faint odor; some, usually processed after the rest of the operation had been completed, had both a faintly unpleasant taste and an odor. If all three were put together indiscriminately, lard with poor keeping qualities would result. Since not everyone was willing or able to undertake separate time-consuming operations, there was bound to be some inferior lard.

As we see it now, another factor may have operated to influence the quality of lard. At rendering time, the fat was cut up into small pieces and then, little by little, put into the kettle. A paddle was used to press the pieces down into the pot and help force the liquid away from the fiber. At a fairly advanced point, a squeezer or press was used to expel any lingering pockets of fat from the fiber, and when the fiber was as nearly dry as possible in the nature of things for it to be, it was removed and set aside to cool. (In most cases, it was eventually rationed out to the chickens, a very little at a time.) The liquid fat was then poured into large containers to solidify. The point of the matter is that some of the fat was actually in a super-heated condition for a good many hours. Fat which gets too hot will scorch, even though it many not change in appearance. No thermometers were available to make any kind of check on the

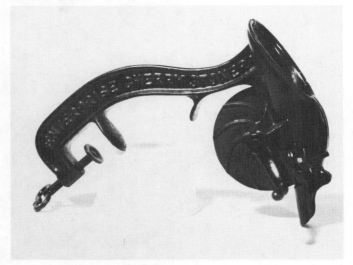

*There were two schools of thought as to the merits of "boughten" cherry pitters. One extolled their usefulness; the other maintained that they crushed the fruit needlessly and wasted the juice.*

temperature—and scorched lard was likely both to pick up foreign odors and to turn rancid quickly . . . or so it was said.

An operation now all but forgotten was that of pitting and canning cherries. In a day when insect control was something taken care of by the bird population and sprays were unneeded and unknown, the cherry crop could be enormous. A favorite Sunday occupation for many a townsman was to gather up all the tin pails he thought he could fill, and spend the day at a farm on which the owner was only too glad to have someone help harvest the crop, either on shares—the favorite way of doing it—or at a very nominal fee on the part of the picker. Both black and red varieties produced abundantly. There was a degree of danger in the picking; the trees grew tall, and often the longest ladders would not enable the picker to get anywhere near the top, where the largest fruit grew.

The out-kitchen came into play after the Sunday fun was over, and the stoning or pitting took place. It was a messy job, especially if the cherries happened to be the sweet but ultra-juicy Black Tatarians. One could control spurts of juice if the pitting was done by hand, but hand-pitting was slow. Store-bought cherry pitters speeded up the process, but it was smart to wear one's oldest or most disreputable clothes when using them.

Depending upon the total number and the location of auxiliary buildings on a farm, some of the butter-making processes were carried on in the out-kitchen.

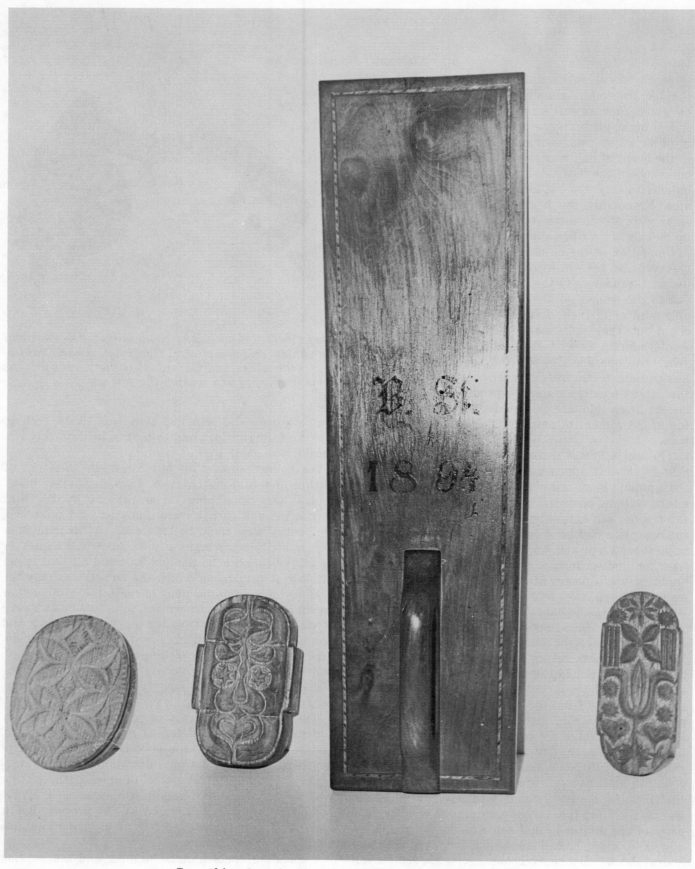

*Smoothing boards, used to minimize the wrinkles in laundered objects which were not scheduled for ironing. The small hand-size specimens, sometimes mistaken for butter molds, often show elaborate carving. Some up-country housewives still make a distinction between "smoothing" and "ironing."*

*A moistened finger tip lightly touched to the surface of an old-time flatiron heated on the kitchen range indicated—to the initiate—whether the iron was too hot, too cold, or just right for use.*

A churn was a cumbersome thing, especially to cleanse after it had been used, and there was no room for it in the spring house. The cellar was pressed into service in some cases, but the logical place was the out-kitchen. Not only did the churn have its special nook, but the appurtenances which accompanied its use also needed storage space—the butter bowl and paddles, the bags of fine salt, and the stone crocks, which would be inverted and stacked up in a pile with the smallest on top. After natural milk-cooling came to be too slow for a somewhat stepped-up tempo in living, home cream separators were used on some farms. They were manually operated, and by centrifugal action did a good job in starting with milk fresh from the cow and turning it into cream and skim milk. The principal objection most women had to their use was the multiplicity of little working parts, all of which had to be sterilized in boiling water after each using. At the end of a long day's work, taking care of the cream separator seemed like the proverbial last straw. Needless to say, the only handy place for the separator was in the out-kitchen.

After the 1800s, the fireplace came to be used less and less, with a square-topped cast iron stove, wood-fired, taking its place. It would be set as close to the fireplace opening as possible, with a piece of stovepipe carrying the smoke into the wide chimney. With this kind of stove, large-scale canning operations could take place, and the processing could go forward without interrupting the cooking and meal-getting which had to take place in the kitchen of the main house three times a day.

The drying of fruit and vegetables took place here also. Farther south, there were specially constructed ovens for the purpose, with built-in drawers or racks. In the up-country there seems to be no record of any such setup. When thinly sliced string beans, or cut sweet corn, or "schnitzed" apples, or peaches or berries were to be dried for winter use, the ideal situation was to spread them on large platters or trays and put them in the sun. If the sun proved uncooperative, a low fire could be built in the laundry stove, and business could go ahead almost as usual. Laundry stoves had no ovens—just a firebox; so there was less chance of ruining a forgotten pan of apples than if the oven of the kitchen range had been used.

Summer heat was no more excessive in the up-country than it was in other places, and women probably spent no more time in hot kitchens than they did elsewhere—but cooking, baking, canning, and heating hot water in July and August created stifling and unendurable conditions just the same, not only downstairs but in the sleeping rooms above. The cellar kitchen offered one solution to the problem. The out-kitchen offered another. When neither existed, a special addition was frequently constructed at the back of the house, a lean-to or a "shanty," inelegantly speaking, or a "summer kitchen" if one wanted it to sound better. The idea was simply to get the indispensable stove out of the house during the hot months.

Moving a kitchen range from one location to another may not sound like a major operation, especially to one who has not tried it. For a crew of strong men it would not be. Only too often, though, it was up to the woman of the the family to set the machinery in motion, and when the time came, about the only help available was her husband. Inch by inch, after the stovepipe came down, the heavy stove would be eased across the floor, through a door, and to its new location. Then the gaping hole left by the stovepipe would be closed with a fancy flue stopper, the pipe would be erected in its new location, the furniture would be adjusted, and life could go on again. The starting point was neither the stove nor the stovepipe, however; it was the kitchen door. If the stove was wider than the door through which it would have to pass, there could be no move. A story repeated for years in the up-country is that of an uneven-tempered man who neglected to perform the preliminary measuring, with the result that the stove he and his wife were moving became firmly jammed in the doorway. Try as they might, they could not move it forward—and the wife would not listen to the idea of moving it back to its starting place. In utter exasperation, he gave a mighty kick, breaking his ankle in the process. But the stove moved on through the doorway—and before the time came to move it back in the fall the door molding was altered so that there was no need for him to break the other ankle.

Once a move of this magnitude had been undertaken, the temptation was to delay the return move as long as possible. After really cold weather set in, there was no alternative, of course; one had to move back again. Once a summer kitchen had been constructed, though, it was kept in use, whether the stove was there or not. The flour and meal drums were kept there—in a progression of sizes from large to small according to the needs or tastes of the family. In early years, the largest one would have been allocated to rye or buckwheat flour. Later, wheat would edge out one or the other, possibly both. In the Poconos, corn-meal would have needed the smallest, at any time, since it was used chiefly for mush—not a universal favorite.

Lard cans were kept in the summer kitchen in the winter—and after a butchering such items as scrapple, souse, liver pudding, and the like. Nuts gathered by children in the fall were handier to get at if stored in the summer kitchen than if they had been carried up to the attic. Heavy winter garments and footgear which required a great deal of room took up residence also, along with snow shovels, brooms, and the barn lanterns. In fact, to be blunt about it, the summer kitchen often became a winter catch-all.

Summer kitchens and out-kitchens are still in existence in more places than one might realize unless he happens to be looking for them. In some cases they have been modernized—but it is quite possible,

on byways in the West End, to find the little outbuilding with its enormous chimney standing smack-dab beside an impressive residence, housing some of the gear and performing some of the functions of three-quarters of a century ago.

One regrets the deterioration of cellar kitchens which through years of indifference or neglect have often become little more than places of musty storage. One such, in a venerable house in Hamilton Township, is a subject of nostalgic regret for a descendant of the family which built the house in the early 1800s. Her remembrance of the room goes back to the time, shortly after her fourth birthday, when with her parents she went to attend the funeral of her grandfather. They arrived very early. In those days, town florists made no delivery of flowers out in the country, and the cellar kitchen was filled with women busily turning great masses of home-grown flowers into arrangements for the funeral. Local women, they were conversing in Pennsylvania Dutch, a tongue completely unfamiliar to her—and she was disturbed. What had these outsiders to do with her grandfather's funeral? Were they, perchance, gypsies? Children were warned over and over to have nothing whatsoever to do with gypsies. Gypsies were foreigners. . . . The only foreign language she had ever heard was spoken by a family referred to as the "Eye-talians." Gypsies, Italians—

In a burst of sudden fear she rushed upstairs to her mother, who of course wanted to know what was the matter.

"I'm afraid of those Eye-talian women!" was the reply.

COLLECTORS LOOK FOR:

Fireplace mantels from old kitchens
Fireplace cranes, trammels, and hooks
Fireplace tongs, andirons, and long-legged trivets
Cast iron kettles—butchering kettles, "gypsy" pots, Dutch ovens, and the like. (Sorghum kettles are currently popular as fireplace dressing, but few if any of them are native to Pennsylvania.)
Wooden wash benches, tubs, wringers, and ironing boards
"Smoothing" boards for hand use. They helped to minimize the wrinkled effect in laundered cloth. No heat was involved.
Smoothing irons of various types, including flatirons
Stands or trivets for irons
Wooden buckets
Cakes of homemade soap
Wooden two-handled lard presses. The handles are

usually connected by a heavy leather thong.

Cherry pitters

Cream separators. They belong to the machine age—but they constitute a closed series and collectors are becoming interested.

Flour drums with stenciled decorations, often in a wheat motif

Decorated flue stoppers of metal (for stovepipe apertures)

Pottery collars or liners used as insulators in stovepipe apertures

Pottery or glass foot rests for kitchen stoves

*Jackpot:* A chased sawtooth fireplace trammel known to be old

# 24
## All but the Squeal

Butchering day was a time of bustle and activity unusual even for the up-country, which could hardly have been indicted for sloth at any season. Once the farmer had ascertained that the hogs had reached a suitable condition of rotundity—and somewhere short of actual fatness but definitely beyond leanness—he took the Farmer's Almanac off the clock shelf to discover the auspicious days for the task.

That is, he consulted the almanac if he had a lingering trace of the superstition his forefathers had probably had in stronger degree. If he professed a complete lack of belief in the zodiacal signs he might check anyway, in order to forestall comment or criticism by those of his relatives or neighbors whose help he would need to get the job done. Butchering was serious business. With the meat supply for much, perhaps most or all, of the winter at stake, what man in his right mind would take chances? Almost everyone could point to an unhappy experience on the part of someone who had disregarded the signs: someone's hams had not kept well, or the side meat had turned "strong," or, worst of all, whatever was cooked or fried had tended to shrink unreasonably.

The farmer needed to bring in additional help according to how many members of his family were available or according to the number of animals to be slaughtered. Youngsters could assist, up to a point, but tended to be squeamish at certain stages of the work. Therefore a trading arrangement was usually made: Uncle Bill would lend a hand, but would expect comparable return assistance when he decided to do his butchering. If a number of animals were scheduled for slaughtering, more than one extra man would be needed; some of the work was heavy. There was a rather well-observed gentleman's agreement that the host farmer would make all the decisions in such matters as just how the hams were to be trimmed, how much meat would be left on the spare ribs, and how much tenderloin would be reserved for his wife to can. In particular, seasoning the sausage was a highly individual matter. One family might like its sausage meat mixed with only salt and pepper, whereas another would find it tasteless without added spices. The helper might be forced to stand by and watch a whole batch of sausage being "ruined" by the addition of seasonings he personally found distasteful, but his duty was clear: all he had to do was keep his mouth shut!

Necessary chores to be performed in advance were numerous. One of them was to see that all the equipment was in order—and being in order meant that the knives were sharpened, that all the utensils and containers had been thoroughly scrubbed, and that a check had been made to be sure that no single bit of equipment would be missing at the moment it would be needed. Pieces of meat to be put down in brine, those to be hung up for temporary curing, sections to be ground—all these called for their own special gear, and it would have been quixotic to assume that all the tubs, hooks, planks, scrapers, and the rest would be just where they had been left at the time of their previous using—especially if there were youngsters about the place.

The housewife would be called on for cloths of various sizes and shapes, and for strainers and pots and pans. These would be stacked in readiness the day before, and woe to the person who "borrowed" one without authorization. It normally fell to the older boys to make sure that there was an adequate supply of fuel immediately available—often including knotty chunks which had resisted attempts to reduce them to stove wood but which were ideal to maintain a steady fire under the giant iron kettles used on butchering day. To the boys also went the job of seeing that the water barrels were filled—and that they were replenished during the day according to need. It took a lot of water, from preliminaries to final cleanup.

Farmers generally preferred to do as much of the work outdoors as possible. If, as was often the case up to about the 1900s, the work facilities included a detached out-kitchen with a walk-in-size fireplace, some of the operations would be centered there, and the heavy slabs used for working tables would be set up before the fire.

*Knives used at butchering time were heavy, efficient —and dangerous in the hands of any but the expert. The chopping bowl knife, four inches deep, was also a most business-like implement.*

The use of the wooden scalding trough marked the beginning of a long succession of steps or processes. In very early years, the trough was a hollowed-out section of a log. As early as possible, such cumbersome pieces were discarded in favor of a simple rectangular trough made of tightly joined heavy planks. Troughs were generally caulked with tar in order to make them as nearly watertight as possible.

Sometimes there was a working fireplace outdoors.

If there was not—and a single fireplace would be too small to meet the large-scale needs of the day—fires would be built under pots hung on trammels suspended from stout poles—three poles being set up teepee-wise for one trammel. In some cases it was easy to erect these in a wind-free place, but in others it was expedient to construct a temporary windbreak. One could not risk having ashes or dirt blown into a pot at any stage after the scalding had taken place.

Removing the bristles from the slaughtered hog was the first step in the meat-dressing process. The animal, trussed with straps, was carefully lowered into the trough of near-boiling water, enough additional water was added to cover the carcass, and the body was rolled from side to side. After several minutes of this treatment, the animal was rolled out of the trough and on to the slatted platform beside it. It was this stage which particularly called for the muscles of Uncle Bill. Chains were sometimes used instead of straps to move the animal. Just the right temperature of the water meant that the bristles would come off easily as the hand scrapers were wielded. A few degrees one way or the other meant that the operation would take longer, but one did the best he could.

The next step was to suspend the animal by its hind feet, through which a gambrel stick was thrust to keep them as widely spread as possible. Any bristles which had escaped earlier were now removed and the whole animal was thoroughly scrubbed, shaved with a razor-sharp knife, and then wiped dry.

The disemboweling process was one to which many a farm child had to grow accustomed—or stay away from the scene until in his or her—usually her—thinking the pink-and-white carcass had passed from the stage of pigdom to that of pork.

Another unesthetic phase of butchering immediately followed the disemboweling—that of reducing the small intestines to casings for sausage and liver pudding. A sharpened wooden scraping blade—a metal blade caused too many cuts—was used in the process, which actually removed the inner lining of the intestine. This lining was discarded, along with any fat clinging to the outer intestinal wall. A final step not for the squeamish was the blowing up of the casing to make sure that it was free of cuts or holes. The separation of the casing or intestine walls, usually entrusted to a woman of the family, was tricky business and probably called for more delicate expertise than any other single operation. Long wooden trays were used to hold the casings. These trays were sometimes of solid cherry—and are quickly snapped up today when they appear in antique shops. On the farm they were bluntly referred to as "gut boards."

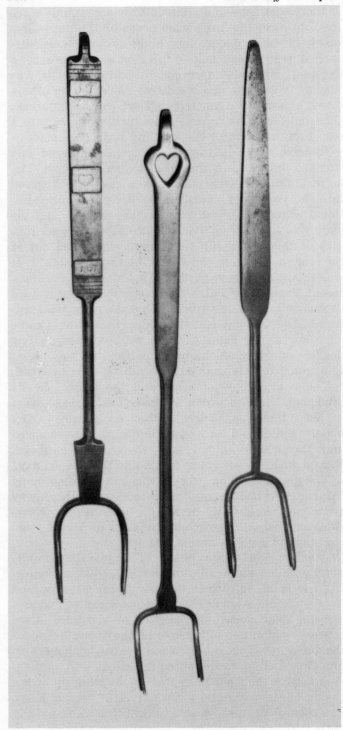

*Expert attention was often lavished on the heavy two-tined forks used at butchering time and for fireplace cookery. The date on the specimen at the left, not very clearly indicated, is 1857.*

(In the shop the term "butcher board," somewhat inexact or misleading, is usually used.)

The carcass was allowed to hang until the residual body heat had been completely dissipated and the meat was becoming firm enough to retain its shape when cut. The head was then severed and subjected to its own processing operations. Many farmers removed what meat they could from the head, cut the meat into small pieces, and put the sections and scraps into a kettle, where they simmered for hours —anywhere from four to seven or eight. Fat was reserved for lard making, which came later. The rest was discarded.

The suspended carcass was cut vertically into three sections, a narrow one in the middle, consisting of the entire length of the backbone, and the right and left sides, each containing a ham and a shoulder. Separately these were removed to the cutting boards and there converted to the cuts and proportions desired: hams, shoulders, ribs, side meat (now, in a later age, we smoke it and call it bacon), belly, and feet. The hams and shoulders were trimmed to their appropriate size and shape, the trimmings being reserved for sausage. Other pieces were similarly cut to shape. What fat could be removed was put aside for lard. All the meat scraps wanted for sausage, including some choice pieces of the backbone section, were kept together and then ground.

Once the carving-up phase had been completed, there were four stages, either already on-going or to be undertaken: preservative preparations for large cuts; grinding, seasoning, and stuffing the sausage; rendering the fat for lard—deferred to a later day, in most cases; and processing the contents of the simmering kettle.

Hams, shoulders, feet, and some sections of the backbone cuts were consigned to a salt-brine solution. Large stone jars, with capacities up to 30 gallons, were used for this purpose. Hams and shoulders were kept apart from other pieces, and a small quantity of saltpeter was added to the pickling brine to help keep the meat pink. After a period of time ranging from a few days to several weeks—a matter of personal preference—the pieces would be removed to the smokehouse. Smaller pieces were usually kept in brine—a weaker solution than the one used for curing meat to be smoked—until needed for the table.

Making sausage required special implements: a grinder to reduce chunks of meat to a hamburger-like condition, and a stuffer, which forced the ground meat into the casings previously mentioned. Some of the lengths of sausage would be consigned to the smokehouse, and some would be canned by the housewife at her convenience, but within a matter of days, while it still was fresh. Determining the correct amounts of seasoning for a dishpanful—or perhaps a tubful—of ground sausage meat often called for family consultation, and tiny test cakes were often fried to see whether or not the seasoner had guessed right.

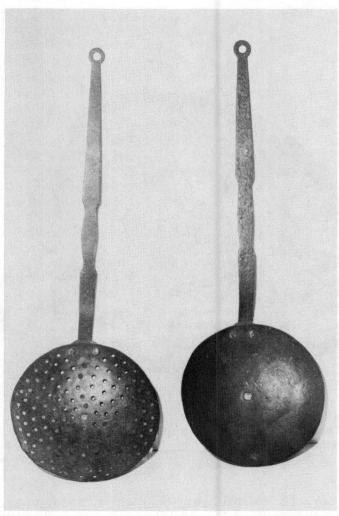

*Long-handled large strainer and dipper, handmade, from the out-kitchen of the late Harry Kautz, Shawnee-on-Delaware.*

The old-fashioned sausage stuffer, which has for the most part become a museum piece, was an unwieldy but interesting implement. The hopper was filled almost to the top with ground meat; the motive power was supplied by a yard-long arm to which was attached a wobbly cover fitting neatly into the top of the hopper. Downward pressure on the arm, care-fully controlled, forced the sausage into a tube over which the casing had been stripped, and into the casing itself. Later "improved" models of stuffers did away with the long arm—and also much of the picturesqueness of the job. Various stuffers were patented from the 1860s to the 1880s. Some look much like later presses for lard, the processing of which is discussed in another place.

Perhaps the most time-consuming phase of the day-long activity was what was done with the potful of fragrant, simmering stew. Generally speaking, there were two products which would evolve—liver pudding (*pudden*) and scrapple (*pannhaus*). Late in the day, all the contents of the pot would be removed and the broth thoroughly strained. If it appeared too greasy to the critical eye of the housewife, she would skim off as much fat as she felt ought to be removed. Similarly, she would go over all the bits and chunks of cooked meat and cut away and discard any lingering areas of fat or pieces of gristle. ("Discard" does not imply "waste"; the dog or the chickens would be the eventual beneficiaries.) To what she had left she would add pieces of liver, usually cooked separately, after which the entire mixture would be ground.

At this point, what was designed for liver pudding was separated from the portion intended for scrapple, and seasoned. The seasoning normally included ground onion, salt, pepper, and perhaps sage or marjoram, as a minimum. (Sage and marjoram were used as seasoning for sausage, also, in some cases.) Some families liked nutmeg or allspice in their liver pudding. If any casings remained after the sausage had been stuffed, they were filled with liver pudding. If none were available, the mixture was put into pans to solidify and cool. Uncased liver pudding was heated again before eating, usually in a frying pan, and consumed with buckwheat cakes. One either liked it or he did not; it was by no means universally popular. In a family in which no one liked it, the ingredients, minus the onion, went into scrapple.

Up-country scrapple is different from any other scrapple. It has little in common with store-bought Philadelphia-style scrapple, which tends to be soft and greasy. Nor is it like the usual Dutch Country scrapple, which in most cases is thickened with cornmeal or a combination of cornmeal and wheat flour. The genuine up-country article utilizes buckwheat flour as the thickening agent, and in consequence has its own distinctive texture (very firm) and flavor. The process of making it is simple enough: the ground-up mass of lean meat scraps is returned to the almost fatless broth; the mixture is seasoned with nothing but salt and pepper; and the pot is brought to a boil.

*Short-handled two-quart dipper, a necessity for
large-scale cooking, and a "pudden pan," used as a
strainer for meat scraps destined for liver pudding,
scrapple, or souse.*

A pan or pail of buckwheat flour and a scoop are
manipulated by one person, and a long-handled stirring paddle by another. Slowly the flour is sifted into
the pot, no faster than it can be incorporated into the
mass by the paddle. This procedure continues until
the mixture is so thick that it can no longer be
stirred. Then the pot is removed from the fire and the
scrapple is scooped quickly into the waiting line-up
of pans. Scrapple solidifies quickly, and when it is
cool there will be a paper-thin encrustation of fat on
the top surface. If there is more than that—well, it is
less than perfect scrapple. Scrapple will keep for
weeks in any cool place in which air circulates, but it

can not be covered tightly—nor will it stand freezing.

Just as there is a quality peculiar to up-country
scrapple, there is a distinctive way of preparing it
for the table. It should be sliced about half an inch
thick, placed in a heated, lightly oiled or greased
skillet, and fried very slowly to a light brown color.
It will be crisp on the outside when it is done right;
it should be turned just once, and served hot. It has
been whispered that there are those who eat it with
syrup—but that may be just idle gossip.

Made rarely was a variant of scrapple known as
blood pudding. Into the broth used as the base for
either liver pudding or scrapple, blood caught at the

time the animal's throat was cut was poured. The liquid was then thickened in much the same way that scrapple was. It is said that this dish, like other butchering by-products, had its devotees.

More to the popular taste, but never really widely popular, was another pork product called souse. Except for the fact that it called for pork instead of veal, it suggested calf's-foot jelly. The pig's feet or knuckles were carefully cleaned and boiled, the outer hoof being entirely stripped off and discarded. The skin and such shreds of meat as there were, were ground. Vinegar, seasonings, and sometimes sliced hard-boiled eggs were added to the boiled liquid after the bones had been removed. The gelatine in the knuckles was sufficient to create a semi-solid delicacy which was eaten cold.

One final step, this time an amenity, remained for the very end of the day's work. A "taste" of fresh sausage, perhaps slices of liver or heart, and a pan of scrapple were given to Uncle Bill to take home. Similar gifts were taken to especially close friends or relatives—who would make a return in kind when *they* butchered. In deep Dutch territory, this gift was called the *metzel-supp;* in the up-country it was simply known as the "taste."

Hogs of ordinary size were seldom weighed. However, an animal of exceptional proportions might be weighed, using a steelyard either before or just after disemboweling. There was probably some satisfaction in knowing that one's own animal was larger than Uncle Bill's, especially if Uncle Bill had forgotten himself and let slip an unflattering remark about the shape the hams were assuming!

COLLECTORS LOOK FOR:

Gambrel sticks

Hoisting devices

Butcher planks—some of these are as much as six inches thick.

Scraping racks

Butcher boards (gut boards)

Steelyards

Scoop scales

Sausage grinders

Sausage-stuffing devices

Sticking knives

Butcher knives. Often homemade, these were of a quality all but unknown today.

Chopping bowl knives

Long-handled implements used in open-air or fireplace cookery—skimmers, forks, slitted spoons, ladles, paddles, dippers

Tin "pudden" dishes with wire-mesh bottoms (for straining liquid from cooked meat scraps)

Bristle scrapers. "Hog-scraper" candlesticks, similar in shape, are said to have doubled as actual bristle scrapers, but no instance of such use has been reported in the up-country.

Steel-mesh scouring "cloths," used for cleaning large kettles

Tin or granite-ware scrapple pans

——and buckwheat flour. (Try a small-town independent grocery or hardware store.)

*Jackpot:* Dated long-handled fork, spoon, or skimmer, brass-trimmed, with impressed name of maker

# 25
## Kootsches, Smokehouses, and Almanacs

When today's gardener—home, weekend, or commercial—gets ready to set out his young garden plants he need not think of the step as an intermediate one in a progression which started weeks or even months earlier. He simply drives to a place where all the preliminaries have been taken care of as a matter of business, buys his flats of seedlings, and goes ahead from there.

That was not the way they did it in up-country Dutchdom a hundred years ago or, in scattered instances, a couple of decades ago. They used the kootsch instead. (Pronounce the "koot" to rhyme with "foot," not with "boot.")

But even the kootsch did not start as its own creation; it began as an appendage to the smokehouse. Farmers grew their own hogs, slaughtered them or had them slaughtered, and after a preliminary treatment in which hams were soaked in salt-and-saltpeter brine (saltpeter to preserve the pinkness of the meat) did their own meat smoking, too. Hams, bacon, sausage, and sometimes liver pudding were subjected to repeated periods of smoking, the number of sessions largely depending upon family preference. A good many farmers, even in the Pocono uplands where hickory trees grew so thick that they were almost a pest, would have scorned today's presumed preference for hickory-chip smoking. Their first choice would have been corncobs. Beyond that point, chips were chips. All chips made smoke, didn't they? Smoke created the flavor, didn't it? Then why not corncobs, which made a good, slow smoke, were immediately at hand, and demanded no extra time of a man?

Whatever the fuel, the slow process kept the smokehouse warm, and in early spring (March or April in the Poconos, but earlier than that farther south) although the winter's supply of meat had long since been smoked, the smokehouse was again put to use. The kootsch was, in essence, a small hotbed, elevated three or four feet above the ground, and attached to the south side of the smokehouse. It was sturdily constructed of heavy, usually discarded, lumber, and mounted on posts, either upright or slanted back to the smokehouse at the bottom. Typical measurements would be four to five feet long, two to three feet wide, and at least eighteen inches deep. Discarded window sash, set at an angle so that a late snow would melt and run off without damaging the tender plants, usually finished off the construction.

At the bottom of the box about six inches of well rotted manure was spread, with perhaps six inches of good garden soil above it. Enough space had to be left so that the young plants could reach a height of up to six inches without touching the glass. There were actually three warming agents involved: the manure, which would generate warmth except in the very coldest weather; the sun—which was unpredictable and might wilt the plants if one forgot to tilt the sash; and the real control, the smokehouse, in which one could build a smouldering fire if freezing weather occurred after the seeds had germinated.

The kootsch was probably never all that it was cracked up to be, but in a climate like the one at the top of the Poconos it made garden crops a possibility much earlier than if the seeds had been sown outdoors "after all danger of frost is over," as directions on seed packets so naïvely phrase it. Usually, kootsch-makers planned successive sowings of seeds. Lettuce (seldom called lettuce in German-speaking communities, where the German word *Salat* was used instead) was normally followed by cabbage. Lettuce had to be transplanted early or it would bolt to seed in almost no time; cabbage could not be transplanted too early because it needed the cool nights of late summer to grow properly and to avoid the curse of club root, brought on by hot, dry weather. Celery was started as early as possible, because of the long growing season required. Tomatoes and peppers were least demanding.

The disadvantages of the kootsch are probably almost self-evident. The plants had to be watered regularly, and the great weight of box, soil, and water, coupled with the fact that waste lumber had often been used in the construction, usually brought the enterprise to the ground within a year or two. Children, to whom some of the farm chores had to be entrusted, were prone to forget to close the sash on a night of sudden frost, or to open it in time on a day of hot sun. Chickens at large found it an ideal place to dust themselves; cats were prone to make use of it. Transplanting time might be delayed for reasons which will appear, and kootsch plants sometimes got so large that their suitability for transplanting was almost destroyed.

The kootsch is a casualty today, both in the Poconos and in the Dutchland itself, largely because the need for it no longer exists. Even if the need did exist, though, where would one find the smokehouse, the corncobs, and the iron pot embedded in the smokehouse floor to provide the mild but steady heat needed on March days? The smokehouse has given way to the chemical "smoke" embedded by needle, the corncobs have been shredded to provide mulch (there are those who aver that they have become breakfast foods!), and the iron pots have been metamorphosed into *objets d'art* in suburban fireplaces.

All this business of the mechanics of kootsch making and kootsch use, however, is secondary to a philosophical point behind it. Those glib phrases "when all danger of frost is past" or "when the apple trees are in bloom" may serve as at least some kind of guide to today's small-time gardener, but they would have been insufficient for the home gardeners of Upper Dutchdom up to at least the early 1900s—and in some cases right up to the present. Any *echt* Dutch-country gardener knows that, kootsch or no kootsch, the starting point is the farmers' almanac, which provides two all-important bits of information

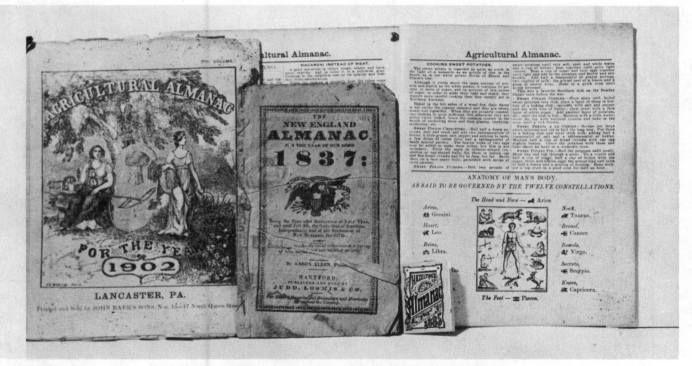

*It was a brash gardener who ignored the advice given in the almanac as to the proper days for sowing or planting. Farmers' almanacs were and still are all-time best sellers in the world of print.*

Gardening manuals, mail-order catalogues, and printed promotional materials of all kinds kept the farmer posted on the latest methods and most up-to-date devices available. The publications shown above are from a long-time accumulation in a West End general store.

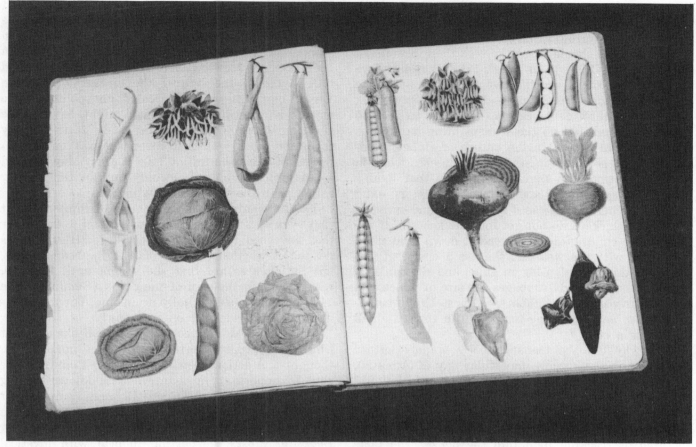

*The seed catalogues of yesteryear were filled with colored illustrations which served an unintended double purpose—selling garden seeds and filling scrapbooks.*

—the nature of the weather at any given time from January 1 right through the year to December 31, and a notation of the sign of the moon, that is, the zodiacal sign, for each day of the year. He knows, too, that each zodiacal sign has indisputable significance for the farmer.

Farmers' almanacs are among the most venerable of the forms of the printed word in Pennsylvania, appearing in Philadelphia as early as 1705, and have in addition a distinction not always accorded to the printed page: they have usually been read from cover to cover, not once, but many, many times, and by every member of the family. Moreover, their contents have widely been the Law, the Prophets, and the Gospels as decade followed decade, and century followed century.

Best known has perhaps always been John Baer's almanac, emanating from Lancaster. In earlier years the German language alone was used; now, it is easier to buy an almanac in English than in German. In New England and along the seaboard the "Old Farmer's Almanac" can usually be picked up at a newsstand—and back numbers over a span of almost a century are frequently available at antique shows. It is the smart thing to scoff at the naïveté in these little booklets, which carefully maintain the time-honored format, but there is nothing naïve about the number sold in a year!

What the nature of the weather will be at a given time in June might seem to be of little concern to the housewife who has transplanted her lettuce from the kootsch at the back of the smokehouse on April 20 and is wondering whether, although it seems premature, she should sow the early cabbage seed where the lettuce came out. To make matters specific, let us take the *North American Almanac* for 1858—surely long enough ago that those who wish can charge our housewife with benightedness. Naturally, she wishes her cabbage to grow as large and heavy as possible. Obviously, one should plant the seed then in the sign of the scales (Libra). In April, 1858, the only days occurring in Libra are the twenty-fifth—out of the question because it is Sunday—and the twenty-sixth.

There is still a complication, however: to take no chances, one should do the transplanting as well as the sowing in Libra. In the nature of things, seedlings should be ready in six to eight weeks; when in June is the moon in Libra? It appears that Friday and Saturday, June 18 and 19, are satisfactory—and so she puts her cabbage seed into the ground on April 26. If the chickens do not get into the kootsch, if the neighbors' children do not break it down, and if all goes well with the weather, she has a choice of two days for the transplanting in June, and she can look ahead to having early cabbages the size of which will be the envy of her neighbors—a most happy condition, since early cabbage tends to run toward small heads, as a rule.

But why did she transplant her spindly lettuce seedlings on the specific, particular day of April 20, thus setting the stage for the cabbage calculations? Referring to the almanac, we find that there were showers on April 20, 1858, and one could catch a bad cold setting out lettuce plants in the rain, to say nothing of tracking mud into the house. The facts are these: the lettuce plants were actually big enough to transplant by April 18—but both April 18 and 19 fell in the sign of the crab (Cancer). Anything planted on those days would take on the characteristic of the zodiacal sign; crabs go backward—and who wants his lettuce to grow backward? It is better to risk the rain, and perhaps get the planting done between showers on the twentieth.

Suppose, in spite of all the preplanning, the cabbages turn out to be puny, miserable? If something should go wrong, the gardener could be sure of one thing: whatever the cause of the misfortune, the signs could not be wrong. She might have misinterpreted, or might have blundered in some way. She might spend sleepless nights trying to recall what it was that she had done wrong, but the signs themselves were infallible. Since she kept her almanacs from year to year, with notations against the dates as to when she did what, she at least had something to go on to ward off future disaster.

The quarters of the moon were significant, too, as were special days. Our gardener would have had a special problem with her lima beans in 1858. It is well known that one should plant lima beans on Ascension Day, so that they will climb the poles instead of sprawling untidily around on the ground, as pole limas are wont to do—at least if they have been planted in the wrong sign. But Ascension Day in 1858 came on May 21—after the apple blossoms had fallen—and in the sign of the virgin (Virgo). In Virgo, blossoms obviously could not pollinate. No matter how auspicious the day might be for pole climbing, there could be no beans. In fact, the only favorable omen was that the moon was on the increase; it would be full at 1:06 P.M. on May 27, and for a prolific crop one should plant in the waxing rather than the waning of the moon.

There remained, though, the disturbing thought that, wax or wane, the moon was subject to the power that governed it—in this case, Virgo. History does not tell us whether the lady planted the beans or not, but the chances are that she waited until June 10, which came in the sign of the twins (Gemini). June 11 would have been equally promising, but the almanac "wanted" showers on that day!

It has been said that certain esoteric books which at times in the past exerted a powerful influence on thought and action deep in the Dutch Country were equally important up-country. Best known among these works are Johann Georg Hohmann's *Long-Lost Friend*, which first appeared in or near Reading in 1819, and a compilation called *The Sixth and Seventh Books of Moses*, purporting to deal with mystical practices of the ancient Hebrews.

It is indisputable that such books, which were intended for use only at the hands of one versed in white magic (*Braucherei*) or—Heaven forbid!—black magic (*Hexerei*) were known to, and used in, up-country Dutchdom. Where the population was heavily Germanic, as in the West End, the two "magics," which usually were lumped together under the general term of powwowing, were familiar to many, and practitioners were available. (Acts of *Braucherei* or *Hexerei* were a professional, not an amateur matter.) In communities farther toward the periphery, however, even the words for the whole concept were unknown. Such a condition is by no means strange; these were underground, occult matters, and the occult operates with difficulty in places in which there is a minimal background of belief or half-belief in the unknown.

What is of more significance to us here is the fact that the "powwow" books, so called, do not deal with planting lore, as is commonly supposed. They are largely concerned with healing and protection, not with the soil, the weather, or the influence of the moon on growing things. Planting according to "the right sign of the moon" may be deeply ingrained in either down-country or up-country thought, but the idea came from the almanacs, not from secret books of an essentially religious nature.

Thus, our gardener of 1858 could lean heavily on such astrological lore as the almanac maker chose to supply, but she would have shuddered at the idea of making her wish for a good garden the subject of petition to the Deity.

"Dog days" were the bane of the housewife, not only since the garden was likely to be infested with slugs and worms from mid-July to mid-August, but because in those pre-refrigerator days food would spoil with unbelievable speed. Some housekeepers undoubtedly blamed the heat and the humidity of that time of year for their woes, but there were others who, had they put the matter into words, would have placed the responsibility directly upon the almanac for "wanting," that is, predicting, the climatic conditions.

A somewhat more graceful—perhaps, however, only euphemistic—way of looking ahead to the almost certainly dismal prospect of dog days was to refer to July 15 as the day when "Mary goes over the mountain." If it rained on that day, it would rain each day for the ensuing forty days; conversely, fair weather when Mary made her trip would mean forty days without rain. One could be as bad as the other in a farming community! How the old legend of St. Swithin and that of Mary came to join identities in the Dutch Country has never been explained. For that matter, the mystery of the identity of Mary has never been very satisfactorily explained, either. The idea of dog days—the sultry part of late summer, not necessarily exactly forty days—may derive from the medieval belief that the rising of Sirius, the Dog Star, at this time of year was responsible for a particular kind of bad weather.

*Meat hooks were a farm necessity. Made by hand at first, they soon became available in country stores. Multiple hooks like these are ordinarily of commercial manufacture.*

One further word on the subject: there was a widespread belief that, in dog days or out, a woman should have nothing whatsoever to do with the preservation of food during her menstrual period. It mattered not that the peaches might be dead ripe or that lima beans were at the epitome of readiness for their hot water bath; there was no use in canning anything during this time, because it would not keep, anyway. This folk belief seems to have had its genesis in Germany, and has been a hard one to shake.

There was yet another factor which the home gardener took into consideration—the matter of just *where* one planted or sowed *what*. (One did not always have to take conscious thought about it, though; he could just put things in where they had always been put in. No problem.)

There appear to have been three recognizable categories in location: garden, truck patch, and "place." The garden was, ideally, as close to the house as possible—just a step or two away from the back door if such an arrangement were feasible. With a location so handy, the housewife could set out a few plants, pull up a weed which had hitherto escaped her vigilance, or cut a panful of lettuce for supper without interrupting the smooth flow of other, on-going operations. The garden was heavily fertilized, and plowed or spaded each year, according to its size. Usually it was small enough to spade, and the little winter accumulations of vegetable refuse could be turned under and started back on their mission of returning to earth. There was never much of an accumulation, since anything even remotely edible was fed to the chickens.

The garden (farther north and in other places it was often called the kitchen garden) was normally fenced in; chickens were even more fond of greens from the garden in summer than they were in the winter, and would take their own way of getting them, from scratching a hole under the fence to quietly winging their way into an apple tree and then descending to the garden when no one was looking. The garden was primarily intended for small or tender plants not desired in large quantities—and things which could be cleaned up so completely by the time of heavy frost that the garden could be put in apple-pie order for the winter.

Into the kitchen garden went lettuce, radishes, onions, peas, pole beans, carrots, a few tomatoes, spinach, a number of early cabbage plants, and whatever trailed over the ground—cucumbers for certain; citron, probably; a few squashes of various kinds; and cantaloupes if the family happened to like cantaloupes —or "mushmelons," the more usual name. With the

*Making good sauerkraut was an art, though the tools were simple. The shredder to slice the cabbage fine and the "stomper" to tamp it down in large tubs or stone jars were indispensable in the early steps of the process.*

exception of the cucumbers, most of which were used for pickling, these were the items intended for immediate rather than remote consumption. If both citron (the thick rinds were a favorite for preserves) and squash were planted, only one would be put into the garden, since they would cross-pollinate.

The truck patch took care of everything which could be planted in rows and tended by boy, horse, and cultivator. That meant early sweet corn and potatoes, in particular; the vegetables destined for canning in quantity, like green beans, late corn, and tomatoes; and the main crop of cabbage and shell beans. The cucumber and squash vines were a nuisance in the garden but had to be placed there since they would have been hopelessly trampled in the truck patch.

Special places were reserved for special plants, neither in the garden nor in the truck patch, although sometimes they could be snuggled up against a fence. Rhubarb, an all-time favorite for pies in early spring (it was called "pie plant" oftener than "rhubarb"), needed a sunny, wind-free place, preferably against a wall. Once the plant became established in a place it liked, it would continue to grow for years, with only the encouragement of an occasional shovelful of manure. It is not unusual to see a thriving stand of rhubarb at an abandoned farm on which everything else—possibly excepting a spreading clump of purple lilacs—has reverted to the wild.

Horse radish needed soft, permeable ground so that its roots would grow straight and free. It had to be established in a place which was never plowed and which would not be touched by a mower's scythe. "Multiplier" onions, a strong variety which produced little bulblets on their stems as well as bulbs in the ground, were put in any undisturbed spot where cows or chickens could not get at them. They would lend an unpleasant quality to milk, and it was believed that they imparted a taint to eggs.

Spearmint and peppermint, used medicinally, were wanted near the house, but in the dampest spot possible. If there were a spring run, peppermint was planted on the edge. Spearmint would tolerate a somewhat drier location—and pennyroyal, a distant cousin, could grow in dry ground and bright sun. Wormwood, used both medicinally and for flavoring (raspberry syrup, in particular), was put next to a fence post, if possible, since it grew tall and needed to be tied up. Dill, used for flavoring, tended to reseed itself annually, and was placed where the new plants would not be destroyed by cultivation the following year. The term "herb" was not ordinarily used for the plants just mentioned, but was reserved for such exotic specimens as rosemary, thyme, marjoram, or summer savory. Some herbs used at pickling or butchering time seem not to have flourished in the upcountry—saffron (pollen of the autumn crocus), coriander, and turmeric, in particular.

Farmers' almanacs—except for very early (before 1840) or very rare issues, these are still inexpensive.

Early seed catalogues

Ironwork equipment used in smokehouses, especially the iron "smudge" pots and multiple-armed or single meat hooks

Old photographs showing small out-buildings of various kinds, including smokehouses

Back issues of the *Pennsylvania Folklife* quarterly, published by the Pennsylvania Folklife Society, Box 1053, Lancaster. Pa.

Horticultural manuals, books, and periodicals of the mid-nineteenth century, many with hand-colored illustrations. While they made an obvious bid for the attention of a flower-minded clientele, the content actually had a rather broad appeal.

John Lindley's *Ladies' Botany*, published in London by James Ridgway and Sons at an unspecified date apparently not long after 1830

*The Ladies' Wreath*, a periodical edited by Mrs. S. T. Martyn, New York, 1847. Only single issues have been reported but it is not unlikely that bound volumes exist.

Joseph Harrison's *The Floricultural Cabinet*, bound volumes published in London at an unspecified date by Whittaker and Company

Bound volumes or single copies of H. C. Hanson's *The Florist and Horticultural Journal*, published in Philadelphia in 1852 and later

# 26

# The Lone Woman in the Up-Country

A good many women in the up-country were prone to declare that they were too busy to pay attention to changing fashions in dress. There can be no question as to the busyness of the lives they led, but one would probably have had to travel far to find a woman who did not know what was in fashion and what was not, even though personally she might not be in a position —or might not wish—to do anything about it.

Along with the awareness of what it was acceptable to wear went an even stronger sense of what it was correct to do. The origin of such a feeling might well be lost in antiquity, but if the Victorian code of morality attached more strongly to another place than it did to the up-country, that place might be hard to find. We are using the word "morality" here not in a limited connotation of right and wrong only, but in the broader sense of proper and improper, genteel and nongenteel, appropriate and inappropriate—even decent and indecent, all the terms being set against the background of the up-country in the nineteenth century.

It would be a mistake to picture all our feminine great-greats, back to the earliest days of the colonies, as being strong, unswerving, dedicated heroines who rocked the cradle, sickled the grain, shot rattlesnakes, and ground corn with mortar and pestle, all with no thought beyond their ultimate heavenly reward for a life well lived. They were human, too, and they reacted to circumstances and the conditions of the times as human beings have always done in the past—with a healthy regard for what other people were thinking, no matter what their reactions of the moment might be.

All this, as a preliminary to the prime consideration of what the up-country woman might and might not "decently" do to earn money in the nineteenth century—plus a few years on either side of its turn. The normal expectation was that a girl would marry, usually in her teens, and that from then on her husband would assume financial responsibility for her and for the family they would establish. But some girls did not marry, and among those who did there were some whose husbands died early, frequently leaving families of small children. Perhaps the spinsters were the least fortunate; they moved in with a married sister or brother and lived out their days on a dependency basis somewhere between that of an almost-but-not-quite equal and a household drudge. The widow might remarry; or she might—and it was at this point that the whole community would automatically assume a gratuitous concern in her affairs— attempt to earn the money necessary to support herself and her children.

There were several things she could do, with no actual prejudice to her reputation, though she might have to endure a patronizing air on the part of some. She could take in washing, for instance, if someone was actually ill or in the up-country condition known as "poorly," or she could go to the home of the ill person and do the laundry there. It would be nothing out of the ordinary if she were expected at the same time to get meals for the family employing her, tidy up the house, and perhaps do some mending. Or she might "go out" housecleaning. Some women did. The work was seasonal, and it paid but little—no more than manipulating the wooden washboard did—but beggars could not be choosers in those days.

These jobs were admittedly at the bottom of the scale. If it seems that the community should be indicted for allowing something like slavery to exist,

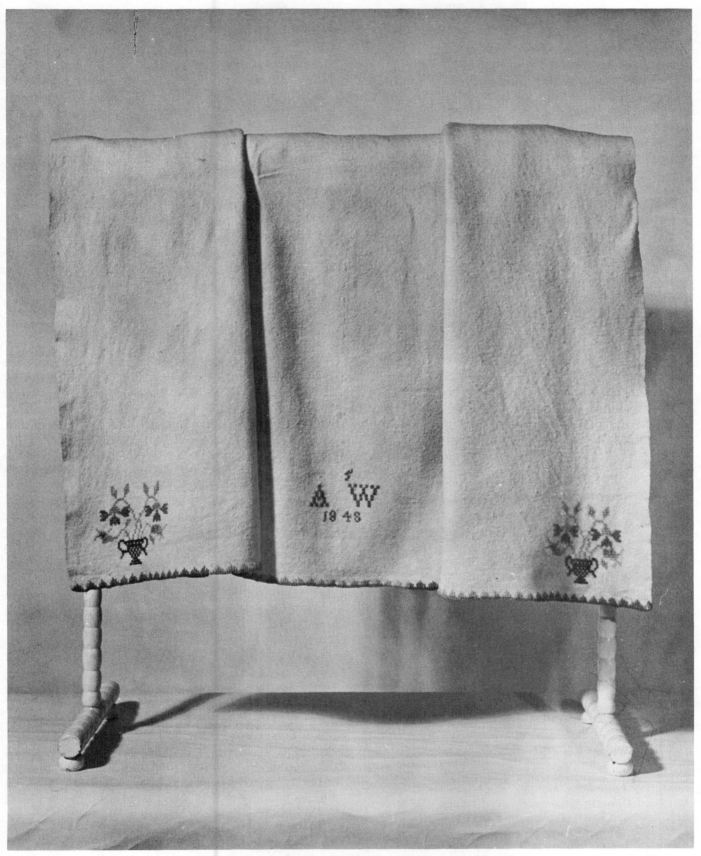

*Home-woven blanket with added hand-embroidered designs, including initials and date. This kind of piece is often referred to as a "rose" blanket.*

we need to bear in mind that cash money was not easy to come by, especially in an age of barter. Perhaps one of the cruelest aspects of the whole era was that of using hand-me-downs as payment or part-payment in place of cash. Worn-out clothing which could be made to serve again—for someone else's child—by taking a stitch here and a stitch there, along with totally inappropriate garments to be cut down in size, was a source of heartburning for many a fatherless child.

A step up in the scale was the practical nurse, who was often a midwife as well. Nowadays the practical nurse is one who has undergone a period of professional or, at least, semi-professional training. The condition did not prevail then; some women may have had training in their field, but more were elderly persons with reputations just for gentle, watchful care. Still remembered with affection by oldsters in the Newfoundland-German Valley area, although she has been gone for many years, is one "Granny" Grim, who, perhaps because she made a point of being on the job ahead of time, probably delivered almost as many babies as did Dr. (Arthur) Simons or Dr. (Fletcher) Gilpin. When Granny arrived at the place of her employer, she took charge—complete charge; that was implicit in her being there. She had a preliminary conference with the mistress of the house,

*Samplers have been popular since women first began to spend time on decorative needlework. "Memorial" samplers are less well known than many other types. Elizabeth Ann, like other needleworkers of her day, executed her memorial in black against a white background.*

but it was understood that after Granny had learned where everything was kept she would plan and prepare the meals, and see that the children got to bed on time, that they would leave the house in the morning in time for school (with ten minutes to spare if they did not dawdle), and that she would be kept informed as to the whereabouts of the man of the house in case he had to go for the doctor in a hurry. Granny's services might be arranged for, several weeks in advance; a longer period would probably have been considered indelicate.

Some women, to make ends meet, set up looms for the weaving of carpet. Often these were widows— frequently women who had brothers or perhaps brothers-in-law who would help with the initial job of installing the loom. Carpet weaving was heavy work, and only women of strong physique were likely to tackle the job. It was not very rewarding financially, but it was an eminently respectable way of earning money.

Before 1900, teaching school was less a woman's than a man's job. At a time when, in some of the remote country schools of Monroe and Pike, it was a badge of distinction to have "licked the teacher," women did well to stay out of professional education. As years passed, however, and the grown-up rowdies who had been the bane of rural schools everywhere found other outlets for their energies, women began to replace men in the classrooms. Perhaps it is merely hearsay, or perhaps it is owing to memories which have grown faulty with passing years, but there seems to be a feeling that one of two things is true of pre-1900 women teachers: either they were so loved by one and all that sweetness and light were the prevailing condition, or they had natures so iron-clad that the hoodlum kept his disruptive potentialities under control in preference to being beaten up by a woman.

The dressmaker and the milliner came closer to meeting our present notion of the business or professional woman than did any of the others mentioned, including the teacher. The dressmaker was often looked up to as much for her ability to handle complicated patterns—and her concomitant skill in reducing or enlarging the size to suit her client—as for her skill as a seamstress. Frequently she subscribed to publications in her special field, and could be counted on to know what was being worn in New York or Philadelphia as well as who had had a dress or a coat made locally over a given pattern.

There is a subtle professional distinction here which perhaps we should note: some women "took in sewing"; some were dressmakers. The woman who took

*Wool embroidery made a popular decoration. Since the name of the artist appears, it would seem that she approved of her work.*

in sewing may have performed the same kinds of services as the dressmaker, and with equal skill, but she worked at her own home, in the time she had at her disposal. She ordinarily had one room in which she kept her own equipment and supplies as well as the materials which were brought to her. She could often be counted on to complete a job for someone who had, for instance, broken her arm at just the time when she had an important dress to complete. She was not usually asked for advice, however; she was thought of more as an extra pair of hands than as a consultant.

The dressmaker, however, was a professional consultant. A typical mode of operation would be the following: Mrs. X had decided that, in order to attend the wedding of a relative in a place outside the community, she would need, let us say, a dress, a suit, and a coat. In the upper Poconos, she would, in the early 1900s, have gone to Mrs. Hazleton and explained her needs. Together, the women would reach an agreement as to the basic fabrics, the trimming, the cost, and the style. Mrs. Hazleton would take the needed measurements and would order the desired materials. A series of fittings would follow, and in due time the costumes would be completed. The dress would pose no extraordinary problems, but the suit and the coat would call for skillful tailoring—which Mrs. Hazleton was more than competent to handle.

Some dressmakers operated differently, however.

If Mrs. X had not specifically desired the services of Mrs. Hazleton, she might have let her need be known to a seamstress who would move into the house for a period of time; work on the garments desired, using materials Mrs. X had already purchased; and then go on to her next assignment. It may be that, generally speaking, there was a degree of distinction in having to visit the dressmaker rather than having the dressmaker make the call.

The milliner met a special need in the last quarter of the nineteenth century and the very beginning of the present century. She had to keep a stock on hand, and in that respect differed from the woman who did sewing professionally. Her stock included basic straw, felt, or cloth shapes as a starting point, and then an array of ribbons, veils, bows, pins, buckles, tassels, swags, artificial flowers and foliage, bunches of grapes, birds or bird plumage—whatever happened to be in fashion at the time—for the trimming. Whatever else might be lacking, she always had on hand black straws, ribbons, veils, tulle, etc., in order to be prepared for the elaborate mourning outfits called for in that day. All the objects would be displayed on tables in her home, or in boxes if other space were

lacking, and the customer, after selecting the essential foundation in vogue at the time, would usually count on the milliner's advice for the trimming.

In Hamilton Township (Monroe), Annie Fenner enjoyed the double distinction of being a popular milliner and of being the first woman in Monroe County recognized as a business woman. Farther north, a Mrs. Emil Walter for years fashioned hats for women who considered her aesthetic judgment outstanding.

The entrance of the great mail order stores of the day proved at once a boon to the women who could not afford custom services and the death knell of individual dressmaking and millinery enterprises. The National Cloak and Suit Company, Bellas Hess, the Charles William Stores—these and mail order houses still operating today made it possible for most women to feel that, at long last, fashion could be achieved with a modest expenditure of money. As for the woman whose means of livelihood had been disrupted, she had the choice of going into business in a nearby town if she could provide the necessary capital, or of turning her hand to something entirely different.

Yet another occupation should be noted as suitable

*One of the most popular types of wall decoration throughout the up-country was the framed Victorian motto, often religious in tone, worked in brilliant wools against a preperforated buckram background.*

for a woman to engage in—but with a built-in condition. She might clerk in a store if she were a close relative of either the owner or his wife, but not if the relationship did not exist. In Newfoundland, Frederic Ehrhardt founded a general store about 1860. Considerably later he made the comment, according to his biographer, that he had never had a clerk outside the family. One of his daughters, now in her nineties, was still operating the store as late as 1960.

Now and then a girl of independent spirit, old enough to leave home and branch out on her own in the city—usually with an older relative to keep an eye on her activities—could achieve success in merchandising. One of these was Annie Sieg of German Valley, a daughter of Frederic and Christina Sieg, mentioned earlier in these pages. Annie's name became a familiar one in the Philadelphia firm of Strawbridge and Clothier before she left to marry Harry TsChudy. Another, Jennie Cole, of the Williams family of Hamilton Township, became a buyer in a city department store. Long before the days of the Women's Liberation movement, these girls took their own steps toward liberty, and succeeded in the effort.

Teaching instrumental music was a respected profession, but it was not until late in the development of the up-country that it became a practical one. By the end of the 1800s, a good many young ladies had been to such seats of learning as the Moravian Female Seminary at Bethlehem or Linden Hall at Lititz, and had there acquired a taste for music. Among them, some became teachers of piano or organ—and the country home in the 1890s which could not boast at least of a reed organ was an exception rather than the rule.

It was the seminaries, too, which were responsible for a great burst of activity in fancywork. The urge toward beauty, which was one of the outward manifestations of the Victorian age, and the efforts of the young ladies who had been taught the domestic skills needed in its achievement made a combination before which nothing could stand. Housewives in an earlier day had made braided and hooked rugs; to these were now added creations of loops or petals or strings, colorful and attractive if less durable than their predecessors had been. In the early 1900s a German Valley matron boasted that no two rugs among the many which graced her floors had been made in the same way.

Crocheting, tatting, embroidery, and knitting with fine thread were popular. Where there was a practical application for these arts, as in edgings for handkerchiefs, or insertion or borders for undergarments, the opportunity was exploited to the utmost. An em-

*A tramp-carved spool holder–sewing basket, with accompanying beaded pin cushions of the kind popular at the end of the nineteenth century.*

broidered pillow top might call for months of concentrated effort, but the result was considered well worth it. Crocheted doilies, covers for chair arms, and tablecloths took shape in myriads.

Two of the typically Victorian forms of fancywork seem to have had fewer practitioners in the up-country than in places to the south—Berlin work, so-called, and painting on silk or velvet. Berlin work, achieved with colored strands of yarn on a prepatterned background, the whole having somewhat the effect of gros point or needlepoint, was a sometime rather than a usual form of decoration. Among family effects, a pillow top or other piece of silk, hand-painted in bird or floral designs, will sometimes come to light, and the chances are fair that someone in the family can recall that a dead-and-gone aunt or cousin made it long ago as a boarding school assignment—too pretty or too fragile ever to put to actual use. Paintings on velvet have weathered the years more successfully, but there seem to be even fewer of them.

Two typical deep Dutch Country kinds of work appear also above the mountain, but with fewer survivals. These are samplers—those repositories of stitches made ordinarily by little girls—and show towels. It is perhaps not too difficult to account for the paucity of samplers, which are typically eighteenth or early nineteenth century efforts. Showcase specimens of the best fancywork young people could do, they had less place in the serious atmosphere of the up-country than in communities in which life had become more evenly paced—and more likely to provide stretches of time in which youngsters could indulge in fancywork. A good example of the early

*On table runner or napkins, the red-outline type of handwork was a perennial favorite. The chances are that, in a dozen napkins, no two would have the same decorative motifs.*

sampler is one done by Elizabeth Jordan in 1800. Although the piece came to light in Mt. Bethel, over the line in Northampton, there is no positive proof that this is the Quaker family prominent in early Monroe County affairs. Later specimens, although often called samplers, are likely to be in the nature of easy exercises for young fingers rather than records of stitches known to the accomplished wielder of the needle. For the most part done in red stitchery against a white cloth background, they branch out into the square pillow shams in use at the turn of the century.

Show towels—needlework-decorated coverings for the ordinary huck towels used by members of the family—are found but rarely. Two made by female members of the Rinker family, well known in Jackson and Hamilton townships, are in simple designs, and may represent the final stages of a custom which had begun to die out down-country somewhat earlier. The same kind of tight, evenly spaced little stitches, usually in red, are found on napkins, tablecloths, and, less frequently, bedding. In Quaker families the initials or names were stamped but not given the benison of needlework—perhaps because fancy needlework might appear frivolous.

It is probably unnecessary to add that the creation of fancywork, with all its ramifications, was not a revenue-producing activity. The pieces might in later years be donated to a church bazaar or comparable activity for fund-raising purposes, but as a source of personal income—well, it seems highly improbable that anyone would try it. No matter how desperate the circumstances, that kind of thing was just not done!

## COLLECTORS LOOK FOR:

Early laundering equipment—wooden wash boards, wooden tubs, and hand-operated wringers
Objects in gros point and in needlepoint
Embroidered articles
Tatting
Crocheting
Berlin work
Samplers
Show towels
Rugs of unconventional construction
Pillow shams
Tablecloths and napkins displaying fine needlework
Knitted thread objects, up to and including bedspreads
Table runners
Bureau scarves
*Jackpot:* Hooked rugs with homemade design

# 27
## *Warp and Weft*

It seems advisable here to divide our up-country into two parts—an upper up-country, which we may call simply the Poconos; and the lower up-country, referred to in the Poconos as the territory "below the mountain."

Below the mountain, the growing of wool and flax, the practices of spinning and weaving, and the general nature of the early home clothing industry are very largely comparable with those all along the seaboard. From earliest times, the creation of clothing was of major importance, and the old ledgers available to us reflect this significance.

In Smithfield Township, indigo as a coloring agent for home-woven goods was being imported from Esopus (now Kingston), New York, as early as the 1740s. A bushel of flax seed—and a bushel would seed a considerable stretch of ground—was worth four shillings in 1756. (Later, flax seed had other uses also, notably for oil.) A weaver in Shawnee was establishing credit for his necessary purchases at the store by spinning linen thread in 1753. In other words, flax production, from the seeding through the tedious processes of hatcheling—or "swingling" or "scutching"—and spinning and weaving, was an established, on-going occupation below the mountain in eighteenth century up-country life.

While most professional weavers could work with either flax or wool, different processes and implements were involved—and rates of compensation seem to have varied considerably. Perhaps those with greater skill were able to command higher prices; the ledgers are mute on that point. We learn that John Pue (Dupuis?) in Shawnee got three shillings for weaving 26 yards of cloth in 1753—threepence a yard. Daniel Labar charged sixpence a yard in 1781. In the new century, in the same community, after currency had changed to dollars and cents, Thomas Crisbin got $1.55 for weaving 10 yards of linen (1818) and George Treible $3.25 for 25 yards (1822). Other weavers in or near the Smithfield community in roughly the same time period were Rebeckah Bartron, Aaron Hankinson, Henry Biles, William Bensley, and Matthias Winans. The names of Biles, Bensley, and Winans appeared on Monroe County tax lists as early as 1796. Bensley owned ten acres of land; nothing was said of the other two. One Henry Smith traded some of his woven goods for shoes at Shawnee between 1827 and 1830, and hearsay has it that an "old settler" named Peter La Bar had two looms in his house at Bushkill about the same time, and that he wove cloth for other settlers. (The La Bars were early land owners on Mt. Minsi, just below the Delaware Water Gap, too.)

There seems to be less about wool in the old records than there is about flax. In fact, the name of only one grower of sheep has come to light in all the years up to 1837—that of Chauncey Dimmick, who sold ten pounds of wool in 1837 (possibly 1838) at 50 cents a pound. He sold two sheep for $4.00 the same year . . . wool obviously commanding greater compensation than the creatures producing it. The weavers of woolen cloth appear to have set their prices according to the quality or fineness of the cloth produced. Thus, woolen flannel for shirts, woven by persons named above, ranged from seven cents to 18 cents a yard.

What we have been saying has almost entirely been about cloth intended for clothing. Below the mountain, clothing was of necessity a home product; in the years up to the early nineteenth century a choice between a homemade garment and a store-bought one did not exist. In the Pocono country, where history for the most part started in the 1800s, not the 1700s, there was no alternative either; in most cases it was a store-bought garment or nothing. Home-woven fabrics were all but unknown—and for a number of good reasons. Foremost among these was the impracticability of transporting looms over the kinds of roads existing in the early part of the century. In much of the open territory of Wayne—well out of the Pocono country—conditions comparable to those in the "home" communities of New England existed, and moving a loom from one place to another was no more of a problem than it was in Connecticut—or below the mountain. In the Poconos, moving *anything* by wheeled vehicle in the early years was avoided if there was an alternative. By 1820, the availability of store-bought woven goods was a boon to the settler. True, it had to be secured by barter rather than by cash—but at least it was there.

The difficulty of growing flax in the Poconos was a significant factor, too. Flax grew well below the mountain and as late as the 1850s it still constituted an important crop in some sections, one of which was Chestnuthill Township. In the higher altitudes it flourished less abundantly, though in Newfoundland a German shoemaker was using linen thread made from his own flax as late as 1918. Since there was no particular reason to grow it in any quantity, the soil generally was put to more rewarding uses.

Then there was the matter of a limited supply of wool. Sheep were not entirely lacking in the Pocono territory, although they were never widely popular— and for good reason. Sheep on an open range, with a shepherd and a dog in attendance, are one thing; in an upland pasture, turned out on their own, they are something entirely different. Sheep—at least Pocono mountain sheep—seem to possess a great deal of curiosity and apparently some deep-seated convictions about the nature of the grass beyond their designated grazing grounds. In consequence, the sheep pastures in the up-country were enclosed with wooden board fences of five-board height, or with barbed wire fences of at least five strands. Anything less was simply an invitation to breachiness—and a stray lamb or sheep was seldom likely to come back to the fold. Since fences of these proportions called for a tremendous amount of labor, in the case of boards, or were inordinately expensive, in the case of wire, the sheep pasture—and thus the size of the flock—was kept small.

A deterrent to the raising of sheep on farms in which the pasture was out of sight of the house was

*Anna Elisabeth Betger's flax hatchel, dated 1794. Many hatchels were decorated in some degree, but few more elaborately. (The letters "in" after "Betger" indicate the feminine form of the German surname.)*

the ever-present risk of attack by wandering dogs, and more than one farmer gave up the practice of raising sheep because of the havoc created by these animals. They were not wild packs; they were the usual mixed-breed farm dogs with hound or Shepherd blood, but once they had discovered that running sheep was an exciting pastime there was no stopping them. A sheep-running dog that had tasted blood had to be destroyed; there was no known way of rehabilitating a killer.

Wool was a favored object of barter, and a surplus might make its way to the general store, as we have indicated. More of it, however, would be likely to go

*A completely handmade yarn reel with a heart-shaped base. The piece, black with age and dust, was found tucked away under the eaves of a Wayne County farmhouse.*

to a local carding operation—occasionally carried on as a sideline by a miller, but sometimes as an independent enterprise. Carding straightened out the fibers, which were likely to be in a matted and tumbled condition after the washing which preceded the trip to the carding machine. If the carded strands were turned out in parallel ranks in a strip of uniform thickness, the sheet was known as batting, or a batt. The best of the batting was reserved as filling for quilts and comforters; the rest was destined for the spinning wheel.

Many families had both wool wheels and flax wheels —but either might be used for wool, some women preferring to stand ("walk" was the term used) while they worked and others to sit. For whatever reason, some of the reels, which were used to form the yarn into skeins after it had come from the wheel, were more attractive than were the wheels. One with a heart-shaped base, from a long-deserted attic in the Poconos, is unique in design—and also a masterly piece of hand construction throughout. Niddy-noddies, commonly used in New England to skein yarn, seem not to have been very popular in Pennsylvania, and swifts, widely used both to the north and the south, were apparently nonexistent.

Housewives who would have been reluctant to try their skill at fine spinning, to say nothing of weaving, had fewer qualms at making yarn to be used for such everyday objects as mittens, stockings and heavy socks, "fascinators" (scarves worn over the head), pull-on caps—including the favorite *Zipfel* (tasseled) cap for small boys—wristlets and vests. Homemade yarn of run-of-the-mill quality was seldom uniform enough in texture for more ambitious projects; store-bought Germantown yarn was used when a really fine job was to be done. Even so, it was taken for granted that a knitter of average skill could turn out a pair of socks in a checkered pattern, or mittens with rainbow decoration at the wrist.

The processing of wool as a business got an early start in the part of the country below the Poconos. John Keller, of Kellersville, at the time of his sudden death in 1854 was operating a factory where wool was cleaned, carded, woven, and dyed, according to the Keller family record. His son David gave up the business when he found that it was injurious to his health. (In those days, the term "allergy" was unknown.) Though the family history does not indicate the date of the opening of the factory, it seems to have been operating at least as early as 1845 when Thomas McFall McIlhaney, who was born in Upper Mt. Bethel Township in 1823, went there to work as a tailor. McIlhaney became a prominent citizen; a nearby village bears his name.

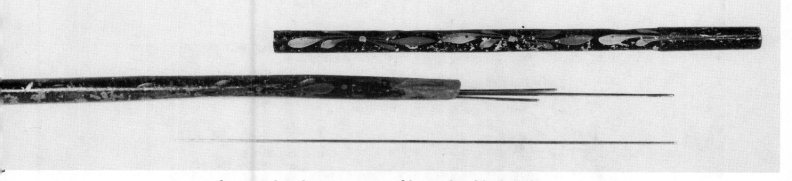

*One wonders how women could use the thin knitting needles of the nineteenth century, but evidently the thinness posed no problem. Knitting needle cases of decorated tôle like the ones shown above are almost nonexistent today, according to antiques dealers.*

The Stroudsburg Woolen Mill was founded in 1865 with Richard S. Staples as its first president. The company changed hands a number of times, passing in succession to Doster Brothers (of Bethlehem); Kitson, Walker, and Davis; Wallace and Kitson; and to John Davis. Its best known product appears to have been material for overcoats.

The antiques collector, while he may have an academic interest in the early production of clothing, is more likely to be concerned with the colorful woven coverlets which, unlike dresses or shirts or trousers, have come down to our own times as desirable objects of art. These coverlets, woven at first on handmade looms and later by the Jacquard "machine" which rendered a good many earlier processes obsolete, called for both flax and wool—flax for the warp and wool for the woof. Yet an unexpected—even a surprising—condition appears to exist: it is all but impossible to authenticate more than a few woven coverlets as bona fide up-country products.

Venerable unmarked coverlets are treasured in many families, and obviously date back to the '40s and '50s, the heyday of the genre; even the most history-conscious housewife, however, is ordinarily forced to admit that she has no idea as to their time or place of origin, beyond the fact that they are "very old." By no means do all old coverlets have woven-in corner cartouches in which the date, the name and place of the weaver, and sometimes of the buyer, are there for the collector to see. For those which do, there is of course no problem—but the data in many instances are those of places deep in the *echt* Dutchland.

It would be easy to jump to the conclusion that up-country coverlets are mostly imports—easy, but prob-

ably wrong, as we shall see. There is obviously a job for the researcher, of course, but the coverlets are there, in the blue and white patterns which presumably date back to the time when indigo was the usual or only dye available, and in the red, blue, green, and natural color combinations so universally favored. We know the names of a number of weavers; early tax lists are helpful in that respect. Upper Mt. Bethel Township, at the northernmost tip of Northampton County, adjacent to Monroe, embracing what today are the hamlets of Richmond, Stone Church, Mt. Bethel, and Portland, had at least eight: Daniel Fravel (Frable); Joseph Long, John La Bar, Jacob Nicholas, Samuel and John Oyer, Christian Poff (originally "Pfaff"?), and George Snyder. Most of these surnames occur today in the up-country. What we can not do, until someone finds the weaver's Rosetta Stone and deciphers its mysteries, is put two and two together.

There may be a ray of light so far as the blue and white coverlets are concerned. Within the last year a single identification has been made—the hitherto unknown P.H.U.M.T. whose initials stand over the word "Bethel." For years, although a coverlet with this marking was known, no one had succeeded in making either a positive attribution or a good guess. Now it appears that "P.H." stands for Philip Hilliard, and the remainder of the cryptogram, "Upper Mt. (Bethel)" or "Upper Mt. (Bethel) Township." Hilliard, on the tax list in 1839, owned a house, 44 acres of land, a horse, and three cows. With the first identification clear, we know that it was he who made a coverlet for P. Snyder in 1839; one for Hester Ann Brown in 1840; and one for Elizabeth Teep in 1846. There were undoubtedly many others.

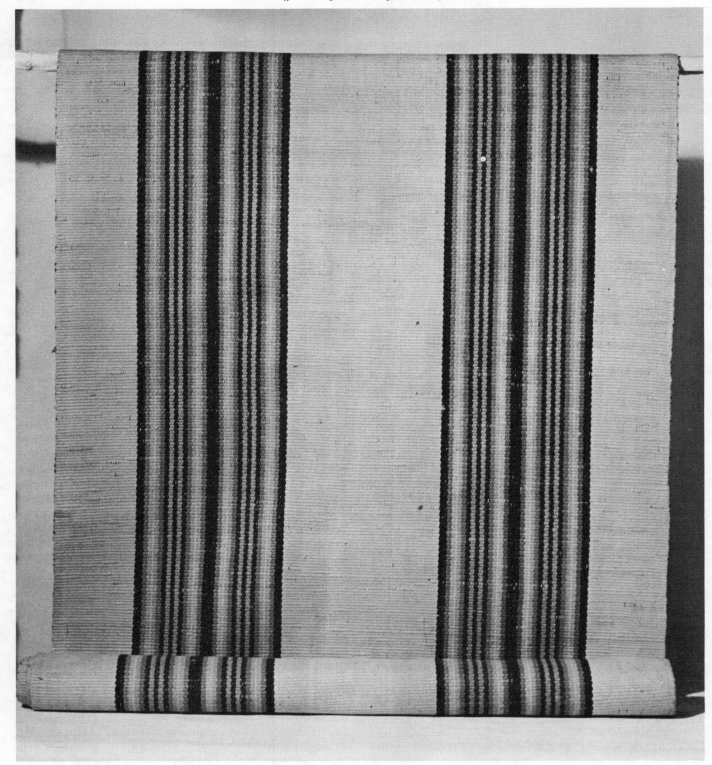

*Few household objects can compare in vivid color with rainbow rag carpet. A single strip can be attractive; a floor completely covered with it might be overpowering.*

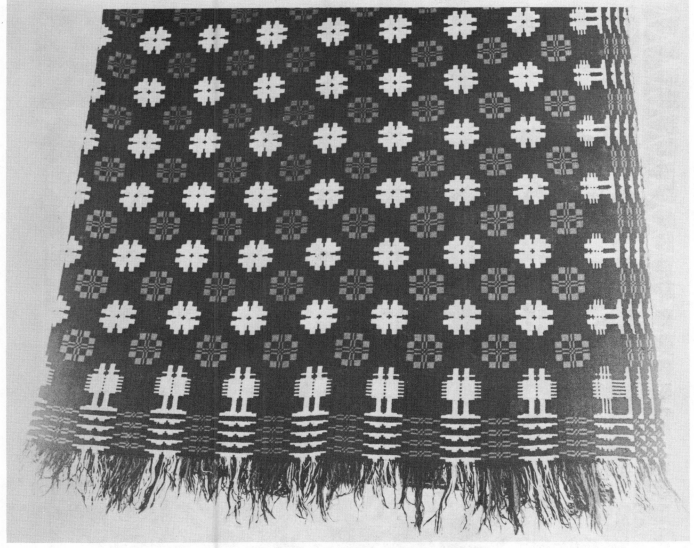

*Red, white, and blue woven coverlet, unmarked as to
maker or date, long in the possession of the Henrich
Fenner family of Sciota. The pattern is usually referred to as Pine Tree or Twin Pines.*

There is one happy exception to the over-all condition of anonymity—that of Jacob Setzer (1819–1892)
of Jackson Township. He was descended from George
Setzer, an early man of affairs in Jackson; was on the
Jackson Township tax list for 1849; and is buried
in Custard's Cemetery, south of Bartonsville. He used
a Jacquard loom, and his pattern book must have been
identical with, or a least remarkably similar to, those
used by other weavers in his time—the middle of the
nineteenth century. A surviving granddaughter, a
few years ago, recalled that some of his wool-and-
linen coverlets had been in actual use within her

memory, but were so worn and faded that the original
hues could barely be discerned.

The colors favored by Setzer were red and white,
and the patterns of which he was most fond, if one
may judge from the four known surviving specimens,
all in private hands, include hearts and roses. No date
appears in the corner cartouches of his coverlets, but
the information "Jacob Setzer, Jackson Township,
Monroe County," is woven in. Like other Jacquard-
loomed coverlets, these are in two pieces, carefully
sewed together at the middle.

It would appear that the up-country relied heavily

*Blue and white woven coverlet with eagle design in the border, made by Philip Hilliard of Upper Mt. Bethel Township for a Monroe County family. (Courtesy of the Monroe County Historical Society)*

on quilts and comforters for bed covers. The story of quilting has been told elsewhere, but a note on yarn-tied comforters may not be amiss here. Frankly, a comforter was, more often than not, a time-saving device. Like its more sophisticated relative, the pieced or appliquéd quilt, it had three component parts— the top, the liner or filling, and the backing. The top, however, while now and then an attractively pieced specimen comes to light, was frequently a single piece of woolen fabric. (Very early comforters were sometimes of linsey-woolsey.) The backing was frequently plain outing flannel, and the filling consisted of carded wool batts. The three parts were joined at regular intervals by darning-needlefuls of brilliantly colored yarn, pulled through all three parts and firmly knotted. According to the colors of the yarn, even otherwise drab comforters could be attractive. Perhaps their chief virtue, though, lay in the fact that, when soiled, they could easily be taken apart for washing and then reassembled and given a new lease on life with fresh yarn.

What the up-country may have lacked in sophisticated looms and loomed objects, it made up for in its own specialty—woven rugs and carpets. By the mid-1800s, even the most remote hamlet seems to have had at least one person who, with spools of warp and a homemade loom, could convert balled carpet rags into carpet. There was no intricate arrangement here of mathematical formulas which, correctly followed, would result in floral or geometrical patterns; instead of pine trees and hearts and birds, there was a continuous strip of carpet ornamented almost entirely according to the color or colors of the warp.

At that, a surprising variety was possible, with "just plain" carpet being woven only when nothing beyond economical utility was under consideration. A popular pattern was one known simply as "check"; the warp chosen would typically be blue and white, set in alternating bands two inches wide. Half the rags chosen for the carpet would be blue, and the other half a neutral tone or a general mixture of all colors except blue. The weaver would alternate the strips of blue and non-blue rags to correspond to the width of the blue and the white warp, the effect being more pleasing than a hit-or-miss arrangement would have been. One of the rooms in the Slateford Farm restoration of the National Park Service near the Delaware Water Gap is laid with this blue-check carpet.

A universal favorite is the rainbow carpet, as colorful as its name would imply. While it might be overpowering in effect if injudiciously used, it can also be strikingly effective. Like the blue check, it

depends for its charm on a studied arrangement of background color and an equally careful use of colored warp. The background may be plain (black, brown, cream-colored, or any other single tone the user wishes) or monochromatic. The warp used for the body of the strip is often a narrow alternation of black and white, but the 8-inch-wide bands used as outer borders are of such composition as yellow-orange-red-brown-red-orange-yellow—or a less subtle combination like orange-purple-green-purple orange.*

A pepper-and-salt pattern was achieved when all the rags were black or gray and the warp was of alternating black and white. Since the over-all effect here was neutral, pepper-and-salt carpet was usually made when the owner had small, brightly colored rugs she wished to lay on top for accent.

Responsibility for good rag carpet was about evenly divided between the supplier of the rags and the weaver. It was up to the supplier to see that the rags were evenly cut, free from frayed edges, and of the right color for the desired effect. The weaver's job was to create a smooth, tight carpet, with no variations in the spacing of the warp. A good, firm carpet made with warp of superior quality was what every housewife hoped to get. Most weavers have long since been forgotten, but one still remembered approvingly in the neighborhood of Greentown, Pike County, was a Mrs. Alice Schiffler, whose work was always carefully done. It was said, with what authority it is now out of the question to determine, that her loom, housed in a little building of its own, had been converted from one originally intended to weave "blankets"—presumably coverlets.

How long rag carpet could be expected to wear depended upon the kind of treatment it got. Some, too pretty to risk, was tacked down in unused, spare rooms, with the curtains drawn to keep the sun from fading the colors. There it lay, sometimes for two generations or more. Some was kept in the roll after it was brought home, awaiting a super-special use which never arrived. It is this unused carpet today's buyer hopes to pick up at a country auction—and, once in a while, he is lucky.

Some carpet looms are still in existence in the up-country. With a contemporary resurgence of interest in rag carpet, a number of all-but-forgotten looms are being put back into use. In most cases, however, operators find new, compact looms more satisfactory to handle than the massive behemoths of the past—and

---

* Rags for the background of rainbow-stripe carpet were sometimes completely covered with warp of a single color, often a light tone.

*Woven coverlets depicting George Washington are said to have heralded the Philadelphia Centennial of 1876. This one is dated 1871.*

of course today's buying public expects new, not used, fabric in the woven product. One of the skilled weavers of the old school, the possessor of a loom which goes back to the earliest days of carpet weaving in Monroe County, is still at work in the village of Brodheadsville.

Now and then a roll of what appears to be hand-woven rag carpet of superior quality, and in unused condition, comes to light—but with a sewed-on tag identifying it as the product of a carpet factory in Carlisle, Pa. Such carpet is about as close to the old-time product as most collectors are able to get and, in fact, it is so like what was once produced on country looms that without the label even an expert would be hard put to tell the difference.

## COLLECTORS LOOK FOR:

Flax hatchels, especially those with decorations, names, initials, or dates

Hand carders (preferably by the pair) for wool

Woven coverlets—whole, halves, or fragments

Weaving pattern books

Unskeined yarn as it came from the spinning wheel

Old knitting needles and needle cases

Yarn reels

Spinning wheels

Niddy-noddies

Handmade knitted objects

Rag-carpet, especially in fancy patterns

Rag rugs (warp-fringed short lengths of carpet)

Spools of carpet warp

*Jackpot:* Completely authenticated and documented woven coverlet in pristine condition

# 28
## Quilts by the Dozen

The physical demands on women were almost infinitely more varied than those on men—and whoever coined the term "the weaker sex" obviously had little acquaintance with the feminine contingent of the up-country. The resourcefulness and the stamina called for in spending an adult lifetime of 18-hour days are something beyond our complete comprehension.

In spring, summer, and fall the woman on a lonely farm without even the smoke of a neighbor's chimney in sight could usually take her way of life with some degree of equanimity. There were so many chores that had to be done during the day that she had little time for reflection, and at night her necessary work could hardly be completed before bedtime.

Winter was a different matter. Children left the house daily for school, and the man of the establishment seemed always to have errands which took him to the haunts of his fellowmen—the store, the mill, the blacksmith shop, or perhaps just to return something borrowed. His wife remained at home except as she created an occasion to go elsewhere. The woman whose children had grown had an advantage; when life at home became too monotonous to take she could walk to the house of a neighbor, even if that neighbor lived at a considerable distance. The woman with very young children was the person who suffered most deeply from lonesomeness, and in a day when families of ten to fifteen were the rule, practically every woman was a victim at some time or other.

One of the ways of getting through the interminable winter days was the practice of quilting. Every home needed bed coverings—"covers" was the term usually employed—and in those long-ago times before electric blankets, when the only heat upstairs came from a stove pipe leading from the kitchen or living room below, there was apparently never a question of acquiring too many. Long overlooked by the majority of antique hunters, these quilts, packed away for years in mothballs, have come into their own—not quietly, either, but with considerable fanfare.

A major impetus to the search for the laid-away quilts of the past and also to the contemporary return to the quilting frame has been given by the Pennsylvania Folklife Society, which features a nationwide quilting contest yearly in connection with its folk festival at Kutztown. If there are quilters today who can match their forebears in skill—and there are!—they have an opportunity for recognition their predecessors never enjoyed. The folk festival has come to be known all over the world, and prize-winning quilts each year are sold to visitors who come from such scattered places as Panama, Rome, Japan, Peru, Sweden, or Canada. Quilts have been bought at the festival for display at two international expositions—and for hundreds of homes far and wide, where they may actually be put to use or, more probably, displayed proudly as works of art.

At that, there are Dutch Country quilts which surpass in beauty and quality even the best specimens shown in the great display room at Kutztown. A necessary condition of entering a quilt in the contest is that the owner be willing to sell it—and the possessor of an heirloom of superlative quality is rarely likely to dispose of it for a consideration of dollars and cents. Bear in mind that we are speaking here of antique quilts, which constitute one of the stated categories in the annual display. Perhaps fewer than a tenth of all those submitted are antique—and "antique" is a comparatively flexible term, with a hundred years of age as a general but not

*Three ways of laying out a quilting pattern are shown here: perforated cardboard through which powder (often plumber's chalk) was tapped; a heavy metal marker to the edges of which powder or crayon would be applied; and six-pointed tin stars around which light pencil marks would be drawn.*

absolute guide. The rest are thoroughly contemporary, are submitted by individuals or by groups, and are not confined to the Dutch Country either as to their making or as to their design.

Quilting was essentially what a leading authority has called a "salvage" art. In some places out in the country in the 1800s, practically all the clothing, either everyday or Sunday, worn by members of the family was made at home. The economical housewife cut her cloth to the best advantage she could, but she also saved every scrap. She kept these scraps ("snibbles," children called them) in what was known in Monroe County as the piece-patch bag—and woe to the person who for any reason whatsoever removed anything from it.

The earliest record we have (1743) gives us names of fabrics which have long passed from memory—such esoterica as Nonesoprity ("None-so-pretty"?), callimancoe, oznabrig ("Osnabrück"?), flannan, kersey, shalloon, frise, and garlix ("Görlitz"?). If there are in the up-country either quilts or piece-patches in which these goods figure, they have thus far eluded the researchers. We shall have to start at a later point to put at least a toe on familiar ground.

A country store log of the 1860s provides a clue to the drygoods the housewife was trading her butter and eggs for at that time: calico (14¢ a yard), chintz and gingham (16¢), muslin (20¢), flannel (45¢), and cashmere ($1.00). There are some in the book which are totally unfamiliar to today's buyer: "Delane" (delaine), which was a light woolen or sometimes woolen-and-cotton dress fabric; "Selecia" (silesia), a twilled cotton fabric also used for dresses; and "Italian cloth," a light material of cotton and worsted used expressly for linings—and sometimes rather patronizingly termed "farmer's satin."

Appearing over and over are heavy-duty cloths, the scraps of which might show up in carpets but not in quilts—drilling, panting, ticking, lining, and canvas. Calico and muslin were way out ahead in frequency of purchase—a condition directly reflected in quilt making. Calico came in bright colors and a great variety of small-figured patterns. Muslin (either just plain muslin or "B" muslin—the "B" perhaps standing for "bleached") was used not only for underclothing but also invariably for the backing of quilts. Two dyes were sold at the store, indigo and madder. Some muslin tends to resist dyes; we do not know, therefore, whether the plain blues and yellow-reds of old muslin represent a home dyeing operation or not.

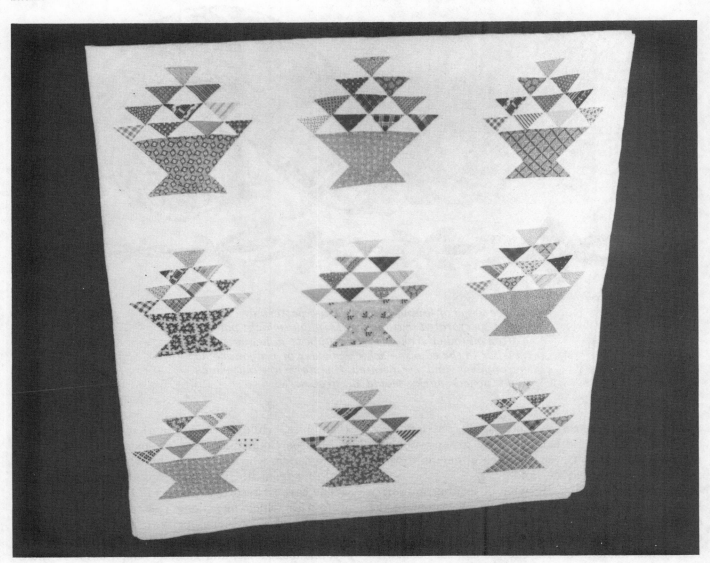

*An early pieced quilt with exceptionally fine stitching.*
*The pattern is known as Flower Basket.*

*The Dutch Tulip (look for the design in the dark patches) in work which is both pieced and appliquéd. Comparatively few quilts are signed or dated, but this one is marked M. A. Learn, 1855. The Learns were a prominent family in Monroe County.*

When the scrapbag began to bulge, the housewife took account of stock. Before she embarked on a quilt-making project she needed to consider what she had to work with. Scraps of considerable size meant that she could utilize certain patterns or designs in her repertoire; a preponderance of small pieces would indicate entirely different patterns. If there were one pattern at which she particularly wanted to try her hand—let us say, for example, Drunkard's Progress, a rather demanding one—and the materials at hand seemed inadequate, she would probably pay a visit, scrapbag in hand, to a relative or close friend, to see whether some trading might be done.

Once the pattern had been chosen, most of her in-between fragments of available time for the next few weeks or months—often months—would be devoted to cutting out and sewing together the pieces which would combine to form individual blocks of the quilt. (Appliquéd designs on a full-size background, while not unknown in the up-country, were less frequently undertaken; for that matter, they could hardly be considered a phase of salvage art, either.) In time, the blocks would be joined, and the infinitude of little patches began to take on the aspect of a quilt.

There were still a number of important steps ahead, and it was these steps which, both in anticipation and in actuality, helped to dispel the sense of isolation and monotony mentioned above. Homemade quilting frames were set up in the largest room which could be heated. The furniture was moved aside or even removed, except for the chairs, when a quilting was to take place, and the house put in readiness for callers. The work to be done by the quilters included assembling the three necessary component parts of the quilt—the piecework top, the filling, which was ordinarily wool batting, and the backing—and if time allowed, binding the finished product. Usually the quilting was a day-long affair involving up to a dozen women; sometimes several days were required.

The actual amount of time called for in completing a quilt was largely determined by the intricacy of the pattern or patterns to be used in the stitching process. It was not just a matter of assembling three layers of material into one unit; a good quilt was a showplace for fine needlework according to a thought-out plan for the quilt as a whole. True, this tracework of white was hardly noticeable on the patchwork top, although the practiced eye of the needleworker could easily detect it there—but on the back it showed as a thing of beauty in itself. It was a matter of pride for the quilters to put forth their best efforts at the home of a neighbor.

The quilting designs were ordinarily laid out in chalked lines, either by means of a pierced stencil or by a cooky-cutter-like tin pattern marker which imprinted the lines on the fabric. Simple "utility" quilting merely followed the lines of the pattern in the blocks, and some quilts did not go beyond this point. Where any sizable area of white or a solid color appeared, however, as in appliquéd quilts, the mettle of the quilter was tested, for here the overall pattern assumed real importance. Using a complicated, large-scale quilting design on a patchwork quilt in which the prior assembling of tiny blocks was an art in itself may seem like gilding the lily—in the telling. In actuality, it represented a considerable enhancement of the attractiveness of the whole.

Gradually, as churches grew larger than they had been in the beginning, and as basements came to be utilized and Sunday School rooms created, many quilting operations were moved to the church in preference to discommoding private families. By the early 1900s, too, quilting had begun to be a revenue-producing activity, and the Ladies Aid Society of almost every rural church included quilting among its activities, often putting into the shade such events as strawberry socials, picnics, and bazaars. There are in the up-country today, difficult as it may be for us to realize, women who have engaged in church quilting over a period of more than 60 years—simply because they enjoy it.

It is not easy, in view of the fact that quilting was a far-flung art, to state with any degree of authority that certain designs or patterns were peculiar to the up-country. Actually, there may well be *no* up-country pattern which was not known in some other place —anywhere from Allentown to Virginia or Indiana. Entries in the antiques category in the competition of the Pennsylvania Folklife Society, previously mentioned, are in many cases free of regional significance. The best that one can do is to indicate some of the patterns of old quilts which have been found in the territory with which we are concerned.

Among these, Drunkard's Progress, mentioned above, is familiar as a design, although it is less likely to be identified by that name than it would be in communities less strongly church-oriented than up-country villages. One of the oldest, if one may judge by surviving specimens, is the Sunflower—a quilt made of large blocks in which a gigantic daisy-like flower is the central motif. The roughly representational Log Cabin pattern, in which long, narrow strips are used, would probably be found in most early homes. The block is divided diagonally, one-half being devoted to dark strips and the other to light.

*A carefully appliquéd quilt in one of the many, many variants of the Tulip pattern.*

The sharply pointed star was a familiar design and had a great many variations. Most spectacular was the one known variously as Moravian Star, Morning Star, or Bethlehem Star—one enormous star built up of diamond-shaped blocks with one basic color but varying intensities, carefully arranged so that the total effect was one of light gradually merging into dark or vice versa. The diamond-shaped pieces were not ordinarily of salvage material alone, and the resources of even the best-stocked country store were taxed to provide a dozen tones of red or yellow or—the prime favorite—violet.

Popular in Monroe was the Pinwheel pattern, which called for blocks of dark colors set against their mirror images in white. Pinwheel blocks faintly suggest the whirling swastika design familiar to the student of things Pennsylvania Dutch farther south—and also known, for whatever devious reason, as the Jacks pattern.

When time was lacking, the Crazy quilt was most likely to come into being. Pieces of irregular size and shape were joined in more or less promiscuous fashion, as the name suggests, until the desired size had been achieved, but a steady check was maintained to see that there was a variety in color and pattern and that a fabric as thin as calico, for instance, was not joined to a heavy flannel piece. Crazy quilts were often made of heavier materials than those calling for

*An exceptional quilt—velvet and brocade in the Fan pattern, with added refinements of decorative appliqué, embroidery, and fancy stitching. Dated in the 1800s. (Courtesy of the Monroe County Historical Society)*

*An appliquéd pillow case in the Oak Leaf pattern, shown with ends folded under.*

meticulously exact workmanship, and in some cases at least were made at all only because heavy materials were expensive and not a single fragment could be allowed to go to waste. Some were all flannel; some were all wool, *not* including flannel. In any case, a compensating gesture for the random effect was made in the fancy stitching which outlined each piece on the quilt. Bright-colored silk or crocheting cotton was used for this purpose, and often the complete repertoire of fancy stitches known to the quilter was utilized.

Very, very special were Crazy quilts in which all the pieces were of velvet, brocade, moire, or heavy ribbon, many of the pieces additionally being heavily embroidered in silk. When such a quilt was contemplated, either at home or, as seems sometimes to have been the case, at a boarding school for young ladies, pieces of treasured fabric were accepted—or perhaps solicited—from friends and relatives, and the name of the donor was embroidered on each. The resultant quilt was then called a Friendship quilt. A matching pair of these in Stroudsburg is of such splendor that it is obvious no one has ever had the temerity to put them into actual service. They are, like all those of their kind, demonstrations of superb needlework rather than mere specimens of quilting.

Another type of Friendship quilt, found in Monroe County and also farther afield, is one which served as a fund-raising device for the church in which it was created. As many persons as the quilters could get in touch with were solicited for small cash contributions and a handwriting specimen. The handwriting was sometimes done directly on the cloth block, after which

the quilter outlined it in red. Sometimes there were quilters adept enough to copy the signature—a simpler procedure than carrying the cloth from door to door. After the quilt was completed, it was either raffled off or put up at auction.

There were still other variations of the personalized quilt. One in a private collection is a kind of recording, in needlework, of scenes familiar to family members—house, barn, animals, brook, winding lane, rail fence, and so on. Such mementos are usually meaningful as long as they remain in the family, but are likely to evoke expressions of regret when they are allowed to pass into alien hands.

While patchwork existed principally in quilts, one of the prized collectibles in the territory is the patchwork pillow case. A pair of these appearing at auction is likely to arouse more interest than a quilt because of their rarity. Pillow cases were laundered much more frequently than quilts, and those which have survived are usually in existence because somebody once liked them well enough to preserve them by retiring them from service.

As one looks back now, it appears that three major techniques were principally employed by old-time up-country quilters, each technique in the course of time lending its name to a category or subdivision of the whole field. While all the categories are found throughout Wayne, Pike, and Monroe, the patchwork quilt, with its myriad patterns, was way out ahead in number and, allowing for notable exceptions here and there, in quality.

Next would be the appliquéd quilt, in single block patterns rather than in overall designs. (In the whole domain of quilting, there were probably no more magnificent specimens than the super de luxe appliquéd bride's quilts—but few persons in the up-country ever had the time or the means to indulge in this luxury.) Yet it appears that it was the bride's quilt which gave rise to the idea of a dozen quilts as the appropriate number a newly married young woman would bring to the marriage as an important part of her dowry. Twelve, of any kind she chose to make, would be of her own fabrication. The thirteenth, the "bride's quilt," was the work of her friends—and perhaps of her mother, on whom the onus of the actual quilting frequently devolved.

The third general category would be the one in which all the decoration was done by outlining in red cotton, against a white background. The signature-Friendship quilt belongs in this category, as would quilts made of blocks, each with its individual, self-contained design. Some quilters were content to outline conventional patterns in pencil, and then go over them with a needleful of red cotton. More appealing, however, are specimens which show original touches—an assembly of fruit or flowers or leaves or trees or anything which occurred to the artist. A favorite pet might be immortalized in red, or a farm dinner bell suspended in its frame—or a pot of geraniums of exceptional size.

It would be unfair to suggest that these three types —patchwork, appliqué, and red outline—constituted the sum total of up-country quilt-making in earlier times, of course. Perhaps a specimen of every ramification of the art known throughout the world of quilting could be found somewhere in the area but, by and large, the categories are as listed.

COLLECTORS LOOK FOR:

Patchwork quilts
Patchwork pillow cases
Single quilt blocks of patchwork
Early fabrics used in quilting
Cardboard patterns used in cutting individual parts
    of quilt blocks
Appliquéd quilts, blocks, and pillow cases
Friendship quilts, especially those with names of
    historically significant persons
Quilting frames
Sewing baskets
Sewing birds (small ornamental clamps)
Emery bags and pincushions
Metal quilting pattern markers
*Jackpot:* Any dated quilt of good workmanship made
    before 1900

# 29
# Frolics, Bees—and Carpet Rags

No matter how industriously the farmer worked or how long the day he put in, he could not hope to accomplish by himself certain large-scale operations. A washed-out stretch of road had to be filled in after a torrential summer storm; a piece of "new ground" had to be cleared of stumps and rocks to create added crop space; a roof blown off by a violent wind had to be replaced as quickly as possible. All these operations might call for the combined efforts of the male community, usually for a single day but occasionally longer. The man to benefit from this concentration of assistance was normally expected to provide refreshments—solid and liquid. It may have been the liquid aspect of the arrangement that gave rise to the term "frolic"—the usual up-country word for the dawn-to-dark operation. (No less a personage than the eminent pioneer and man of affairs Daniel Brodhead bought three gallons of rum for his house-raising on October 20, 1743—at a cost of one pound, four shillings, according to the record.)

Normally, too, it was a work force of this nature which graded the yards of small country churches; built walls for the cemeteries and cleared the enclosure of dewberry vines and poison ivy and sumac; and erected sheds to shelter the horses and conveyances which got the congregation to church on time in stormy weather. Since there was usually a firm conviction, at least among the women of the congregation, that church affairs and alcohol did not mix, church frolics were frequently less well attended than those of secular nature. The term "frolic" was still used, but there was a difference in the connotation of the word. It was one thing to do one's duty; it was a horse of a brighter color to do one's duty and enjoy himself at the same time. At a church frolic the minister would be on hand, and his influence was normally a sobering one, for he often worked harder than anyone else. And there were ministers, it is said, who were not averse to sharing the cup that cheers.

In New England, a frolic and a bee may have been one and the same thing. Not so in the Pennsylvania up-country: a frolic was an occasion for heavy, serious work; a bee implied work, too, but equally implicit was the understanding that it would be followed by fun.

The spelling bee of the one-room country school should probably be counted as an exception; it was really neither a bee nor a frolic, in spite of its name. It was an occasion for achieving or sustaining intellectual distinction and could be very exciting; nothing, however, was demanded of the spectators beyond the moral support of their favorite candidates, in a great many cases. True, now and then *everyone* took part at the start of the affair, with the weaklings eliminated early and only a few serious participants remaining. It was possible, then, that an accomplished dark horse might appear; if he did, there was real excitement—but the caliber of the spellers was ordinarily known, well in advance. Probably the least interesting of the spelling bees were those in which the most accomplished spellers were members of the same family; playing off the Greiners against the Moyers was a great deal more fun than having Susie Greiner spell down her older sister Margaret, no matter how significant the act might be to Susie— or to Margaret.

Since many country schools could accommodate children of only a few families (not an unusual circumstance in a day when fewer than eight children constituted a small family and twelve or fourteen

*The champion at a spelling bee usually got his—*
*oftener* her, *according to hearsay—start through the*
*assiduous use of such texts as those shown here.*

were the rule rather than the exception) inter-school spelling bees sometimes generated real interest if it became known that there was a genuinely accomplished speller in each.

The spelling books used a century ago are something to give us pause. Bearing little relation either to personal vocabularies or ordinary reading matter, the words they presented for pronouncing, defining, and memorizing would probably stump almost anyone—anyone, that is, except the person who, attending the country school of the time, took them as a matter of course. One either was a good speller or he was not; it was as simple as that. (The keepers of old store ledgers, who had to record words they had never seen and probably never would see in print, were sometimes extraordinarily inventive!)

The quilting bee, it goes without saying, was a

purely feminine affair except as an occasional small boy too young to remain at home alone, or an elderly grandparent too feeble to be taken to a neighbor's for the day, made a more or less reluctant addition to the group. The onus of the entertainment for the day —to say nothing of the weight of the world—was on the hostess, who had as a rule spent several days or a week in preparation. True, she might desire or need the talents of a large group of wielders of the needle to get a pressing chore out of the way, but every facet of her house or her housekeeping, from carpet to mantel, front door to back entry, was under scrutiny —often very accomplished scrutiny—and every bit of her skill as a cook had to be brought to the fore. Quilting bees were important social occasions; it is said that they could be fun, too. And of course the hostess could always look forward to the next one,

*In many up-country farm homes, the cutting and sewing of carpet rags helped the elderly and infirm to get through tedious winter days. Tin lard cans, secured from country stores, were a favored storage vessel if there were mice in the attic.*

*The great copper kettles used for the boiling of apple butter were among the most treasured as well as the most expensive pieces of household equipment.*

when she would be a guest and another woman would be on the spot. The amount of stitchery that a team of good quilters could turn out made the day worth while, whatever the concomitant problems of the occasion.

While spelling and quilting bees were rather highly specialized as to participants, carpet rag parties were broader in scope—and almost always coeducational, so to speak. A woman faced unexpectedly with the prospect of making a home for an elderly relative might actually need additional quilts—and quickly, at that. Rugs or carpets were a different matter; they were usual and necessary gear, but one's reputation as a housekeeper was not normally at stake if they were missing. Carpet-rag parties, therefore, while they helped to get some tedious chores out of the way, were free enough from pressure that everyone, including the hostess, could have fun.

In carpet making, there were several stages be-

tween the worn-out garment and the trip to the neighborhood loom. The first stage was to cut the usable pieces of the discarded garment into the longest possible strips, usually somewhat less than an inch wide. By judicious turning of the goods, a good cutter could achieve strips of surprising length. The second step was to sew the strips together, with some attention to matching or contrasting colors and a judicious separation or juxtaposition of dark and light tones. The final step—and it was this one which was usually the occasion for the *lumpa* (that is, carpet rag) party —was to wind the endless lengths of sewed rags into tight balls. A good ball was six to seven inches in diameter; an experienced weaver could tell at a glance just how many balls would be required for a yard— or any given amount—of carpet.

For whatever reason, bags and boxes—and tin flour drums and lard pails and old suitcases—full of balled carpet rags are likely to make their appear-

*A line of redware apple butter pots which showed every gradation in size might be a hundred yards long. It would include specimens from gill-size to those which would hold four gallons or more. The glazed pottery lid in the foreground is one of the few surviving covers for redware pots.*

*The participant in a work bee or frolic often took his
own flask along, to make sure that he did not become
too thirsty to work. Flasks came in pottery, tin, glass,
and wicker-covered glass, as indicated here.*

ance, even today, when an old house is completely
emptied of its contents. Sewing and balling carpet
rags was for a hundred years and more a winter occupation for elderly or partly incapacitated women,
not only in Upper Dutchdom but in places far removed. Perhaps the balls, now usually faded to an
almost uniform no-color, were stored away and forgotten; perhaps it took so long to accumulate the
needed quantity that some other floor covering was
substituted; perhaps they represented only harmless
busy-work and no one expected to put them to actual
use. There is often something touching about them—
perhaps a tinge of regret for the patient hours expended, or perhaps just a hint of nostalgia for a way
of life long gone.

It should go without saying that a *lumpa* party
usually ended with refreshments or a square dance,
or both, and that the dusty carpet rag festival served
basically as a reasonable means toward the desired
end of entertainment.

The *schnitzing* bee had some of the same characteristics. Apples intended for apple butter had to be
peeled, cored, and cut into small segments, usually
eighths, called *Schnitzen* (cut pieces). Since bushels
of apples and barrels of cider were involved, and since
pared apples quickly turn brown and lose flavor when
exposed to the air, a speedy means of processing the
ingredients was needed—the *schnitzing* bee, of course.

Patented iron apple parers and corers in the '70s
and later worked like a charm—well, some of them,

anyway—and dozens of paring knives in the hands of
willing workers completed in a few hours what one
person, working alone, could not have achieved in
days . . . even if it were possible to keep the peeled
fruit fresh that long. Cider was boiled down ahead of
time; the day-long cooking and stirring would take
place tomorrow; there was time enough for a square
dance before the party broke up at midnight.

Corn-husking bees may well have been more prevalent in the up-country than they were farther south.
For one thing, the growing season is shorter the
farther north one goes (It comes as a shock to many
to discover that spring arrives about two weeks later
in Newfoundland than it does in New Holland, for
instance) and instead of the dent corn of the Dutchland, flint corn was grown in Wayne and Pike until
well into the present century, when early strains of
dent were introduced. Flint corn, like its stalks and
husks, is tough, and shucking the tightly encased
ears in cold, windy weather can be something of a
nightmare. In consequence, corn was sometimes cut,
shocked, and then moved onto an empty barn floor.
When a suitable occasion presented itself, the young
people of the neighborhood were invited in to help
with the husking—and to assist the host in disposing
of the refreshments provided. Sometimes the husking
bee became a little boisterous in nature, a circumstance possibly owing to the degree of energy called
for in husking flint corn.

Another old-time social occasion was often less a

bee in the usual sense than a reward for some especially demanding or long-sustained activity. It might be a church supper, of the kind still served to the public as a fund-raising project from Maine to California. Or it might be a strawberry festival—at first, conducted properly when strawberries ripened in June, but later, owing to more expeditious methods of food processing and transportation, at any time of the year.

In Pike County's German Valley, it was the church oyster supper. As a matter of fact, sometimes it was *two* oyster suppers, the first served by the women of the Moravian congregation as a fund-raising affair, and the second by the men, some time later, as a gesture of appreciation for the preceding one. In passing, let it be observed that the men of that particular congregation, some 50 or more years ago, had a startling reputation for superb biscuits, ambrosial strawberry shortcake, and cheese soufflés no woman of the community could match. Loyally, no woman ever breathed to the outsiders who flocked to German Valley church suppers, after the first spectacular success, that a quiet, self-effacing man in the congregation had for years been a chef in a prominent Philadelphia hotel before making German Valley his home!

The best-publicized of deep Dutch Country cooperative enterprises is probably the barn-raising—that gargantuan effort which involved up to a hundred men and put a huge barn into place in a single day. If comparable activities took place in Monroe, Pike, or Wayne—and they may have done so—they have been poorly recorded or not recorded at all. Frequently a photographer was on hand when large-scale activities took place, but photographic records of up-country barn-raisings seem to be entirely lacking. We have noted Daniel Brodhead's house-raising in 1743, but the chances are that there was little resemblance to the operations which took place in Berks or Lancaster counties. Picnics, outings, reunions, staff pictures—all these may turn up in old albums, but the barn-raising is not there.

One good reason may be that the smaller size of buildings made a full-scale community operation un-

necessary; another, that it was only in the closely knit *Freundschaft* of the Dutch Country that men had been trained in the closely coordinated step-by-step methods which could bring about the desired end.

## COLLECTORS LOOK FOR:

Early newspapers, periodicals, and almanacs with accounts of frolics or bees

Apple peelers and corers. Those made in Reading, Pa., were frequently seen in the up-country.

Long-handled apple butter stirring paddles. Most were operated by hand, but some were equipped with free-wheeling swivel devices which made it possible for the operator to remain at a comfortable distance from the fire.

Copper apple butter kettles

Redware apple butter pots in graduated sizes—a pint to about two gallons

Tin, iron, and pottery baking vessels in large sizes and in fancy shapes—fish, heart, horseshoe, etc.

Pottery "harvest" jugs or rings to slip over one's arm

Stoneware field jugs. While the clay was still "green" —that is, while it was still malleable—the neck was tilted carefully to one side so that the drinker could swing the vessel over his shoulder, support it with one hand, and bring the mouth into proximity to his own. Without this crook in the pottery, holding a large, heavy, filled jug in drinking position would have been a two-hand job, at least.

Sewing and quilting paraphernalia. (See chapter on quilts.)

Early spellers, primers, and other books used in rural schools

A-B-C books in German and in English, for Sunday School use

Early rural school furniture—benches, pupils' desks and teachers' desks

Vintage globes from rural schools

State and county maps

Schoolhouse bells; hand bells for the teacher's use

*Jackpot:* County map of Wayne, Pike, or Monroe, mounted on wooden rollers and in good condition

# 30
# Just Fooling Around: The Whittlers

What an inventive individual could do with a pocket-knife and a slab of wood was amazing. One wonders, in fact, what some of the bygone whittlers might have achieved had they developed and employed their talents more thoroughly, instead of just keeping their hands occupied during a bad-weather bull session or while arguing politics in the evening at the country store with their cronies.

We are not talking now of lumbering enterprises or planing mills or even "specialty" factories; we are speaking of the man who, knife in hand, would have referred to his activities as just fooling around with a knife—a man who worked according to no tradition but who set his own pattern. At the same time, both he and an observer would know perfectly well that back of the disclaimer of serious intent some real skill was being employed, even if it was a kind of skill about which it was not good form to brag. There were many solid citizens who considered whittlers shiftless unless they also turned out a full complement of "real," hard, physical work. (Work was "real" when it was conventional, according to the pattern of the time.)

The upshot of the matter is that names of good whittlers have usually long since been forgotten. As a matter of fact, had a stranger dropped in on one at the country store on a rainy day, observed his occupation and asked his name, the chances would have been almost totally against his getting a straightforward answer. What a man chose to do in his spare time was purely his own business. His name, likewise, was his own business—as the outsider would indubitably have discovered.

Offhand pieces might not always be a man's own idea, of course; he might actually have an extensive backlog of suggestions or needs or requests from his wife, all pointed toward the rainy day when he had nothing more important to occupy his time. Every woman, for instance, needed a bakeboard on which to knead her bread, cut out cookies, or roll her noodles thin. A nice rectangular shape was ordinary; a round board with, say, an 18-inch diameter was better; a round one with a well-shaped extension for a handle, drilled so that it could be hung on the wall when not in use was better still. If it was only a small board that was needed, a solid slab of curly maple cut out in the shape of a pig was especially popular in the Poconos. If curly maple was lacking, pine could be used but then the pig would be minus its distinctive markings. It is popularly supposed that these pig boards were invented as surfaces on which to slice bacon, and that they were called bacon boards; actually, they were in use for all sorts of small cutting operations when cured side meat was still called side meat and "bacon" might as well have been a word in a foreign language. The whittler here would first have needed a saw, but he would finish the operation with his pocketknife.

Rolling pins of curly maple were also popular, but a number of tools beyond a pocketknife had to be employed in the making—notably a drawing knife and a smoothing agent like a chunk of broken scythe blade or a segment of broken window pane. These rolling pins, extraordinarily heavy as a rule, have little to recommend them to today's cook, since roller and handle were usually of a piece and the object was unwieldy to manipulate.

Youngsters at crafts shows today are often fascinated with hand operations, probably because so much that they have used or played with has been

*Wooden holders for soap: a soft soap scoop, a partly
lathe-turned dish for a cake of hard soap, and a
whittled-and-sanded container.*

mass-produced, and seeing something take shape
through an operator's manual dexterity is a novelty.
They would be even more fascinated if they could
see the whole range of handmade gadgets or implements once used in cooking, though had they lived at
the time the objects were made they would have taken
the whole business for granted. Potato mashers, cabbage cutters, small pestles, sauerkraut stompers,
mush sticks, long-handled spoons and stirring paddles, meat pounders geometrically serrated on their
working surface—all these have gone by the board,
along with such esoterica as the interesting little devices used for skimming cream from the top of cold,
whole milk. One needed or wanted such household
objects; they were not available in stores—or, if they
were, they were expensive; so one made them and,
to forestall any unwelcome suggestion that perhaps
the maker was unable or unwilling to buy the commercial product, he made them better than anything
which could have been bought.

Professionally made cupboards in later years would
be provided with metal catches to keep the doors
closed. With the homemade piece it was different;
there is a fascinating array of wooden catches or
"buttons," as they were called, made by whittlers—
sometimes to go with the original cupboard at the
time of making, or as a later replacement. So far
as utility is concerned, these buttons are still a handy
gadget for simple pieces. Closures for interior house
doors were made in the same way. However, latches
for outside doors on the dwelling house or outbuildings were usually more elaborate and were made by
conventional carpentering methods rather than by
whittling. (Ironwork was preferred to almost any
kind of wooden lock or fastening.)

Meal or flour scoops in sizes from those obviously
intended for filling a small container, up to some as
big as a man-size grain shovel, hung on the walls of
grist mills, rested on piles of grain bags, or were
thrust into bins of the finished product, whatever it

*Careful attention was often lavished on slaw cutters
like the walnut specimens shown here. The example
at the left is wood-pegged throughout. The powerful
cutting knives were often made from broken scythe
blades.*

*A bureau box made in the vicinity of Bushkill. Few country carpenters tried their hands at inlay, though trained cabinetmakers could take such ornamentation in stride.*

happened to be—perhaps middlings, perhaps flour or meal, perhaps bran. Those in a mill which handled wheat slowly turned white with continued use. Some of these scoops were carefully designed; many of them were fitted up with leather thongs for hanging over a nail. It was usual to turn out a scoop made from a single piece of wood—but two pieces were also usual if the whittler wanted to show off a copper nail-studded handle tapering gracefully into a bowl of a different wood. A "good" scoop was one which had no rough edges or angular spots which might catch on clothing or on a container being filled.

Wooden dishes to hold a bar of homemade soap and little square scoops to dip soft soap from the keg are found now and then. An excellent specimen of each has been found at Kellersville. Another device should be mentioned, too—the scouring-soap holder attached to the scouring board. The steel-bladed knife or fork to be scoured was first dampened, then run over the gritty gray soap, and next whetted sufficiently to remove any rust which might have accumulated. A mere scouring was not enough; the process was repeated until the steel shone. While most of these boards are now badly worn, some are still sufficiently intact that one can see the signs of care in the making.

No one has reported a jug-stopper specialist, but somewhere there must have been one. Bung holes in casks or barrels were ordinarily equipped with plain wooden stoppers. (Corks in large sizes are likely to be latecomers.) Jugs and demijohns were subjected to the same treatment, or were fitted out with corn-cobs. Now and then, however, a fancy specimen comes to light—a stopper made from an interestingly shaped knot or from a wooden excrescence which had been a tiny tree burl. Once in a while there is an actual carving, usually that of a human head. Bottle stoppers in elongated shapes probably came into be-

*Wood carvings of exceptionally fine caliber. These are
believed to have been done by a talented member of
the Hawk family in Monroe County's West End.*

ing to replace lost or broken cork ones. Here is an
all-but-untouched field of exploration for the antiques
enthusiast in the up-country. All those fabled old-
time Pike County whiskey bottles with the labels
bearing "brand" names which could not be repeated
in polite society—were they merely corked, and not
equipped with more individual stoppers? Certainly,
it behooves some researcher to find out.

A good whittler had a keen eye for unusual root or
stem formations which, with a little imagination and
the trusty pocketknife, had the makings of a walking
stick. It would seem that most elderly men in the
Poconos used to be fond of canes, if one may judge
from the number of survivals, and some of the designs are intriguing. In other parts of the world, the
serpent motif was fairly common on walking sticks,
but snakes in any form have never been very popular
in the up-country. What the canemaker liked best to
do was make his way along the banks of a stream and
watch for exposed roots of unusual shape. Judicious
cutting and some auxiliary shaping would bring into
being the desired conversation piece. Animal's heads
were always popular on sticks, but especially interesting are those in which most of the features were
present naturally and only a minimum of knife work
was needed to bring about the proper configuration.

Some men liked to make boxes—small, large, and
in-between. Since one thing leads to another, some
went beyond simple containers and tried their hands
at document-size boxes with inlaid tops. One such
specialist lived near Bushkill, and now and then one
of his boxes with a star inlay on the top lid turns up
in an antique shop. The art of inlay is a rather specialized and tricky one, and seems to have been less
well-developed among pocketknife artists than among
professional cabinetmakers. A walnut footstool with a
light star inlay purporting to represent the star of
Bethlehem, in a private collection, is well made—and
exceptionally attractive.

Those ingenious persons who worked almost entirely with the soft wood of cigar boxes turned out
remarkable objects—remarkable first of all in their
conception but notable also for the adeptness of their
execution. "Tramp" artistry is what this edge- or
notch-carving is usually called and since the wandering hoboes who paid for their handouts at all often
did so by making bureau boxes, comb cases, and the
like for their hosts, utilizing empty cigar boxes and
scrap material, the name is perhaps an apt one. This
notch carving, in which surfaces were built up by suc-
cessively narrower superimposed layers of thin wood,
was not limited to the up-country or to Pennsylvania.

In fact, its manufacture was as widespread as the territory covered by the hoboes, a circumstance which means that it can turn up anywhere.

The original vogue for this kind of work was seemingly short-lived. It appears not to have been produced until toward the end of Victoria's reign, when gimcrackery of all kinds was fashionable, but was both out of sight and out of mind by the time of World War I. Pieces were all but impossible to keep clean, broke easily, tended to come apart when the varnish dried and the little nails pulled out of the soft wood, and in general were something the housewife was glad to relegate to the attic or to an outbuilding. When it was "rediscovered" in the 1930s

*The epitome of folk carving—an eagle by Wilhelm Schimmel, shown here on a wooden base. Schimmel was not an up-country resident, or a permanent resident anywhere, for that matter, but one of the largest single aggregations of Schimmel pieces ever found occurred in Newfoundland.*

and '40s, persons of mature years began to remember it, search for it in more or less obscure hiding places, and bring it to light in rather surprising quantities. Well-meaning attempts to brighten its dinginess by the use of aluminum or gilt paint did little beyond making a real refinishing job all but impossible.

How long it will remain interesting to collectors is a good question, but there is no doubt as to its present popularity. Bureau boxes probably head the list of wanted objects, with comb-and-brush cases and picture frames following. A notch-carving itinerant who knew a comfortable stopping place when he saw one was probably the person who would undertake such out-size jobs as a secretary-desk completely covered with carving; a bedroom commode featuring carefully alternating light and dark woods; and large hall stands complete with pegs for holding hats, studded with small drawers, and decorated with brass rosettes, mirrors, white knobs, and cross-sawed sections of butternut shells. Many pieces are quite ugly, but others, especially those in which a built-up heart motif is utilized, have a considerable degree of charm.

The printing on the cigar boxes was seldom if ever removed, and it is obvious from the variety of names one sees on the backs and bottoms of comb cases and the like that a great many brands were popular. Colored labels on the boxes were also allowed to remain, especially when they featured pulchritudinous Spanish maidens. Bureau boxes and sewing cases were frequently inlaid with velvet, and lithographed greeting or advertising cards were freely used as added embellishments for the insides of lids and covers.

Not all notch-carved pieces were made by itinerants. An incident comes to mind in connection with the restoration, in 1970, of Slateford Farm, mentioned elsewhere. When the place had achieved a suitable degree of completion for receiving visitors, an Open House was scheduled. One of the visitors, a nearby resident whose identity must remain undisclosed, came bearing a gift—a large and exceptionally well carved "tramp art" mirror frame. The mirror had long since been broken, and for it a specimen of the lush, near-nude decoration popular on wall calendars of the early '20s had been substituted. (Perhaps one should qualify the popularity by observing that these calendars were popular in saloons, washrooms, and other places where women were not expected to appear.)

With his gift, the prospective donor approached a restoration adviser and asked whether the government would accept it. This person, impressed by the fine quality of the carving, said yes, adding that a print of just about that size had been awaiting a suitable frame and that the substitution could easily be made.

The visitor seemed dubious. "I don't know," he said, surveying his treasure. "I like it the way it is. Tell you what I'll do: I've got a whole houseful of this stuff. My father used to whittle it out in his spare time. He'd get his cigar boxes in East Stroudsburg and then just settle down. Some of the stuff he made took as much as a thousand boxes. I'll go home and get you a different piece, since the frame is all you're interested in, and I'll put this one back where I got it. Okay?"

He was as good as his word—but the restoration person has had sleepless moments since, wondering just where this extraordinary cache of carving is, how an outsider might get to see it, and, most particularly, what the unknown masterpiece which called for a thousand cigar boxes could be. Tentative feelers have been recognized and rejected. "You've got one now," says the donor, "and you're welcome. Maybe some time I'll show you some of the others, but I'll tell you one thing: No antique dealer is ever going to get his fingers on anything of mine. I'll see it burned first. A restoration is different." As of now, the adviser might observe that a restoration does not appear to be as different as she could wish!

Tramp carving has at least one feature in common with the little elaborately jigsawed walnut bracket and corner shelves popular after the 1840s: When it is good, it is very good, but when it is bad, it is horrid. Both the tramp carving and the ornately scrolled vines and flowers of the corner pieces are part and parcel of the gingerbread fussiness which transformed porch brackets, window pediments, and cornices into things of wonder if not of beauty in the late 1800s. Again, when they were good they were very good, as in some down-country houses like those on Walnut Street in Kutztown; when they were bad —and that was much of the time—they departed from the world unmourned and unsung when their time came.

Across the Monroe County line, in the country in Lehigh County, lived one of the most prolific of the pocket knife artisans, Noah Weiss. Weiss (1842–1907) might have scorned notch carving, though; his work was in the round or in the kind of double-sided bas relief which was one of his specialties. The whole thing began when he took his pocket knife one day and carved a toy for a sick child. Something within him apparently clicked at that point, and from then to the end of his life he spent some time every day in carving. He kept an inn, and the walls of the public

*A masterpiece of tramp carving—a six-drawer desk
with slope-fall lid, inner compartments under the lid,
and six drawers. The piece is twenty inches high.*

rooms became the showplace for his work. When the last available space had been filled, he started with the rooms of an adjacent building, which became a second exhibition hall.

Some of his creations were life size. It was the age when cigar-store Indians and merry-go-round figures were well known and popular, and Weiss's creations were at least as realistic and as gaily painted. Among his best specimens, all of which were achieved with no tool other than a pocket knife, were a life-size hunter and his dog; a scale model of his childhood home, a stage coach with six horses (not life size!); and, in his office, a figure of George Washington mounted on his horse. Such spectacular decorations of course inspired comment, and Weiss's Inn was known far and near for its picturesque décor.

It was the adulation of his patrons, we are told, that kept Weiss at his carving in later years when other men might have stopped. He liked to work; he loved carving; he liked people. The combination was a happy one. Nothing seemed to be too difficult for him to tackle; completely self-taught, he would try his hand at anything which came to mind or had been suggested. An instance of this urge to see what he could do was a series of great wooden panels illustrating Biblical scenes, adapted from engravings he liked. It is said that while they lacked artistic finesse, they had great vigor—and certainly they were greatly admired. Weiss stole no time from his business for the exercise of his hobby; his carving was done in the small hours of the morning, before even the earliest frequenters of the tavern arrived.

Some day a researcher may be able to establish, beyond doubt, the provenance of certain small wood carvings from the western extreme of Monroe—or just as possibly from such nearby places as Weissport, Lehighton, Slatington, Jim Thorpe, or perhaps Tamaqua. This territory, while it has been explored for antiques generally, has apparently not been thoroughly researched in any one field. Individual pieces known to the author are in private collections—and are likely to remain there, since they are greatly treasured. For the most part, they are human figures

and domestic animals up to eight inches high, carved in the round with professional competence, sanded, and realistically painted. One would adduce the dates of 1860–1880 as the probable time in which they were made, but whatever information anyone may have about them is apparently not available at this time. If they are pieces by Noah Weiss—a circumstance which seems unlikely but which from the matter of propinquity alone can not be written off—they represent his work at its very best.

### COLLECTORS LOOK FOR:

Large one-piece baking boards in fancy shapes or with fancy touches

Cutting boards in small sizes

Hand-whittled potato mashers, flat-bottomed ladles, and other kitchen implements more usually occurring in tin

Cabbage cutters, especially those with heart-shaped cutouts or fancy moldings. Hand-whittled wooden pegs instead of screws for fastenings are very special—but rare.

Scouring boards and scouring soap holders

Hand-whittled jug-stoppers (alternatives for corks)

Walking sticks with shaped heads—human, dog, fish, bird, otter, etc.

Locally made bureau boxes

Jigsaw-carved brackets and shelves with added handwork

Corner whatnots with hand-whittled posts, finials, or other members

Tramp-carved small objects—boxes, comb cases, mirror or picture frames, jewelry cases (sometimes velvet-lined)—all these in a great variety of forms. A much desired embellishment is a separately carved bird, or, even better, a number of birds on one piece. Bird decoration is most likely to be found on comb cases or on mirrors.

Full-size furniture enlivened with tramp carving

Hitherto unreported local carvings—whenever and wherever they appear

*Jackpot:* An attested piece of the work of Noah Weiss

# 31
# A-Putzing They Went

A colorful Christmas practice prevailed among the German-speaking elements of the up-country, starting with the near-solid Pennsylvania Dutch West End of Monroe County, gradually diminishing the farther north and east one went, and finally almost disappearing in the English-Irish upper extremities of Wayne. This practice was the erection of a *putz*, which was followed by a neighborhood putz-visiting period which might last for a mere matter of a day or two—but could run to a week or more.

The word needs a definition. A *putz* (the derivation is from the German verb *putzen*, meaning to decorate) is an imaginative miniature setting, ranging from village, farm, or forest to a desert scene, for the crèche of the Nativity—Mary, Joseph, the Infant, the manger, the Magi, the shepherds, the angels, and the animals of the stable. Anciently religious in its conception, it took on a number of secular overtones in some places as years and then centuries passed. It appears to be as old in Pennsylvania as the German immigrations themselves, and was highly developed among, although by no means limited to, the Moravians, whose "mother" church was in Bethlehem. Putz-building is still a distinctive Christmas activity among some Bethlehem Moravians, and putz-visiting in the so-called Christmas City is of interest to visitors beyond merely local environs.

Making a putz is not a stereotyped operation, but varies according to the imagination or resources or remembrance of things past of the person who constructs it. When one bears in mind that for many years there was stiff competition as to whose putz would be considered the outstanding one in a given community, he can understand the enormous amount of time that was often expended by some families in "getting ready for Christmas."

In the first place, sheets of moss would be needed to represent grassy surfaces. Before frost, children would go out searching for handsome, good-sized pieces which could be stripped from rotten logs or the tops of flat rocks. These sheets were placed back-to-back to keep them clean, moistened if they seemed dry, and then stored in a cool place with burlap over them. They had to be allowed to "breathe," or they would turn yellow.

At the time of the moss hunt, children would also seek out interesting knots from rotten logs, moss-covered stones, segments of weathered roots from a stream, and white shelf fungus from fallen trees. A little later, often after Thanksgiving but before the likelihood of deep snow, bagfuls of Jerusalem Moss (Princess Pine) were pulled. These would be utilized for great festoons in church as well as at home. Individual specimens of these eight-inch-high "trees" were often used to simulate trees in the putz landscape. Other kinds of ground-hugging greens were gathered, too, including club moss and—when they could be found—wintergreen and partridge berry. A pail or two of sand would be secured and put into the cellar, where it would not freeze.

The actual construction would begin shortly before Christmas. A platform of planks would be set up—sometimes in the parlor but preferably in a room normally kept unheated. This platform might be three feet deep and run the width of the room. At the back and ends, evergreen branches would be massed with perhaps a number of small, well-shaped trees set into pots or pails to suggest the edge of a forest. Sometimes the evergreen branches would go all the way to the ceiling. Spruce or balsam would be the prime choice, with hemlock a weak second and rhododendron or kalmia a poor third. The entire plat-

*At the Christmas candle-light service in Moravian churches, beeswax tapers were distributed to members of the congregation. This old dispenser tray was used at the Moravian Church at Newfoundland.*

*Handmade Moravian beeswax candles with their proper Christmas Eve paper frills at the bottom. The wall sconce shown is one of a pair.*

form would be draped, usually with sheets.

Next would come the placing of the Christmas tree, if one was to be used. The center of the platform was the obvious spot unless the decorator had some special plan in mind. A Christmas tree might not be set up in a household of adults, but was hardly likely to be omitted in a home where there were young children. It was at this point that two divergent schools of thought became evident. In one, only the traditional religious significance of the season figured, and the Nativity scene dominated; in the other, there was a mingling of tree, Santa Claus, toys, and tinselly decorations with the religious. When a putz was erected in a church there was no problem; the focus was on the Nativity and on nothing else. More than one parent in Moravian homes was hard put to explain why Santa Claus could appear at school but not at church, or why reindeer might graze on the mossy green under the tree at home but could not be harnessed eight to a sleigh. Perhaps the parents were not always happy about the ambivalent situation.

Ideally, the putz, whether totally religious or partly secular, embodied a theme of some kind, but only the most zealous purist could long maintain it. As year followed year, toys, figurines, dolls, play objects, fancy glass ornaments, and tinsel-and-lithograph decorations kept accumulating—and youngsters wanted to see them on or under the tree. Naturally, on or under the tree they went, and children could take in stride a two-inch-high china doll leading a six-inch-high dog along the mossy way with greater equanimity than could the decorator aiming for a degree of perfection—or, if not that, verisimilitude.

A typical putz would have a winding road, either of sand or of sawdust; a lake or pond which had begun life as a mirror; and a paper village with collapsible buildings. How to work the family Noah's Ark and its two-by-two creatures into the setting posed a problem, as did the display of gaudily dressed tin or lead soldiers which were *de rigueur* after the Civil War. The only thing to do, of course, was to create separate areas, and keep the Ark in one place, the military in another, and the crèche in yet a different spot. Even so, there were a dozen favorite objects from strings of trains to spinning tops which simply would not blend into a unified whole—and the "best" putz of the year was likely to be in the home of the decorator who had the greatest degree of ingenuity in bringing inharmonious elements into some kind of order.

The road of the putz had to be at least long enough to accommodate all the animals of the Ark, proceeding in orderly fashion to the vessel perched on an eminence toward the back. These animals might number a mere twenty or so to more than a hundred. Most were imported from Germany or Switzerland, along with the Ark, and the best ones were hand-carved.

There was great variety in the houses which stood by the roadside, by the lake, or at random on the green. In Newfoundland, Georg Huguenin's little wooden houses, none more than a few inches high, were pleasing but under-scaled for most of the objects they accompanied. Huguenin's work will be discussed elsewhere.

Collectors seek out vintage pasteboard buildings from perhaps 1860 to the end of the century. These folding buildings may include no more than a house, a church, a school, and a store, or may range further into village halls, firehouses, and railroad stations. Some are painted to indicate brick dwellings or other edifices, and most are attractively colored. Fences, beds of flowers, a flagpole and a pump may be included.

Considerable ingenuity often went into creating a stream, frequently a brook paralleling a road or perhaps a railroad track. Pieces of broken mirrors were saved for this purpose; lacking mirrors, the decorator could make do with plain windowglass over black cloth. Since the surface was likely to be fairly well covered with ducks, frogs, canoes, or steamboats, the absence of an actual mirror might go unnoticed. By the early 1900's, some of the amphibious creatures were of celluloid, a circumstance ordinarily distressing to the decorator because of their often casual, as opposed to careful, construction.

The figures of the crèche were less subject to variation than were the toys, but even here a completely homogeneous setting could seldom be achieved. There were as many interpreters of crèche figures as there were manufacturers, with the result that the units of one set could seldom be matched with those of another, in the event of breakage or loss. Much admired were porcelain or china figurines imported from Europe.

This great diversity of objects is mentioned, not critically, but to call attention to the fact that the creation of an attractive putz was not a simple matter. If the under-the-tree decoration had been a miscellany of meaningless objects, the chances are that the putz as an art form would have been abandoned long ago. That is not to say that such decoration is as widespread as it once was, of course. With the advent of the artificial, nonflammable Christmas tree, maintaining the old tradition becomes even more difficult.

For those, if any, who would like to try their hands at creating a putz, and who have an accumulation of

*Noah's Ark figures are shown leaving the Ark under
the watchful eyes of the dove on the roof—and the
guardianship of Noah and his family.*

seemingly incompatible objects to work with, there
may be food for thought in some of the groupings or
arrangements remembered from the past in the up-
country: a picnic, complete with tables and food—
and dogs—at the center of the paper village; a procession to or from the village church; a dolls' tea
party; a race involving a train, a carriage and horses,
and a boat; a Santa Claus with a check list and an
open cornucopia-like pack filled with small objects; a
varied country landscape with cows in a pasture,
children pulling a wagon, farmers loading hay,
women chatting over a fence—and a dozen others.

The tree, when a tree formed part of the putz or of
the total effort, had its distinctive trimmings, few of
which can be found today, short of antique shops. The
old-time paper-frilled beeswax candles, still made at
Bethlehem, can be purchased today through the Moravian church, and may be mounted in their proper
long wire-handled bobs with a painted pottery ball
at the end—if one can find the right antique shop.

Once, these candles were lighted on the tree as well as
at the Christmas Eve candlelight service at the
church; few would try it today, no matter how de-
lightful the smell of burning beeswax may be.

Equally nostalgic are three-dimensional folded-
paper stars, which today come in a do-it-yourself kit
complete with directions for assembling; tinsel-bord-
ered lithographed paper cups, baskets, pails, and
cornucopias featuring Santa Claus and children in
the costumes of the '80s; delicate blown and colored
glass birds with spun glass tails, often imported from
Austria; puzzle toys of carved wood; and an enormous variety of fragile glass tree ornaments in fancy
shapes—animals, violins, lamps, umbrellas, fish,
Santa Claus heads, and the like.

In the main, these were "boughten" toys, in many
homes a few being added each year, since they were
ordinarily too expensive for a great outlay of cash at
one time. Made at home were popcorn strings; cranberry festoons; spice cookies pierced for hanging on

the tree; gilded walnuts, peanuts, and seed globes from sycamore trees; and sometimes maple sugar in marzipan molds. Brilliantly tinted marzipan in delicate white-metal baskets, intended for hanging on the tree rather than for eating, was a bought decoration, as were pretzels and clear toy candies in the shape of animals, birds, and human figures. Peppermint sticks, just right for hanging over spruce branches, had a way of disappearing from the tree—as, in fact, did most of the candy. A final touch to the old-time tree, for the person of inexhaustible patience, was the plump white popcorn kernel, pierced with a pin and fastened to the soft bud end of each branch of the tree, no matter how tiny the branch, in a simulation of snowflakes.

Somehow, the putz was completed and the tree decorated before Christmas morning. The children's stockings were stuffed—in many cases with an orange, a single toy, a handful of peanuts, and perhaps some candy. Stockings were personal; they remained out of sight in the round of neighborhood putzing calls, which began on Christmas day. It should undoubtedly be noted that in the up-country these calls were likely to be on a much less comprehensive scale than those in towns or villages to the south. There was a tacit understanding that all callers would be welcomed and that refreshments would be provided.

Tradition seems to have stereotyped early putzing refreshments as homemade cookies and wine. In the northern up-country, where of course the churches had been established later than those to the south,

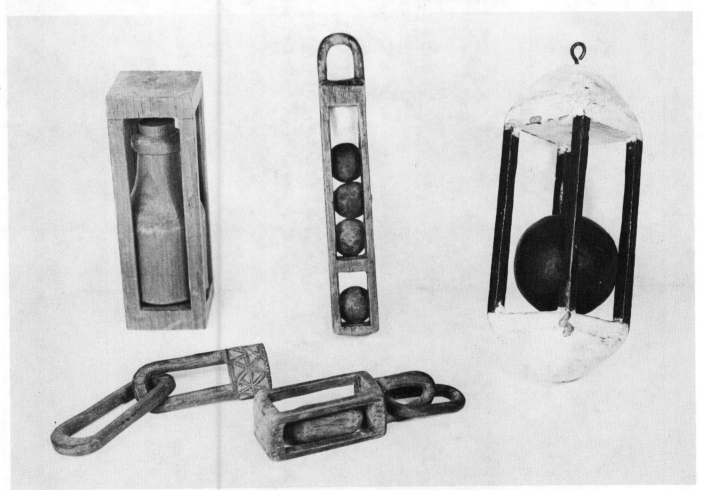

*Christmas tree or Christmas putz decorations, each carved from a single block of wood. This type of ornament was once fairly common in German Valley and Newfoundland, but the genre is not limited either to the up-country or to Pennsylvania.*

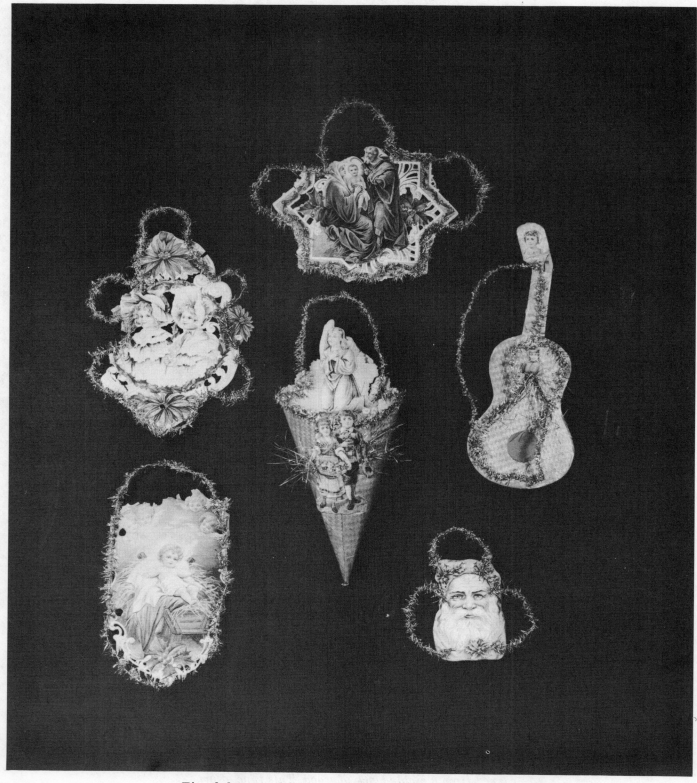

*Tinsel-decorated "scraps" look as good on Christmas*
*trees today as they did nearly a century ago . . . if*
*one can find them.*

there seems to be no record or even a notation that wine was served. Whatever occasional private tastes or inclinations may have existed, wine was not really a popular drink north of the Blue Mountain. As a matter of fact, the "wine" used in church Communion services was unfermented grape juice, as often as not. Nor does it appear to be the case that wine was served in southern Pike or Monroe, especially since the visitors in many instances were children.

The cookies, however, were something very special, and fancy cutters used at no other time were brought out after Thanksgiving when the holiday cooky baking began. These tin cutters existed in an enormous variety of shapes. Made by itinerants or by local blacksmiths according to remembered patterns and current inspiration, they were passed along from mother to daughter from earliest times down to and including the present. Many of the cooky baking "receipts" had come with the pioneers from Germany or Switzerland, and as often as not existed orally rather than in writing. In the course of time they became standardized and were carefully written down so that they might not be lost to future generations. The preferred cut-out cooky was one which was considerably thicker than the usual cookies of today— up to half an inch. Many cutters had fancy insets of hearts, tulips, or wavy lines which made an impressed mark on the cooky. On the crisp, paper-thin cookies favored today, these inset marks do not show at all, and a degree of the original charm is lost. Almost without exception these were spice cookies (*Zimt* or *Tsimmet* to earlier generations, apparently because considerable cinnamon was used in the recipe). However, for New Year's Day, white cookies, also made in fancy shapes, usually appeared.

The culinary skill of the housewife was taken for granted; the job of turning out a bushel—or two, or more—of cookies was simply a part of the Christmas preparations, and the woman who could not bake good cookies simply did not exist, in theory, at least. The variety in patterns, however, was another matter, and it is to be feared that sometimes the major reward accruing to the housewife who had spent endless hours catering to the vagaries of a wood-burning stove was the fact—and the comment—that she had a pattern that others would like to own.

Once the cooky supply began to run low, toward the end of the putzing season, apples were brought up from the cellar, polished, and set out as a substitute. It was a dead give-away, of course; the presence of the apples indicated—in the idiom of the day—"The cookies are all."

No discussion of up-country putzing would be complete without a mention of perhaps the most skilled—and colorful—Christmas artist in the German Valley-Newfoundland area in the years from the late '90s to about 1910. This person was Mrs. Joseph Able (pronounced "Apley," according to the German). A tall, heavy woman, she bothered not at all with the little figures of the crèche and the small ornaments of the Christmas tree. Instead, she directed her efforts toward creating the human figures and all the animals of the Nativity—life-size. She had to make a concession in the case of the camels, but the sheep and the donkeys, with wooden frames sturdy enough that a small child could sit on their backs, were not only life-size but very competently made.

Mrs. Able started to set up her display in November, using for the purpose all the first-floor rooms in her farmhouse except the kitchen. Furniture was relegated to the back porch, and progress through the kitchen was fraught with danger—but, then, visitors were not expected to go to the kitchen. The "front" room was devoted to a representation of the stable and the scene at the manger. The others, including a long hall, accommodated the shepherds, the Magi, the angels, and animals which would not fit comfortably into the stable setting. The figures were remarkable in that Mrs. Able, a completely untrained person in any art technique, was able with scrap materials to create, for instance, a smooth, lifelike donkey as neatly rounded as any sculptor could have achieved, and so natural in its stance that one almost expected it to twitch its ears and walk away.

As we have intimated, Mrs. Able was a person with firm convictions, one of which had to do with Joseph. She had little time for Joseph, for reasons which she would make amply clear if one asked, but which need not figure here. While there *was* a Joseph in her collection, visitors might find him with his face turned to the wall, or perhaps consigned to the kitchen, according to the intensity of her feeling at the moment. Another feeling had to do with the church, where she felt her display should be placed. Since the church was small, permission for the display was annually denied, to Mrs. Able's considerable —and forcibly expressed—annoyance.

It was a recognized part of Christmas to go to see Mrs. Able's work, and people came from far and wide. Whether this visitation should be classified under the head of putzing or not is a fair question: people came to see and admire the figures and, if truth be told, to listen to the spontaneous and unrehearsed recital which accompanied the showing. After her

*Christmas cards from a Monroe County scrapbook.*

death, the figures were thrown away and hence lost forever except as they linger in the memory of those who saw them and marveled at the skill which went into their creation.

#### COLLECTORS LOOK FOR:

Tinsel-trimmed lithographed Christmas tree decorations
Spun glass tree ornaments, especially birds
Hand-carved wooden tree ornaments
Filigree baskets—with or without tinted marzipan
Moravian beeswax candles
Candle bobs with pottery balances; also other bobs of painted metal; clip-on candle holders
Noah's Arks and Noah's Ark figures
Early Moravian publications, including hymnals
Folding paper villages
Old cutters for cut-out cookies
Christmas cooky recipes
Wooden puzzle toys for Christmas tree or putz decorations
*Jackpot:* Hand-carved Noah's Ark animals, especially those of known American provenance

## 32
# Hickory Nut Dolls to Slingshots

While youngsters had household or farm chores to perform as soon as they were physically able to do so, they still had time for play. The games they played seem to have been essentially the ones their parents before them had known, but the objects with which they amused themselves were closely associated with the circumstances in which they lived. In this respect they were probably no different from youngsters in any other age or place.

Little girls played with their dolls, then as now, but the dolls seem to have been more highly individual in early times. Rag dolls made at home were largely one of a kind; each woman put together what scraps of fabric she had, stuffed the object with sawdust or, in some cases, with wool, drew as realistic a face as possible—and the child had a doll completely her own and like no other. Securing sawdust for stuffing was hardly a problem in the up-country; there was usually a supply in the barn for bedding purposes. Men who took lumber to the mill usually brought home a load of sawdust; the sawmill operators were only too glad to get rid of it. Sawdust dolls frequently became a little attenuated in the course of time as the sawdust dried and turned to powder, and had to be supplied with a transfusion.

Clothespin dolls were less elaborate in the making, but almost as individual. True, they were small, and their slender shanks limited the creative possibilities in clothing, but their inked-on faces and glued-on woolly hair created a degree of lifelikeness which made them right at home in the little girl's family.

Apple dolls were made now and then, but tended to be short-lived. Except for their heads, they took on the aspect of rag dolls, just as hickory nut dolls tended to resemble their clothespin sisters. To make

an apple doll, one peels an apple carefully, and puts it in a warm place to dry. When the drying process starts, eyes, nose, and mouth are outlined with a sharp knife. As the drying continues, the apple gradually becomes wrinkled and the features take on a curiously lifelike quality, a quality augmented by judicious touching-up with pencil or paint. Ordinarily, an apple doll has no structural arms or legs—just a head affixed to a stick wrapped in cloth. This "body" is then supplied with a dress. Arms are fashioned of cloth. Feet may or may not be indicated.

Creating a hickory nut doll was more difficult before the days of power tools than it would be now—if one knew where to find a hickory nut. The problem was that of drilling a hole in the nut so that a sharpened stick could be inserted for the body of the doll. Sometimes that problem was eased by the discovery of a nut which had already been "drilled" by a worm! To create a face, one turned the nut on edge and used the hard little projection where the four segments of the outer shell came together as the nose.

Most little girls had play dishes for their dolls. These ran the gamut from the simplest of homemade objects to store-bought sets of china of impressive appearance or quality. A good pocketknife artisan could make cups and saucers of acorns, and bowls and pitchers from gourds for a dried-apple doll—or a whole tea set of birch bark if he could spare the time. Few of these primitive types were long-lived, since they were likely to be discarded in favor of "boughten" pieces as soon as possible. Collectors today have a wider choice than is often realized among surviving play dishes—the tea sets which frequently matched the treasured dishes of the mistress of the house. These sets may comprise either child-size or

*Crandall's District School as it looked with part of the*
*figures in place. Each little book is open at an actual*
*spelling lesson.*

doll-size pieces—oftener child-size. Among them are spatterware, stick spatter, blue spongeware, transfer-decorated pieces (usually in blue or brown), and all-white sets somewhere between ironstone and semi-porcelain in quality.

Tin dishes, sometimes gaily painted in floral or plaid patterns, were common—but were less likely to be favorites than those which matched the dishes used by grown-ups. By the time of the tin or china-ware play dishes, girls often had at least one "china" doll, too—with real hair and eyes that opened and closed. China, bisque, and papier mâché dolls were all popular—but none of them could be treated with the casual attention the rag doll often got.

Whatever the kind of doll, there was one added form of embellishment supplied by many a little girl who passed the door of a planing establishment or cabinetmaker's shop. The thin shavings formed by the motion of the plane as it glided over the straight-grained wood were often long and curving, and made very satisfactory curls—either for the dolls or for the children themselves.

The woodworking places of the up-country provided a variety of playthings other than the much-admired long blonde tresses. Most youngsters had sets of building blocks of various sizes and shapes. By the 1890s such toys were painted or covered with pasted-on paper decoration, but in the beginning they were strictly homespun. About the only concession made to their special use was a thorough sanding after the blocks had been selected at the planing factory and brought home.

Objects made at the factories for entirely different purposes had a habit of turning up as playthings. Sometimes they were factory rejects but, just as frequently, offhand products made by a mill worker on his own time. Nathan Houck's factory at La Anna, mentioned elsewhere, produced portiere rings, among other small objects, and a box of wooden playthings would often include a number of them. Similarly, knobs intended as finials for furniture, round wooden balls, checkers, wooden "eggs" to be made into darning implements, and the pointed arrowheads destined to fit over the ends of dowel rods to which small cloth flags would be attached served out their time as playthings. Many parents were careful to see that such play items were unpainted, since the lead paint of the day was known to be—or believed to be—poisonous.

Lest it be supposed that no toys intended as toys were produced in the wood-turning establishments, one should point out that many, perhaps most, of the tops in the whole toy industry were produced in the Poconos. Most of them went elsewhere for the metal caps, metal pegs, and strings with which they would be equipped, but the initial shaping and grooving took place at the factory. Beech and maple were favorite woods for tops. Another play item was the little round wooden box with either a screw-on or a friction top. Some of these started life as containers for such tiny items as doll mittens or bonnets—but even the mundane, utilitarian ones were likely to wind up as places of safe-keeping for coins or the small personal treasures of childhood. When we say "utilitarian" we have in mind such uses as holders for pills, powders of different kinds, court plaster, needles, pen points, and buttons. Boxes with their original labels intact are as popular with grown-up collectors today as the boxes, with or without labels, were among children a century or so ago.

Child-size or doll-size furniture was likely to be homemade and individual; it was competent or less-than-competent according to the skill of its maker. In a day when almost every man had some experience in the processing of wood products of one kind or another, one could expect, rightly, that much of it would be good. Chairs, small stools, chests of drawers, and play tables for the actual use of children were matched in quality by the same kinds of objects made in doll size.

Home-fashioned objects, even though their creators often were prone to speak deprecatingly of them, have come down to us as mementos or treasures in greater numbers than those which were factory- or machine-made. Seemingly, the charm of the homemade, whether it is a chair, a quilt, or a toy, never wears completely thin.

Small boys made whistles—usually with their fathers showing them how to angle the notches in the bark. It was older boys or young men, however, who "carved" butternuts or walnuts into tiny baskets by sawing or cutting out quarter sections of a nut, leaving a base and just enough of the top for a handle. The basket was then sanded, polished, and used as a gift. Peach stones were sometimes carved in the same way. Incidentally, old-timers were not likely to use the word "walnut" unadorned; walnuts were of three kinds—English, black, and white. White walnuts and butternuts are one and the same thing.

Slingshots were popular among small boys, in spite of the fact that their use was generally frowned upon by the mothers concerned. The result was usually that slingshots were used when youngsters were out of sight of the house. Some boys became adept enough in their use that they could pick off squirrels at a considerable distance. And sometimes, of course, the temptation to show off overcame discretion and the slingshot was used too close to the house—often with

painful consequences to the user.

More of a novelty than a toy was a kind of wooden serpent occasionally found in Monroe County. Expertly jointed, it was made of a great number of carefully articulated bits of wood, tapering properly from head to tail. When grasped in the middle, it could be manipulated so that both head and tail would wiggle realistically. Hickory sprouts had bark of the right texture and color to make a convincing-looking snake. Some years back, a visitor to an antiques show in Stroudsburg picked up one of these objects from a table, grasped it to test its squirming qualities—and started a near-panic among visitors to whom it looked like a very real, very lively blacksnake, some two feet long. In the 1890s, a comparable snake toy, made commercially, was supplied to stores by Butler Brothers, wholesalers, of Chicago and New York.

*Who carved these figures would be hard to say. The jack-on-a-stick and the figure holding the handle of a long-vanished carriage are of kinds once often seen up-country. The specimen at the left may have moved in from somewhere else.*

*Specimens of the Christmas putz carvings of Georg
Huguenin of Newfoundland.*

A great deal of ingenuity went into the making of wooden puzzles of various kinds. A favorite was a neatly fitting combination of six pieces which interlocked to look like three tightly conjoined sections. The person who took it apart, however, and then tried to put it together again was often completely stumped, since the six pieces appeared to be identical and looked as though they could not possibly interlock. Others, equally baffling, were comparable with jigsaw puzzles but with an added dimension, depth.

If the person who was handed the dozen or more pieces did not know the shape of the object he was supposed to construct, he could work through hundreds of combinations and still draw a blank.

Puzzling in a different way were cleverly constructed ornamental objects which had been so deftly carved from a single block of wood that they constituted a framework within which there were one or more free-standing, movable objects—a bird, perhaps, or a ball, or a number of balls. These objects,

*Samuel Christ's tiny lead figures, not old enough to
rate as antique, have come to be prized collectibles,
all the same. Christ lived in La Anna.*

light in weight, were often brightly painted and frequently were used as Christmas tree ornaments. Jokesters were prone to offer small children a coin if they could figure out how to get the birds or balls out of the wooden cages without breaking the cage. If the joker was an uncle, he often concluded his little game by awarding the coin anyway. Such toys seem to be of the same genre as the interlocking or conjoined wooden chain links found in New England and elsewhere.

Popular in the second half of the nineteenth century was a country or "district" school setup which included teacher, students, and desks, all with bases which could be fitted into grooves on a wooden floor and then moved into various positions. This building-block unit was the creation of Charles M. Crandall, born in 1833. Crandall, a member of an American family which included at least eleven toy makers in the century between 1830 and 1930, was a versatile man who made many kinds of toys, including his celebrated "Old Hero" and "Crandall's Acrobats" units. Of them all, probably none were more popular than the school figures; the books were open at a spelling lesson, the teacher had a suitably stern posture, and the dunce with his pointed cap stood in a corner—without a book. One such set has had local names applied to the figures, including the teacher but tactfully excluding the dunce. Crandall's factory was at Montrose, Pa., from about 1866 to 1885. Crandall left Montrose to establish a toy factory at Waverly, New York.

Other flat figures, sometimes hand-cut, sometimes jigsawed, included birds and animals. These were simple representational pieces, colored identically on the two sides. Some were as much as a half inch thick; most were less. They appear to have been local in inspiration. Some of the birds are noteworthy in that their creator has caught enough of the feeling of the original to make it immediately recognizable—a woodpecker looking like a woodpecker, a robin like a robin, and so on.

While the up-country had its share of itinerants, there is no evidence to indicate that among them there was a wood carver of the stature of a Wilhelm Schimmel. (One brings up the subject only because one of the largest caches of Schimmel figures ever found at one time or place came to light in Newfoundland.) Occasionally, wooden figures used in a Christmas putz purport to have been locally carved, but one can not, in the absence of supportive evidence, be sure. Such figures are oftener found unpainted than painted.

The Pocono up-country did have one known personality, however—a man who lived and died in comparative obscurity, but whose toy-making skills have now, not far from a century after his death, achieved recognition. This person was Georg Huguenin, a French-speaking emigrant from Travere, Switzerland. Huguenin came to America with his mother before the Civil War and established a home for her in the village of Newfoundland. He served in the war, receiving a wound which was the eventual cause of his death in 1882. In 1874 he married Mary Sieg, considerably his junior.

Huguenin had behind him a family tradition of toy carving, and while there was no opportunity in Newfoundland for him to exercise his skill widely he did create a number of objects for his own children as well as for the children of friends and neighbors.

His specialty was sheep—little creatures less than two inches high, carved in the round in the fashion of Noah's Ark animals and given a coat of real wool. One sheep in each flock he created had a black fleece. He also carved other domestic animals, which, with the sheep, were utilized in the yearly Christmas putz. Some of these animals are still in the possession of his grandchildren and great-grandchildren, but others have been lost. According to family tradition, his masterpiece was an enclosed stockade or farmyard containing one or more of all the animals in his repertoire. The story may well be true, since many European toy carvers created similar displays—but the set has been lost or, more probably, taken apart in order to divide the animals among inheritors.

Partly in the tradition, too, of European toy carvings are his little wood-block buildings—church, schoolhouse, dwelling house—which go to make up a village. These have been painted either white or a dull red except for the roofs, which are in black. Windows and doors are outlined in pen and ink. While the buildings themselves are constructed in the same way as their European prototypes, they do not, in toto, give the impression of a European *Hof* or village. They do not purport to represent any specific American buildings, either—but they do look like many of the simple rectangular structures of the Pocono area, particularly the farmhouses with their precisely centered front doors, many-paned windows, and a chimney at each end of the building.

Perhaps all these small creations were found under the Christmas tree oftener than in the hands of children at unsupervised play. We do not know. What we do know is that there are just enough survivals to make us wish that others might come to light.

Two of Huguenin's larger play pieces survive. These are doll-size. One is a one-story house with a

*All-white semi-porcelain child's tea set. Unmarked, it
appears to be of the mid-nineteenth century. From the
Henry family, Henryville, Pa.*

sloping roof, two windows, and an open front door.
It still has its original green paint. The other is a
doll-size bed of simple construction.

In a class all their own are tiny animals of cast lead
made by Samuel Christ (pronounced to rhyme with
"mist") of La Anna as late as the twentieth century.
Averaging not more than two inches high, they convey a feeling of fragile delicacy, partly because of
their graceful lines and partly, too, because of their
thin wash of subtle color. While the inspiration for
these animals may possibly have stemmed from the
Noah's Ark idea, Christ's beasts do not always come
two-by-two—and, in addition to the lions, tigers,
giraffes, and other familiar denizens of the Ark, such
American creatures as a buffalo and a cottontail sit-
ting on his haunches are to be found, to say nothing
of a leather-clad hunter using a long rifle.

Christ made these toys as a pastime, first creating
his own molds. After he died, an admiring neighbor
secured Christ's entire output. Occasionally he has
been persuaded to part with some of the little figures,
which were at first regarded merely as local curiosi-
ties but which are now earning wider acclaim among
collectors, decorators, and handcraft enthusiasts.

COLLECTORS LOOK FOR:

Homemade dolls of all types
Factory-turned playthings, including building blocks
    and spinning tops.
Sets of Crandall's Improved Building Blocks (Dis-
    trict School) patented 1875 and 1876
Pill boxes; any kind of small friction or screw-top
    wooden boxes, especially with intact labels
Locally made dolls' furniture and dolls' houses
Hand-carved puzzles
Carved nut shell baskets
Jointed serpent toys
Jigsawed birds and animals
Hand-carved Christmas putz figures
Huguenin carvings
Lead figures by Samuel Christ
*Jackpot:* Woolly sheep by Georg Huguenin

# 33

## *The Receding Ice Age*

The mountainous region of northeastern Pennsylvania was ideally equipped, three-quarters of a century ago, to supply the refrigeration needs not only of spots at home, but also places north, east, south, and west. The Pocono region itself, with its numerous ponds and small lakes, as well as many sections of Monroe—everywhere, as a matter of fact, where natural or artificially created ponds of suitable size existed—had a stake in the annual ice harvest.

The requirements were uncomplicated: plenty of still water surface, plenty of sub-freezing weather in January and February, adequate storage houses, and a railroad siding right at hand. A good supply of labor, which might have been a problem, was taken for granted, since many farmers and others could put in several weeks' work in the dead of winter.

Vast ice houses could exist where the lake or pond surfaces were sizable and where the weather was consistently cold enough that ice could be cut more than once in the same place. Perhaps the most talked-of up-country enterprises were those at Reeders, Tobyhanna, and Gouldsboro, and men from far and wide found short-term employment there. That these men would almost inevitably suffer frozen ears, toes, and fingers mattered less than that here was a source of income at a time when little else was available.

Not least among the hardships facing the ice worker away from home was the caliber of some of the boarding houses he had to patronize. Some of these places were undoubtedly good, but the folklore which has accrued points in a contrary direction. Most were bad, according to the tales told when the workers returned home, and those which were not bad were worse. The badness seems to have been an amalgam of monotonous and often unappetizing food; bunks or beds insufficiently supplied with blankets or quilts, and in some cases not overly clean; and a prevailing air of rowdiness tending to erupt in fights and brawls. To indict all the establishments catering to the seasonal workers would obviously be unfair, especially since the ice ponds ranged in size from those which employed only a few men, who were housed in the homes of the owners, to those which were so large that only a barracks-style catering setup would serve. Folklore is folklore, however, and one of the first things recalled by elderly men who once put in time at the ice ponds is frequently the boarding house rather than the frozen toes or the heavy work.

Storage houses were so constructed that the ice could be preserved until well into the summer. The various needs of distant cities; the butcher shops throughout the counties served; the dairies; the ice cream industry, which was just beginning to take shape; the breweries—all these had to be served from the giant ice houses at the lakes. An idea of the scope of the ice industry may be gained from the fact that in Wayne County alone there are 110 lakes, 80 of them natural, used at one time for the harvesting of ice. Gouldsboro Lake covered 278 acres. The pond at Tobyhanna was artificially created. Bodies of water, wherever they were, were utilized whenever possible. A Mr. Barr had a plant on Lenox Avenue in East Stroudsburg in 1895. Another operation in the Stroudsburgs was that of Norman B. Gregory, who harvested 5000 tons a year.

The buildings, whether home-size or commercial, were usually double-walled, the space between the walls, eight to twelve inches, being filled with sawdust. At home, another space to be filled in with sawdust was left between the inner wall and the edge of

249

the cakes were sometimes set on edge instead of being laid flat. The sawyers could not control the thickness of the cakes; they could, however, assure reasonable similarity in length and width. One historian suggests 22 by 32 inches as the "proper" size for commercial cakes. Those for home use, where no mechanical conveyors helped to relieve the sheer physical drudgery, were likely to be smaller.

It might seem that insulation with sawdust would be less than satisfactory. Actually, it was remarkably efficient. How the industry would have fared without

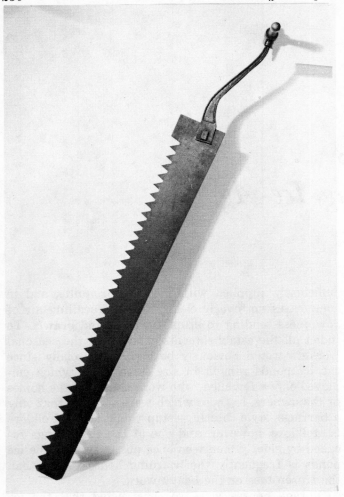

*Sturdy six-foot hand ice saw from a Monroe County ice operation.*

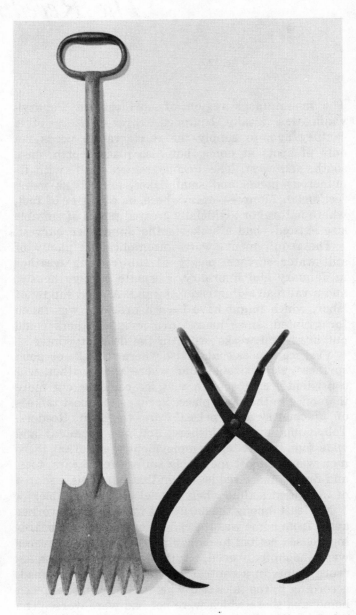

*Tongs and an ice-cake breaker from the Silver Lake ice house at Minisink Hills.*

the slowly forming ice mountain. Ice cakes coming in from the lake were stacked in layers, usually but not necessarily horizontal. As the pile increased in size, all the cracks and crevices were filled with chipped ice or with sawdust, since every possible bit of air must be excluded. Cakes of ice varied in size, but were seldom if ever less than eight inches in thickness. Nine or ten were better, but beyond that point not only were the individual cakes too heavy for efficient handling in all but the most thoroughly mechanized plants in later years, but they called for a disproportionate amount of effort in the sawing operation. In exceptionally cold winters the operators were forced to accept the inevitable and work with the ice available, no matter how thick it became.

Because ice cakes of varying thickness created problems in the packing processes inside the houses, the seemingly inexhaustible supply from the sawmills of the day makes for interesting speculation. Perhaps the major hazard to keeping ice the year round was the degree of care it was possible to take in the summer when the cakes were removed for shipping. If the sawdust was replaced to a proper depth after each excavation, a minimum of wastage occurred. A single careless operation, however, could be all but disastrous in warm weather when, instead of a layer of cold air hovering over ice and sawdust, the space under the roof was an ever-enlarging bowl of superheated air. It has been suggested that working in an ice house on a sizzling August day must be an ideal occupation. Nothing could be farther from the truth, for the physical exertion called for, in addition to the stifling atmosphere in the windowless building, made the work not only uncomfortable but dangerous.

Probably there was little about any phase of ice harvesting that was actually comfortable. Certainly the cutting operation had little that was romantic about it. In the beginning, all the sawing was done by hand and, since the saw descended into the water at each stroke, it was only a matter of time before the operator's hands were wet. Unless he had completely watertight clothing from head to toe, a condition seldom occurring, he was likely to get soaked before the day was over—and the bitter wind sweeping over the lake did not increase his comfort. One of the worst things that could happen was for an operator to loose his footing and plunge into the icy water. If he did, he had to be taken back to the boarding house on the run for a change of clothing or he might freeze to death. One of the hazards a neophyte had to deal with was the presence of a practical joker on any sizable crew. To such a person, giving the greenhorn a "bath" was great fun—or so we are told.

The condition of the ice was of much importance to the entrepreneur. Ideally, ice in cake form should be brittle enough to chip easily, be free of flaws or extraneous matter, and break in a straight line. Its condition will change from day to day, according to the temperature and the humidity of the air above it. After several days of warmish weather, it will lose its brittle quality—the first step to thawing—and should not be cut unless the weather grows colder, since it is not likely to keep well. Honey-combed or "rotten" ice was avoided like the plague, and very properly so. Not only was it dangerous to work with; its keeping qualities were poor. A single day's warm sunshine would not start the honey-combing process— but two days' exposure often would.

Small operations, as a rule family affairs, tended to be more endurable than those on a commercial scale. The farmer's ice house followed the principle of the commercial plant but of course was of a size geared to his own needs. Generally speaking, the house was an independent structure, though occasionally it might be a converted part of another building. With less ice than there would be in a larger place, there would be less cold, in toto, to preserve it, and in consequence more sawdust was required to make up for the deficiency. At the time of summer consumption, this excessive quantity of sawdust was a marked nuisance. Using a maximum of sawdust for insulation, therefore, and a minimum for summer convenience presented a neat problem. In any case attrition was likely to be considerably greater in the small ice house than in the large establishment.

Contributing to the diminution of the supply was the fact that the person who removed a cake for home consumption first had to get into the ice house and, once there, needed a little room in which to work. An ice house, for the sake of insulation, was windowless and doorless. When the place was being filled, the ice was taken in through an entrance perhaps three feet in width and running from the floor to the top of the building. As the cakes were stacked in place, the entrance was gradually boarded up, until finally the interior was solidly packed with a thick layer of sawdust on every side. Thus far, there was no problem. However, when the topmost board of the entrance was removed, the evenness of the insulation was disturbed, no matter how carefully the sawdust was replaced. In a house which covered acres of ground, the damage would have been inconsequential. In the small place, however, unless extreme care was taken, a slow thaw would set in and endanger the entire supply.

One of the problems haunting the Pocono farmer who had his own ice pond was the matter of whether or not, when the temperature plummeted, there would be enough water to assure an ice harvest. If the pond had a natural breast, the principal difficulty was that of keeping the shores free of cattails and other aquatic growth. If, however, the farmer built his own dam, unless he was something of an engineer he had to cope with muskrats, beavers, freshets, and changing currents. Few homemade ice ponds lasted as long as their owners hoped they would, and one experimental idea after another was tried and abandoned. If wooden dam breasts were employed— the usual method up to at least the year 1900—slanting the boards at an angle more or less obtuse than the one previously used might be tried. Or the spillway might be angled differently, or set in a different place. Or the breast might be set in a trench which in the summer had been partly filled with small hemlock branches, called "browse," and tamped down tight. The result, only too often, was the same: The chances were about even that in January the farmer would have to strike a bargain with a neighbor whose pond was covered with ice, the water having drained out of his own.

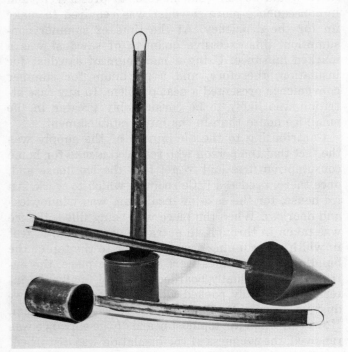

*Milk retailed by street vendors was dipped from large cans into smaller receptacles by means of utensils like these.*

The tools employed in the ice industry, apart from the elaborately mechanized plants and equipment of the later years, were simple. First, there was the saw itself, a more or less cumbersome affair that had to be operated almost vertically. The initial opening in the ice was made with an ax, but the saw was used from that point on. A problem attaching to the use of this implement was that until one got the knack of the operation the saw was likely to stick in the ice if the slightest deviation in the kerf took place. The immediate and natural reaction was a tug to dislodge it; the equally immediate consequence might be as simple as a painfully bruised jaw as the loosened saw flew up—or as serious as the loss of a number of teeth.

As the cakes were cut through and floated free, a long pole with a metal hook at the end—the "ice pike" —served to push them to the edge of the open water, where they were removed with a pair of tongs. In the ice house, in addition to another pair of tongs and the

inevitable shovel to distribute the sawdust, a sharp-pronged ice cake splitter was a necessary tool, not only in lining up the cakes when they were stacked in place but also in separating them in summer, when they had refrozen and were stuck together. Farmers liked to get their ice home by bobsled, if there was snow on the ground, because less lifting had to be done than if a wagon were used. Sometimes in small-scale operations the cakes would be drawn to the ice house on a stone sledge.

As late as 1927, a Stroudsburg historian listed twelve Monroe County plants dealing in natural ice, though not all of them at that time were still locally owned—four in Tobyhanna Township, three in Coolbaugh Township, and one each at Reeders, Saylorsburg, Stroudsburg R.F.D., East Stroudsburg R.F.D., and Silver Lake (now Minisink Hills). But the great days of ice ponds and ice houses were over; the whole industry ground to a halt when "artificial" refrigeration became possible on a wide scale. As the power lines spread, one by one the big natural ice establishments closed. Hotels, butcher shops, restaurants, and ice cream parlors were among the first to install their own refrigerating equipment. Last to give up the struggle were the small outlying farms, but eventually electric current reached them, too, and even the most nostalgically inclined person would hardly have had it otherwise. Ice harvesting may look idyllic in an old lithograph, and undoubtedly it had its better moments, but in the main it was a grueling, demanding task in which the unpleasant or dangerous aspects outnumbered the attractive ones.

Let it not be thought, though, that a once great industry could come to an end without leaving, here and there, a touch of poignance for something irrevocably lost. Perhaps there were few small-town sights more comforting on a broiling summer day than the ice delivery wagon clattering down the street, the melting ice dripping on the cobblestones as it came—or more satisfying than the beds of crushed ice cradling the oysters or fish in the peddler's cart. And in the same kind of conveyance there were the cans of crushed ice which kept milk cool until it was ladled, with a long-handled dipper, into the pail of a waiting small boy—who would surreptitiously slip a chunk into his mouth if no one appeared to be looking. (If he was a Pennsylvania Dutch boy, the little covered pail he carried would have been termed a "blicky.")

The farmer has torn his ice house down, now, or converted it into a garage. Timbers from one of the best known of the large West End plants have been salvaged and used to excellent advantage in a resi-

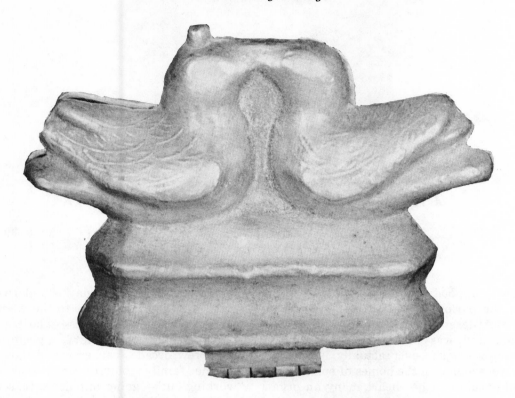

*A hinged ice cream mold of pewter, in the confrontal birds design—one of the most popular ever created. Molded ice cream, enormously popular at the end of the nineteenth century, is unknown to many persons today.*

dence between Tannersville and Reeders. Many of the commercial plants burned. Some of them were probably struck by lightning, as has been claimed; some of the fires may have been incendiary in origin. However they met their end, they have disappeared so completely that in many cases not even a pile of stones is left to tell where they once stood.

### COLLECTORS LOOK FOR:

Handwrought ice tongs
Ice pikes
Forked ice bars with two, three, or four prongs
"Breaking" bars for splitting refrozen cakes of ice
Splitting chisels
Broad scoop shovels for spreading or removing sawdust
Manual ice saws—one-handed or two-handed
Wooden racks from early walk-in refrigerators

Complimentary ice picks with the name of the ice company printed on the handle
Slender tubs for filling with crushed ice to cool tall bottles
Small granite-ware or tin pails—"blickies" to the Pennsylvania Dutchman in the up-country
Milk cans
Long-handled vertical dippers for milk cans. Some of these were cone-shaped, the handle being soldered to the cone.
Ice cream parlor chairs and tables with twisted wire frames
Metal-and-glass containers used in ice cream parlors for sundaes, frappes, sodas, etc.
Prints, lithographs, or postcards illustrating the cutting of ice
*Jackpot:* Ice tongs with multiple grips of teeth on each side, as opposed to those with single grips

# 34
## *The Ubiquitous Parlor Organ*

Anybody who was *anybody* in the up-country had an Instrument in the parlor by the 1870s—Instrument with a capital I. At least four times out of five it was a parlor organ, and was highly cherished by its owner, whether or not she ever actually learned to play it. There were pianos in the homes of some of the well-to-do, and perhaps in her heart many an organ owner would have preferred the more expensive instrument, though she might not have chosen to say so. After the 1890s, or perhaps 1900, the organs began to disappear, one by one, and today it is hardly possible to find even a fair specimen, whether in a private home or an antique shop. And, human nature being what it is, a great many piano owners nowadays would gladly acquire a parlor organ—if they could find one.

Violins, accordions, and zithers—all of these had their places in country homes, too, but they were not Instruments; they were just violins, accordions, and zithers. No lack of respect accrued to them or to those who played them, but there was something impressive about the highly polished organ—or piano—in a darkened parlor that made anything else seem small and insignificant.

Let us bypass the piano, for the moment, as well as the person who could pay for one without disrupting the entire family economy, and concentrate on the reed organ—the "pump" organ, as it is often called. (Need it be said that organ tones were created by air flowing over metal tongues or reeds, and that the air came from operating, that is, pumping, a pair of pedals?) Those who do not like the sound of the term "pump organ" usually say "reed organ" instead— and perhaps the term is somewhat more euphonious.

While reed organs would seem almost ridiculously inexpensive by present-day standards, they represented a major investment to the women—often unmarried girls in their teens—who bought them. Toward the end of the century, a good many girls who only a few decades earlier would have remained under the family rooftree until they married were "working out"—going into domestic service at boarding houses or the homes of the well-to-do in their own community or in town. A "strong, willing" girl—the kind preferred by employers—could earn a dollar and a quarter a week, plus, of course, her board and room. If she had her heart set on a parlor organ, she might be able to save enough, in a year or two, by careful economy, to buy one.

Butler Brothers' catalogue (New York and Chicago) for 1893 listed two—the Parlor Gem for $39.75 and the Home Circle ("ten stops and ten octaves") for $49.50. One wonders how many buyers were led astray by the printer's error which credited a six-octave organ with ten octaves. A ten-octave instrument would indeed have been an instrument with a capital I! While organs could be bought at places as close to home as Stroudsburg or Scranton or Easton, it seems that most girls "sent away" for them. Some liked the Miller organs from Lebanon; others were partial to the instruments which came from Bridgeport, Connecticut. Many, of course, simply pored over the advertisements in the periodicals of the day and made their choices according to the convincingness of the descriptions given.

An organ was much more than just a musical instrument. As we have hinted, it was a status symbol —and status was a many-faceted thing. Butler Brothers' organs, mentioned above, were of oak. Oak was popular for living room and dining room furni-

*The Miller reed organ (Lebanon, Pa.) in walnut was the favored instrument for many an up-country parlor.*

ture; for bedrooms it was almost a must. To many girls, however, especially those who made up their own minds, there was more class in dark wood like mahogany or walnut, especially walnut. The owner of a walnut organ might not actually look down on the possessor of one in oak, but she could, if she chose, feel smug about her own.

The number of octaves was a matter of pride, too. Whereas the piano keyboard of seven and a third octaves is standard, a reed organ normally has five or six. It did not matter that the uppermost treble keys in a six-octave instrument often tended to be squeaky rather than musical; one had more organ— and more status—with six. Even here, however, there was room at the top, so to speak; now and then a reed organ with a full complement of 88 keys was built into an upright piano case. It should go without saying that the owner of such an instrument might have a feeling of condescension toward the owner of even a very good six-octave organ.

Important also was the number of stops—the regulators which gave the reeds their distinctive tonal quality. There might be as few as seven; ten were usual; there could be as many as seventeen. When an organ was new, there really was a distinguishable tone quality among the stops, and lovely melodic variations could be produced by pulling out just the right ones. In the course of time, however, some of the nuances were lost and could not be restored. It is for this reason that one counts himself fortunate if his old reed organ today has enough stops in working order to produce even a minimum of harmonious sounds.

The names of the stops leaned on pipe organ nomenclature and were probably intended to be descriptive. Frequently, though, they were less descriptive than picturesque. They varied from manufacturer to manufacturer, but a typical assemblage would be, starting at the upper treble and going to the lower bass, Dulciana, Echo, Celeste, Celestina, Treble Coupler, Vox Humana (or Tremolo), Bass Coupler, Hautboy, Principal, Dulcet, and Diapason. Out of the lot, three did not actually influence the tone: Vox Humana or Tremolo simply allowed air to escape quickly when one stopped playing, and the couplers linked a played note with its mate an octave above (treble) or an octave below (bass), thus lending volume.

Volume could be further amplified by using the swells, which were operated by knee pressure and which stepped up the amount of air which put the reeds in vibration. Some organs had a short cut—the Full Organ stop, which turned on everything except the knee swells.

Reed instruments were of two general types— parlor organs and church organs. Today's purchaser, if he is in the happy but unlikely position of being able to make a choice, would do well to take the church organ. Parlor organs were built so that, when they were new, the sound would fill a room of ordinary size. Over the years, as they were subjected to wear, as the inner felts wore thin, and as the reeds lost some of their sensitivity, the volume diminished to the point at which the total effect was too attenuated to be entirely pleasing. Church organs, on the other hand, were built for greater volume—too much for home use unless the player exercised good judgment. In the course of time many have mellowed or softened to the point at which they are highly desirable for home playing.

There is an added plus today in purchasing a church organ. The accompanist normally faced the congregation; the back of the organ, therefore, was in the direct line of vision of the people—and so it was constructed and finished with all the careful detail lavished on the rest of the piece. Parlor organs were intended for placement against a wall, and not much attention was paid to their backs. Since many homeowners today find it expedient to set an organ with an *end* to the wall, the church organ might well get the nod. It should be noted, though, that in the beginning a young lady would certainly have been considered eccentric had she bought the wrong kind of organ for her home—or put the right kind anywhere but flat against the wall.

In an age where gingerbread, so called, on parlor furniture—or any furniture, for that matter—had reached all kinds of extremes, the parlor organ somehow usually managed to come out ahead. All that the musician needed, above the keyboard and the row of stops he faced, was a rack of some kind to hold his music book or sheets so that he could read them. What he got was more—much, much more. Illumination ordinarily had to be provided. Lamps could have been set on the top of the instrument—but, instead, fancy lamp stands to right and left of the keyboard, but above its level, were built in. Lamps might be knocked over, though; so little galleries enclosing the stands were frequently constructed. A really special gallery would have been made so that ribbon could be threaded through the posts and tied in a bow.

A storage place behind the music rack seemed like a good idea to some inventive designer—but then the superstructure of the instrument—now rapidly heading toward its apotheosis—had to be raised to match. That usually left a flat top, and on a flat surface pictures of family groups and bric-a-brac could be placed. Since the bric-a-brac was usually something

*Manuscript pages in which musical notation, fraktur-type decorations, and highly moralistic verse compete for attention. Found at Shawnee-on-Delaware, the manuscript is dated 1852.*

in-the-round, a mirror was added to double the beauty of the objects. The mirror was usually balanced on either side by shelves, and the whole given an open gallery of turned posts and fancy finials stopping just short of the ceiling. Plain surfaces seemed to be a matter of abhorrence; machine-made scrolls, knobs, reeding, pierced work, and spooling helped to take away any curse of plainness left by this time. The wonder of it all is that, in spite of the ostentatious plus-upon-plus, the music could still be sweet and pleasing. To-day, the superfluous gimcrackery can frequently be removed, bringing the instrument into line with our present, more restrained tastes, but of course the authenticity of the piece suffers in the process.

Organs had, and have, two prime enemies—mice and dryness. The inner mechanism which controls the flow of air is banded with felt. In earlier times, it was not just any old felt, but very good wool felt. A mouse on the lookout for a safe place to build a nest was likely to ignore everything else in sight and, waiting until the time was ripe and she could escape detection, head straight for the parlor organ. The carnage wrought on the felts was always damaging, and many an instrument was ruined before the mice could be eliminated.

Dryness was less a problem in days when houses lacked central heating than it is now; one could play the organ in a warm or a cold room with equal facility. Nowadays, however, one's antique organ may be almost impossible to manipulate in the winter months, though it works fine in the summer. Again, it is the felts which are at the root of the trouble; they dry out in a heated room, allowing air to escape, with a consequent diminution in volume, plus an unpleasant wheezing as one tries to pump harder. In the summer there seems to be enough humidity in the air to keep the felts in proper working order.

A piano will go out of tune more quickly than will a reed organ. In fact, if an organ is well treated, the pitch remains constant throughout its long lifetime, with the possible exception of the highest keys in the treble. Even then the difficulty is seldom in the tuning; it is much more likely to be an accumulation of dust under the tiny tongues of the reeds. The manufacturer provided a reed hook so that clogged reeds could be pulled out and the dust removed. This was an operation of some delicacy, and an inept touch could put the reed out of tune. Persons who would attempt repairs of any kind on an organ were scarce a century ago, and are even harder to find, today.

Taking music lessons was an almost inevitable concomitant of possessing an Instrument. True, the manufacturer almost always provided a (free) manual of instruction, just as he did the reed hook and a revolving, padded-topped adjustable stool. Some persons were able to master the exercises in the manual, with a little help from one who had gone through the mill before, and progress to "pieces"—"Music in the Air" and a simplified version of "The Bluebells of Scotland," for instance. More, however, gave up trying to work things out on their own, and took lessons from a bona fide teacher if one were available.

A schism in thinking frequently occurred at this point. Most teachers were pianists and, while they could and would give instruction on the reed organ, generally preferred their own chosen instruments. In fact, some of them exercised almost a missionary zeal in trying to convince their students of the superior qualities of the piano. For the girl who had saved pennies and nickels for two years to buy an organ, the teacher would shortly discover that she was espousing a lost cause; as soon as the student had mastered a few basics she would discontinue instruction by the professional and take her own path.

In fairness to the piano teacher, one should observe that the piano transcends most of the limitations of the reed organ, and that the musical literature which can be played effectively on a reed organ is extremely limited in scope. In a day, however, when a "good" musician was one who could play simple church hymns without making mistakes and could run through the "Orvetta Waltz" with vim and vigor, the

*A completely hand-copied music manual of selections someone liked well enough to record—in 1783. The chances are that this work was done in a school for young ladies.*

*Pages in a typical bilingual (German and English)
shape-note hymnal—the* Pennsylvania Choral Harmony, *published in Allentown in 1869.*

virtues of the piano were of little moment . . . unless
one owned a piano. As for compositions like "The
Maiden's Prayer," "Star of the Sea," and "The Midnight Fire Alarm," well, the reed organist who could
handle them was likely to be regarded as a talented
and able musician.

The board-bound, impressive-looking manuals
which were part and parcel of the musical picture
should not be overlooked by the collector. Comprehensive in nature, they started with identifying C-major
on the keyboard and progressed by rapid steps
through the scales (major and minor), various finger
exercises, simple transcriptions of the classics, and
duets. At the back of the book there were usually
selections the range of which went beyond the limits
of the keyboard and which because of the impossibil-
ity of sustaining a reed organ tone once one's fingers
have left the keys should never have been included.
One complication for today's would-be player of the
selections in the manual is the use of the letter "x"
for the thumb when fingering is indicated. To the person familiar with 1–2–3–4–5 fingering, the combination x–1–2–3–4 can be catastrophic.

Equally interesting, though not properly belonging
to reed organ literature, are the shape-note singing
school books once used widely throughout the land.
Actually, they were intended for use without instrumental accompaniment other than a tuning fork, and
many of them preceded the time when the Victorian
parlor organ was enjoying its heyday. The theory back

of the shape-note was that a person could learn to follow printed musical notation with ease if each note
of the scale was printed in its own distinctive shape—
one angular little figure representing "do," no matter
what the key signature, a different one indicating
"mi," and so on.

To the noninitiate today, the result on a printed
page is at first sight something to fill him with awe.
The books are arranged for four-part singing, and the
weird-looking little shapes take on seemingly impossible combinations. What we should call the melody
usually appears in the third stave—but critics of the
system pointed out that in many cases there really
was no melody. Even ministers of the churches in
which the books were a necessary prerequisite to par-
ticipation in singing in the choir are said to have
complained that all the tunes sounded alike and that
they all sounded bad. A mildly deprecatory term for
the whole shape-note school of thought was "buckwheat music"—the angular little notes somewhat suggesting grains of buckwheat lying at differing angles.

Since the whole emphasis was on sight-reading and
the use of one's voice, no instrumental accompaniment
was provided; in fact, theoretically there was no need
either for an accompanist or for an instrument. In
practice, most country churches acquired organs—or
even pianos—at the earliest possible moment; an accompanist of reasonable skill could render a satisfactory improvisation by building on the "melody" stave.
It seems likely that it was the combination of instru-

ment and accompanist that put the shape-note out of business.

Some of these little books became enormously popular, and went through many printings from a time as early as the 1830s through the 1870s and later. Actually, it is said that in some remote places in the South they are still being used—and successfully. Those found in the up-country were, in a great many cases, printed in German. However, some were in English —and a number were bilingual. Perhaps the most popular of all the German-language volumes is the one affectionately called the "Blue Strawberry" book —not that the berries pictured on the cover represent some strange, exotic fruit; the cover is blue, and the strawberries in the printed border are black. The book, entitled *Deutsche Harmonie (German Harmony)* was compiled by J. G. Schmauk and published in Philadelphia in 1847.

In the bilingual category, Thomas R. Weber's *Pennsylvania Choral Harmony*, published in Allentown in 1869 (and probably earlier, also), was popular. Considerably older, and possibly for that reason less well known to collectors, is *The Franklin Harmony*, compiled by John Rothbaust and published in Chambersburg in 1830.

The Monroe County favorite was apparently the English-language volume called *The Timbrel of Zion*, compiled by T. K. Collins, Jr., and printed in Philadelphia in 1857. One cherished specimen bears on a flyleaf a cluster of three penciled names of long-gone residents in the Hamilton Township region: "Susan E. Fenner, Elmira Fenner, and Delila Fenner." It is not uncommon for one book to contain a succession of names and, occasionally, dates—an indication of long service, if nothing else.

Rounding out the list of music books is another type, more rare by far—the completely handwritten manuscript music book. The volumes themselves were purchased blank, putatively for use in young ladies' schools or academies. Both staves and music are hand-drawn, in ink, and represent countless hours of work. For most students, compiling their personal song books meant copying well-liked selections—often highly sentimental ones. For a few, it meant adding personal compositions. The quality of the writing and of the notation is variable; sometimes it is creditable, but nothing like the caliber of the little fraktur-decorated handwritten song books of early days, farther down-country. The sheer size of some of these books is astonishing, running to several hundred pages. The earliest known to the author bears the date of 1783. Books of this kind give us a clue as to the musical tastes of the times in which they were made, but perhaps their most important service today is as conversation pieces.

A final half-note on the entire matter: any person of English-Irish background in the up-country would at any time have understood instantly what a speaker meant by "organ." Not so the Pennsylvania Dutchman or German; to him, up to, let us say, the early 1900s, an "organ" was an English name for some inner anatomical entity. He might not have had the effrontery to correct the speaker—but surely anyone should know that the name for the musical instrument was *orgel*, not *organ!*

### COLLECTORS LOOK FOR:

Reed organs

Harmoniums and melodeons—earlier than reed organs and rare, though not completely nonexistent in the up-country

Piano-cased organs

"Organ lamps"—pairs of matching kerosene lamps in pressed glass, milk glass, or art glass

Organ stools (Piano stools will not always serve, since they may be too low for comfort.)

Early hard-back instruction manuals

Shape-note singing school books

Sheet music, vintage of the 1870s to 1900—or later

Manuscript music books

*Jackpot:* Simply styled walnut reed organs in playing condition—all stops, couplers, swells, and key ivories intact—and no mouse damage

# 35
# Scrapbooks and Fancy Paper

Nobody, anywhere, took a back seat to the fancy-paper artists of the up-country. One is tempted to say that if there was a peak in variety and quality, that peak must have been reached in Monroe, where two of the conditions necessary for the nurturing of this special acivity came into being earlier than was the case to the north—a fair degree of familiarity with the progress of individual art expression beyond the local level, and comparative freedom from the economic pinch which held so many families captive so long in more remote regions of Wayne and Pike—especially Pike.

At the same time, after the mid-1800s anyone in the up-country would have had to be either a recluse or completely impecunious not to have been touched by the urge to make plain things look pretty, either by bringing out their natural attractiveness or—in what is called the "typically" Victorian way—by making them look like something else which was presumed to look better. The ramifications are so extensive, and are so tied in with the ever-continuing American craving to improve on the old, whatever it was, that to attempt a thorough-going classification of the scrapbook art of the later 1800s would probably take a lifetime—and a five-foot bookshelf. The best we can do is to see, by examining the survivals, what was apparently characteristic of the region in the scrapbook age.

There were at least four major types of repositories for small memorabilia, several of which we should write off here as meriting full treatment at other hands and in another place. One of these is the photograph album, either a large, heavy book with magnificent over-stuffed plush or papier mâché covers and gilt fore-edging, or a comparable kind of ar- rangement, but with the spine mounted on a low stand so that the pages would open vertically rather than horizontally. Some of these albums had elaborately shaped little mirrors set into the top cover, and some were of a superior early glue-and-wood-powder composition which we should now call plastic. Meriting a nonlocalized treatment also is the later picture postcard album, popular during the first quarter of the present century, which might be as consciously gorgeous as the photograph album or as simple as an aggregation of pages slitted to accommodate penny post cards, and enclosed in inexpensive cardboard covers. Trailing the post-card albums in popularity were the autograph books, many of which were a by-product of the nineteenth century boarding school for young ladies.

Objects which lacked the specific quality of belonging sometimes found their way into photograph, postcard, or autograph albums, but by comparison with what was found in the brightly covered scrapbooks the contents seem almost severely homogeneous. Scrapbooks were the places in which one preserved everything of paper considered too pretty to throw away, provided that it was small enough to fit neatly within the covers of a book up to 14 or 15 inches long and perhaps ten wide. If a book professionally created for the purpose was not available, a store ledger which had fulfilled its primary mission —or which had not yet reached the point of being needed—was pressed into service now and then, especially in earlier days when paper was still an expensive commodity. Youngsters were sometimes given worn-out or unwanted books for their own private pasting-up exercises, and now and then one comes upon a child's scrapbook in which the pasted

*Popular mid-Victorian decoration. Such creations were sometimes framed, as shown here, but just as frequently made their way into scrapbooks. Montages of lithograph and cloth, left and middle; spatter decoration at right. These were found in an old house in Cherry Valley.*

or glued pictures (often from farm magazines or other illustrated periodicals) have covered the pages of a book which might eventually have achieved value as a collector's item in its own right.

What pieces were so pretty that they merited preserving—to look at privately or to display proudly to callers? Way out at the head of the list would be the brilliantly colored imported paper ornamentation which the Germans called *Glanz-bilder Reliefs,* a name which translated somewhat freely into English is "embossed-glazed pictures." In America they have oftener been known simply as "scraps," from the fact that, regardless of what the much earlier German originators had intended, they have constituted a major resource of multitudes of scrapbooks. They exist in uncounted patterns and motifs; they may have a total surface of less than a square inch or be as large as several inches tall and wide.

The hues are sparkling and bright; many embossed-glazed pieces were printed by a six-color process (red, pink, green, blue, yellow, and brown). Only the decorated surface was glazed, the back being allowed to remain unfinished in order to take paste or glue. The variety in design in *Glanz-bilder Reliefs,* while flowers are almost always involved, seems endless; to choose almost at random, one

would mention floral clusters, vases with elaborate arrangements of blossoms and ferns, urns with trailing vines, animals, exotic birds, grotesque figures, cherubs' heads, full-length angels, children in enormously varied costumes, carriages, trees, and Santa Claus figures. There were many, many others. Perhaps no roses more luxuriant in color and size ever existed in nature than those on the glazed scraps one could buy so inexpensively, and the winged hosts of heaven have seldom received more colorful—or sympathetic—treatment than they were given here.

Scraps were used abroad as early as 1800 to bedeck cakes and confectionery, but they never achieved real popularity in America among sugar bakers. One exception might be that of the bride-and-groom figures used on wedding cakes. If one were guessing—and guessing is about the best that can be done—he would surmise that Americans did not especially want these fancy paper ornaments on articles of food because they would be damaged or destroyed in use . . . and they were too pretty to place in jeopardy. Instead, they were pasted on crocks and jars, assembled into combinations which could be framed, added to bureau accessories, stuck on fire screens, placed on the Christmas tree—and pasted by the million, it would seem, in scrapbooks. One might

Name cards of members of the Rinker and Fenner families of Hamilton Township. Note that actual photographs in thumbnail size have been used (center) for the calling cards of Susan and Henry Fenner.

A cut-paper valentine. The term "Scherenschnitte" (scissors cutting) for this kind of work has achieved currency within the past year or two.

suppose that anything so enormously popular would not long remain a solely foreign product, but for a long time there appears to have been little if any American competition, perhaps because the scraps were so inexpensive. There were, however, American enterprises which used the imported objects as integral parts of their own products, especially valentines.

Another American scrapbook ornament may have had its beginnings in Europe, although when an art form appears in a number of places at about the same time it is probably safest to refrain from making any flat statement as to time or place of origin. We are speaking here of what Americans have called paper cutting from the time the Peales were doing silhouettes in Philadelphia or M. A. Honeywell was creating her fantastically delicate cut-outs in New England, both in the very early 1800s. (Miss Honeywell was the artist who, born without hands, created her work by manipulating the scissors with her feet.) A contemporary American writer who has made a study of the art, with emphasis on its early European manifestations, uses the German name *Scherenschnitte* ("scissors cutting") for the genre—an apt term. Probably every little girl who went to an up-country district school during the latter part of the nineteenth century learned how to fold and cut paper dolls as busy work. This would probably rate as the very simplest form of *Scherenschnitte*. From that point, one goes on to other folded

*Scrapbook covers were often as brilliantly magnificent as the contents of the books.*

and cut creations, some of which are marvels of laciness. Cut-paper valentines, often with a written message and carefully applied colors, tended to feature hearts and doves as decorative motifs—and what better place to preserve such fragile creations than in one's personal scrapbook? We should note that cut-paper pieces of considerable size or obvious importance were often mounted against dark velvet and framed. Framing made good sense; even the most careful scrapbook treatment was likely to damage such delicate objects, especially since the paper grew brittle after a few years.

Many of today's valentines, with their flippant messages and sophisticated designs, would have found little favor among the Victorian scrapbook artists, although a comic valentine, so called, ranging from the merely snide to the downright scurrilous in design and comment, managed to coexist with the heart-and-dove type of art. The latter got into the scrapbook; the former did not. Some of the appealing valentines one comes upon in scrapbooks, as we have noted, are of the embossed-glazed type. Others, equally appealing and more personal, are obviously handmade, and one can recognize such components as *Glanz-bilder* cupids' heads, frilled paper of the kind used in candy boxes, bits of brocade or ribbon, and occasional handwork to draw the unit together. Three-dimensional figures, in which parts of the design are folded back for storing but brought forward for standing the valentine in place, were popular as late as the early 1900s, and there are those who would like to see them more widely reproduced than they are at present.

The pressing of exceptional specimens of flowers, ferns, and leaves was a popular activity. One frequently comes upon them in old, family-size Bibles, or dictionaries, or medical books—but when they were utilized in scrapbooks they soon went to pieces and substitutions had to be made. Feathers, though, were something else. Using needle, thread, glue, and perhaps a bead, a girl with talented fingers could turn feathers from a live, three-dimensional bird into a very creditable two-dimensional representation. If she had access to a milliner's stock she could extend her repertoire. Nor would the bird she created have to stand on its own merits; it might become part of a valentine or of some equally treasured combination of paper materials. Feathers were also used to create "flowers" of more charm than exactness in representation. In recent years feather decoration from Mexico has become popular.

Found in the homes of old families, oftenest in Monroe, are two types of artistry which once reposed in scrapbooks but which now, unless the book is being treasured as an entity, are likely to be abstracted, matted, and framed so that they can be appreciated away from the clutter of the ordinarily crowded pages. Both may have derived from the young ladies' schools. One is a kind of modified decoupage in which a small face—either an actual photograph or a magazine clipping—pasted on a sheet of paper constitutes the starting point. In subsequent steps the artist may fabricate either a total modish outfit of cut paper or cloth, or any part of it, such as a bonnet or a shawl. The figure is ordinarily, but not necessarily, human; one rather attractive survival of this kind is a well-dressed cat.

The second type mentioned is that of spatter decoration, in which a paint- or water color-loaded brush is used. The sheet of paper which will be the background is selected; an object cut from another sheet of paper—a leaf, a fern, or perhaps a human figure or a pet—is laid flat against the background; then the brush is tapped and the droplets distributed as evenly as possible. After the paint has dried, the pattern is removed. It is perhaps unnecessary to observe that some skill is demanded here—and that in all probability there were a good many preliminary failures before a piece of acceptable scrapbook quality was achieved.

One calls attention to water colors in particular, because small pieces of colored paper, often no more than two or three inches square, are sometimes likely to go unnoticed among more brightly hued objects in scrapbooks. They may be, and in some cases indubitably were, practice pieces in the boarding schools in which the art was taught, but there are enough of them of good quality that one should be careful that they are not lost among the bits of fancy wrapping paper, tinfoil, cigar bands, labels from fancy braid or balls of yarn, and clippings from seed catalogues which in the course of time filled many scrapbooks to overflowing.

Next to embossed-glazed decorations, the various kinds of cards popular from about the 1840s to the end of the century, and in some cases even later, seem to loom largest in scrapbook material. Among the earliest were Award of Merit cards, which were distributed in both secular and Sunday schools. In such German language-oriented communities as those of the West End, the merit award frequently was actual fraktur, mentioned previously. As the years passed, the number of varieties increased, and by 1900 there was an impressive range which included printed, lithographed, chromolithographed, and hand-decorated specimens, some with printed and some

*Trade cards for advertising purposes were colorful
and collectible from the start—the 1880s and 1890s.
Many of these are from business establishments in
Stroudsburg and East Stroudsburg.*

with handwritten names of donor and recipient.

Sunday School cards, now seen infrequently, once served as strong incentives toward regular attendance on the part of children. The lesson for the day, sometimes with questions and answers, usually appeared on one side of the card. On the other, generally brightened with color, were Scriptural quotations, pictures and sketches of Biblical personalities, Old Testament situations, or New Testament events and parables.

Advertising cards have their own peculiar charm, in some instances partly nostalgic since the objects advertised are not infrequently within the span of

recollection of persons still living. The "shape" advertising cards, popular from the outset, are especially sought by collectors of paper ephemera today. There seems to have been sound reasoning—since the method appears to have worked—behind creating a card in the shape of a bottle for a cough remedy; a cup-and-saucer shape to advertise crockery; an over-size spool to indicate the merits of thread; a desk to bring to the fore a new development in that type of furniture; a pickle to focus attention on a canned product; a pen knife, a hat, a glove, and so on, for obvious reasons. It may be a little more difficult to determine the rationale for others, even though the cards are no less attractive: a fan to indicate the superior quality of a certain brand of coffee; a watermelon to advertise a kind of scouring soap; and a fancy Easter egg to publicize a June 18, 1883, excursion by "iron steamboat" to Orienta Grove, Long Island.

Advertisers, to assure a continuity of interest, tended to issue their cards in series. Adults not especially concerned with certain products cared little about the cards advertising them—but the youngster who had acquired a complete set, minus one or two, cared a great deal! Subjects for the series may have been chosen by the advertisers according to how long they wished to continue publicizing a particular product. The series of cities of the world, famous buildings, birds, dogs, exotic animals, and recipes would be good for a long time, even if a new card was issued weekly; western life (chiefly cowboys, horses, and Indians), maps of the states of the Union, and Oriental scenes might indicate a run of lesser proportions. Other well-known series included calendar cards, signs of the zodiac, insects to be studied or avoided, foreign stamps, flags, and—among the most attractive of all—nursery rhymes, fables, and mythological subjects.

Cards were issued widely, of course, and a space for the name of the local merchant was left to be filled in, in the locality concerned. Remembered with affection by up-country collectors are—among many others—the cards of the L'Hommedieu Music Com-

*Fine specimens of flourishing. The two smaller pieces are in autograph books. The larger was apparently framed long ago and at some forgotten point made its way northward from the down-country spots indicated.*

pany (sewing machines, pianos, and organs); J. Y. Sigafus (pianos, organs, and sewing machines!); Steward Flagler (druggist); Flory and White (kitchen ranges); W. H. Flory, Jr. ("Golden Sunshine Parlor Heater" and the "Othello" kitchen range); Linford Marsh (crockery and groceries); Hiram Kistler (school supplies); and Brown and Keller ("furnishing undertakers and dealers in furniture, carpets, and oil cloths")—all these in Stroudsburg. Remembered with equal satisfaction are those of W. H. Voss (clothier and furnisher); J. H. Shotwell (groceries); and H. S. Drake (sewing machines and wagons) of East Stroudsburg—as well as S. B. La Bar (dry goods and notions) of Marshalls Creek, and the Globe Flour Mills of Bangor.

One special type of card met with ready acceptance, but was so costly that it went through a number of transmutations, finally becoming something radically different. This was the satin-fringed card, three by five inches—as well as somewhat larger and somewhat smaller—in which the emphasis was on a lithographed or chromolithographed "scene," and the name of the advertiser assumed a minor role. Such cards seem oftenest to have been distributed to customers at Christmas, and occasionally on other holidays, and served the double purpose of advertising the product and of indicating the good will of the distributor. Some were designed as greeting cards— to be used as such by the recipient. Most popular in the 1880s, they disappeared within a matter of decades. After 1900 they gave ground to a newcomer, the penny postcard—which was in turn nudged almost out of existence, except for local-color and scenic cards, by the considerably more specialized and much more expensive greeting card we buy in stationery stores today.

Before we consider yet another of the prime scrapbook fillers we should make note of one of the lost arts of the Victorians, that of fine handwriting. Only a generation ago, handwriting supervisors still had a place on the payroll of many a metropolitan or suburban board of education, even though that supervisor was probably teaching a "system" which he had thoroughly absorbed but which few of his students would be able to master or even to imitate very satisfactorily. Before the day of the public school supervisor there had been handwriting specialists, too, at least some of whom had started with expertly developed calligraphic master books as guides. But there was an added plus in the work of the accomplished Victorian penman—the "flourishing." Flourished writing depended for its charm not only on the perfect development of each letter, from A–a to Z–z,

but on the elaborate steel-pen swirls, curves, and shaded down-strokes which embellished all the capitals and some of the small letters. Nor did flourishing stop at that point; to the handwriting itself, in special cases and for special purposes, were added skillfully executed birds, trees, animals, and the like.

Eventually, the art of flourishing, before it died for lack of practitioners, transcended the ordinary uses of handwriting, and was used chiefly in presentation pieces, for awards of merit, and ultimately as art objects in which no word of writing, not even the penman's name, appeared. Three prime favorites in this final category were the leaping deer; the galloping horse, sometimes in black ink alone and sometimes in black and red; and the eagle. Magnificent specimens have appeared in the up-country—and to the extent that it is possible to determine authorship, at least some of them were done not by professional calligraphers but by skilled laymen.

Most large pieces of flourishing—and many of the accomplished smaller ones, which are likely to be found in autograph books—are framed by today's collectors. There are, however, smaller pieces for which one should watch—the ones used on the popular calling cards (less frequently on business cards) of later Victorian days.

There is an astonishing variety of calling cards or "name" cards in the up-country. The earliest may have been the card in either regular or cursive type, completely unadorned. In a metropolitan center it might have been engraved; in the up-country it was almost always printed. It was not a spectacular addition to the scrapbook—but one saved calling cards because it might appear unfriendly to throw them away.

A notable step beyond this starting point was the printed card on which a thumbnail-size photograph of the owner of the name appeared. The picture was pasted on. A very special touch here, if the person had the skill, was a handwritten flourished name accompanying the picture. A person of only average skill in penmanship would have his name printed, usually in an ornamental type face.

Less distinctive but more colorful were cards in which bright-toned illustrations—pastoral scenes, buildings, or clusters of flowers, among others—took up a fair proportion of the space not needed for the name itself. A hand grasping a sheaf of lilies and forget-me-nots; a cluster of morning glories with a fancy ribbon bow; a horseshoe with red carnations; a yellow rose with a butterfly hovering near—these and many others bore handwritten or printed names, with such added (printed) sentiments as "In fond

*A standing photograph album from Panther; white composition with a heavy brass clasp and traces of gilt in the repoussé decorations.*

remembrance," "Forget me not," "Ever faithful," and so on. Louisa Croasdale's card—probably in the late 1860s or early '70s—added a vigorous note to the prevailing sweetness of Victorian sentiments: "Love many, trust few, and always paddle your own canoe."

Infrequently found, and the more treasured on that account, are cards done entirely by hand—a calligraphically adept name with at least a modicum of flourishing, and individually drawn and personally colored bits of scenery. The talented persons who created these often applied comparable decorations to their personal note paper, used, it must be supposed, for only very special occasions.

Yet another card, though it was minus floral decoration, had a "textured" background suggesting plaid or a fabric pattern against which the name would be set.

By far the most popular of all, in its own day, at least, was the embossed-glazed card, in which the name is printed on a white card and then concealed by an elaborate scrap which can be lifted at one end to reveal the name. These cards were exchanged among friends, relatives, and acquaintances with somewhat the degree of casualness employed in our own time in exchanging Christmas greeting cards.

Fitting into their own special niche in the whole scheme of things is one markedly distinctive series— the botanical cards which utilize "the language of the flowers." The idea that each flower has its own message to convey is far from new; more than 300 years ago Shakespeare had Ophelia say, "There's rosemary; that's for remembrance." These are partly preprinted cards, with the actual coloring process left for the purchaser. The creator of the series took no chances; he put the accepted "meaning" of the flower in fine type just below the blossom itself. Since the name of the species appeared in larger type near the top of the card, the person who wrote *his* name on the card had to do the best he could in the space that was left. When it came to filling in the colors, the would-be artist did not always guess right! Examples in this comprehensive series are chestnut ("Render me justice"); dahlia ("Dignity and elegance"); plum tree ("Keep your promises"); laurestine ("I die if neglected"); and mouse ear ("Forget me not"). Let us not be over-critical of those long-gone persons who were uncertain as to what tints or shades they should select from the watercolor box; who among us, even in a day of coloring books, would know how to paint the laurestine or the mouse ear?

### COLLECTORS LOOK FOR:

Photograph albums with papier mâché or plush covers
Standing photograph albums
Scrapbooks
Postcard albums
Autograph books with hand-done drawings or flourishings
Embossed-glazed "scraps" (*Glanz-bilder Reliefs*)
Cut-paper pieces (*Scherenschnitte*)
Valentines, handmade or embossed-glazed
Feather work
Decoupage creations featuring cut paper or cloth
Spatter pictures
Watercolor prints
Silhouettes
Trade cards, especially the "shape" cards
Fringed advertising-greeting cards
Sunday School cards
Awards of Merit
Calligraphic ("flourished") drawings
Name cards—printed, handwritten, lithographed, chromolithographed, hand-colored, textured, or embossed-glazed
*Jackpot:* A large scrapbook filled with fine specimens of the small items mentioned above

# Bibliography

*Adler Calender* (*sic*). Reading, Pa.: Ritter and Company. (Various issues of this popular German-language almanac, published by the Reading *Adler* (*Eagle*) from 1796 to the present century.)

*Agricultural Almanac*. Lancaster, Pa.: John Baer's Sons. (Early issues, starting with 1825, are especially interesting.)

*American Agriculturist*. New York: Orange Judd Company, 1897. (A weekly periodical.)

Anderson, John J. *Pictorial School History of the United States*. New York: Clark and Maynard, 1875. (Interesting for its maps showing early Indian territorial claims.)

Appel, John C. *General Daniel Brodhead*. Stroudsburg, Pa.: The Monroe County Historical Society, 1970.

Barber, Edwin Atlee. *Lead Glazed Pottery*. Philadelphia: The Philadelphia Museum and School of Industrial Art, 1907.

————. *Tulip Ware of the Pennsylvania-German Potters*. Philadelphia: The Philadelphia Museum and School of Industrial Art, 1903.

Beach, S. A. *The Apples of New York*. Albany, New York: J. B. Lyon Company, 1905, from the New York State Department of Agriculture Report of 1903. (An unexcelled study, which includes northwestern New Jersey and northeastern Pennsylvania as well as New York.)

Beers, J. H. *Commemorative Biographical Record of Northeastern Pennsylvania, Including the Counties of Susquehanna, Wayne, Pike, and Monroe*. Chicago: J. H. Beers and Company, 1900. (Subjective—but comprehensive and informative.)

Black, Mary and Lipman, Jean. *American Folk Painting*. New York: Clarkson N. Potter, Inc., 1966.

Blake, J. L. *Book of Nature*. Boston: Waitt and Dow, 1831.

Bogart, Ernest L. *Economic History of the American People*. New York: Longmans, Green and Company, 1935.

Borneman, Henry S. *Pennsylvania German Illuminated Manuscripts*. Norristown, Pa.: The Pennsylvania German Society, 1937. (Superb illustrations in color.)

Brodhead, Luke W. *The Delaware Water Gap; Its Legends and Early History*. Philadelphia: Sherman and Company, 1870.

Burrell, A. B. *Reminiscences of George La Bar*. Philadelphia: Claxton, Remsen, and Heffelfinger, 1870.

Carlisle, Lilian Baker. *Pieced Work and Appliqué Quilts at Shelburne Museum*. Shelburne, Vermont: The Shelburne Museum, 1957.

Clement, Arthur W. *Our Pioneer Potters*. York, Pa.: Privately printed, 1947.

Coffin, Margaret. *The History and Folklore of American Country Tinware 1700–1900*. Camden, New Jersey: Thomas Nelson and Sons, 1968.

Comstock, Helen. *American Furniture: Seventeenth, Eighteenth, and Nineteenth Century Styles*. New York: The Viking Press, 1962.

Davidson, Marshall B., ed. *The American Heritage History of Antiques from the Civil War to World War I*. The American Heritage Publishing Company, 1969.

Decker, Amelia Stickney. *That Ancient Trail* (*The Old Mine Road*). Privately printed, 1942. (Has to do with early houses and families along the Delaware River, on the New Jersey side.)

Drepperd, Carl W. *American Pioneer Arts and Artists*. Springfield, Mass.: The Pond–Ekberg Company, 1942.

Dunaway, Wayland F. *A History of Pennsylvania*. New York: Prentice-Hall, 1935.

*East Stroudsburg Centennial, 1870–1970*. East Stroudsburg, Pa.: The Sun Litho–Print, Inc., 1970. (Comprehensive "souvenir" program containing interesting historical items.)

*Farm and Garden, The*. Philadelphia: Child Bros. and Company, 1883. (Various issues of this monthly periodical.)

Fenner, R. B. *The Fenner Genealogy* (Typescript). Freeport, New York: n.d.

Goodrich, Phineas G. *History of Wayne County.* Honesdale, Pa.: Haines and Beardsley, 1880.

Gould, Mary Earle. *Antique Tin and Tole Ware.* Rutland, Vermont: The Charles E. Tuttle Company, 1967.

Greaser, Arlene and Paul H. *Cookie Cutters and Molds.* Allentown, Pa.: Privately printed, 1969. (Interesting account of a private collection, now dispersed.)

*Guide to the Historical Markers of Pennsylvania.* Harrisburg, Pa.: The Pennsylvania Historical and Museum Commission, 1948.

Hall, Carrie A. and Kretsinger, Rose G. *The Romance of the Patchwork Quilt in America.* New York: Bonanza Books, 1935.

Hall, Eliza Calvert. *A Book of Hand-Woven Coverlets.* Boston: Little, Brown and Company, 1931.

Haller, Mabel. *Early Moravian Education in Pennsylvania.* Nazareth, Pa.: The Moravian Historical Society, 1953.

Heller, William J. *History of Northampton County and the Grand Valley of the Lehigh.* New York: The American Historical Society, 1920. (Comprehensive three-volume study.)

Hinckley, F. Lewis. *Directory of the Historic Cabinet Woods.* New York: Crown Publishers, 1960.

Hine, Charles Gilbert. *The Old Mine Road.* New Brunswick, New Jersey: Rutgers University Press, 1963. (Romantic account of a hiking trip along the Delaware in pre-motor vehicle days.)

Hoffman, Luther S. *The Unwritten History of Smithfield Township, Monroe County, Pa.* East Stroudsburg, Pa.: The Artcraft Press, 1938.

Holstein, Jonathan. *Abstract Design in American Quilts.* New York: The Whitney Museum of American Art, n.d. (1971). (An exhibition catalogue with commentary.)

Horn, Jeanne. *Hidden Treasure.* New York: The Arco Publishing Company, 1962.

Humphrey, Edward F. *An Economic History of the United States.* New York: The Century Company, 1931.

Ickis, Marguerite. *The Standard Book of Quilt Making and Collecting.* New York: Dover Publishers, Inc., 1949.

Illick, Joseph S. *Pennsylvania Trees.* Harrisburg, Pa.: The Pennsylvania Department of Forestry, 1923. (Authoritative and readable.)

Iverson, Marion Day. *The American Chair, 1630–1890.* New York: Hastings House, 1957.

Johnson, Clifton. *Old-Time Schools and School-books.* New York: Dover Publications, 1963.

Jordan, John W. and Green, Edgar Moore. *The Lehigh Valley.* New York: The Lewis Publishing Company, 1905.

Kauffman, Henry J. *Early American Copper, Tin, and Brass.* New York: Medill McBride Company, 1950.

Keller, David Henry. *The Kellers of Hamilton Township.* Alexandria, Louisiana: The Wall Printing Company, 1922.

Keller, Robert B. *History of Monroe County, Pa.* Stroudsburg, Pa.: The Monroe Publishing Company, 1927.

Kent, William Winthrop. *Rare Hooked Rugs.* Springfield, Mass.: The Pond-Ekberg Company, 1941.

Kieffer, Henry Martyn. *Some of the First Settlers in the Forks of the Delaware.* Easton, Pa.: Privately printed, 1902.

Koehler, Le Roy Jennings. *The History of Monroe County, Pennsylvania, during the Civil War.* Stroudsburg, Pa.: The Monroe County Historical Society and the Monroe County Commissioners, 1950.

Kishpaugh, Philip. *The Valley View.* McMichaels, Pa.: Privately printed. (Various issues of this scarce monthly periodical appeared during the first decade of the twentieth century.)

Krebs, Friedrich, and Rubincam, Milton. *Emigrants from the Palatinate in the 18th Century.* Norristown, Pa.: The Pennsylvania German Society, 1953.

Landis Valley Associates. *Pennsylvania German Fraktur.* Lancaster, Pa.: 1969. (An illustrated special-exhibit catalogue.)

Laury, Preston A. *History of the Allentown Conference.* Kutztown, Pa.: The Kutztown Publishing Company, 1926. (The Conference referred to is that of the Lutheran Ministerium of Pennsylvania.)

Lesh, William S. *Cemeteries of Hamilton Township.* Manuscript compilation, n.d., but in the 1940s.

————. *History of the Neola Methodist Church, Jackson Township, in the Cherry Valley Circuit, Monroe County, Pennsylvania.* Ocean Grove, N.J.: Press of the Ocean Grove *Times*, n.d. (1951).

Lindsay, J. Seymour. *Iron and Brass Implements of the English and American House.* London: Alec Tiranti, 1964. (Helpful in establishing perspective for both English and American collectors.)

Lipman, Jean and Meulendyke, Eve. *American Folk Decoration.* New York: Oxford University Press, 1951.

Martin, M. J. *Jay Gould and His Tannery.* Scranton, Pa.: Lackawanna Historical Society, 1945.

Martin, Roscoe C., *et al. River Basin Administration and the Delaware.* Syracuse, N.Y.: Syracuse University Press, 1960.

Mathews, Alfred. *History of Wayne, Pike, and Monroe Counties, Pennsylvania.* Philadelphia: H. T. Peck and Company, 1886. (Invaluable to the researcher in the history of northeastern Pennsylvania.)

McClinton, Katharine Morrison. *Antiques of American Childhood.* New York: Clarkson N. Potter, Inc., 1970.

McKearin, George S. and Helen. *American Glass.* New York: Crown Publishers, 1941. (Well known in its field; perhaps more useful to the expert than to the novice.)

Mellick, Andrew D., Jr. *The Old Farm.* New Brunswick, N.J.: Rutgers University Press, 1948. (Condensation of an earlier work of fiction, long out of print.)

Menzies, Elizabeth G. C. *Before the Waters: The Upper Delaware Valley.* New Brunswick, N.J.: Rutgers University Press, 1966.

Mills, F. B. *Mills Seeds in 1900.* Rose Hill, N.Y.: F. B. Mills. (Commercial catalogue, listed here as representative among many in the field.)

Monroe County Court Records, Prothonotary's Office, Stroudsburg, Pa.

*Mountain Echo, The.* Stroudsburg, Pa.: The Echo. (Various issues of weekly publicity organ for the summer resorts of the entire Pocono region, early 1900s.)

*North American Almanac.* Philadelphia: Sower and Barnes, 1858. (One of the most widely circulated of all the almanacs of the nineteenth century.)

*Old Farmer's Almanac.* Boston: Jenks, Palmer and Company; various issues from 1793 to 1900, especially those in the decade of the 1850s.

Otto, Celia Jackson. *American Furniture of the Nineteenth Century.* New York: The Viking Press, 1965.

*Our Drummer.* New York and Chicago: Butler Brothers, 1886–1890. (Wholesalers' catalogue, widely known among country storekeepers toward the end of the century.)

*Pain Killer Almanac and Family Receipt Book.* Providence, R.I.: Perry Davis and Son, 1868. (Perhaps second in interest only to the *North American Almanac.*)

Paxson, Frederic L. *History of the American Frontier, 1763–1893.* New York: Houghton Mifflin Company, 1924.

Peto, Florence. *American Quilts and Coverlets.* New York: Chanticleer Press, 1949. ("Peto" is one of the names most familiar to quilt collectors.)

————. *Historic Quilts.* New York: The American Historical Company, 1939.

Polley, Robert L., ed. *America's Folk Art.* New York: G. P. Putnam's Sons, in association with Country Beautiful Foundation, Inc., Waukesha, Wisconsin, 1968.

Proud, Robert. *The History of Pennsylvania in North America,* vol. I. Philadelphia: Zachariah Poulson, Jr., 1797. (This volume contains a celebrated analytical study of William Penn.)

Reaman, Elmore. *The Trail of the Black Walnut.* Toronto: McClelland and Stewart, Ltd., 1957. (Helpful in tracing the travels of the Pennsylvania Dutch into Canadian territory.)

Reinert, Guy F. *Coverlets of the Pennsylvania Germans.* Allentown, Pa.: The Pennsylvania German Folklore Society, 1949. (For its date, an outstanding treatment. Research in this field, largely regional and unpublished, has continued steadily, following Mr. Reinert's death.)

*Report of the Secretary of Agriculture.* Washington, D.C.: The Government Printing Office, 1892. (Has a notable section on fruit and berries.)

Robacker, Ada F. "The Craze for Quilts." The *Antiques Dealer* vol. 24, nos. 6 and 7 (June and July, 1972). (Analysis by a contemporary expert: quilts, quilting, quilt collecting.)

Robacker, Earl F. *Pennsylvania Dutch Stuff.* Philadelphia: The University of Pennsylvania Press, 1944.

————. *Pennsylvania German Cooky Cutters and Cookies.* Plymouth Meeting, Pa.: Mrs. C. Naaman Keyser, 1946. (A Home Craft Series pamphlet prepared with the assistance of Ada F. Robacker and Bessie E. Gower.)

————. *Pennsylvania German Literature.* Philadelphia: The University of Pennsylvania Press, 1943.

————. *Touch of the Dutchland.* Cranbury, New Jersey: A. S. Barnes, 1965.

Rubi, Christian. *Holz Bemahlen (und) Kerb Schnitzen (Painted and Edge-Carved Wood).* Bern, Switzerland: Hans Huber, 1951. (Alone in its field—unfortunately limited in appeal to those who read German.)

Rupp, Israel Daniel. *History of Northampton, Lehigh, Monroe, Carbon, and Schuylkill Counties.* Harrisburg, Pa.: Hickok and Cantine, 1845.

Schiffer, Margaret B. *Historical Needlework of Pennsylvania.* New York: Charles Scribner's Sons, 1968.

Schwartz, Marvin D. *Collectors' Guide to Antique American Ceramics.* Garden City, N.Y.: Doubleday and Company, Inc., 1969.

Schwarze, Edmund. *History of the Hopedale Moravian Church.* Stroudsburg, Pa.: Monroe Record Press, 1912. (Apparently the only published record of this congregation, established in 1837.)

Shaw, Simeon. *History of the Staffordshire Potteries.* New York: Praeger Publishers, Inc., 1970. (Reprint of work first published in 1829.)

Shelley, Donald A. *The Fraktur-Writings or Illuminated Manuscripts of the Pennsylvania Germans.* Allentown, Pa.: Schlechter's, 1961. (Outstanding study in this field.)

Shoemaker, Alfred L. *Christmas in Pennsylvania.* Kutztown, Pa.: Pennsylvania Folklore Society, 1959.

————. *Eastertide in Pennsylvania.* Kutztown, Pa.: Pennsylvania Folklore Society, 1960.

Stevens, Sylvester K. *Pennsylvania, Birthplace of a Nation.* New York: Random House, 1964. (A good background study.)

Stillinger, Elizabeth. *The Antique Guide to Decorative Arts in America, 1600–1875.* New York: E. P. Dutton and Company, 1972.

Stokes, A. F. *Geography and History of Northeastern Pennsylvania.* Scranton, Pa.: International Textbook Company, 1936.

Stoudt, John Joseph. *Early Pennsylvania Arts and Crafts.* New York: A. S. Barnes, 1964.

*Stroudsburg in the Poconos, Sesqui-Centennial, 1815–1965.* East Stroudsburg, Pa.: The Sun Litho-Print, Inc., 1965. (Not an in-depth treatment, but good for leads and clues.)

*Structural Slate Company, Slate Plumbing Fixtures and Products.* Philadelphia: The Structure Service Bureau, 1922.

Van Tassel, Valentine. *American Glass.* New York: Gramercy Publishing Company, 1950.

Walsh, Louise Gilchrise (*sic*) and Walsh, Matthew John. *History and Organization of Education in Pennsylvania*. Indiana, Pa.: Louise G. Walsh and Matthew J. Walsh, 1928.

Walters, Mrs. Horace G. (*sic*). *The Bicentennial Celebration of the Shawnee Presbyterian Church*. East Stroudsburg, Pa.: The Sun Printery, 1952. (Interesting factual material by a leading genealogist.)

Watkins, Lura Woodside. *American Glass and Glassmaking*. New York: Chanticleer Press, 1950.

Wells, Louis Ray. *Industrial History of the United States*. New York: The Macmillan Company, 1924.

Weygandt, Cornelius. *The Red Hills*. Philadelphia: The University of Pennsylvania Press, 1929. (Eminently readable discussion of early phases of life in Pennsylvania by a distinctive prose stylist.)

Wheeler, Robert G. *Folk Art and the Street of Shops*. Dearborn, Mich.: The Edison Institute, 1971.

White, I. C. *The Geology of Pike and Monroe Counties*. Harrisburg, Pa.: The Board of Commissioners of the Second Geological Survey, 1882. (Not for the casual reader, but a presentation of major importance.)

Williams, Garford Flavel. *A History of Sterling, Wayne County, Pa.* Nicholson, Pa.: The Nicholson Examiner, 1950.

Williams, H. Lionel. *Country Furniture of Early America*. New York: A. S. Barnes, 1963.

Wilson, Everett B. *Vanishing Americana*. New York: A. S. Barnes, 1961.

Wright, Caleb E. *On the Lackawanna: Tale of Northern Pennsylvania*. Doylestown, Pa.: McGinty, Printer, 1886. (Romance of the Pennamite War period.)

# Index

Abel (family), 17
"Ab Heller's Mill," 56
Able, Mrs., 241
Ackermanville, 15
Adams, George L., 89
Albright's (church), 18
Albrightsville, 15
Almanacs, 186ff., 193
Analomink, 16, 80, 89, 136
Analomink Creek, 59
Analomink Iron Works, 59
Anderson, Joseph, 87
Angelmeyer, Johan, 144; Simpson, 147
Angels (village), 17, 57
Appelbachsville, 15
Appenzell, 15, 17
Applejack, 152
Apple picker, 153
Arndt, John, 161
Arnold, Catherine, 144; Samuel, 48
*Arsch-backe korrup*, 137
Atkinson, Joseph, 71
Award of Merit. *See* Reward of Merit
Axes, 67
Ax sockets, 26

Bacon board, 227
Baer, John, 189
Bag stamps, 58; stretcher, 54, 58
Bake-oven, outside, 120
Bangor, 113, 114, 118, 268
Bangs, John, 64
Banks, Samuel, 23, 40; William, 23; William, Jr., 23
Bantam (hen), 99
Bark spud, 85
"Bark Street," 87
Barlow knife, 112
Barr, Mr., 249
Barred Rock (hen), 99
Barrels, 83
Barrel stopper, 153
"Barrens," huckleberry, 169
Barroom objects, 83
Bartonsville, 16, 207
Bartron, Rebeckah, 202

Baskets, rye straw, 136, 139; Shawnee Inn, 137; slat, 137, 139; white oak, 135, 139; willow, 137, 139
Beach, S. A., 149, 151
"Beautiful Delaware," 32
Bechtelsville, 15
Beds, 43
"Beech," the, 24, 25, 36
Beehives, 165
Beehler (family), 17
Beehn (family), 17
Beers, F. W., map by, 123
Bees, corn-husking, 225; *schnitzing*, 225
Bell (family), 59
Bell, James, 55
Bell and Thomas, 55
Bellas Hess, 198
Bell's Bridge, 59
Belvidere, 15
Bensdorf cocoa, 107
Bensley, William, 202
Berlin work, 199
Berry, E., 153
Betger, Anna Elisabeth, 203
Bethany, 69, 168
Biesecker, Catarina, 144
Biles, Henry, 202
Bins, sugar, 171
*Binsa grawss*, 102
Bird tree, 103
Bittenbender, Aaron, 80; Christopher, 54; George, 54
Blairstown, 26
"Blicky," 252
Blood pudding, 184
Blooming Grove, 23
Blue-decorated stoneware, 133
Blue Mountain, 128, 144, 147, 148, 241
Blue Ridge Enamel Brick Company, 121, 122, 123, 124
"Blue Strawberry" hymnal, 260
Boards, baking, 234; cutting, 234; scouring, 234; smoothing, 176
Boats, Durham, 27, 55, 68
Bobsleds, 26
Bogert, David, 55
Book of Kells, 140
Bootjacks, 86, 89

Bossard, Joseph, 73; Melchior, 88
Bossardsville, 15, 16
Bottles, 76
Bowls, wooden, 96
Bowmanstown, 15
Box, bureau, 234; farrier's, 47; ornamental wooden, 230
Bracket shelves, 232
Brantum, Mathew, 87
*Braucherei*, 190
Brazier, iron, 174
Brick, 120–25; enameled, 123, 125
"Bricktown," 123
Brinker, Jacob, 53
Brinker's Mill, 53
Bristle scrapers, 185
Broad ax, 22
Brodhead, Daniel, 221, 226
Brodheads Creek, 36, 59, 73
"Brodheads Creek Colts," 31
Brodheadsville, 15, 17, 211
Brown, Hester Ann, 205; William, 56
Brown and Keller, 268
Bucket bench, 43
Buff Orpington (hen), 99
Bung starter, 153
Bunnell, Gershom, 25
Bunting, Mrs. John, 168
Burger and Bleckler, 89
Burns (potter), 133
Burrows, William, 71
Burt Bottling Works, 70, 71
Bush, Dr. Philip, 56
Bushkill, 15, 26, 56, 57, 59, 202, 229
Buskirk, Joseph, 34
Buss, Jacob, 87, 151, 152
Butcher boards, 181, 185
Butchering, 180–85
Butler Brothers, 245, 254
Butter, 90–96; box, 43; molds, 95; pails, 96
Butteris, farrier's, 47
Buttermilk Falls Bridge, 87

Cabinet woods, 38, 40
Calno, N.J., 33
Canadensis, 18, 89, 109, 155
Candlelight service, 236
Candles, beeswax, 236
Candy molds, 105
Cant hook, 27, 28
Cards, advertising, 266ff.; botanical, 270; calligraphic, 267; calling, 268; Sunday School, 266; trade, 266ff.
Carlson, Charles X., 29
Carlton (family), 18
Carlton, David Hartson, 40
Carlton Hill, 16, 37, 40
Carpet, rainbow, 206
Carpet rags, 223
Castle Inn, the, 123
Catlin Glass Works, 69, 75
Certificate, baptismal (*Taufschein*), 147; birth (*Geburts-schein*), 147; confirmation, 147; marriage (*Trau-schein*), 147
Charles William Stores, 198

Cherry canning, 175
Cherry Lane, 38
Cherry Valley, 164, 262
Chestnuthill Township, 68
Chests, blanket, 43
Christ, I., 60; Samuel, 246, 248
Churns, butter, 92
Cider Royal, 152
Cigar box artistry, 230–32
Clark, John, 41; Philip B., 41; T. B., 69
Clocks, Connecticut, 112
Clothespin factories, 36
Cochin (hen), 99
Cole, Jennie, 199
Collins, T. K., Jr., 260
Columbia, N.J., 15, 33, 68
Columbia Glass Works, 68, 69, 76
Conestoga wagon, 108; ironwork, 24
Confirmation certificate, 147
Cookie cutters, 65
Cookies, Christmas, 241; New Year's, 241
Coolbaugh, Cornelius, 55
Coolbaugh Township, 252
Coons, Sidney, 162, 164
Coopering, 34, 35
Corner cupboards, 43
Correll's (inn), 80
Coverlets, woven, 205ff.
Cowbells, 83, 96
Cowden-Wilcox pottery, 131
Cradles, 43
Craig's Meadows, 109
Cramer, R. C., 123
"Cranberry," the, 168
Crandall, Charles M., 247
Crandall's District School, 244
Crane, fireplace, 173
Crely, Daniel, 90
Cresco, 94
Crisbin, Thomas, 202
Croasdale (family), 59
Croasdale, Louisa, 269
Crocheting, 201
Cross, Abram, 132
Cross and Burns, 132, 133
Cupboards, corner, 43; jelly, 43
Currier, N., 147
Currier and Ives, 147
Custard's Cemetery, 207
Cutters, cabbage, 228; cookie, 65; tobacco, 112

Damascus, 30
Daub (potter), 133
Davis, John, 205
"Dawdy Haus," the, 172
Decker, C. W., 37
Decker's Ferry, 33
Decoupage, 270
De Laval cream separator, 78
Delaware and Hudson Canal, 129
Delaware Water Gap, 14, 15, 27, 30, 31, 33, 34, 68, 77, 114, 116, 123, 124, 141, 146, 161, 202, 209
Delaware Water Gap National Recreation Area, 137

De Long (family), 87; John, 34
*Dengelstock*, 64
Depui, Ten Eyck, 36
Detrick, Carrie, 40; Nelson K., 136
Deubler's (inn), 79, 80
*Deutsche Harmonie*, 260
Dietz (family), 18
Dill's Ferry, 33
Dimmick, Chauncey, 202; Victor, 123
Dimmick's Ferry, 33
Dingman's Ferry, 26, 30, 31, 33
D. L. and W. Railroad, 89
Dog days, 191
Dolls, types of, 243–48
Dominique (hen), 99
Dongan, B., and Son, 109
Dorflinger, Charles, 70; Christian, 69, 70; Louis J., 70; William F., 70, 71
Dorflinger Glass Works, 69, 70, 75
Doster Brothers, 205
Dough box, 43
Dowing and Company, 89
Drach, Adam, 126; Henry, 126; Magdalena, 126; Rudolph, 126–29, 133; Rudolph II, 126
Drake, H. S., 268
Drawshaves, 139
Dreher Township, 23
Drinker's Turnpike, 79
Drinking vessels, 83
Drover's Home, 80
Druch, Daniel, 126
Drying, fruit and vegetable, 177
Dry sink, 43
Dunbar, E., 36
Dunning (family), 18
Dupuis, Aaron, 23, 34, 64, 87, 90, 165; Nicholas, 51, 151
Durham boat, 27, 55, 68
Durham Furnace, 59
Dutch Country, defined, 13
Dutch Flats, 16, 79

Eagle Valley Corners, 137
Ear caps, 50
East Branch Pond, 23
Easter egg decoration, 100–104; trees, 102
Easton Bible Artist, the, 141, 144, 146
East Stroudsburg, 15, 37, 69, 71, 73, 74, 75, 89, 121, 123, 132, 137, 144, 146, 232, 249, 266, 268
East Stroudsburg Glass Company, 71, 72, 75, 76
E. B. Marsh and Brother, 60
Effort (village), 15, 17, 48, 49, 61, 63
Effort Spoke Factory, 26
Egg money, 97
Egg objects, 105
Eggs, decorated, 98
Egypt Mills, 56
Ehrhardt (family), 18; Frederic, 199
Eighteen Forty-eighters, the, 16
Eilenberger, Fred, 26; Frederick W., 151
Elk Horn Tannery, 89
Embossed-glazed pictures, 262ff.
Embroidery, 197, 201
English-Irish, the, 14

Erwin, Francis, 87
Etruria (Glass) Works, 80
Experiment Mills, 55
Eyer, John, 144, 147

Faatz, Christian, 69; Christopher, Jr., 69
Fabel, Samuel, 55
Fabrics, quilting, 213, 214
Farrier's box, 47
Feather work, 270
Fenner (family), 263
Fenner, Annie, 198; Barnet, 53; Delila, 260; Elmira, 260; Henrich, 54, 143, 146, 207; Henry, 145, 263; Joseph, 54, 88; Margaret, 145; Susan, 263; Susan E., 260
Fennersville, 16, 61, 88
Ferries, river, 33
Field (family), 18
Fishville, 54
Flagler, Steward, 268
Flasks, drinking, 225
Flatirons, 177
Flax processing, 203
Flocked-paper toys, 105
*Floricultural Cabinet*, the, 193
*Florist and Horticultural Journal*, the, 193
Flory, W. H., Jr., 268
Flory and White, 268
Flour drum, 57, 179
Flourishing (handwriting), 267
Flue stoppers, 179
Fly nets, 50, 89
Foods, up-country and down-country, 18, 19
Forest, the, 22
Forge Cut, 59
Forks, butchering, 182
Fort Penn, 121
Frable. *See* Fravel
Fraktur, 265
Frankenfield, Samuel B., 36, 43
*Franklin Harmony*, the, 260
Fravel, Daniel, 205
Frederic, Christina, 199
Frederick, P., 125
Frey, Garrett, 62; Lambert, 62; William, 62
Friebole (family), 17
Fries, Jacob, 68
Fries Rebellion, 68
Frogtown, 16
Frühling Creek, 27
Fruit jars, 76
Fulmer, Henry, 119
Funnels, 153

Gambrel sticks, 185
Gaudy Ironstone, 170
*Geburtsschein*, 147
*Geddelsbriefe*, 147
George, Cicero, 136
German Valley, 15, 17, 18, 37, 39, 94, 137, 154, 155, 196, 199, 226, 239, 241
Getz, "Old Man," 131
Gilbert (village), 15, 17, 67
Gillette, 129

Gillinder "Just Out" glass, 105
Gilpin (family), 18; Dr. Fletcher, 196; John R., 23
*Glanz-bilder Reliefs*, 262ff.
Glass, cut, 74–76
Globe Flour Mills, 268
Golden Sunshine Parlor Heater, 268
Gondelsheim, 17
Goodrich, Enos, 31
Gould, James, 33; Jay, 88
Gouldsboro, 15, 88, 249
Gouldsboro Lake, 249
Gould's Ferry, 33
Grain bags, 58
Grapes, glass, 170
Greasing of wagon wheels, 45
Greentown, 16, 101, 155, 209
Gregory, Norman B., 249
Greiner, Adam, 69; Nicholas, 69
Grim, (family), 18
Grim, "Granny," 196
Grimes, Ichabod, 34
Gros point, 201
Gunn, J. C., 57
Gut boards, 181, 185

Haag, A. L., 57; John, 57; Maurice, 57
Hagerman, George, 80; Sanford, 48
Half-way House, 79
Halter, Joseph, Sr., 69
Hamilton Church, 144
Hamilton Foundry, 60
Hamilton Square, 126
Hamilton Township, 41, 42, 53, 55, 59, 68, 88, 89, 126, 127, 128, 142, 143, 144, 146, 153, 163, 168, 178, 198, 199, 201, 260, 263
Hancock, N.Y., 15
Handwriting, 267
Haney, John, 103; William, 54
Hankinson, Aaron, 202
Hanson, H. C., 193
Harloe's insulators, 76
Harness, 89
Harrison, Joseph, 193
Harvest jugs, 226
Hatchel, flax, 203
Hawk (family), 230; Alfred, 136; Edward, 114; Nicholas, 67; Peter, 67
Hawley, 15, 76
Hawley Glass Works, 71
Hay knife, 60
Hazleton (family), 18; Mrs., 197, 198; Samuel, 37
Heberling (family), 17, 18
Heckewelder, John, 161
Heffele (family), 17
Heller, C. B., 67; John, 87; Melchior, 34; Melchior, Sr., 151
Hellick, George F., 107, 110, 112
Hemlock Grove, 18
Hemlock Hollow, 31
Hendricks, Cornelius, 36
Henry (family), 248; William, 59, 66
Henry Gun Factory, 66
Henryville, 16, 248
Hens, breeds of, 99

Hess, Philip, 67
*Hexerei*, 190
Hickory Run, 15
Highway fingerposts, 83
Hilliard, Philip, 205, 208
Hines, Christopher, 69; Jacob, 69
Hobbs, Mrs. Harry, 53
Hohmann, Johan Georg, 83, 190
Hoke Town, 16
Hollow Road, 126
Home Circle (organ), 254
Honesdale, 15, 36, 37, 57, 64, 69, 129, 130, 162
Honesdale Glass Works, 69
Honey, bees, 161ff.; containers, 165
Honeywell, M. A., 264
Hoop poles, 34
Hope (village), 15
Hopps, Samuel, 67
Hornbeck, John, 30
Horseshoes, 23
Horticultural catalogues, 153
Houck, Nathan, 40, 244
Houcktown, 15
House blessing (*Haus Segen*), 147
Houser's store, 31
Huguenin (family), 18; Emile, 23; Georg, 237, 246–48
Hull, Gershom, 87; James, 87
Hyndshaw, James, 34, 56

Ice cream molds, 253
Ice houses, 249–53
Illick, Joseph S., 160
Indian Queen Hotel, 123
Inns, loggers, 29, 30
Insiders and outsiders, 19
Instruments, musical, 254–60
Insulators, glass, 76
Irish, the, 14
Isaac Van Campen Inn, 30

Jacks, wheel, 26, 46
Jackson Township, 201, 207
Jacoby, John, 40
Jacquard looms, 205
Jars, preserving, 171
Jelly cupboard, 39
Jersey Lightning, 152
Jones, Evan, 129, 130; Richard D., 37
Jordan (family), 59; Elizabeth, 201; John, Jr., 59
Journals, farm, 188
Jubilee (place name), 133
Jug-stopper, wooden, 229
Jungchen, 141: *See also* Youngken, Younken

Karamac Inn, 33
Kautz, Abraham, 71; Harry, 47, 126, 183; William Valentine, 71
Kellam, Moses, 57
Keller, Christopher, 55, 107; David, 204; John, 204; John George, 53, 55; Joseph, 55
Kellersville, 23, 41, 42, 55, 107, 114, 204, 229
Kempton, 15
Kennedy, Ezra, 87

Kerr, Joseph, 114
Kester, Peter, 89
Kettle handle, iron, 25
Kettles, copper, 223; iron, 174
Killam, Ephraim, 154; Jephthah, 154
Kimble, Ephraim, 154; Jacob, 23; Walter, 154
Kingston, N.Y., 27
Kipp, Isaac I., 23
Kistler, Charles E., 88; Hiram, 268; Stephen, 88, 89
Kitchens, cellar, 172ff.
Kitson, Walker, and Davis, 205
Kneading boards (slate), 119
Knipesville, 89
Knitting needles, 205
Knives, butchering, 181
Knowlton Township, N.J., 116
Kootsches, 186ff.
Krebs, F(riedrich), 143, 146
Kresgeville, 15, 16, 114
Kroll, Arthur, 126
Krumsville, 15
Kuhnsman, "Old Man," 131
Kunkletown, 15, 61, 67, 71, 89

La Anna, 15, 37, 80, 155, 244, 246, 248
La Bar, Daniel, 202; John, 205; Peter, 202; S. B., 268
Lackawaxen, 27, 28, 30
*Ladies' Botany*, 193
*Ladies' Wreath*, 193
Lake Wallenpaupac, 16, 40
Lamb, Harley, 26; Jacob, 55
Lancaster (family), 18; George H., 37; H. A., 37
Landers, John, 34
Lantz, Jackson, 75
Lap robes, 50
Lard-making, 175
Latches, wooden, 228
Lauffer, Raymond, 137; Sabina, 137
Laundry processes, 174
Learn, M. A., 215
Leather, 84–89
Le Bar, Amos, 114; J. Depue, 30
Ledgedale, 132
Ledgers, innkeepers', 83; store, 112
Leghorn (hen), 99
Lehigh, 59
Lehighton, 15, 136
Leonard, George W., 162
Levis Creek, 27
L'Hommedieu Music Company, 267
Lincoln, Mary Todd, 70
Linden Hall, 199
Lindley, John, 193
Little Gap, 77
Little Kunkletown, 15
Liver pudding, 183
Loder (family), 129
"Log dog," 28
Loggers' inns, 30; sledges, 28, 30
Long, Joseph, 205
*Long-Lost Friend, The*, 83, 190
Looms, 205ff.
"Lord High Admiral of the Delaware," 30

Love Feast, 35
Lower Smithfield Lutheran and Reformed General Church Book, 144
Lower Smithfield Township, 141
Lutheran Ministerium Camp, 40
Lutz, Nicholas, 75
Lynch (potter), 129
Lyon, Philip, 73
Lyon and Bossard Glass Company, 71, 73, 74, 76

Mc Carty, Case, 26
Mc Dowell, John, 90
Mc Ewing, George, 48, 87
Mc Fall & Warne, 132
Mc Ilhaney (village), 61, 204
Mc Ilhaney, Thomas Mc Fall, 204
Mack, Thomas, 114
Mc Michaels (village), 61
Mc Michaels, John, 79
Mc Michaels Creek, 36, 53, 54, 56
Madden (family), 18
Majolica, Etruscan, 108, 110, 112
Manhart (family), 17
Manhart's Hill, 25
Mann, Jonathan, 162
Mantels, fireplace, 178
Marsh, Abraham, 60; Isaac, 60; John, 60; Linford, 268
Marshall's Creek, 56, 268
Martyn, Mrs. S. T., 193
Matamoras, 68
Match factory, 37
Meal chest, 56
Mease, Dr. James, 151
Megargle, Allen, 23, 57
Mershon and Eilenberger Blending Mill, 48
Mervine (family), 70, 76
*Metzel-supp*, 185
Metzgar, Joseph, 55
Metzgars, the (storekeepers), 109
M. F. Van Kirk Stick Factory, 37
Michael, George, 151
Michaels, Omar, 38; Joseph, 161; Samuel, 120
Middle Creek, 71
Middle Smithfield, 16, 34, 40, 51
Milford, 26, 41
Milk cans, 96
Milk glass mustard containers, 105
Miller, Depue S., 87; Henry, 41; Philip, 162
Miller and Mackey, 89
Millstones, 58
Mill Turn, the, 37
Mine props, 26
Mine sprags, 26
Minisink, The, 26
Minisink Hills, 26, 55, 59, 128, 250, 252
Moersch (family), 17
Molds, ice cream, 253
Montages, Victorian, 262
Moravian Female Seminary, 199
Moravian mint tins, 159, 160
Moravians, the, 17, 35, 141, 161, 235, 236, 237, 238, 242
Morey, John, 114
Motto, wall, 198

Mountainhome, 15, 36, 37, 89
Mt. Bethel, 15, 116, 148, 201, 205
Mt. Minsi, 114, 202
Mt. Paul, 79
Mt. Pocono, 79
Mounts, Aaron, 101
Mt. Tammany, 22, 114
Moyer (potter), 133
Music, manuscript, 257, 258; shape-note, 259
Mustard containers, 100

Nanatumam Ferry, 33
Napkins, 200, 201
National Cloak and Suit Company, 198
National Park Service, 21, 40, 41, 57, 93, 115, 122, 137, 149, 209
Nazareth, 15, 16, 17
Neckyokes, 160
Needlepoint, 201
Neola, 17, 53, 117, 132
Nest eggs, 104
Nevins (family), 18
Newfoundland, 14, 15, 16, 17, 18, 27, 35, 62, 79, 80, 94, 101, 109, 129, 131, 133, 137, 154, 155, 196, 199, 203, 225, 231, 236, 237, 239, 241, 246, 247
New York-Delaware Water Gap Slate Company, 114
Neyhart (family), 40
Nicholas, Jacob, 205
Niddy-noddies, 204
Noah's Ark, 237, 238, 247
Nobletown, 16
North American Almanac, 189
North and South Turnpike, 77
North Water Gap, 26
Notch-carving, 230–32
Nutshell toys, 243
Nyce, Frank, 31; George L., 26

Oak Valley Branch Tannery, 89
Oak Valley Tannery, 89
Odenwelder, Asher, 67
Old Farmer's Almanac, the, 189
Old Mine Road, 27, 152
Oppelt (family), 17
Organs, Miller, 254–55; parlor, 254–60
Ornaments, carved wood, 239; Christmas, 238–39
"Othello" kitchen range, 268
Out-kitchens, 172ff.
Outsiders and insiders, 19
Owl Hoot (village), 57
Ox shoes, 23, 26; yokes, 26
Oyer, John, 205; Samuel, 205

Pahaquarry, 30, 116, 149, 151, 152
Palen and Northrop, 89
Palmerton, 17, 134
*Pannhaus*, 183
Panther (village), 15, 16, 23, 25, 26, 35, 40, 62, 269
Papier mâché toys, 104
Papillon (family), 18
Paradise (village), 24, 80
Parers, apple, 225
Parkes, Josiah, 30

Parlor Gem (organ), 254
Parties, carpet rag, 224; *lumpa*, 224–25
Pattern books, weaver's, 211
Patterns, quilting, 213ff.
Pattisons, the, 108
Paupac, 16, 132, 155
Paupac Eddy, 31
Peale (family), 264
Peavey, 27
Peck's Pond, 15
Pelts, sheep, 26
Pen Argyl, 113
Penn, John, 126; Thomas, 126; William, 13
Pennamite Wars, 14
Pensyl Creek, 59
*Pennsylvania*, The (sailing vessel), 31
*Pennsylvania Choral Harmony*, 259–60
Pennsylvania Dutch, origin of term, 17
Pennsylvania Folklife Society, 193, 212
Pennsylvania Slate Company, 113
Peters Valley, N.J., 137
Philadelphia Centennial, 1876, 210
Philipsburg, Pa., 16
Phillips, S., 130, 133; S. P., 123
Phillips Street, 122
Photograph albums, 261, 269, 270
Pie peel, 168
Pillow shams, 201
Pin cushions, beaded, 199
Pipher, Peter, 114; Samuel, Jr., 114; Samuel II (son of Samuel, Jr.), 114
Pitters, cherry, 175, 178
Place, John, 161
Playthings, children's, 243ff.
Pleasant Valley, 61
Plug tobacco cutters, 112
Plymouth Rock (hen), 99
Pocono Lake, 36
Pocono Plateau, 80, 155, 168
Poff, Christian, 205
Polk Township, 114
Pomegranate decoration, 130
Port Jervis, 26, 30
Portland, Pa., 26, 33, 68, 69, 116, 205
Postcard album, 261
Pot covers (slate), 119
Pots, apple butter, 224
Powwow books, 190
Prescott, L. T., 37
Promised Land, 15
Props, mine, 26
*Pudden*, 183
*Pudden* pan, 184
Pue, John, 202
Puffee (family), 18
Pugh, Hugh, 40
*Putz*, Christmas, 235ff.
*Putz* carvings, 246
Puzzles, hand-carved, 248

Quarrying, slate, 113–19
Quilting, 212ff.
Quilting frames, 220

Quilts, appliqué, 212ff.; bride's, 219; friendship, 219; patch-work, 212ff.; signature, 219

Raetz, 17
Rafting, 27–33
Railroad ties, 26
Ramsay, C. G., 123
Ray (N. A. Ray and Company), 69
Reaper's hook, 60
Red Indian Cut Plug Tobacco, 107
Red-outline handwork, 200
Redware pottery, 133
Reeder's (village), 15, 16, 249, 252, 253
Reese, William Stroud, 25
Reinhold, the, 47
Resaca, 89
Resica. *See* Resaca
Reward of Merit, 144, 147, 265
Rhode Island Red (hen), 99
Rhodes, C. L., 73
Ribble, William, 149, 151
Richmond (village), 15, 205
Ridgway, Mathew, 68
Rifles, Nicholas Hawk, 67
Rinker (family), 201, 263; James Wycliff, 40
River Road, the, 29, 120, 173
Roemerville, 15, 17, 155
Roosevelt, Teddy, 71
"Rose" blankets, 195
Rosencrans Ferry, 33
Ross, Baldwin & Co., 62
Roth, Georg Adam, 142, 144, 147; Leah, 126
Rothbaust, John, 260
Ruby-stained glass, 73
Rugs, 201
Russell, Henry Z., 71
Ruster, Nicholas, 109

Saffron, 92, 192
Samplers, memorial, 196, 201
Sand Hill, 59, 60
Sap-boiling pans, 160
Sap buckets, 160
Sauerkraut-making, 192
Sausage-making, 183
Saylorsburg, 34, 71, 77, 103, 122, 123, 124, 126, 128, 129, 252
Scales, brass, 171
Scarves, bureau, 201
Schaeffer (family), 18
Schelbert (family), 17
*Scherenschnitte*, 263–64
Schiffler, Mrs. Alice, 209
Schimmel, Wilhelm, 105, 231, 247
Schlatter, Michael, 144
Schlotter, George, 144
Schmauk, J. G., 260
Schneider, 17
*Schnitz* dryer, 153
*Schnitzelbank*, 50, 134
Schoonmaker, Benjamin, 87
Schoonover, Benjamin, 59; Daniel, 162
Sciota, 15, 16, 17, 40, 41, 60, 88, 120, 124, 132
"Scissors-cutting," 264

Scoops, sugar, 171; wooden, 228
Scotch, the, 13
Scott-Warman Glass Plant, 76
Scrapbooks, 242, 261–70
Scrapple, 183
Scraps (*Glanz-bilder Reliefs*), 240, 242, 261–70
Scythes, 67
Seat, wagon, 26
Seed catalogues, 189, 193
Seely, Colonel R. L., 64
Seelyville, 62
Separators, cream, 177
Setzer, George, 207; Jacob, 207
Sewing birds, 220
Sgraffito pottery, 133
"Shades of Death," 22, 168
Shafer and Rinehart, 37
Shaking fork, 35, 37
Shawnee champagne, 152
Shawnee-on-Delaware, 26, 27, 29, 33, 34, 47, 51, 55, 64, 87, 120, 124, 137, 151, 152, 155, 173, 183, 202, 257
Sheep-growing, 203
Sheller, corn, 55
Shelves, bracket, 232
Shoemaker, Henry, 64, 161; Moses, 25
Shoemaker's Ferry, 33
Shoemakers' implements, 89
Shoepeg factories, 36
Shoe-trees, wooden, 87
Shohola, 15, 90
Shotwell, J. H., 268
Shouse, William, 40
Show towels, 201
Shug, S., 123
Shupp, Catherine, 67; Simon, 48
Sieg (family), 17; Annie, 199; Christina, 94; Frederic, 94, 199; Jacob, 62; Lavine, 62; Reuben, 62
Sigafuss, J. Y., 268
Silhouettes, 264, 270
Silver Lake, 56, 250, 252
Silver Spangled Hamburg (hen), 99
Simons, Dr. Arthur, 196
Simonstown, 16
Singmaster, Joseph, 87
*Sixth and Seventh Books of Moses*, 190
Skinner, Daniel, 30
Skunk's Misery Road, 37
Slate, architectural, 119; book ends, 119; carved, 119; clocks, 119; fireplace screens, 119; game boards, 119; marbled, 116–19; over-mantel, 119; pencils, 119; picture frames, 119; school, 119; table tops, 119
Slateford Farm, 41, 93, 115, 209, 232
Slaters' tools, 119
Slavs, the, 11
Slaw cutters, 228
Sledge, logger's, 28; stone, 44
Slingshots, 245
Slutter, David, 55; Levi, 41, 55; Levi M., 60
Smiley, Samuel, 121
Smith, Henry, 87, 202
Smithfield (Township), 16, 34, 54, 64, 87, 90, 114, 116, 126, 151, 161, 202
Smokehouses, 186ff.

Snyder, George, 54, 205; P., 205; Samuel, 114
Snydersville, 41, 42, 48, 59, 61, 114
Soap containers, wooden, 228
Soap-making, 174
Soapstone, 36
Sofas, 43
Souse, 185
South Sterling, 18, 27, 40, 62
Spangenberg, Johannes, 146
Spatter pictures, 262, 270
Spectacles, 112
Sperry, Mr., 37
Spiles, sap, 160
Spinning, 204
Spinning wheel gear, 204
Spittoons, 83
Spoke factory, 44, 48; Effort, 26
Spoke shave, 45
Spout mill, 23
Sprags, mine, 26
Spragueville, 89, 136
Squeak toys, 104
Staples, Abel, 164; Richard S., 205
Star Glass Works, 71, 73, 74, 76
Starner, Cornelius, 120
Stauffer, George E., 73
Stecher, Mathias, 114
Steelyards, 185
Sterling, 16, 79, 109, 155
Stillwater, N.J., 121
Stockertown, 15, 80
Stoddartsville, 15
Stone, Oliver D., 121; William, 121
Stone Church, 15, 206
Stone sledges, 44
Stoneware, 96, 133
Stools, milking, 96
Stormsville, 94, 109
Strawbridge and Clothier, 199
Stroud, Charles (grandson of first Jacob), 87; Daniel, 17; Jacob, 17, 56; Jacob (grandson of first Jacob), 87
Stroudsburg, 15, 31, 36, 43, 53, 55, 56, 59, 60, 63, 70, 71, 73, 74, 75, 76, 80, 82, 87, 89, 94, 95, 109, 113, 114, 121, 123, 129, 132, 133, 136, 145, 146, 205, 245, 249, 254, 266, 268
Stroudsburg Tannery, 87
Stroudsburg Woolen Mill, 205
Stroud Township, 114
Sugar Hill, 23, 27, 154
Sullivan Expedition, 53
Summer Hill Ridge, 123
Summer kitchen, the 177
Swedish, the, 13
Sweet corn grater, 36, 43

Tablecloths, 200, 201
Tables, 43
Tamaqua, 15
Tannersville, 16, 40, 77, 87, 88, 114, 147, 253
Tatting, 201
*Taufschein*, 147
"Tea" companies, 112
Teep, Elizabeth, 205

Thomas (family), 59
Thornhurst, 15
Ties, railroad, 26
*Timbrel of Zion*, The, 260
Tobyhanna, 36, 249
Tobyhanna and Lehigh Lumbering Company, 36
Tobyhanna Township, 252
Tock's Island, 30
Tongs, fireplace, 178; iron, 25, 178; pie, 168
Tools, ice, 249–53
Tott's Gap, 77
Toys, 243–48; Crandall, 247–48
Traceyville, 64, 69
Trachsville, 15, 126, 157
Trade cards, 266ff.
Trammels, fireplace, 173
Tramp carving, 230–32
Transue, Adam, 33
*Trauschein*, 147
Treadmills, 92
Treible, George, 202
TsChudy, Harry, 199
Turn, John, 25, 64, 151, 152, 162; John, Sr., 40
Turtle hook, 63

Uhl (family), 18
*Unitas Fratrum*, 17
Upper Mt. Bethel, 113, 204, 205, 208

Valentines, 265
van Buskirk (family), 18, 121
Van Campen, John, 55
Van Vliet, Derrick, 74; Warren, 74; W. E., 137; W. R., 137
Van Vliet Glass Factory, 71, 74, 76
Van Why, Daniel, 137
*Vorschrift*, 142, 144
Voss, W. H., 268

Wagner, Fred, 63
Wagon seat, 26; wheel jack, 46
Walker's Ferry, 33
Walking sticks, 230; toys, 66
Wallace, Joseph, 129, 132; William, 36
Wallace and Kitson, 205
Wallenpaupac Creek, 154
Walpack Bend, 31, 33
Walton, Edward, 41
Walter, Barnet, 161; Mrs. Emil, 198
Walters, Henrietta, 32
*Wammus*, 19
Washington, George, 154, 210, 234
Waterbury Clock Works, 111
Watercolor prints, 265, 270
Water glass (preservative), 97, 99
Weather vanes, 83
Weber, Thomas R., 260; Valentin, 30
Wedge plow, 60, 61
Wedges, 28
W. E. Henry and Company, 37
Weiss, Noah, 232–34; Samuel W., 71
Weissport, 15
Wells, Henry, 41; Nathan, 41
Wells Fanning Mill, 41

Wells Ferry, 41
Welsh, the, 13, 131
Werckheuser, Henrich, 144
Westcott, Joseph, 73
West End, 15, 16, 32, 44, 54, 61, 63, 71, 90, 121, 126, 132, 136, 144, 188, 230, 235, 252, 265
Weston, Horace, 129; Horace, Jr., 129; William W., 129
Whips (horse, mule), 50
White, F. C., 71
White Bunting, the, 168
White Lightning, 152
White Mills, 69, 70, 71, 75
White's Tannery, 89
White Wyandotte (hen), 99
Whyte (potter), 129
Wilderness Country, the, 22
Williams, Frances, 41, 42; Peter, 41, 42
Wilson, Woodrow, 71
Wilsonville, 40
Winans, Matthias, 202
Wind Gap, 77, 79, 80, 134

Window glass, 76
Wintermute, William S., 121
Wolff, 17
Womelsdorf, 17
Wood, Eliphalet, 36
Wyckoff, A. B., 109; Amzi, 109; Daniel, 108, 109; Jacob, 108, 109
Wyoming Massacre, 22

Yetter, Andrew, 26; Milton, 71
Yokes, ox, 26
York Imperial, 150
Youngken, Abraham, 141, 144, 146

Zacharias, Joseph, 123
Zadik Pratt & Jay Gould, 88
Ziegler (family), 17
Zieglerville, 15
Zimmerman, George, 56; Peter, 56
Zion's Lutheran Church, 33, 114, 120, 141